MULTINATIONAL CORPORATIONS

Investments, Technology, Tax, Labor and Securities: European, North and Latin American Perspectives

with summaries in French and Spanish

Edited by
Alain A. Levasseur
and
Enrique Dahl

UNIVERSITY PRESS OF AMERICA

LANHAM • NEW YORK • LONDON

LOUISIANA STATE UNIVERSITY
PAUL M. HEBERT LAW CENTER

University Press of America,® Inc.

4720 Boston Way
Lanham, MD 20706

3 Henrietta Street
London WC2E 8LU England

Printed in the United States of America

Library of Congress Cataloging in Publication Data

Multinational corporations.

"With summaries in French and Spanish."
Bibliography: p.
1. International business enterprises. I. Levasseur, Alain A. II. Dahl, Enrique, 1949-
HD2755.5.M8334 1986 338.8'8 86-13192
ISBN 0-8191-5496-2 (alk. paper)

All University Press of America books are produced on acid-free paper which exceeds the minimum standards set by the National Historical Publications and Records Commission.

CONTRIBUTORS

Carlos E. Alfaro
Allende & Brea

George M. Armstrong, Jr.
Louisiana State University

Hugh J. Ault
Boston College Law School

Beverly May Carl
Southern Methodist University

Françoise Genot-Delbecque
Fiduciaire de France

Ricardo J. Diez
Curtis, Mallet-Prevost, Colt & Mosle

Art Dula
Dula, Shields & Egbert

Sylvie Durant des Aulnois
Rogers & Wells

Henri Grondon
Grondin, LeBel, Poudrier, Isabel, Morin & Gagnon

William Haney
Rogers & Wells

Sergio A. Leiseca
Baker & McKenzie

Glenn G. Morris
Louisiana State University

Allan S. Mostoff
Dechert Price & Rhoads

Jean-François Serval
Leon Constantin & Co.

Stanley Siegel
University of California, Los Angeles

Paul D. Slocomb
Baker & McKenzie

Short biographies of the authors appear at the beginning of their papers.

ABOUT THE EDITORS

Alain A. Levasseur

Professor of Law, Louisiana State University Law Center, Associate Director, Center of Civil Law Studies; D.E.S. University of Paris, 1965, M.C.L. Tulane University, 1966; Technical Assistant, IBRD; Washington, D.C., 1969-70; Ass't, Assoc. and Professor of Law, Tulane University, 1970-77. Member Boards of Directors: A.J.C.L., FIEDA; Member: Ass'n Henri Capitant, Société de Législation Comparée, Louisiana State Law Institute.

Enrique Dahl

Admitted to practice in New York, Madrid and Buenos Aires. LL.B., LL.D. (Buenos Aires Univ.); LL.M. (London Univ.); Stazhor (Leningrad Univ.) Former Associate Attorney at Curtis, Mallet-Prevost, Colt & Mosle (New York) and Assistant Professor of Law at Louisiana State University. Visiting Professor abroad (Summer, Fall 1986) and at Southern Methodist University (Spring, 1987).

INTRODUCTION

Since the early 1960's the growth of international business transactions has been both phenomenal and erratic. This paradox can easily be explained by the major role played by the multinational corporations (MNC) or enterprises (MNE) which for our purpose can be described as corporations that own or control, to a larger or lesser extent, the production, marketing or service facilities of subsidiaries located abroad, outside the legal jurisdiction of the home country. By their sheer size, the scale of their operations, their resilience acquired through confrontational experiences, the MNE have come to exercise a dramatic influence on the framing of the political, economic, social, and even cultural, development of international relations.

Their ability at shifting resources of all sorts over national boundaries[1] could not go unrestrained as it pitched the inherently dynamic outlook of a MNE against the naturally guarded attitude of the nation-state. A game was played on the world chess board, on which MNE moved as both the instruments and the scapegoats of international politics.

For decades now these MNC have been the focus of attention of a wide spectrum of interested groups. Be they international or regional organizations, national public or private associations, these groups have either extolled the socio-economico-cultural benefits of MNC or decried the dangers and evils wrought by the octopus-like creation of the free-enterprise economy. It is a fact that economic growth has long ceased to be the exclusive concern or problem of national governments to become the necessary concerted action of a world-wide web of international relations. In this shift of the centers of decision, MNC have been involved as necessary parties to the framing, policing and strengthening of international economic cooperation. During the 1950's and 1960's the growth of international trade, and the variety of its beneficial or detrimental repercussion, either willingly accepted or reluctantly endured, was mainly due to the involvement of North American born MNC. They enjoyed, then, the solid support of a healthy economy at home, the backing of a world reserve currency and the prodding of well devised programs of research and development. At the outset, the preferred terrain of action of the North-American MNE was Western Europe; it offered comparatively low wages, a sophisticated market, stable political institutions and a similar cultural heritage.

In the late 60's, the scale tilted somewhat with the awakening of Europe and Latin America. Political social unrest resulted in riots in universities and factories. European and Latin American governments became more open and sensitive to the political pressure of militant trade unions and the social aspirations of workers. Following the example of these national governments, regional and international organizations added a new dimension to the control and supervision of the economic growth and political hold of the MNC.

It is the purpose of this collection of papers to review the major policy decisions taken by a MNC in response to the problems it is confronted with. These problems arise, first, from within the internal raison d'être of the MNE, second, from its national home environment and, third, from its crossing borders into the host country jurisdiction. To this purpose, the book here presented offers two additional features which emphasize its originality. As suggested above, the issues addressed by the papers submitted here will be considered from the viewpoints of three different continents, North America, Western Europe and Latin America. Besides, this book is somewhat unusual in that it offers an opportunity to non-English readers to acquire some knowledge of the matters discussed by reading either the French or the Spanish summary of the main paper.

The book has been divided into five different titles which are: investments, technology, tax, labor and securities.

I. <u>Investments</u>.

The MNE, by its very nature, operates under the laws of the country of its domicile as well as the laws of the host countries where its subsidiaries are located. This web of legal regulations of different origins and conceptions plays an important part in the formulation of the investment policies of the MNE. It is the purpose of the first chapter of this book to examine the originality and complexity of the investment laws of different regions where a MNC might operate.

Concerning the Latin American continent, the paper of Messrs. Leiseca and Slocomb opens with the challenging thought that, against common belief, these countries do not have a uniform culture. Likewise, their treatment of foreign investments is not uniform either [p. 16].

The central point of this essay is the issue of corporate reorganization as a strategy to improve foreign investments. Without naming any country in particular, the authors offer a panoramic view of eight possible devices ranging from amendment of the purpose clause [p. 23] to sale of assets [p. 28]. Some of these reorganization strategies are illustrated with examples [pp. 28-30]. Occasionally, considerations of broad general impact are mentioned, which go beyond the topic discussed. For instance, the convenience of "interposing pure holding companies between ultimate investors and companies organized in Latin American countries having foreign investment legislation" is raised [p. 29].

The paper draws a full circle, ending as it began, by commenting on the diversity with which the various regional countries try to control foreign investments [p. 31].

A radical change is felt when reading Professor Morris' description of the same topic, from the point of view of North America. Concerning the U.S. [pp. 36-71], the position is far less guarded than in Latin America. With good reason, perhaps, the instinct to protect against foreign penetration seems rather weak by comparison. On the contrary, the first issue discussed, the Foreign Corrupt Practices Act [pp. 37-40], restrains principally domestic corporations rather than foreign ones.

One measure of control, the International Investment Survey Act [pp. 44-47], seems mild when compared to the stringent protection systems encountered in other countries. Topics that obsess Latin nations such as repatriation of profits, exchange control, etc . . ., apparently are not much of an issue in the U.S.

Canada [pp. 48-53] shows to be in a middle position between Latin America and the U.S. Its efforts to retain national control over its businesses, while concurrently trying to lure foreign investments is a situation reminiscent of Latin countries.

II. Technology.

In the second chapter of this book, the reader will find a practical treatment of the controversial issue of transfer of technology. It is commonplace to say that the diffusion of technology is an inherent part of international economic growth and that MNE are in an ideal position to control the flow of the latest technical and scientific discoveries. This ability of a MNE to channel the benefits of technology or withhold its productive use determines to a large extent the economic development of the world at large.

An analysis of the Mexican situation is presented by Professor Armstrong. The Dependencia Theory is explained in the first part of this paper [pp. 78-86], establishing connections between the international patent system, the role of MNE and the effect of these two factors on the local technological development. The second part of this article covers the impact made by the Registry of Technology Transfer [pp. 86-101].

Both topics, Dependencia and the Registry, are treated in an interrelated way since one is a consequence of the other. The author presents a variety of opposing opinions, indicative of how polemic this subject has become.

An interesting point of this work is a random survey on the merits of the Registry, conducted among legal departments of U.S. corporations doing business in Mexico [p. 98].

Professor Carl approaches the topic of technology transfer [pp. 129-143] after making reference to antitrust and foreign investment laws [pp. 115-129]. Rather than focusing on a single country, Professor Carl analyzes the whole Latin American region. The paper opens with a timely comment on Latin America's foreign debt and on how modern technology, just as a transfusion of capital, can rescue a local business from bankruptcy [p. 114].

Technological transfer is discussed, in keeping with other papers in this book, from the angle of a MNE undergoing a reorganization process. The interesting symbiosis between technology on the one hand and foreign investments and antitrust laws on the other, is presented by reference to Argentina [pp. 140-141]. This country crossed, in 1976, from a restrictive to a more liberal system of technology control. In 1981 such system became even more open.

The author concludes by considering how antitrust and related legislation is more often used against foreign than domestic firms. Also raised is the new issue of Latin American MNE, as in the case of Brazil and Mexico, which pose problems of their own.

As with the preceding chapter, while crossing from Latin America to the U.S., a great change is immediately noticeable. The issues are not the same. As Art Dula, Esq., shows in his paper [pp. 168-177], the American concern is not so much to protect its technological potential but, rather, to prevent countries perceived as unfriendly from reaching such potential. Obviously, here, the problem is not import of technology but its export.

The paper describes the system of the 1979 Export Administration Act, amended in 1985, and its system of export licensing. The reader is introduced to the categorization of countries in eight groups, of which Canada receives the most liberal treatment, while Cuba, Kampuchea, North Korea and Vietnam (all belonging to group Z) are subject to a total embargo [p. 171].

Of great practical interest is the fact that American export controls are not limited to commodities. They also reach technical data and all computer software [p. 174].

One dominant theme in this essay is the tension between two opposing goals of American policy. Such are, on the one hand, to prevent unfriendly countries from having access to American latest technology and, on the other, to increase American exports. The author's opinion is that export controls are too rigid and that they should be revised [p. 176].

III. <u>Taxation</u>.

The puzzle of tax laws and regulations always baffle the taxpayer. That riddle becomes a maze where the MNE is involved. The latter must live under the control of a variety of tax systems and accounting regulations, cope with the extraterritorial application of its home country laws and ascertain whether or not it can find some solace in international tax treaties. It is the goal of this third chapter on taxation to take the reader through an examination of the policy decisions which confront a MNE in devising its tax liabilities.

In this section we find an analysis of the Latin American situation, two studies from the American point of view and a description of the French system.

The first paper, by Mssrs Leiseca and Slocomb [pp. 184-192] parallels their earlier contribution of chapter I. The general conclusion is that although diversity is still the rule, some common patterns can be found from country to country, e.g., territoriality of income taxes.

An interesting observation is the predominance of form over substance while assessing taxes [p. 185]. This, perhaps, is only a consequence of "formalism" as a general trait of Latin American law.

The tax impact of corporate reorganization is the backbone of this essay, as well as of the two following ones.

In his paper Professor Ault explains the U.S. position [pp. 200-214]. Here we find great differences with the Latin American view. For instance, the principle of territoriality is overtaken by that of worldwide taxation [p. 319]. The general impression is that the U.S. system is far more sophisticated and, probably also, more complicated.

The essay offers four principal angles: a general overview [p. 200], outbound transactions [p. 203], inbound transfers [p. 209] and wholly foreign transactions [p. 211].

Professor Siegel uses a similar approach, but focused on income tax. This article deals with the situation of American MNE [pp. 221-224], foreign MNE [pp. 224-228], tackling in the end certain special issues related to corporate structure [pp. 228-230].

The French system, as described by Mr. Serval [pp. 236-264] is based on two controlling principles, equality of taxation and division between direct and indirect taxes. An interesting trait is the wealth tax (impôt sur les grandes fortunes), which applies to French residents regardless of whether their assets are in or outside of France [p. 237].

The question of income obtained by non-residents of France [pp. 251-253] is explained in some length. The French application of value added tax (V.A.T.) is described in conjunction with the relevant EEC rules [pp. 245-251].

IV. Labor.

The growth of a MNC has often been considered a stimulant in the modern development of labor relations. National labor unions are confronted with problems which transcend their geographical boundaries and force them to be involved in operations which lie outside their home country's jurisdiction. In the papers presented under this heading the authors have addressed these problems in a most realistic and meaningful manner.

The Latin American perspective is addressed by Carlos Alfaro, Esq., who uses Argentina as a model, also applicable to situations arising elsewhere in the continent. Collective bargaining (convenciones colectivas) is the central topic.

The author discusses how trade unions operate and how power struggles are almost unavoidable with MNE. Two important labor cases, involving a meat packing concern and a car manufacturer are used to illustrate, respectively, bad and good policy decisions [pp. 274-275].

The most important message that comes across is that the MNE should maintain open a communication channel with the trade unions. Interestingly enough, the two other papers in this chapter, giving the Canadian and the European view, stress exactly the same point.

The peculiarities of the Canadian system are described by the bâtonnier Henri Grondin [pp. 288-296]. Freedom of association to trade unions is the rule. If this could weaken union power, the exclusivity of representation held by unions probably compensates for any other disadvantage. The duality of federal and provincial legislation, usually unknown in Latin America or in Europe, is solved in a similar way to the U.S.

Mme. Genot-Delbecque describes the situation of collective bargaining in Europe [pp. 304-324]. Frequent references are made to national as well as supranational rules and control systems. Among the latter, the OECD, the EEC, and the ILO are the ones most often mentioned.

A point raised, and worth developing elsewhere, is the treatment of Eastern European corporations that do business abroad. Reportedly their governments refuse to consider them MNE and to subject them to the U.N. Code of Conduct [p. 311].

V. Securities.

Any player on the international trade chess board very quickly discovers the existence of many obstacles, direct or indirect, not only to the free movement of goods and services but also to the free flow of capital. Raising money to fuel the huge machinery of the MNC is a daily dilemma of its management. The complexities of the national laws on securities require that one wade with great care through the pitfalls and snares that appear to be the common inherent feature of these laws. Our reporters have excelled in providing the reader with a safe and informative guide through these intricacies of the laws and regulations on securities.

In Latin America, as analyzed in Ricardo Diez, Esq., the international securities market seems to be less developed than in other areas. Reflecting this trend is the fact that Mexican law only contemplates the sale or purchase of securities issued locally [p.331]. And although Venezuela authorizes the trade of foreign securities, in practice only local ones are negotiated [p. 332].

The possibility of acquiring securities in Latin America as a way of foreign investment is explored [p. 336]. Venezuela, for instance, appears to reject this idea, while Argentina has come to accept it and even promote it. Tying in with this notion, the author suggests the conversion of Latin American debts into equity as one of the three possible ways of obtaining payment [pp. 337-339].

The situation in the U.S. appears to be entirely different. Allan Mostoff, Esq., presents the U.S. approach as the detailed regulation of a powerful market [pp. 347-363].

The topic is divided in two main parts: foreign securities offered in the U.S. and purchase of U.S.

business by foreign enterprises. The American system also contemplates the case where the issuer is a foreign government, which is somewhat less controlled than when it is a foreign corporation [p. 356].

William Haney, Esq., and Sylvie Durant des Aulnois, Esq., approach the issue of selling securities in Europe, concentrating on England, France, Germany, Holland and Germany. The systems of these countries are compared among themselves.

The main issues are restrictions to access, registration and disclosure requirements, accounting standards, insider trading and proxy solicitation [pp. 370-381].

Much of what is said is later tabulated on a useful chart that allows a quick comparison between any of the systems involved [pp. 382-398].

If the book is viewed in its entirety, after going through each chapter individually, it can be seen that all of its five chapters are interrelated. Changes in one area almost certainly affect the remaining four. Taxation is perhaps the most ubiquitous example, but there are others no less pervasive. For instance, foreign investment and transfer of technology relate to labor so strongly that they create as many problems as they solve. In the U.S., and other industrial countries, foreign direct investment can be seen as a job-export problem, creating jobs abroad to the detriment of domestic workers.[2] Conversely, technology transfer can be seen in developing nations as another form of job-export, since machines devised by foreign workers gradually replace the local working force. Securities is not an isolated topic either. It has direct links with foreign investments and transfer of technology, as mentioned repeatedly by our contributors (e.g. pp. 27, 45, 130).

The purpose of this book is to offer some ideas and different points of view to the reader. The complexity of the subjects approached and the span of the three chosen continents defeat any attempt to draw a generalized analysis or conclusion. What is possible, and so we hope, is that the following papers contribute to a better understanding of commercial issues among nations of different cultures.

The editors

FOOTNOTES

1. Roughly 35-40% of America's imports and exports moved within American multinational companies in 1977-80, according to a new study by the Federal Reserve Bank of Boston. The Commerce Department's latest survey of multinationals (still based on whiskery numbers) shows that these companies' total trade accounted for 77% of America's exports and 50% of its imports in 1982. That was lower than in 1977, when they accounted for 84% of exports and 58% of imports, but in recent years the proportion has certainly risen again as companies have responded to an over-valued dollar by shifting production and suppliers offshore.

Plant closures in such mature American industries as steel, textiles, shoes, metal castings and tyres have increased in the five years to late 1985 as the high dollar made chunks of the American economy uncompetititve. But American multinationals probably lost a much smaller part of their share of world exports than American industry as a whole, because of their ability to move production to more competitive places. The Economist, March 1986 at 61.

2. Conf. International Investment and Multinational Enterprises, Structural Adjustment and Multinational Enterprises, by OECD, p. 50 Paris 1985.

ACKNOWLEDGMENTS

Reorganization of Multinational Enterprises: Legal and tax aspects was the topic of a conference held at Louisiana State University under the auspices of the Paul M. Hebert Law Center in October 1984. This conference provided an opportunity for two associations of legal scholars, FIEDA and AACSL, to combine their annual journées.

The organizers, and editors, wish to express their gratitude to Professors Yves Guyon and Christian Louit, respectively President and Vice-President of the International Foundation for the Study of Business Law (FIEDA) and to Judge Edward D. Re, President of the American Association for the Comparative Study of Law (AACSL). The trust and confidence of the members of the boards of these two associations made our tasks most rewarding intellectually and enriching humanly.

Our most sincere thanks are extended to Chancellor William D. Hawkland of the LSU Law Center for his unmitigated support, both moral and financial, and his constant encouragement from the very inception of this conference.

The administrative and logistical aspects of the conference were the responsibility of the wonderfully efficient and reliable staff of the LSU Law Center. We must all gratefully acknowledge, in particular, the assistance of the Word Processing Center and the Library, the competence of Ms. Solovitch and Mr. Mihoubi, translators at the Center of Civil Law Studies, and the professional diligence of Mesdames M. Skäl, and S. Saale.

Alain A. Levasseur

Enrique Dahl

TABLE OF CONTENTS

Introduction. 1

Acknowledgments. 11

Table of Contents. 12

Chapter I. Foreign Investments

Foreign Investment Aspects Of Multinational Reorganizations: The Latin American Perspective. 15
Résumé. 32
Resumen. 34
United States And Canadian Laws Affecting Multinationals. 36
Résumé. 72
Resumen. 74

Chapter II. Transfer Of Technology

The Mexican Response To Technological Dependency: The National Registry Of Technology Transfer. 77
Résumé. 111
Resumen. 112
Latin American Antitrust Laws and Their Equivalents: Impact On Reorganization And Licensing By Transnational Enterprises. . . . 113
Résumé. 161
Resumen. 164
MNE Reorganization And Technology Transfers: Meeting Changes In American Regulation. 167
Résumé. 178
Resumen. 180

Chapter III. Taxation

Tax Aspects Of Multinational Reorganization: The Latin American Perspective. 183
Résumé. 193
Resumen. 196
Tax Aspects Of International Reorganizations And Liquidations: The United States. 199
Résumé. 216
Resumen. 218
United States Income Tax And Reorganization Policies Applicable To Multinational Enterprises . 220
Résumé. 231
Resumen. 233

The French Tax System. 235
Résumé. 265
Resumen. 267

Chapter IV. Collective Bargaining

Multinational Enterprises And Collective Bargaining From A Latin American Perspective. . . 270
Résumé. 281
Resumen. 284
Multinational Enterprises And Collective Bargaining In A Reorganization Process: The Canadian Approach. 287
Résumé. 297
Resumen. 300
Collective Bargaining: The European Perspective. 303
Résumé. 325
Resumen. 327

Chapter V. Purchase And Sale Of Securities

Securities: Problems In Selling Securities In Latin American Private And Public Markets. . . 330
Résumé. 341
Resumen. 344
Application Of U.S. Laws To The Purchase And Sale Of Securities In The U.S. 347
Résumé. 364
Resumen. 366
Problems Of Multinational Enterprises In Selling Securities In Europe. 368
Résumé. 399
Resumen. 400

Chapter I

FOREIGN INVESTMENTS

LATIN AMERICA

NORTH AMERICA

FOREIGN INVESTMENT ASPECTS OF MULTINATIONAL REORGANIZATIONS: THE LATIN AMERICAN PERSPECTIVE

Sergio A. Leiseca and Paul D. Slocomb

Mr. Leiseca is a partner in the Chicago office of Baker & McKenzie. He has 14 years' practice in international matters, with emphasis on Latin American foreign investment, tax, technology transfer, commercial and corporate law. His J.D. degree is from Tulane University School of Law where he was a member of the Law Review.

Mr. Slocomb is a partner in the Chicago office of Baker & McKenzie. He has 13 years' practice in international matters, with emphasis on Latin American foreign investment, tax, technology transfer, commercial and corporate law. His J.D. degree is from The Harvard Law School.

I. Introduction

There are many countries in Latin America. Contrary to popular perception, they are not uniform. They are not uniform in language. One fluent in the Spanish of Bogota and the Portuguese of Sao Paulo will find in many parts of Latin America that he, if not totally unable to communicate, will at least be confounded and confused. The countries are not uniform in geography, ranging in a relatively tiny part of the region from the Pampas of Argentina to the Andes forming its border with Chile to the deserts of the Chilean Pacific coast. They are not uniform in natural resources or relative state of development. They are not uniform in culture, with strong influences not only from Spain and Portugal but from, *inter alia*, Germany, Italy and the United Kingdom. They are not uniform in political tradition and stability, nor in degree of respect for the rule of law. And they are not uniform in their attitudes toward and degree of control exercised over foreign investment.

A. Foreign Investment Law

We could not in this chapter cover all Latin American countries, or for that matter all variants of their regulations of foreign investment. Some countries in the region are openly receptive to foreign investment, with no significant restrictive legislation except in basic areas intimately tied to national patrimony and defense. Others have foreign investment legislation that may rank with the most restrictive in the world.

Of those Latin American countries that do regulate all foreign investments, some do so by means of specific foreign investment legislation. Others rely on provisions of more generalized exchange control legislation. While the variety is great, it will be useful to describe a few of the most basic features commonly found in foreign investment legislation in Latin America.

1. Prior Approval

Prior governmental approval of foreign investments often required by foreign investment legislation in Latin America. In some countries it is mandatory for all or some foreign investments, with failure to secure approval sometimes resulting in the investment being null and void. In other countries, foreign investors have an option to seek prior approval, but failure to secure it may leave the foreign investor in a less favorable position from an exchange control and tax point of view. In yet other countries, prior approval is not required for at least some investments, but failure to notify foreign investment authorities may leave the foreign investor in a less favorable position. In countries where the foreign investor has the option to seek approval or notify authorities, the protection gained by doing so may be offset by a *quid pro quo* in the form of an excess remittance tax. See 3 below.

2. Registered Foreign Investment

In some countries either the foreign investment or exchange control authorities (*e.g.*, a Central Bank) maintain a registry of foreign investments. Requirements vary as to how a foreign investor must evidence having made a foreign investment. The amount of foreign investment may be registered in the foreign currency in which it was made, in another foreign currency, or in local currency, with or without provision for indexing or other adjustment. The amount of registered foreign investment usually is relevant to the next three topics.

3. Limits on Profit Remittances

The amount of profits that can be paid or remitted to a foreign investor often is tied to the amount of registered foreign investment. The limit may be in the form of a prohibition of payment or remittance of any amount in excess of a stated percentage per annum of the amount of registered foreign investment. Sometimes the annual limits may be accumulated. Sometimes they may not. The limit may not be absolute. Rather, profit payments or remittances in excess of the stated percentage may be permitted with special authorization of foreign investment authorities.

The distinction between payment (in local currency) and remittance (after conversion from local currency to foreign currency) may be crucial. A foreign investor may be entitled to receive profits in local currency to be expended locally, but that local currency may not be convertible to foreign currency to be used abroad.

In some countries the limitation is not on the amount of payment or remittance. Rather, it takes the form of a special "excess remittance tax", generally graduated, on profit remittances in excess of stated percentages per annum of the amount of registered foreign investment. In some cases, the combined effective rate of income tax on the income of the local company, normal withholding tax on dividends, and excess remittance tax may range into the 70-80% bracket. This as a practical matter may preclude substantial dividend payments.

4. Limits on "Reinvestment" of Profits

In some countries, the amount of registered foreign investment can be increased by "reinvesting" profits generated by the local company. The increase allows higher levels of profit payments or remittances in the future, or reduces the impact of excess remittance taxes. The amount that may be reinvested in one year sometimes is limited to a percentage of the amount of registered foreign investment as of, e.g., the end of the preceding year. In other countries a limitation may exist, but may be waived in special cases upon application to foreign investment authorities. In other countries the amount of annual reinvestment is not limited.

The combination of reinvestment and profit remittance limitations sometimes leads to accumulation of so-called "limbo" profits, the status of which is not always clear. They may taint the registered foreign investment base, in the sense that the foreign investment may become partially registered and partially unregistered. The result can be that a foreign investor may be entitled to exchange and repatriate some, but not all, of a profit distribution from a local company.

5. Limits on Repatriation of Capital

Once a foreign investment is made, the foreign investor may have to wait for some period before being entitled to repatriate capital in the event of, _e.g._, total or partial liquidation. The limitation may be imposed by statute or by negotiated contract with the foreign investment authorities.

In some countries, the amount that may be repatriated is limited to the amount of registered foreign investment, even if the value of the the investment has increased substantially through appreciation and accumulation of earnings. In others, excess remittance taxes apply not only to periodic distributions of profits, but also to liquidation proceeds in excess of the amount of registered foreign investment.

6. Limits on Expansion of Business

Foreign investment legislation can limit expansion of business in a number of ways. First, infusion of new capital to fund an expansion often requires prior approval equivalent to that required for the original investment. Second, even if no new infusion of capital is contemplated, expansion into a new line of business or to a new location may require prior authorization of foreign investment or other authorities. Third, wholly apart from considerations strictly of a foreign investment nature, the applicable corporate law may bear on expansion into new lines of business. The corporate laws of many Latin American countries do not permit purpose clauses of the breadth commonly encountered in, for example, the United States. They may require that the purpose of the company be stated in its articles precisely and narrowly. Corporate authorities may be reluntant to approve an amendment to the articles allowing expansion into new lines of business. Furthermore, the amendment of the articles may itself be an event triggering foreign investment review and approval.

7. Limits on Transfers of Ownership

Foreign investment legislation may require prior approval for transfers of equity ownership in a local company from one foreign investor to another, or from a foreign investor to a local investor. In some countries this requirement is in practice a mere formality and can be satisfied in a relatively short period of time.

In some countries transfers from one foreign investor to another may be more closely scrutinized than transfers from a foreign investor to a local investor. For example, in some countries the foreign investment authorities, when presented with an application for transfer of an equity interest from one foreign investor to another, will use the opportunity to press for the transfer of some equity ownership to local investors. This may be particularly true in the case of transfers of equity interests in local companies that are wholly-owned or majority-owned by foreigners, whether by virtue of "grandfather rights" in effect at the time the foreign investment legislation was enacted, or by virtue of an approval secured from foreign investment authorities.

In other countries, transfers from a foreign investor to a local investor may be more closely scrutinized. The authorities may wish, for example, to assure that locally-held shares are broadly-held, sometimes with particular emphasis on shareholdings by the employees of the local company.

Transfers of equity interests from local investors to foreign investors typically are much more difficult, if not impossible. In some countries there are outright prohibitions on transfers of shares held by local investors to foreign investors. In others, such transfers are permitted only in exceptional circumstances such as imminent bankruptcy of the local company.

8. Requirement of Local Investors - "Transformation"

In some Latin American countries, foreign investors cannot invest in local companies unless there is some equity participation by local investors. The required percentage may vary depending upon the nature of the activity in which the local company engages. Even if no minimum level of local ownership is absolutely required, certain incentives may not be available to local companies having less than a stated level of local ownership, and access of the local company to, *e.g.*, local financing may be restricted.

In some countries, a significant level of local ownership may not be required as of the commencement of operations of a new company. But, pursuant to "transformation" requirements, the percentage ownership by local investors may be required to increase to a majority position over a stated period.

B. Reorganization

Our topic is somewhat complicated by the fact that "reorganization", although often addressed in at least rudimentary fashion by the corporate laws of Latin American countries, and sometimes by tax laws as well, seldom is directly addressed by foreign investment legislation. To this add the fact that reorganizations, while certainly not unheard of, on balance are a less common occurrence in most Latin American countries than in Europe or the United States.

C. Approach

From the foregoing introductory comments it should be apparent that encyclopedic treatment of Latin American foreign investment aspects of multinational reorganizations would be impossible in this short chapter. Rather than attempting to treat even the laws of one jurisdiction in depth, we propose to provide a roadmap. We will first identify and discuss the issues that typically must be addressed in various kinds of reorganizations. We then will illustrate how these issues might be resolved using a few examples.

II. Issues in Reorganization

The foreign investment issues depend on the kind of reorganization. The kind of reorganization obviously depends upon the motive of the multinational enterprise. Reasons to reorganize in Latin America, while not significantly different from reasons to reorganize elsewhere, should be identified. They may be quite varied. We will mention only those that, in our practice, occur regularly.

A multinational enterprise may wish to reorganize for non-local tax reasons. For example, it may wish to change the form of local organization to achieve partnership, rather than corporate, income tax treatment for its investment in its own country. Often this can be accomplished through a change in the form of local corporate organization.

A multinational enterprise may wish to reorganize based on "image" considerations. For example, in most Latin American countries the S.A. (corporation) generally is perceived to be a larger, more substantial, more regulated, and thus more reliable form than a limitada (limited liability company -- a kind of hybrid of a corporation and a partnership). Thus, the multinational enterprise may wish to transform a limitada into a S.A. Alternatively, it may wish to infuse new capital or capitalize retained earnings to give greater comfort to suppliers, customers, and financial institutions.

A multinational enterprise may wish to consolidate lines of business to achieve greater managerial efficiency or improve borrowing capacity. Conversely, it may wish to separate lines of business preparatory to, e.g., divestiture of the business of a home country division or subsidiary. In this regard, note that multinationals that operate through separate subsidiaries in their home country often house various lines of business in a local country in a single operating company. Such reasons for reorganizing lead to consideration of mergers, drop-downs, split-ups or spin-offs, and the like.

A multinational enterprise may wish to add new lines of business. To do so it may be necessary to infuse new capital and/or amend the purpose clause of the articles of a local company.

A multinational enterprise may wish to eliminate existing lines of business and/or repatriate excess funds. Thus it may consider capital reduction, partial liquidation, or redemption.

A multinational enterprise may wish to increase or decrease the degree of local equity participation. Thus it may again consider redemption, as well as stock sales and acquisitions.

Finally, a multinational enterprise may wish to sell portions of the business conducted by a local company. In this case, it may consider a drop-down, split-up, or spin-off followed by a stock sale, or it may consider a sale of assets.

There can also be combinations of reasons for a reorganization. In any event, for purposes of this discussion the issues can be identified and discussed by considering (a) amendments of purpose clauses, (b) "transformations" in the corporate sense, from one form of entity to another, (c) increases in capital resulting from new investment or reinvestment of profits, (d) mergers, (e) split-ups or spin-offs, (f) capital reductions, liquidations and redemptions, (g) stock transfers, and (h) sales of assets.

A. Amendment of Purpose Clause

Many kinds of reorganizations may require the amendment of the purpose clause of the articles of an existing company. We here consider only transactions not otherwise requiring local foreign investment approval.

The *ultra vires* doctrine often is rather strictly applied in Latin American countries. If a company engages in activities not within its corporate purpose, officers and directors may be personally liable. In addition, the activities of companies often are closely supervised by corporate authorities. Acting outside the scope of the purpose clause may, in extreme cases, result in suspension of permission to operate.

As noted earlier, the purpose clause under corporate law may have to be specific. Even if it need not, the foreign investment or other authorities (*e.g.*, the Ministry of Foreign Relations or its equivalent) may insist upon a narrow purpose clause upon incorporation. In addition, the foreign investment legislation, or the corporate law itself, may require prior approval for any change in the corporate purpose. This can lead to pressure to, *e.g.*, bring in local investors at the time of a change.

B. "Transformation"

Transformation of a local company from one corporate form to another also requires amendment of the articles. As in the case of amendment of the purpose clause, the amendment required to transform may lead to pressure to bring in local investors. The likelihood of pressure, however, is probably less than in the case of a change in the purpose clause needed to expand the lines of business of the local company.

C. Capital Increase

Many kinds of reorganizations may require a capital increase in an existing local company. The capital increase may be my means of infusion of new capital or by "reinvestment" of retained earnings.

1. Infusion of New Capital

In some Latin American countries the infusion of new capital from abroad by a foreign investor requires the same kind of prior approval and/or registration that is required to incorporate a new company. In others, new capital infusion without approval is limited to stated amounts or stated percentages of the amount of prior investment.

In countries that do not require approval of new or additional investment but permit it, and offer benefits for securing approval or registration or giving notification, a foreign investor may fall into a trap. It may fail to register or give notice of a capital increase in a company in which its original investment is registered. If so, it may end up with an investment that is partially registered and partially unregistered. This can lead to difficult questions of remittability of profits and applicability of excess remittance taxes.

2. Reinvestment of Earnings

Unlike infusion of new capital, reinvestment of earnings generated by a local company virtually never must be approved. But if approval is sought, the amount which may be approved and registered may be limited. This is the case, for example, in countries where "automatic" reinvestment is allowed only up to a specified percentage per annum of registered foreign investment.

Because reinvestment of earnings most often need not be approved, the danger of ending up in a partially-registered, partially-unregistered status is greater than in the case of infusion of new capital. A local company may take all corporate steps necessary to implement the capital increase resulting from reinvestment, but fail to document the increase appropriately with foreign investment or exchange control authorities. If so, it may end up with some unregistered investment. The problem is exacerbated in highly inflationary countries where foreign investment is registered in local currency, because relatively modest reinvestments when measured in dollars at current exchange rates may quickly outstrip the amount of original investment when measured in local currency. That is, the resulting proportion of unregistered investment may be very high.

D. Merger

The most difficult foreign investment issue in the case of a merger generally is "carryover" of the amount of registered foreign investment. Foreign investment legislation often is silent regarding this issue. The interpretations of foreign investment authorities may vary widely. The clearest case would appear to be a foreign investor with registered investments of X and Y in local companies A and B, with A to be merged into B. Logically, after the merger the foreign investor's registered foreign investment in B should be X + Y. But foreign investment authorities may refuse to recognize X. They may have a variety of reasons for doing so. As one example, registered foreign investment in some countries is defined by reference to foreign currency invested from abroad, and local currency having free remittance rights. In a simple merger there is no foreign currency coming from abroad, and there may be no identifiable fund of remittable local currency. As the reader may imagine, the issue becomes significantly more complex if the foreign investor's investment in either company is other than fully registered.

E. Split-Up or Spin-Off

In the case of a split-up or spin-off, as in the case of a merger, the most difficult issue relates to the amount of registered foreign investment. How is a foreign investor's registered investment of X in local company A to be allocated when A is divided into A and B? Should it all be left in A? Or should it be allocated? If so, how should it be allocated? The foreign investment legislation typically is silent in this regard. The foreign investor's desires regarding allocation may be wholly irrelevant. Assume, for example, that A is a manufacturing and selling company, and splits up into A, which continues to manufacture, and a new B, which markets. A manufacturing operation usually is more capital intensive than a selling operation. But the selling operation may enjoy higher profit margins. Thus the foreign investor may wish to have a higher allocation of registered foreign investment to the selling company. But the foreign investment authorities may insist that the allocation be proportional to corporate capital or underlying asset value. Again, significantly more complex problems may arise if a part of the foreign investor's investment in A is unregistered.

Split-ups and spin-offs often raise additional issues of a quasi-foreign investment nature. Take for example a multinational enterprise that was allowed, under an incentive program, to set up a 100%-owned local company to assemble and export two lines of equipment. The incentives (tax and duty reductions and the like) may be tied to a long-term export commitment for the combination of the two lines. The multinational enterprise may wish to divest one line worldwide to an unrelated party. If it splits up the local company preparatory to divesting that line, how is the export commitment, and thus the qualification for incentives, to be handled? The local country may wish to make the two companies jointly responsible for meeting the export commitment. But that most likely will not be acceptable to either the multinational enterprise or the purchaser.

F. Capital Reduction, Liquidation, and Redemption

In the case of a capital reduction, liquidation, or redemption, the basic issue is repatriability of capital and earnings. Foreign investment laws generally are fairly clear with respect to complete liquidations. Partial liquidations and capital reductions, on the other hand, may not be adequately covered. Unless an arrangement can be negotiated with local authorities, the foreign investor may have to settle for all (complete liquidation) or nothing. Negotiation of an arrangement may be complicated by different views of the foreign investor and the foreign investment authorities as to how the partial liquidation or capital reduction will affect the remaining amount of registered (and unregistered) foreign investment.

Redemption by a local company of outstanding shares is not possible under corporate laws of some countries. If it is, it may offer attractive advantages, despite (or because of) the fact that it most often is not directly addressed by the foreign investment legislation. Foreign investment authorities may not know whether the redemption should be treated as a capital reduction, partial liquidatiion, or something else. Often they simply treat it as a sale of shares from a foreign investor to the local company. Therein lie the potential advantages.

The first potential advantage is that, if redemption is viewed as a sale, proceeds may be remittable, while proceeds of capital reduction or partial liquidation might not. This, however, is not always the case. The foreign investment legislation of some countries allows repatriation of proceeds of sales of shares to a local company only if the local company is, *e.g.*, majority owned by local investors. This leads to an interesting theoretical question, the potential consequences of which the authors have seen more than once in their practice. Assume a local company is owned 70% by a foreign investor and 30% by a local investor. Further assume control is to be passed to the local investor by having the company redeem 50% of its shares from the foreign investor. As a result, the local company will be owned 60% by the local investor and 40% by the foreign investor. Is the rule regarding remittability of redemption/sale proceeds to be applied by reference to the majority foreign ownership immediately before redemption, or the majority local ownership immediately after redemption? How many angels can dance on the head of redemption?

The second potential advantage of a redemption viewed as a sale is that it may allow cleaning up a partially-registered, partially-unregistered situation. The authors have participated in a number of transactions pursuant to which unregistered shares are redeemed for a modest amount of local currency, which the foreign investor can expend locally, leaving all remaining shares registered. Obviously the result depends upon a system whereby the registered and unregistered status of investment attaches to particular shares, rather than being allocated proportionally over all shares. That is not always the case.

G. Stock Transfers

The principal foreign investment issue in stock transfers depends on whether the transfer is to a foreign investor or to a local investor. If it is to a foreign investor, the issue is carryover of registered foreign investment. Typically the new foreign investor simply steps into the shoes of the old foreign investor. This can present a problem, as the shares may be transferred for a price substantially in excess of the amount of registered foreign investment. Conversely, the rule does encourage trading in local companies that have substantial losses, but in which there is substantial registered foreign investment. This possibility must be investigated carefully in individual cases. Not the least of the problems is that, in some countries, the amount of registered investment not only can be increased by reinvestment of earnings, but can be reduced by annual losses. This, by the way, is a hidden trap for foreign investors establishing local companies that are expected to generate substantial start-up losses.

If the stock is sold to a local investor, the principal issue is remittability of proceeds. As indicated above in the discussion of redemption, proceeds of sale to local investors generally are remittable. But in some countries remittability may be limited to the amount of registered foreign investment attributable to the shares.

H. Sales of Assets

If a multinational enterprise's local company sells all of its assets, and assuming it does not reinvest the proceeds in other productive assets, the principal issue is remittability. The issue will be governed by rules governing complete liquidations, discussed earlier. If the sale is of some but not all assets, the issue again will be remittability, which may be handled in accordance with normal profit remittance rules, or in accordance with partial liquidation rules discussed earlier.

Although not a foreign investment issue, we should mention that many Latin American countries have laws comparable to bulk sales laws familiar in the United States. Typically the commercial code or other laws require public notice of intended sales of all or substantially all or an economically-related unit of a local company's assets. Failure to give notice usually leaves the buyer and seller jointly and severally liable for some time to creditors of the selling local company.

III. Examples

A. Assumed Structure

Assume that a United States multinational enterprise ("USM") owns a United States holding company ("USH"), which in turn owns a company organized in a Latin American country ("LA1"), which in turn owns a Latin American subsidiary organized in the same Latin American country ("LAS1"). Further assume that USM directly (not through USH) owns a second company organized in the same Latin American country ("LA2"), which in turn owns a second subsidiary organized in the same Latin American country ("LAS2"). We will use this structure to illustrate the foreign investment aspects of mergers and divestitures, two of the more common forms of reorganization in Latin America.

B. Mergers

USM may wish to have LA1 and LA2 merge. If the investments of USM and USH in LA2 and LA1, respectively, are fully registered, the transaction in most countries should present no unusual problems. The end result should be registered investment of USM and USH in the surviving company in an amount equal to the sum of the amounts of registered investment of USM and USH prior to the merger. But if any part of either premerger investment is not registered, complications will arise. Furthermore, if the purpose clause of the articles of the company that is to survive the merger is not broad enough to encompass the activities of the company being merged into it, foreign investment authorities may be more inclined to press for some concessions, possibly including divestiture of some portion of the ownership of the local companies to local investors.

If the desire is to merge LAS1 and LAS2, the second tier local companies, foreign investment clearance will not be required in most Latin American countries. But again, if an amendment to a purpose clause is required complications may arise.

C. Divestiture

Now assume USM wishes to dispose of all of its direct and indirect interests in the Latin American country in question. It may consider selling to an unrelated United States company ("USCO") or to an unrelated company organized in the Latin American country in question and owned by nationals of that country ("LATCO").

The foreign investment legislation of most Latin American countries would not require approval for a sale by USM of its shares in USH to USCO. This is an important reason for interposing pure holding companies between ultimate investors and companies organized in Latin American countries having foreign investment legislation. USM and USH would, however, generally require approval from foreign investment authorities for the sale of shares of LA1 or LA2 to USCO. It generally would not be difficult to secure that approval, but in some countries pressure for concessions might arise.

If the sale were to LATCO, rather than USCO, the result might be different. USM typically would not need approval to transfer its shares in USH to LATCO but LATCO, pursuant to exchange control regulations or regulations affecting outbound investments from its country of incorporation, might require approval for its investment in USH.

In most Latin American countries, no approval would be required for USM's or USH's sale of its shares in LA1 or LA2 to LATCO. But in some countries it would, and the foreign investment authorities might attempt to require that the divestiture of shares be broadly-based, perhaps including transfers to employees of LA1 or LA2.

The situation would be considerably more complicated if USM, as is not uncommon, wished to dispose not of all of its assets in Latin America, but rather only those assets related to a particular line of business. Assume, for example, that LA2 conducts two lines of business and USM wishes to dispose of only one of them, which includes LA2's share interest in LAS2. If the acquiror is LATCO, foreign investment approval normally would not be required for LA2's sale of assets, including the shares of LAS2, to LATCO. LA2 would be left with a single line of business and, presumably, more local currency than it needed for the continuation of its operations. That excess cash might not be remittable under applicable foreign investment legislation. USM would want to consider capital reduction, partial liquidation, or redemption of shares of LA2.

Problems would also be presented if the acquiror were USCO. USCO might not have an existing wholly-owned subsidiary in the Latin American country in question, and the foreign investment legislation of that country might prevent USCO from forming a new wholly-owned subsidiary. Thus, an asset sale to a locally-organized company might not be possible. USM would have to consider splitting up LA2. If local foreign investment authorities permitted it to do so, USM might consider having the company to be divested owned by a newly-organized subsidiary in the United States, the shares of which could be sold to USCO after the split-up, typically without any further requirements of foreign investment approval. Otherwise, USM would have to sell shares of a local company resulting from the split-up, which typically would require foreign investment approval, and might increase the possibility of pressure for concessions.

IV. Conclusion

The effect of foreign investment legislation on reorganizations varies widely from country to country in Latin America. While certain general patterns can be identified, there is no substitute for careful planning of the structure of an original investment in a Latin American country, and careful examination of the foreign investment legislation and alternative approaches to reorganization when a change must be made.

RÉSUMÉ EN FRANÇAIS

RÉORGANISATIONS DES MULTINATIONALES ASPECTS RELATIFS AUX INVESTISSEMENTS ÉTRANGERS: LA PERSPECTIVE LATINO-AMÉRICAINE

La réglementation des investissements étrangers dans les pays latino-américains n'est pas uniforme. Toutefois, dans les pays où il existe une législation importante en la matière, on retrouve certains traits communs. À titre d'exemple, on peut citer:

- l'obligation d'obtenir une autorisation suivie d'un enregistrement;

- des restrictions au transfert des profits à l'étranger;

- le réinvestissement des profits et le rapatriement des capitaux;

- des restrictions au développement des affaires et au transfert de proprieté;

- l'obligation de la participation d' investisseurs locaux.

Dans la majorité des cas, les réorganisations ne sont pas directement régies par la législation relative aux investissements étrangers. Les problèmes dépendent surtout du type de réorganisation.

Si la réorganisation nécessite une modification des statuts d'une société locale, les autorités nationales peuvent faire pression pour que les investisseurs nationaux obtiennent une certaine participation dans cette réorganisation.

Par contre, lorsque la réorganisation implique une augmentation de capital, l'approbation ou l'enregistrement de cette augmentation peuvent être exigés et, si l'investisseur ne se conforme pas strictement aux exigences locales, son investissement risque d'être partiellement enregistré et partiellement non enregistré.

Si la réorganisation se fait sous forme d'une fusion, elle peut s'avérer beaucoup plus complexe que ce que ce qu'on espérait obtenir d'un amalgame des montants des investissements étrangers enregistrés dans les sociétés concernées par la fusion.

Quand la réorganisation se présente sous forme de scission, il ne serait peut-être pas possible d'assigner aux sociétés en résultant l'investissement étranger selon les proportions prévues.

Si la réorganisation implique une réduction de capital, une liquidation ou un rachat d'actions, il est possible que le produit ne soit pas nécessairement transférable à l'investisseur étranger.

Lorsque la réorganisation implique un transfert d'actions d'un investisseur étranger à un nouvel investisseur étranger, une autorisation de procéder à cette réorganisation peut être exigée et l'investissement enregistré du nouvel investisseur sera probablement le même que celui de l'investisseur précédent, au lieu du montant payé pour le transfert. En revanche, si le transfert est destiné à un investisseur local, l'approbation n'est souvent pas exigée, mais la somme transférable peut être limitée. Par ailleurs, le transfert d'un investisseur local à un investisseur étranger peut être interdit.

Si la réorganisation nécessite une vente d'actifs, la problème majeur serait probablement le transfert du produit, lequel peut être limité selon des règles applicables aux dividendes, aux réductions de capital, aux liquidations et au rachat.

En conclusion, les législations latino-américaines relatives aux investissements étrangers, sans être uniformes, ont un effet important sur les réorganisations. Tout investissement devrait être structuré de façon a être flexible si une réorganisation est envisagée dans le futur. A ce moment là, un certain nombre d'alternatives devront être étudiées.

RESUMEN EN ESPAÑOL

ASPECTOS RELATIVOS A INVERSIONES EXTRANJERAS DE LAS REORGANIZACIONES MULTINACIONALES: LA PERSPECTIVA LATINOAMERICANA

La regulación de las inversiones extranjeras por los países latinoamericanos no es uniforme. En aquellos países que tienen una regulación importante, se encuentran ciertos rasgos comunes. Estos incluyen, por ejemplo:

- el requisito de la previa autorización y registro;

- límites a la remisión de utilidades; "reinversión" de utilidades y repatriación de capital; límites a la expansión de negocios y a la transferencia de propiedad;

- requisitos de participación por parte de inversores locales.

La mayoría de las veces las reorganizaciones no están directamente reguladas por la legislación de inversiones extranjeras. Los problemas dependen de la clase de reorganización.

Si la reorganización requiere la modificación de los Estatutos Sociales de una compañía local, las autoridades locales pueden presionar para que se transfiera cierta participación a inversores locales.

Contrariaments, cuando la reorganización requiere un aumento de capital, la aprobación o registro del mismo pueden ser requeridos, y la falla en cumplir estrictamente con los requisitos locales puede resultar en que la inversión de un extranjero esté parcialmente registrada y parcialmente no registrada.

Si la reorganización adopta la forma de una fusión, puede ser más complicado que lo esperado combinar los montos de la inversión extranjera registrada en las compañías a ser fusionadas.

Cuando la reorganización se hace bajo la forma de una escisión, puede no ser posible adjudicar a las compañías resultantes la inversión extranjera registrada en las proporciones deseadas.

Cuando la reorganización requiere una reducción de capital, liquidación o rescate de acciones, las recaudaciones pueden no ser remesables para el inversor extranjero.

Cuando la reorganización implica una transferencia de acciones de un inversor extranjero a un nuevo inversor extranjero, la autorización de la misma puede ser requerida, y la inversión registrada del nuevo inversor probablemente será la del anterior inversor, en lugar de la del monto pagado por la transferencia. Si la transferencia es a un inversor local, la aprobación usualmente no será requerida, pero el monto remesable puede ser limitado. La transferencia de un inversor local a un inversor extranjero puede ser prohibida.

Si la reorganización requiere ventas de activos, el problema principal probablemente será la remesabilidad de las recaudaciones, las cuales pueden ser limitadas por reglas aplicables a dividendos, reducciones de capital, liquidación o rescate de acciones.

En conclusión, las reglas latinoamericanas sobre inversiones extranjeras, sin ser uniformes, generalmente tienen un importante efecto sobre las reorganizaciones. Las inversiones deberían ser estructuradas para tener flexibilidad si en el futuro se contempla una reorganización. En tal momento, posibilidades alternativas deberán ser consideradas.

UNITED STATES AND CANADIAN LAWS AFFECTING MULTINATIONALS

Glenn G. Morris

The author is Assistant Professor of Law at Louisiana State University. He teaches courses in contracts, business associations and corporate finance. Professor Morris holds a J.D. degree, with high honors, from the University of Florida, where he was a member of the Law Review and Order of the Coif.

From the many topics that I might have discussed under the broad title of this presentation, I have chosen to deal only with those major United States and Canadian laws that are directed specifically at foreign investments and operations, as distinguished from provisions that affect multinationals only incidentally, as a result of the applicability of those provisions to conduct within a jurisdiction generally.

In treating United States law, I will discuss (i) the antibribery provisions of the Foreign Corrupt Practices Act of 1977, (ii) the antiboycott provisions of federal tax and export administration law and (iii) reporting requirements for foreign investments. The Canadian portion of my presentation will cover the Foreign Investment Review Act, which requires governmental approval of the establishment or takeover of Canadian businesses, and provisions in federal and provincial corporate law that require certain minimum levels of Canadian representation on corporate boards of directors.

FOREIGN CORRUPT PRACTICES ACT

The Foreign Corrupt Practices Act of 1977 ("FCPA")[1] imposes accounting requirements on U.S. "issuers"[2] and prohibits foreign bribery by these issuers and by U.S. "domestic concerns". "Issuers" for purposes of the FCPA are companies whose securities are publicly held in the United States.[3] "Domestic concerns" are either business entities (other than issuers) that are organized or have their principal place of business in the United States or individuals who are citizens, residents or nationals of the United States.[4] Enforcement responsibility under the FCPA is split between the Securities and Exchange Commission ("SEC"), which handles civil enforcement of the issuer provisions, and the Department of Justice, which is responsible for all criminal actions and for civil actions against domestic concerns.[5] This discussion will deal solely with the Act's antibribery provisions.

Except for so-called "grease payments," (i.e. the bribery of low- level officials with only clerical or ministerial responsibilities),[6] both issuers and domestic concerns are subject to liability under the antibribery provisions of the FCPA if they use the telephone or mail (or any other instrumentality of interstate commerce) "corruptly" in furtherance of any transfer or offer of anything of value to any person, if they know or have reason to know that the item of value will be used, directly or indirectly, to encourage a foreign political or governmental official to use his official position to direct business to any person.[7] There are no safe harbors under the Act and no "restructuring" of a transaction will immunize the issuer or domestic concern from FCPA exposure. In effect, if a foreign official receives a bribe to direct business to someone, and that bribe can be linked, however indirectly, to some payment by a U.S. firm (furthered by some use of an instrumentability of commerce), the firm must be ready to show either (i) that it did not know and had no reason to know that the payment would help fund the bribe or (ii) that it lacked the requisite "corrupt" intention. While the restructuring of a transaction might help obfuscate the connection between the issuer and any possible bribery, it also increases the risk that knowledge and evil motive will be inferred once the connection is made.

Unfortunately, despite the importance of the intention issue, and the obvious inconsistency of the "reason to know" and "corrupt intent" phrases in the statute, no one yet knows whether an evil motive actually is required for an FCPA conviction or, instead, will simply be deemed to exist where the payor is reckless enough to make a payment under circumstance that give him "reason to know" that it might be used for a bribe. The legislative history of the FCPA suggests that an evil motive actually is required;[8] the SEC insists that it is not.[9] Indeed, the SEC has even taken the position that simple negligence is enough to satisfy the Act's "corruption" element.[10]

In view of the Supreme Court's rulings that more than simple negligence must be shown in actions for compensatory damages under the antifraud provisions of the federal securities laws,[11] it is very unlikely that negligence alone would support the imposition of civil or criminal penalties for bribery. However, the Supreme Court has left open in the fraud cases the question of whether recklessness with respect to the accuracy of an issuer's representations is tantamount to an intention to deceive.[12] The lower courts have held consistently that it is.[13] The analogue in bribery cases, i.e., that recklessness with respect to the disposition of funds amounts to an intention to bribe, is very strong. If this is true, the meaning of "recklessness" becomes critical.

In fraud actions, an action is considered "reckless" where the actor ignores "red flags," obvious indications of wrong-doing, and nevertheless proceeds with his transaction as planned.[14] This approach in bribery actions would fit nicely with FCPA's "know or have reason to know" language and would resolve the tension between that language and the Act's "corruption" phrase. At the very least, the case for a "recklessness" standard is strong enough, particularly in view of the SEC's aggressiveness on this issue, that a reasonably conservative company will treat it as the controlling standard.

The difficulty with the "recklessness" approach for business managers, of course, is the uncertainty involved in identifying the red flags that are supposed to put them on guard. What might appear to a court in hindsight to have been an obvious indication of corruption might to a careless manager have seemed innocent enough, or, if not innocent, at least not connected to a bribery scheme.[15] To obtain some margin of comfort on this issue, therefore, the FCPA forces the business manager to exercise considerable diligence in spotting things that could later be construed as suggesting bribery. Indeed, American firms that engage overseas in bribery-prone lines of business are generally well advised to adopt an "affirmative action" plan to document the steps they take to spot and stop any corrupt use of their funds.[16]

Because of the uncertainties concerning the scope of the FCPA, its purportedly straightforward prohibition of bribery has resulted in the imposition of a substantial regulatory burden on U.S. business. Indeed, the Justice Department has actually established a "no action" procedure, a device usually reserved for the administration of complex tax and securities law provisions, for transactions that may pose FCPA risks.[17] Despite the efforts by Justice, though, the business community has remained distrustful. Few companies have been willing even to comment to the agencies, except in very general terms, on the problems that the FCPA has created.[18]

Besides the FCPA's impact domestically, the efforts by U.S. firms to document their diligence in avoiding FCPA improprieties has also resulted indirectly in the regulation of foreign persons not technically subject to the Act. Although the foreign person that remains outside U.S. jurisdiction faces no personal exposure for FCPA penalties, it must always consider as a cost of its dealings with the American firm the things it must do, or avoid doing, to comply with the American firm's FCPA program.

This extraterritorial impact is not a mistake. The FCPA was a product of the Carter Administration's attitudes toward morality both in business and in foreign relations.[19] The committee report on the FCPA contends that foreign bribery by U.S.-based companies has important consequences both in foreign relations and domestically, even if the payments are made strictly overseas. In foreign relations, corporate bribery is said to "taint" the image of American democracy.[20] Domestically, bribery is thought to weaken American firms by encouraging them to rely on illicit payments, rather than on better prices, quality and service, in their competition for business.[21] In enacting the FCPA, therefore, Congress was not purporting simply to offer assistance to foreign governments in their own efforts to stop bribery, but was instead deliberately setting an American standard of conduct for foreign transactions involving U.S.-connected multinationals.

Critics of the Act say that the United States should not attempt to regulate the internal affairs of foreign countries. They also suggest that it is a dangerous conceit to assume that American companies are so strong and their products so vital to foreign consumers that the FCPA will do more to clean up foreign governments than it will to damage American business.[22]

ANTIBOYCOTT

The antiboycott legislation consists of two separate sets of provisions, one adopted in 1976 as part of the Tax Reform Act[23] and the other enacted in 1977 as part of the Export Administration Act.[24] The two enactments are closely related in history and purpose, but are different in the approach each takes in addressing the boycott problem. Following a general discussion of the background and purpose of this legislation, the two different enactments will be considered separately.

The antiboycott legislation was, unlike the FCPA, not so much an affirmative imposition of U.S. law on foreign conduct, as it was a defensive reaction to that type of extraterritorial regulation by others. Although no particular countries or boycotts are mentioned in the statutes, the relevant committee reports indicate clearly that the target of the legislation was the Arab boycott of Israel.[25]

The committee report on the export provisions provides the background and rationale of the antiboycott provisions. It identifies three levels of Arab boycott activity and three types of U.S. response to those activities. Under the first level, the "primary" boycott, the Arab states simply refused to do business with Israel. That, says the report, was a legitimate type of economic warfare to which the United States did not object. However, says the report, the boycott was later expanded to a "secondary" level, in which the Arab states refused to do business with third-country companies (e.g., American, British, French, etc.) that did not themselves boycott Israel. The report asserts that participation in these activities became subject to legitimate United States regulation to the extent that the United States had the power to prevent participation in the boycott by U.S.- connected companies. Finally, the report says, the boycott began to be enforced at a "tertiary" level, in which third country companies were blacklisted by the Arab states not only for doing business with Israel, but also for having Jewish or pro-Israeli management, or for doing business with other third-country companies already blacklisted either for their own "pro- Israeli" leanings or for doing business with still other blacklisted companies. This level of boycott enforcement, the report contends, was "clearly against the spirit and intent of U.S. law, including the civil rights and equal opportunity laws and the antitrust laws."[26]

The report suggests that participation in boycotts will be allowed at the primary level, but restricted or prohibited at the secondary and tertiary levels. This distinction in policy, plus the need to protect legitimate, non-boycott-related business practices, is the key to understanding the antiboycott legislation and regulations.

The tax provisions were adopted first, as part of the Tax Reform Act of 1976. They impose boycott-oriented conditions on the enjoyment of certain tax benefits normally available in connection with income derived from foreign operations.[27] These benefits are reduced in proportion to that part of the taxpayer's international business which is tainted by the taxpayer's "participation" in the Arab boycott.[28] The tax provisions also require the taxpayer to file reports concerning both its operations in boycotting countries and the requests it may receive to participate in a boycott.[29]

The types of activities that are deemed, in the tax provisions, to be "participation" in a boycott illustrate the distinction in policy suggested earlier between tolerance of "legitimate" trade practices and primary boycotts, on the one hand, and opposition to tertiary and certain secondary boycotts, on the other hand. A taxpayer "participates" in a boycott if he "agrees" as a condition of doing business with an Arab state or with companies or nationals of that state, (i) to refrain from doing business with Israel, Israeli companies or nationals, or with other companies that themselves do business with Israel or Israelis, (ii) to refrain from doing business with companies owned or managed by Jews, or (iii) to refrain from hiring Jews.[30] He also participates in a boycott if, as a condition to the sale of a product to an Arab state, company or national, he agrees to refrain from shipping or insuring that product on any carrier that is not participating in the Arab boycott. In contrast to the prohibited arrangements, agreements to comply with "primary" boycott requirements, i.e., prohibitions on the import into the Arab state of goods from Israel and the export of goods from the Arab state to Israel, are expressly allowed.[32] Also, compliance with boycott requirements is considered "participation" only if the taxpayer enters into an "agreement," express or implied, to engage in those activities.[33] Thus, to the extent that a company's activities, for example, the employment of workers for a construction project in a boycotting country, are to occur inside the boycotting country, the host country's laws will "force" compliance, without need of an agreement. This "forced" compliance does not constitute "participation" in the boycott.[34]

In contrast to the tax provisions, the export law amendments adopted a year later are not expressed simply as conditions to benefits, but as actual prohibitions that carry with them civil and criminal penalties, as well as the prospect of losing the export licenses otherwise issued or available.[35] The export provisions are greater in scope and more intricate than the tax provisions. They reach not just agreements to participate, but any compliance with a requirement of, or request from, an Arab state (i) to boycott any person, (ii) to require others to boycott, (iii) to refuse, or require others to refuse, to employ any U.S. person on grounds of race, religion, sex or national origin, or (iv) to furnish certain types of information likely to assist the Arab states in monitoring compliance with the boycott.[36] The protection of free trade and primary boycott concerns is afforded by means of both substantive exceptions to the broader coverage of the general prohibitions and by "jurisdictional" exceptions that limit the reach of the substantive prohibitions.

The substantive exceptions permit compliance with (i) primary boycott requirements, (ii) "specific and unilateral" selection of suppliers by the Arab state or its residents, (iii) restrictions on shipments or transhipments through Israel, (iv) immigration and other local laws with respect to activities that occur exclusively in the Arab state, and (v) the supplying of specific, nonblacklisting types of information in import and shipping documents.[37]

Under the "jurisdictional" exceptions, the foreign subsidiaries of American firms may comply with boycott requirements, otherwise prohibited, as long as they do so only in connection with foreign transactions for which they receive no goods or services (not even transaction-related information) from the United States.[38] The absence of any transfer of goods or services between an American company and its foreign subsidiary is deemed to keep the foreign subsidiary's boycott-tainted foreign transaction outside United States commerce and, so, outside the reach of the boycott prohibitions. Strikingly, the provision of so-called "ancillary" services, such as legal, financial and accounting assistance, are not considered enough to trigger the U.S.-commerce connection as long as these services are provided on a general basis to the subsidiary, and not specifically in connection with the boycott-tainted transaction.[39]

The antiboycott provisions seem not to have triggered nearly as much anxiety and opposition in the U.S. business community as the FCPA has generated. While this may be due in part simply to the more limited impact of these provisions (they affect principally those firms that do business with Arab states or companies), much of the difference may also be attributable to the superiority of the antiboycott legislation from a technical standpoint and to the greater deference it shows for the nonboycott-related exigencies of business.

INTERNATIONAL INVESTMENT SURVEY ACT

The International Investment Survey Act of 1976 ("IISA")[40] resulted indirectly from the same type of wealth transfers that prompted the antiboycott provisions. In the case of IISA, there were fears that the dollars being exported to purchase oil and foreign-produced consumer goods were being used to buy control of American lands and businesses.[41] The prospects of foreigners controlling not only America's oil supplies, but also its food and industrial production apparently made some type of reactive measure politically irresistible. Still, in view of the United States' own stake in the free movement of capital,[42] Congressional fears of retaliatory measures overseas seemed to temper the legislators' enthusiasm for the establishment of new trade barriers.[43] Instead, Congress enacted IISA, which provided "clear and unambiguous authority" for the collection and analysis of information on foreign investment.[44] In effect, Congress took the bold step of deciding to study the matter further, and even then qualified its action by statements in the Act that the new legislation was not intended to restrain or deter either foreign investment in the United States or United States investment abroad.[45] Further, said the Act, the information to be gathered was to be collected "with a minimum burden on business and other respondents and with no unnecessary duplication of information."[46]

The statute itself does not set up the system of reports and forms by which the investment information is to be gathered. That is left to administrative regulations.[47] Although the statute authorizes the collection of information concerning all kinds of international investments, regardless of size or kind,[48] the implementing regulations are much narrower, presumably in accordance with the Congressional directive to gather the investment information only to the extent seemed "necessary and feasible,"[49] and with a "minimum burden on business."[50]

By Executive Order, the responsibility for gathering information under IISA was assigned to the Treasury Department with respect to "portfolio" investments and to the Commerce Department with respect to "direct" investments.[51] "Direct" investments are those that give to the investor 10% or greater voting power over the enterprise in which the investment is made.[52] "Portfolio" investments are simply those that are not direct.[53] In both cases, of course, only those investments that are "international" are subject to IISA. An international investment is defined in the statute to be the acquisition by foreign persons of interests in U.S. property or U.S.-issued securities or the acquisition by U.S. persons of interests in foreign property or foreign-issued securities.[54]

Under the Treasury regulations for portfolio investments (those so small in voting power that they are not likely to affect the management or control of the business in which the investment is made) the reporting obligation concerning foreign investments is imposed on U.S. issuers of securities and U.S. security holders of record for foreign owners, provided the U.S. person exceeds certain "exemption" levels.[55] For the "issuer" reports, the exemption levels generally are $1 billion in assets for nonbanks, and $2 billion in assets for banks.[56] However, a few smaller companies, those with assets between $100 million and $1 billion, may also be contacted and requested to file reports as statistical samples of foreign investments in companies of that size.[57] Companies with asset figures below $100 million are exempted entirely from the "issuer" reporting obligations.[58] For the "holder of record" reports, an exemption is available for any person holding an aggregate of less than $10 million in securities on behalf of foreign investors.[58] The Treasury regulations do not provide any means of determining the levels of U.S. portfolio investments abroad or of foreign investments in U.S. property other than securities.

In contrast to the Treasury rules, the Commerce Department regulations for "direct" investments, i.e., those that might affect control over the target business, require reports to be filed with respect both to foreign investments in the United States ("inbound" investments) and United States investments abroad ("outbound" investments),[59] whether the investment is held in the form of securities or otherwise.[60] While exemption levels are provided for smaller businesses, the Commerce Department exemptions are much less generous than those provided by Treasury. Under the Commerce rules, the exemption levels are U.S. dollar figures that are to be applied to three different criteria concerning the business in which the reportable investment is being made. The three critieria are (i) net income after taxes, whether positive or negative, (ii) total assets and (iii) sales or gross operating revenues excluding sales taxes.[61] If, for the business involved, the figure for any one of these three criteria exceeds the stated exemption level (e.g., $5,000,000) a report must be filed.[62] For inbound investments, the acquisition of more than a stated amount of U.S. real estate will also trigger the reporting requirements,[63] regardless of the exemption level normally available. The exemption level for inbound investments, therefore, is the lower of the real estate limit and the normal exemption level. The specific exemption levels for the various reports required by IISA are discussed below.

The IISA regulations establish essentially three types of reports: initial, periodic and benchmark. The initial report must be filed within forty-five days of a transaction that results in an inbound direct investment in a nonexempted enterprise.[64] The periodic reports must be filed quarterly and annually for both inbound and outbound investments,[65] while the benchmark reports are required only at five-year intervals.[66] The exemption level for initial reports of inbound investments is $1,000,000 or 200 acres.[67] For periodic reports concerning these investments and for reports of outbound investments, the exemption levels are $10,000,000 or $8,000,000 depending on the report involved.[68] In effect, there is a fairly low threshhold for the initial report of inbound investment but levels eight to ten times greater for the periodic and outbound reports. As under the Treasury rules, the reporting requirements are made enforceable with respect to foreign investments by imposing the reporting obligation on U.S. persons connected to the transaction.[69]

In response to objections by business representatives that the reporting requirements would deter the investments that had to be reported, Congress included in IISA not only the reassuring language mentioned earlier, but also a strong confidentiality provision. The information collected under IISA is to be used only by the collecting agency and only for analytical and statistical purposes.[70] The President may authorize use of the information by other agencies, but only for analytical and statistical purposes.[71] Persons who disclose IISA information in violation of these provisions are subject to fines of as much as $10,000.[72] Also, disclosure of information contained in the reports cannot be compelled by legal process without the consent of the person that furnished the information.[73] It is impossible to tell, of course, how much investors really trust these assurances and how much foreign investment actually has been discouraged as a result of IISA's reporting requirements. It would be difficult, though, to describe the reporting obligations as minimally burdensome, for the reporting scheme is complicated and demanding.[74]

AGRICULTURAL FOREIGN INVESTMENT DISCLOSURE ACT OF 1979

Although IISA already required reports of foreign investments in tracts of United States land larger than 200 acres, this apparently was considered insufficient by those who feared foreign control of American food production. The Agricultural Foreign Investment Disclosure Act of 1978 ("AFIDA")[75] was enacted two years later.[76] It requires any foreign person[77] that acquires or transfers any nonexempted interest[78] in agricultural land to report the acquisition or transfer within 90 days of its occurrence.[79] In contrast with IISA, AFIDA imposes the reporting obligation directly on the foreign investor, and provides for the assessment of penalties of up to 25% of the fair market value of the property involved for any violation.[80]

The exemptions from AFIDA for small investments are very restrictive. With respect to investments in small tracts, the AFIDA regulations exclude only those parcels of land that, in the aggregate, are no larger than ten acres and which produce gross annual agricultural revenues of $1000 or less.[81] For indirect interests in "reportable" parcels, (for example, foreign ownership of a small portion of the stock of a domestic company that owns a "reportable" size parcel of agricultural land), the test for the reporting obligation is whether the foreigner's interest in the entity that holds the land is large enough to cause the entity itself to be considered a "foreign person" for purposes of AFIDA.[82] An entity is considered "foreign" if it is organized or has its principal place of business outside the United States, regardless of the percentage of its ownership interests held by United States persons.[83] Also, domestic entities, those that are organized and have their principal places of business in the United States are considered foreign if foreign persons, in the aggregate, own 50% or more of the "interest" in the entity, or 10% or more of those interests are held by any one foreigner or group of foreigners acting in concert.[84] The regulations do not specify the kinds of interests in the business, for example, voting power or shares of earnings, with respect to which the percentage figures are to be applied. Also, the existence in a company of a 10% group consisting of both citizens and foreigners, but controlled in its concerted actions by the foreigners would not, without some aggressively creative interpretation of the regulations, render the entity in which the group held its interest "foreign."

Neither the statute nor the regulations address explictly the rules for smaller, but direct, interests in parcels larger than the ten-acre minimum. Applying the regulations literally, however, all interests other than those excepted must be reported, and there are no exceptions for small, direct interests. Thus, it would appear that a foreign person that held a 5% interest as a tenant-in-common of a twenty-acre tract of timberland would have to report that interest under AFIDA, even though the same interest would not have to be reported if it were held either indirectly, through a corporation or partnership holding title to the land, or in the form of sole ownership of a one-acre parcel.

In sharp contrast to the rigorous confidentiality provisions of IISA, AFIDA requires that the reports filed by the foreign owners of agricultural land be made available for public inspection, and be sent to the departments of agriculture in the states in which the lands are located.[85] These disclosure features suggest an entirely different purpose for AFIDA than for IISA. AFIDA seems designed deliberately to facilitate efforts at the state level to discourage or prohibit foreign ownership of farmland.[86] The assurances to foreign investors set out in IISA are notably absent in AFIDA. Nevertheless, advocates of restrictions on foreign ownership of American farmland are still left to fight their battles at the state and local levels, for while Congress has provided the mechanism for gathering the necessary information, it has so far been unwilling itself to impose actual restrictions on foreign ownership of United States lands.[87]

CANADA

Canada is thought to be in a dilemma. It needs to attract foreign capital for expansion and modernization, but wishes to increase, or at least to hold steady, current levels of Canadian control over Canadian businesses.[88] The Foreign Investment Review Act of 1974 ("FIRA")[89] is designed to provide a flexible, case-by-case review mechanism to help Canada work its way through this dilemma.

FIRA requires advance governmental approval of any acquisition or establishment of a Canadian business enterprise by a "noneligible" person, i.e., a foreign person as defined by a series of rules and tests. The test for approval of the investment is whether it is likely to be of "significant benefit" to Canada. There are five statutory criteria to be used by the government in determining whether a proposed investment meets the "significant benefit" test, but the criteria are only vaguely descriptive.[90] Clearly, and not improperly, the significant benefit test is essentially a policy-oriented standard, malleable to suit different political climates. Indeed, following some liberalization of the FIRA rules by the former government, it is generally thought that the new Progessive Conservative government in Canada will reduce the impact of FIRA on foreign investment even further, and perhaps will repeal it altogether.[91] The United States has objected to FIRA on grounds that it is hostile to U.S. business and violative of the free trade policies of the General Agreement on Tariffs and Trade.[92]

Putting aside the governmental policy issues, the technical, legal issue under FIRA is whether a proposed transaction is subject to FIRA at all. The remainder of this discussion will be devoted to that question. A "FIRA" investment occurs where all of the following three elements are satisfied: (i) the investor is a "noneligible person," (ii) the business acquired or taken over is a "Canadian business enterprise "and (iii) the Canadian business enterprise is "taken over" or "established."

Noneligibility

A person is "noneligible" (i.e., foreign) for purposes of FIRA if that person is (i) a nonCanadian individual, i.e., an individual not both a citizen and a permanent resident of Canada (subject to certain "leeway" periods for new residents not yet citizens and citizens not always resident[93]), (ii) a nonCanadian governmental entity,[94] or (iii) a corporation controlled in fact by a nonCanadian individual or governmental entity or by any group of persons that includes a nonCanadian individual or governmental entity holding an interest in the group large enough to taint the entire group as foreign.[95]

FIRA contains presumptions concerning the eligibility of corporations. These are linked to the nationality of the company's shareholders and directors. At the shareholder level, a corporation is deemed to be a noneligible person if 5% or more of its voting shares are held by any single noneligible person or nonCanadian corporation.[96] If the company is publicly traded, the same presumption arises if 25% or more of its voting shares are held by any group of noneligible persons and nonCanadian companies acting in concert.[97] Where the corporation involved is not publicly-traded, noneligibility is deemed to exist where this type of group holds, in the aggregate, 40% or more of the company's voting shares.[98]

Where a corporation is not controlled at the shareholder or owner level by any one person or group of persons, the control inquiry shifts to the board of directors.[99] If fewer than 20% of the directors are noneligible, then the corporation is presumed not to be noneligible.[100] If the "noneligible" figure is between 20% and 50%, and these noneligibles act in concert, a rebuttable presumption of noneligible control arises, causing the corporation to be presumed noneligible.[101] Finally, if more than 50% of the directors are noneligibles, the corporation is deemed, conclusively, to be noneligible.[102]

Canadian Business Enterprise

The issue of whether an operation or set of assets is to be considered a "Canadian business enterprise" depends on the resolution of two principal subissues: (a) whether the operation is a business, and (b) whether the business is Canadian. The "business" element[103] allows distinctions to be drawn (i) between occasional, short-term operations in connection with the performance of contracts in Canada and more regular, organized, longer-lasting operations,[104] (ii) between nonprofit and profit-oriented operations,[105] and (iii) between the purchasing of assets in liquidation of a business and purchasing the business itself.[106] In all these cases the first type of activity is not considered a business while the second one is.

Where a "business" is found, it is considered "Canadian" where it qualifies either as a "Canadian branch business" or a "Canadian business".[107] A Canadian branch business is a business carried on in Canada, by a nonCanadian corporation, that maintains one or more establishments to which employees of the corporation employed in connection with the business ordinarily report for work.[108] A Canadian business is any business carried on in Canada by (i) individuals who are Canadian residents or citizens, (ii) Canadian corporations with Canadian establishments to which employees employed in connection with the business ordinarily report for work, or (iii) groups that include the Canadian individuals or companies earlier described if that Canadian group controls the business in question.[109]

Also, three presumptions will render a business "Canadian" where it might otherwise not be considered so. Under the first presumption, a business controlled by Canadians is deemed to be "carried on in Canada" for purposes of the "Canadian business" definition even if it is carried on only partly in Canada.[110] Under the second, any part of a Canadian business or Canadian branch business that is capable of being operated as a separate business is treated separately as another Canadian business enterprise, for the purpose of triggering FIRA's approval requirements.[111] Finally, a business that is carried on by a company that is controlled by another company is deemed to be carried on by both.[112] The effect of all three presumptions is to magnify what may be an economically minor connection between a business and Canada to the point that transfers of control over it, or over one of its Canadian-connected divisions or operations, is deemed to be a change in control of a "Canadian" business for which approval from the Canadian government is required.

Establishment or Acquisition

The final FIRA issue is whether a proposed transaction constitutes either the establishment of a new Canadian business enterprise or the acquisition of control over an existing one. Where the noneligible investor controls no other Canadian business enterprises, he is considered to have "established" a new enterprise in Canada as soon as he creates an operation that satisfies the definition of a Canadian business enterprise. This generally occurs where he sets up, in connection with a profit-oriented operation, an establishment in Canada to which employees associated with that operation ordinarily report for work.[113] Where a Canadian business enterprise is already being conducted, that business may be expanded into related operations without obtaining a FIRA approval. Otherwise, where new Canadian "establishments" are created, a FIRA approval is required.[114]

The takeover rules distinguish between Canadian businesses run by Canadian corporations and those operations considered "Canadian" even though they are controlled by nonCanadians companies, individuals or governmental entities. Where a business is being conducted by a Canadian corporation, the acquisition of control can occur either by the acquisition of a controlling number of the voting shares of the corporation or by acquiring substantially all the property used in conducting the Canadian business. For Canadian businesses that are not operated by Canadian companies, the businesses can be taken over for purposes of FIRA only by acquiring substantially all the assets of the Canadian business.[115]

The "substantially all" test for asset acquisitions is not, of course, purely quantitative.[116] The acquisition of all the assets necessary to the continued operation of a business satisfies the "substantially all" test even if a large portion remains (on a percentage of value basis) of the business assets.[117] For example, the acquisition of a business' only factory would not likely escape the substantially all test simply because the seller retained large quantities of valuable assets, such as cash, promissory notes, securities, and the like. No presumptions or quantitative guidelines are provided on this issue.[118]

There are, though, some presumptions and guidelines for what constitutes "control" by means of an acquisition of voting stock. For publicly-traded companies, control is presumed to have been obtained where 5% to 50% of the voting shares are acquired.[119] For companies not publicly traded the presumption range is 20% to 50%.[120] Control is conclusively deemed to exist, whether or not the company involved is publicly traded, where more than 50% of its voting shares have been acquired.[121]

Other Restrictions

Canada, like the United States, has also imposed either at the federal or provincial levels, restrictions on foreign control of certain types of businesses.[122] These include aviation, broadcasting, financing, mining and energy businesses. Unlike the United States, though, Canada has federally-chartered general business corporations.[123] Canadian residents must fill the majority of positions of the boards of directors of these corporations, and actions taken by the boards of these companies are valid only if the majority of directors present are Canadian residents.[124] Most of the provinces also impose these Canadian-director requirements.[125]

FOOTNOTES

1. Foreign Corrupt Practices Act of 1977, P.L. 95-213, 91 Stat. 1494 (1977) (amending Exchange Act §§ 13(b), adding §§ 30A, 104, 15 U.S.C. §§ 78m(b), 78dd-1, 78dd-2 (1982)) (hereinafter, "FCPA").

2. Companies with reporting obligations under the Securities Exchange Act of 1934, 15 U.S.C. 78a et seq. (1982)(hereinafter, "Exchange Act"), must:

    (A) make and keep books, records, and and accounts, which, in reasonable detail, accurately and fairly reflect the transactions and dispositions of the assets of the issuer; and

    (B) devise and maintain a system of internal accounting controls sufficient to provide reasonable assurances that--

    (i) transactions are executed in in accordance with management's general or specific authorization;

    (ii) transactions are recorded as necessary (I) to permit preparation of financial statements in conformity with generally accepted accounting principles or any other criteria applicable to such statements, and (II) to maintain accountability for assets;

    (iii) access to assets is permitted only in accordance with management's general or specific authorization; and

    (iv) the recorded accountability for assets is compared with the existing assets at reasonable intervals and appropriate action is taken with respect to any differences.

Foreign Corrupt Practices Act of 1977 § 102, amending Exchange Act § 13(b), 15 U.S.C. § 78m(b) (1982).

3. An "issuer" under the Exchange Act generally means a person that issues or proposes to issue any securities. Exchange Act § 3(a) (8), 15 U.S.C. § 78c(a)(8)(1982). However, only those issuers that are subject to the registration or reporting requirements of the Exchange Act are subject to the accounting requirements and SEC- enforced provisions of the Act. FCPA §§ 102, 103, 15 U.S.C. §§ 78m(b), 78dd-1. A nongovernmental issuer is not subject to these requirements unless it has a class of securities held of record by more than 300 persons, 300 persons resident in the United States if the issuer is foreign. See, Exchange Act §§ 12(g) 15 (d), 15 U.S.C. §§ 78l(g) (1982); Rules 12g 3-2(a), 12g 4 (a), 17 C.F.R. §§ 240. 12 g 3-2(a), 240, 12g 4(a) (1984). Foreign private issuers are also exempted from these reporting requirements if they have not registered an offering of securities under the Securities Act of 1933, are required to report Exchange Act-like information in the country of their domicile and furnish this information to the U.S. Securities and Exchange Commission (hereinafter, "SEC"). Rule 12g 3-2(b)(1), 17 C.F.R. § 240. 12g 3-2(b) (1), See Rule 15d-16, 17 C.F.R. § 240.15 d-16.

4. The definition of "domestic concern" includes issuers, but issuers are not subject to any of the substantive provisions applicable to domestic concerns. FCPA § 104 (a), (d)(1), 15 U.S.C. § 78dd-2 (a), (d)(1).

5. FCPA § 104; S.Rep. No. 114, 95th Cong., 1st Sess. 11-13 reprinted in 1977 U.S. Code Cong. & Ad. News 4098, 4109-10.

6. The FCPA prohibits bribery of "foreign officials." The term "foreign official" is defined to exclude any employee of a foreign government or governmental instrumentality "whose duties are essentially ministerial or clerical". FCPA §§103(b), 104(d)(2), 15 U.S.C. §§78dd-1(b), 78dd-2(d)(2). The committee report on the FCPA used the term "grease payments" to refer to bribery of these

lower-level employees. See S. Rep. No. 114, supra note 5 at 10.

7. The statutory language seems unnecessarily complicated. It contains two separate antibribery provisions, one for issuers and one for domestic concerns, even though the two prohibitions are identical. Further, in both of these separate but identical sections, three separate prohibitions are stated, the first forbidding payments or offers to governmental officials, the second prohibiting the same thing with respect to political officials and the third prohibiting the same thing with respect to any other person where the payor/ offeror knows or has reason to know that the thing paid or offered will be passed on, directly or indirectly, to a governmental or political official or a candidate for political office. A simple listing of these three different kinds of recipients, i.e., governmental officials, political officials and everybody else, would surely have accomplished the same purpose. See §§ 103, 104. It is easier to work with the Act if one recognizes that the "any person" prohibition essentially swallows the other two. The only thing even arguably left out of the "any person" provision is a prohibition of direct bribes, those not involving any intermediaries. To handle this, one need only remember the simple rule that direct bribes are prohibited too.

8. According to the committee report:

> The word "corruptly" is used in order to make clear that the offer, payment, promise or gift must be intended to induce the recipient to misuse his official position in order to wrongfully direct business to the payor or his client, or to obtain preferential legislation or a favorable regulation. The word "corruptly" connotes an evil motive or purpose, an intent to wrongfully influence the recipient. S. Rep, supra note 5, at 10.

It should be noted that, contrary to the suggestion in this report, the language adopted in the final version of the FCPA does not prohibit bribes paid in order to influence legislation or regulations, but instead only those payments intended to influence the official to assist the payor in obtaining, retaining or directing business to someone. While this might be accomplished by means of legislation or regulation, it is not the simple influencing of governmental law-making that is prohibited. The reference in the report to bribes with respect to legislation and regulations seems to be a holdover from explanations of earlier drafts of the FCPA that did prohibit those types of bribes. See, S. 3133, 94th Cong., 2nd Sess. § 3, reprinted in Greanias, supra note 16 at 169; W. Timmeny, SEC Enforcement of the Foreign Corrupt Practices Act, P.L.I., Foreign Corrupt Practices Act (1981) 371, 378.

9. SEC Exchange Act Release No. 34-14478, 72,264 CCH Fed. Sec. Law Rptr.

10. Id.

11. Ernst & Ernst v. Hochfelder, 425 U.S. 185, 96 S.Ct. 1375, 47 L.E.d 2d 668 (1976) (private action for damages); SEC v. Aaron, 446 U.S. 680, 100 S.Ct 1967 64, LEd2d 611 (1980) (SEC action for injunction).

12. Ernst & Ernst, supra, note 11, at 193 n. 12.

13. See., e.g., Nelson v. Serwold, 576 F.2d 1332, 1336-37 (9th Cir.), cert. denied, 439 U.S. 970 (1978); Rolf v. Blythe, Eastman Dillon & Co., Inc., 570 F.2d 38, 44-47 (2d Cir.), cert. denied, 439 U.S. 1039 (1978); First Va. Bankshares v. Benson, 559 F.2d 1307, 1314 (5th Cir. 1977), cert. denied, 435 U.S. 952 (1978).

14. See., e.g., Franke v. Midwestern Okla. Dev. Auth., 428 F.Supp. 719, 725 (W.D. Okla. 1976), rev'd on other grounds & remanded, 619 F.2d 856 (10th Cir. 1980); McLean v. Alexander, 599 F.2d 1190, 1197 (3d Cir. 1979); Rolf v. Blyth, Eastman, Dillon & Co., Inc., 570 F.2d 38, 47 (2d Cir.), cert. denied, 439 U.S. 1039 (1978).

15. Payment to a broker's account in a Swiss bank, for example, might be requested to facilitate a bribe, to help the broker avoid or evade taxes or to keep the payment secret for any variety of legitimate or illicit purposes.

16. Accord, G. Greanias, D. Windsor, The Foreign Corrupt Practices Act (1982) at 87-88. Issuers, of course, are subject to affirmative statutory requirements that they keep proper records and maintain internal controls sufficient to provide "reasonable assurances" that management controls the disposition of company assets. See note 2, supra.

17. See, 28 C.F.R. § 50.18 (1984). In announcing the review procedure, the Justice Department also described its "enforcement priorities." According to this statement of priorities, the most egregious bribes are those that are paid to take business from U.S. competitors, or paid where no one else is engaging in bribery. The Department also stated that it would more likely prosecute bribes the higher the official position of the recipient and the lower the care exercised by the paying company to stop bribery by its employees. Statement of Philip B. Hegmann, Asst. Attorney General, Criminal Division, U.S. Dept. of Justice (November 8, 1979), reprinted in Practicing Law Institute, Foreign Corrupt Practices Act (1981).

    The SEC initially opposed the publication of guidelines or review procedures. In the now-famous words of Stanley Sporkin, the top SEC enforcement officer at the time, "We do not have guidelines for rapists, muggers and embezzlers, and I do not think we need guidelines for corporations who want to bribe foreign officials." Time (Nov. 26, 1979) at 61. Facing prospects of amendments to the statute, however, the Commission later agreed to a trial period, and finally to an indefinite period, during which it would also decline to bring any enforcement action in connection with a transaction with respect to which Justice had expressed a "no action" position as part of its review procedure. Exchange Act Releases 34-17099 (Aug. 28, 1980) and 34-18255 (Nov. 12, 1981), reprinted in CCH Fed. Sec Law Rptr. 26,628, 629 (1984).

18. See, Exchange Act Release 34-17099, supra.

19. See, Greanias, supra, note 16, at 69-71.

20. S. Rep., supra, note 5, at 3.

21. Id. at 3-4.

22. See, Greanias, supra, note 16 at 98-100, 121-126.

23. Tax Reform Act of 1976, P.L. 94-455, 90 Stat. 1660 (1976).

24. Export Administration Amendments of 1977, P.L. 95-52, 91, Stat. 244 (1977).

25. See, H. R. Rep. No. 190, 95th Cong., 1st Sess. 4 (1977), reprinted in 1977 U.S. Code Cong. & News 362, 365.

26. Id. at 4-5.

27. The following benefits were made subject to boycott-related reductions by amendments to the provisions indicated: (a) foreign tax credit, §908(a) I.R.C., (b) deferral of taxation of offshore income, § 952(a)(3) I.R.C., and (c) favorable taxation of Domestic International Sale Corporations (DISCs), § 995 (b)(1)(F) I.R.C. The DISC system has been changed, effective for transactions after December 31, 1984, to a Foreign Sales Corporation (FSC) system, which also provides favorable tax treatment. The enjoyment of the FSC benefits are also limited by the boycott participation factor, in a manner similar to the treatment of DISCs. §927(e)(2) I.R.C.

28. § 999 (c) I.R.C. The legislation and regulations do not mention the Arab states, Jews or Israel by name. Those terms are used in the text for the purpose of clarity and brevity.

29. § 999 (a).

30. § 999 (b)(3)(A).

31. § 999 (b)(3)(B).

32. § 999 (b)(4).

33. S. Rep. No. 938, part. II, 94th Cong., 2d Sess. 467, reprinted in U.S. Code Cong. & Ad. News 4030, 4173 (1976).

34. Department of the Treasury, Guidelines, Boycott Provisions of the Internal Revenue Code, Questions H10-H13, (January 25, 1978) reprinted in CCH Fed Tax Rptr. ¶43, 992.40 (1985).

35. Civil penalties of up to $10,000 are authorized for violations of the Export Administration Act, of which the antiboycott provisions are a part. 50 App. U.S.C. § 2410 (c) (1982). Criminal penalties for knowing violations may be levied up to five times the value of the exports involved or $50,000, which ever is greater. Prison terms up to five years are also authorized. Id. at § 2410 (a). The revocation of export licenses as a penalty for violation of the boycott regulations is authorized in § 2410 (c)(2) (A). One case has also recognized a private right of action by persons injured by a violation of the antiboycott provisions. Abrams v. Baylor College of Medicine, 581 F.Supp 1570 (S.D. Tex. 1984) (private action recognized for Jewish physicians excluded from medical school's Saudi Arabian program), but, Bulk Oil A.G. v. Sun Co., 583 F.Supp. 1134 (S.D.N.Y. 1983), affirmed, 742 F.2d 1431 (2d Cir. 1984) (no private action recognized for oil company that alleged another oil company had refused to perform its crude oil sales contract for boycott-related reasons).

36. 50 App. U.S.C. § 2307(a)(1)(A)-(E), 15 C.F.R. § 369.2. Also prohibited is paying, honoring, confirming or "otherwise implementing" a letter of credit that requires or is conditional on compliance with prohibited boycott provisions. § 2407 (a)(1)(F); 15 C.F.R. §369.2 (F).

37. 50 App. U.S.C. §2407 (a)(2) (1982); 15 C.F.R. §369.3 (1985). Because the same contractual requirement might be used for legitimate trade purposes or for boycott purposes (for example, a unilateral and specific selection of suppliers might be utilized not to control quality but to exclude nonparticipants in the boycott), there is considerable room in the substantive exceptions for boycott-oriented activities. There is some risk associated with this type of activity, for the statute provides that none of its substantive exceptions are to apply to any activity undertaken for purposes of evading the boycott prohibitions. 50 App. U.S.C. § 2407 (a)(5) (1982). As with the FCPA, then, the lawfulness of a given act might well boil down to the issue of the state of mind of the defendant with respect to that act. In contrast with the FCPA, though, the risks of liablity for inadvertent or negligent violation of the "evasion" limitation is probably fairly low.

Although no reported case has yet discussed this issue, the greater breadth and complexity of the boycott exceptions themselves suggests a greater recognition of the difficulty and complexity of the boycott problem. Further, boycott participation is, unlike bribery, not a malum in se offense. Evil motives cannot be as easily connected to actions with potential boycott applications as they can to acts that tend to further bribery. It is inconceivable that a Commerce Department official would, like Stanley Sporkin in reference to Justice's proposed foreign-bribery guidelines, take the position that antiboycott guidelines were no more necessary than guidelines on murder, rape or robbery. See note 17, supra.

38. 50 App. U.S.C. § 2407 (a)(1) (1982). The statute says that the antiboycott regulations are to prohibit compliance with the Arab boycott "with respect to . . . activities in the interstate or foreign commerce of the United States. . . ". The regulations promulgated under this statutory directive describe the types of activities deemed to occur in U.S. interstate or foreign commerce. See, 15 CFR § 369.1 (d) (1985). A transaction between a controlled foreign subsidiary and a person outside the United States is deemed to occur outside the United States interstate or foreign commerce if it does not involve "the purchase, sale, or transfer of goods or services (including information) to or from a person in the United States. . ." Id. at § 369.1 (d)(11). This jurisdictional exception is not subject to the "no evasion" limitation placed on the substantive exceptions. See, 50 App. U.S.C. § 2407 (a)(5); note 37 supra.

39. 15 C.F.R. § 369.1 (d)(13),(14) (1985).

40. P.L. 94-472, 90 Stat. 2059 (1976), 22 U.S.C. §§ 3101-08.

41. See, F. Pederson, Foreign Investment Reporting, BNA Tax Mgt. Portfolio 428-2nd A-2-A-3 (1984); Accord, D. Wallace, Jr., International Regulation of Multinational Corporations 3-4 (1976). The committee report on IISA noted that from 1970 to 1974, foreign investment in the United States had increased 80%, while U.S. investment abroad had increased only 60%. H. R. Rep. No. 1490, 94th

Cong., 2nd. Sess. 2, reprinted in U.S.Cong Code & Ad News, 4663 4664 (1976).

42. The committee report noted that the overseas private investment of the United States totalled $169.1 billion in 1974.

43. Accord, D. Wallace, note 41, supra.

44. 22 U.S.C. § 3101(b).

45. § 3101(c).

46. § 3101(b).

47. § 3103-04.

48. See, 22 U.S.C. § 3103.

49. § 3103.

50. § 3101(b).

51. Exec. Order No. 11,961, 42 Fed. Reg. 4321 (1977), as amended.

52. A "direct" investment is "the ownership or control, directly or indirectly, by one person of 10 per centum or more of the voting securities of an incorporated business enterprise or an equivalent interest in an unincorporated business enterprise." 22 U.S.C. § 3102(10); 15 C.F.R. § 806.7 (j). The term "person" in this definition includes groups formed by two or more persons who by agreement, understanding or "the appearance of their actions" act in concert with respect to the investment involved. Several people acting in concert may, therefore, be deemed to be one "person" for purposes of the 10% figure, 22 U.S.C. § 3102 (3); 15 C.F.R. §806.7(c), (1). Also, certain people, e.g., members of the same family, are simply deemed to be a group (and therefore a single person for purposes of the direct ownership definition) without regard to any evidence concerning their acting in concert. 15 C.F.R. § 807.7 (1). Curiously, the rule concerning direct investments in limited partnerships states that "limited partners do not have voting rights in a partnership and therefore cannot have a direct investment in the partnership." 15 C.F.R. § 806.12. Because limited partners obviously can

have voting rights in a partnership that are very much like the voting rights of a shareholder in a corporation (voting for changes of general partners rather than of directors), see, Revised Uniform Limited Partnership Act § 303(b) (1970), this provision raises the difficult question of whether this apparent error in the rule's description of the rights of limited partners really is a mistake or instead reflects a deliberate decision that, for purposes of IISA, investments in limited partnerships need not be reported. The mistake theory seems weak when the glaring error of this provision is compared to the expansive sophistication of the other rules. On the other hand, it seems surprising that rules designed to generate information concerning foreign control of American business would deliberately except from any reporting requirement the very types of investments that might otherwise be considered most sensitive, i.e., major foreign interests in American real estate development and mineral exploration and extraction enterprises. These are the types of businesses that, for tax planning purposes, typically are operated as limited partnerships.

53. 22 U.S.C. §3102 (11).

54. Id. at §3102 (9); see 25 C.F.R. §806.7(i).

55. 31 C.F.R. §129.1 at et. seq. (1984).

56. 49 Fed. Reg. 48, 918 (1984).

57. Id.

58. Id.

59. See, 15 C.F.R. §§806.14, 806.15.

60. See, id. at §§806.7 (i), 806.14, 806.15.

61. 15 C.F.R. § 806.14(d), .15(g), .16(c)(2),. 17(b).

62. Id.

63. 15 C.F.R. § 806.15 (j)(3),(4).

64. 15 C.F.R. § 806.15 (j)(2).

65. For outbound investments, quarterly reports concerning transactions with the foreign affiliate are required on Form BE-577 and annual reports concerning financial ownership and operating data are required on Forms BE 133B&C and BE 11A-C. Also, the acquisition of additional foreign affiliates, or a change in business that should result in a new "industry classification" must be reported on form BE-507, which should be filed along with the next quarterly or annual report. 15 C.F.R. § 806.14(e)-(g). For inbound investments, the quarterly reports on transactions with foreign affiliates are filed on form BE-605 (BE-606 if the U.S.-enterprise is a branch or agency of a foreign bank). The annual reports on inbound investments are filed on form BE-15. For inbound investments, the "new affiliate/industry change" form is BE-607, and it, like the BE-507, is to be filed along with the quarterly or annual report next due. Special reports on forms BE-21A,B, and P are required for U.S. affiliates of foreign persons where the affiliate is engaged in the processing, packaging or wholesale distribution of fish or seafoods. 15 C.F.R. § 806.15(h)-(j).

66. The next benchmark reports are due in 1987. 22 U.S.C. § 3103(b), (c). For outbound investments these reports are to be filed on form series BE-10, 15 C.F.R. § 806.16, and for inbound investments on form series BE-12. 15 C.F.R. § 806.17.

67. 15 C.F.R. § 806.15(j)(3),(4). Even if exempt, however, an exemption claim form is required. 15 C.F.R. §806.15(g).

68. Id. at § 806.15 (h) ($10,000,000 for periodic inbound); § 806.14(e) ($10,000,000 for quarterly outbound); § 806.14(f)(1),(2) ($8,000,000 for annual reports on expenditures for property, plant and equipment by foreign enterprise in which U.S. direct investment is held); § 806.14(3) ($10,000.000 for general annual reports concerning outbound investments).

69. A report must be filed on form BE-13 either by the U.S. enterprise in which the investment is made, or by the U.S. affiliate of the foreign investor that made the reportable acquisition. 15 C.F.R. 806. 15(j)(3). In addition, anyone who acts as a

"joint venturer" with the foreigner or who "assist or intervenes" in the transaction in which the foreigner acquires the investment must file a report concerning the investment on Form BE-14 unless the Form BE-13 is filed by an appropriate person. 15 C.F.R. § 806.15(j)(4). The U.S. "assister " has to file the BE-14 only if he knows or has reason to know that the person making the investment is a foreigner. Id.

70. 22 U.S.C. § 3104(c). The information may also be used in proceedings for the enforcement of IISA's information-gathering or confidentiality provisions. Id.

71. § 3104 (c).

72. § 3104(d).

73. § 3104(c).

74. See notes 65-69, supra. The annual report form for foreign investments in the United States, for example, is twenty pages long, not counting the four pages of instructions, and includes, among other things, a schedule calling for a state-by-state breakdown of information concerning the U.S. affiliate's employees, acres of land, acres of mineral interests and gross book value of assets. Form BE-15, Part III, reproduced in BNA T-M 428-2d. Foreign Investment Reporting at B-1002, B-1012-13 (1984).

75. Pub. L. 95-460, 92 Stat. 1263, §§ 1-10 (1978), 7 U.S.C. §§ 3501-08 (1982).

76. A "foreign person" is (i) any individual not a citizen, national or permanent resident alien of the United States (nor a citizen of the Northern Mariana Islands or the Trust Territory of the Pacific Islands), (ii) any foreign government, (iii) any entity created under the laws of a foreign government or having its principal place of business outside the United States, or (iv) a domestic entity that is "substantially controlled" by one or more foreign persons, or in which foreign persons have a "significant interest." 7 U.S.C. § 3508(3). See note 82, infra, for the meaning of "substantial control" and "significant interest."

77. The statute exempts only security interests. 7 U.S.C. § 3501(a). The regulations, by defining the term "interest", also exclude leaseholds of less than 10 years, contingent future interests, future interests which do not become possessory upon the termination of the present possessory estate, easements and rights of way not used for agricultural purposes, and interests solely in mineral rights. 7 C.F.R. § 781.2(c).

78. "Agricultural land" is any land located in the United States that is currently used, or has been used in the preceding five years, for farming, ranching, forestry or timber production. Land not exceeding ten acres in the aggregate is not considered "agricultural land" for purposes of AFIDA if the annual gross receipts from agricultural activities on the land do not exceed $1,000. 7 C.F.R. § 781.2 (b).

79. 7 U.S.C. § 3501 (a); 7 C.F.R. § 781.3(b). Where the land or person involved changes character from nonreportable to reportable, i.e., a nonforeign person becomes foreign or nonagricultural land becomes agricultural, a report must be filed within 90 days from the date of that change. 7 U.S.C. § 3501 (c),(d); 7 C.F.R. § 781.3(c), (d). As a transitional measure, AFIDA required that existing holdings by foreigners be reported within 180 days from the effective date of the AFIDA reporting regulations. 7 U.S.C. § 3501(b). Under the AFIDA regulations, this meant that interests held as of February 1, 1979, had to be reported by August 1, 1979. For interests acquired after February 1, 1979, the normal 90-day period controlled. 7 C.F.R. § 781.3(b).

80. 7 U.S.C. § 3501(a); 7 C.F.R. §781.3(b) (foreign person required to report); 7 U.S.C. § 3502; 7 C.F.R. §§ 781.4, 781.5 (civil penalty of up to 25% of value of land).

81. 7 C.F.R. § 781.2(b).

82. See, id. at § 781.3(b) (any "foreign person" who holds an interest must file); § 781.2 (g)(4) (domestic companies are "foreign persons" if a "significant interest" or substantial control is held by the other types of foreign persons listed); § 781.2(k) (substantial control or significant interest exists where foreign persons

hold, in the aggregate, 50% or more of the interest of an entity or where a single foreigner or group of foreigners acting in concert hold 10% or more).

83. Id. at § 781.2(g)(2).

84. See note 82, supra.

85. 7 U.S.C. § 3505 (reports to states), § 3506 (public inspection). Compare, 22 U.S.C. 3104 (c),(d) (IISA reports to be used strictly for analytical or statistical purposes; $10,000 fine for violations of confidentiality provisions).

86. The committee report on AFIDA noted that by May 1978, half the states restricted the acquisition of farmland by foreigners. H.R. Rep. No. 1570, 95th Cong., 2d Sess. 9, reprinted in U.S. Code Cong. & Ad. News 2914, 2918 (1978); see note 87, infra.

87. See, id. at 16-17, 20, 22, U.S. Code Cong. & Ad. News at 2926, 2929, 2932 (calls for substantive restrictions rejected; bill amended to require transmission of reports to states "so that they can take whatever actions they deem appropriate.")

88. See, J. Tennier, Canadia's Foreign Investment Review Act. P.L. I., Legal Aspects of Doing Business in Canada 437, 439-40 (1983); W. Grover, Foreign Investment Review in Canada 5-10, New Developments in Foreign Trade and Investment (Georgetown Univ. Internat'l Law Inst. 1982); R. Donaldson, Foreign Investment Review and Canadianization, P.L.I., Legal Aspects of Doing Business in Canada 471, 483-86 (1983).

89. C. 46, §§ 1-31, Can. Stat. (1973-74), as amended by c.52, § 128, Can Stat. (1976-77), c. 107, § 63 Can. Stat. (1980-81-82-83). (hereinafter, as amended, "FIRA").

90. The factors to be taken into account are as follows:

(a) the effect of the acquisition or establishment on the level and nature of economic activity in Canada, including, without limiting the generality of the foregoing, the effect on employment, on resource processing, on the utilization of parts, components and services produced in Canada, and on exports from Canada;

(b) the degree and significance of participation by Canadians in the business enterprise or new business and in any industry or industries in Canada of which the business enterprise or new business forms or would form a part;

(c) the effect of the acquisition or establishment on productivity, industrial efficiency, technological development, product innovation and product variety in Canada;

(d) the effect of the acquisition or establishment on competition within any industry or industries in Canada; and

(e) the compatibility of the acquisition or establishment with national industrial and economic policies, taking into consideration industrial and economic policy objectives enunciated by the government or legislature of any province likely to be significantly affected by the acquisition or establishment.

FIRA § 2(2)(a)-(e).

91. See, Zehr, New Canadian Investment Rules No Panacea, Wall St. J., Feb. 1, 1985, Canada Seen Easing Its 11-Year Controls on Foreign Investors, Wall St. J., Dec. 7, 1984, at 31.

92. See, R. Donaldson, Foreign Investment Review and Canadianization, supra note 88 at 540-50.

93. FIRA § 3(1). Noncitizen residents are noneligible if they have been ordinarily resident in Canada for more than one year after the time they first became eligible to apply for Canadian citizenship. Id. Canadian citizens become noneligible if they apply for citizenship in another country or have been resident outside Canada for five or more consecutive years just prior to the date that their FIRA application would have to be filed if they were deemed noneligible. Id.; Foreign Investment Review Regulations § 3 S.O.R. 83-493 (1985) (hereinafter "FIRA Regulations"). The five

year period is extended to ten years for persons who were ordinarily resident in Canada on their sixtieth birthdays. §3(b) FIRA Regulations. Also, the eligibility of a Canadian citizen is not lost if he was resident outside Canada as a full time employee of a Canadian governmental entity, a full time employee of a Canadian business enterprise (where the principal financial reason for this nonCanadian residence is that employment), a full time student at a university whose credentials are recognized by a majority of Canada provinces (provided that the nonresident period as a student is less than ten consecutive years) or a full-time employee of an international association or organization of which Canada is a member. Id. at 3 (a).

94. FIRA § 3(1).

95. Id. If more than 50% of the company's voting shares are held by eligible persons who are members of a group that also includes noneligible persons, the company is deemed eligible unless the noneligibles make up more than twenty percent of its members or twenty percent of its voting shares. § 3(6) (b)(1).

96. Id. at § 3(2)(b).

97. § 3 (2)(a)(i); § 3(7)(a).

98. § 3(2)(a)(ii).

99. § 3(7)(b).

100. § 3(7)(c)(i).

101. § 3(7)(c)(ii).

102. § 3(7)(c)(iii).

103. The term "business" in FIRA "includes any undertaking or enterprise carried on in anticipation of profits." FIRA § 3(1). This would exclude only transactions or enterprises operated for nonprofit purposes. However, the Foreign Investment Review Agency has issued "Interpretation Notes" that narrow the meaning still further to include the other two distinctions mentioned in the text. See, G. Hughes, Foreign Investment Law in Canada 64.1-41-44 (1983).

104. Foreign Investment Review Agency Interpretation Note No. 2., reprinted in G. Hughes, supra, note 103 at 211. This Note takes the position that the words "carried on" in the statutory language (i.e., "any undertaking or enterprise carried on in anticipation profit") "contemplates a continuity of business activity." Id.

105. See note 103, supra.

106. Foreign Investment Review Agency Interpretation Note No. 1, reprinted in G. H. Hughes, supra note 103 at 209. A business that is defunct and is being wound up is not considered to be an activity "carried on in anticipation of profit."

107. See. FIRA § 3(1).

108. Id.

109. Id.

110. FIRA § 3(6)(f).

111. § 3(6)(g).

112. § 3 (6)(h).

113. FIRA §§ 3(1), (4), 8 (2).

114. See, G. Hughes, supra note 103 at 64.1-68-74.

115. Compare FIRA § 3(3)(a)(i) with § 3(3)(a)(ii). As mentioned earlier (see text accompanying note 110-112, supra), the presumptions in favor of characterizing Canadian-connected businesses as "Canadian" for purposes of imposing the FIRA approval requirements tend toward extraterritorial application of the Act. The limitations in § 3(3)(a) on the types of acquisitions that will trigger a FIRA approval requirement are supposed to prevent the most egregious forms of this extraterritoriality. For example, the takeover of a U.S. company with a small Canadian branch operation would not trigger FIRA, although the acquisition of the assets of that branch would. See, G. Hughes, supra, note 103 at 64.1-51-52.

116. Foreign Investment Review Agency Interpretation Note No. 6, reprinted in G. Hughes, supra note 103 at 223.

117. Id.

118. The interpretive note does reject a presumption, however. It says that substantially all the assets of a business may be deemed to have been acquired even if the value of the assets acquired amount to less than 50% of the total properties or assets of that business. Id. Presumably, this means 50% on a percentage of value basis, but this is not specified.

119. FIRA § 3(3)(c)(i),(d). An acquisition of control is deemed not to have occurred where less than 5% of the voting stock of a publicly-traded company has been acquired. § 3(3)(b)(i)(A).

120. § 3(3)(c)(ii),(d). As with the 5% figure for publicly-traded companies, the acquisition of less than 20% of the voting rights of a privately-held company is deemed not to be an "acquisition of control" that triggers FIRA. § 3(3)(b)(i)(B).

121. § 3(3)(d).

122. See generally, W. Graham, Types of Regulation of Foreign Investment In Canada Apart From the Foreign Investment Review Act., P.L.I., Legal Aspects of Doing Business in Canada. (1983); G. Hughes, supra, note 103 at 64, 1-17-32; 64 1-95-131.

123. Canada Business Corporations Act, C-32 Can. Rev. Stat §§ 1-220, as amended (1970).

124. c. 33 §§ 100 (3), 110(2) Can. Stat. (1974-75-76).

125. §§ 100(3), 109(3),(4) Alberta Business Corporations Act, c. B-15 Alta. Stat. (1981); § 133 British Columbia Company Act, c.59 B.C. Stat. (1979); §§ 100(3), 109 (3),(4) Manitoba Corporations Act, c. 40 Man. Stat. (1976); §§ 118(3), 126(6), (7) Ontario Business Corporations Act, c. 4 Ont. Stat. (1982); §§ 100(3), 109(3), (4), Saskatchewan Business Corporations Act, c. A-11 Sask. Stat. (1978), as cited in G. Hughes, supra, note 103 at §§ 259, 261, 276, 292, 293, 336, 338, 362, 363.

RÉSUMÉ EN FRANÇAIS

LÉGISLATION AMÉRICAINE ET CANADIENNE CONCERNANT LES MULTINATIONALES

Le rapport qui précède traite des lois du Canada et des États-Unis qui influent sur les multinationales en général notamment en ce qui concerne leurs opérations et leurs investissements à l'échelle internationale.

Du point de vue des États-Unis, ce rapport traite (a) des dispositions contre la corruption du Foreign Corrupt Practices Act de 1977, (b) des dispositions contre le boycott du Tax Reform Act de 1976 et des amendements administratifs apportés à l'Exportation Act de 1977, (c) des critères de déclaration applicables à tout investissement étranger imposés par le International Investment Survey Act de 1976 et le Agricultural Foreign Investment Disclosure Act de 1978. Dans sa présentation de la législation canadienne, le rapport met surtout l'accent sur le Foreign Investment Review Act de 1974 et souligne les critères imposés par le droit des sociétés fédérales et provinciales quant à la représentation canadienne au niveau des conseils d'administration des sociétés canadiennes.

LOI ANTI-CORRUPTION

Le Foreign Corrupt Practices Act interdit l'usage de tout moyen commercial de communication inter-états (comme le télephone ou le courrier) pour faire tout transfert de fonds à qui que ce soit, dans le but de corrompre, lorsque le cédant sait ou devrait savoir que les fonds transférés serviront directement ou indirectement à financer un paiement illicite à un fonctionnaire ou un représentant d'un gouvernement étranger ou un candidat à un poste dans la Fonction Publique. Les incertitudes quant à la détermination des facteurs susceptibles de révéler à l'entité américaine l'usage illicite de ces fonds, ont conduit les sociétés américaines à adopter des mesures d'application strictes qui affectent non seulement ces sociétés américaines mais aussi toute entreprise étrangère qui considère que ses relations commerciales avec la société américaine sont suffisamment importantes pour qu'elle se plie elle même à ces mesures.

LOI ANTI-BOYCOTT

En réponse au boycott arabe des produits israéliens qui dure depuis longtemps, les États-Unis ont promulgué une loi vers le milieu des années 70 qui a pour but de priver les contribuables et les exportateurs américains qui y participent d'avantages fiscaux ou même de leur interdir carrément la participation au boycott en question. La législation américaine prévoit des exceptions.

DÉCLARATION DES INVESTISSEMENTS

D'aprés la législation sur la déclaration des investissements, les investissements étrangers aux États-Unis et les investissements américains à l'étranger doivent être déclarés s'ils dépassent certains "niveaux d'exemption." Les niveaux d'exemption sont beaucoup plus sévères lorsqu'il est question d'investissements fonciers faits aux États-Unis ou lorsque le pouvoir de vote de l'investisseur dans une affaire est de 10% ou plus. Tous les rapports de déclaration, à l'exception de ceux qui concernent les terres arables, sont confidentiels.

LOI DU CANADA SUR L'EXAMEN DES INVESTISSEMENTS ÉTRANGERS

La loi du Canada sur l'examen des investissements a établi un mécanisme gouvernemental dont l'objectif principal est d'examiner tout projet d'acquisition ou d'exploitation de sociétés canadiennes par des étrangers. Dans son rapport l'auteur fait mention des critères d'approbation, mais il met surtout l'accent sur la question relative à la détermination des projets d'investissement qui sont véritablement assujetis à la loi sur l'examen de l'investissement étranger.

LA REPRÉSENTATION CANADIENNE AU NIVEAU DU CONSEIL D'ADMINISTRATION

Le droit canadien des sociétés exige que la majorité des membres du conseil d'administration des sociétés à charte provinciale ou fédérale soient des citoyens canadiens résidant au Canada et que la majorité des membres constituant un quorum pour l'administration de la société soient aussi des citoyens canadiens résidant au Canada.

RESUMEN EN ESPAÑOL

LEGISLACIÓN AMERICANA Y CANADIENSE CONCERNIENTE A LAS MULTINACIONALES

El informe precedente trata sobre las leyes canadienses y estadounidenses aplicables a las multinacionales en general y, particularmente, en lo que respecta a sus operaciones e inversiones a nivel internacional.

En lo que concierne a los Estados Unidos, este informe trata: (a) las disposiciones contra el soborno desleales del Foreign Corrupt Practices Act de 1977, (b) las disposiciones contra el boicot del Tax Reform Act de 1976 y las reformas administrativas hechas al Export Act de 1977, (c) los requisitos de información aplicables a toda inversión extranjera impuestos por el International Investment Survey Act de 1976 y el Agricultural Foreign Investment Disclosure Act de 1978. Al referirse a la legislación canadiense el informe considera especialmente el Foreign Investment Review Act de 1974, y destaca los criterios impuestos por el derecho de empresas federales y provinciales en cuanto a la representación canadiense a nivel de los consejos de administración de las empresas canadienses.

LEY CONTRA EL SOBORNO

El Foreign Corrupt Practices Act prohibe el uso de todo medio comercial de comunicación interestatal (como el teléfono o el correo) para realizar cualquier transferencia de valor a quien sea, con el fin de sobornar, cuando el cedente sepa o debería saber, que los artículos transferidos serán utilizados directa o indirectamente para financiar un pago ilícito a un funcionario, o a un representante gubernamental extranjero, o a un candidato a un puesto en la administración pública. Las incertitudes en cuanto a la determinación precisa del conocimiento que la persona americana tenga sobre el uso ilícito de sus fondos ha resultado en que empresas americanas adopten procedimientos complejos que afectan no solamente a las empresas americanas, pero también a toda empresa extranjera que considera que sus relaciones comerciales con la empresa americana son suficientemente importantes como para seguir tal procedimiento.

LEY ANTI-BOICOT

En respuesta al boicot árabe de productos israelies, en efecto desde hace tiempo, los Estados Unidos han promulgado una ley a mediado de los años 70 que priva a quienes participan en este boicot de ventajas fiscales, o bien prohibe directamente la participación en el mismo. La legislación americana preve excepciones.

DECLARACIÓN DE INVERSIONES

Según la legislación sobre declaración de inversiones, las inversiones extranjeras en los Estados Unidos y las inversiones americanas en el extranjero deben ser declaradas si sobrepasan ciertos "niveles de exención". Los niveles de exención son mucho más severos cuando se trata de inversiones inmuebles en los Estados Unidos, o cuando el poder de voto del inversor en un negocio es del 10% o superior. Todas las declaraciones, exceptuando aquellas sobre tierras arables, son confidenciales.

LEY CANADIENSE SOBRE EXAMINACIÓN DE LA INVERSIÓN EXTRANJERA

La ley canadiense sobre la examinación de la inversión extranjera ha establecidio un mecanismo gubernamental cuyo objetivo principal consiste en revisar todo proyecto de adquisición o de explotación de empresas canadienses por parte de extranjeros. El presente artículo menciona los criterios de aprobación, pero enfatiza sobre todo la cuestión relativa a la determinación de proyectos de inversión que se encuentran sujetos a la ley sobre examinación de la inversión extranjera.

LA REPRESENTACIÓN CANADIENSE A NIVEL DEL CONSEJO DE ADMINISTRACIÓN

El derecho societario canadiense exige que la mayoría de los miembros del consejo de administración de empresas provinciales o federales sean ciudadanos canadienses residentes en Canadá, y que la mayoría de los miembros que constituyan un quorum para la administración de la empresa sean también ciudadanos canadienses residentes en Canadá.

CHAPTER II

TRANSFER OF TECHNOLOGY

LATIN AMERICA

UNITED STATES

THE MEXICAN RESPONSE TO TECHNOLOGICAL DEPENDENCY: THE NATIONAL REGISTRY OF TECHNOLOGY TRANSFER.*

George M. Armstrong, Jr.

The author holds a Ph.D. in political science from Princeton University and a J.D. granted with honors by the University of Pennsylvania. He is the author of The Soviet Law of Property: The Right to Control Property and the Construction of Communism and numerous articles on international trade, transfers of technology and comparative law.

In the last fifteen years investors in the United States have witnessed a change in the policies of Latin American countries as the governments of those states began to take more assertive action to regulate foreign influence in their domestic economies. Anti-American rhetoric had been common enough before 1970. Many Latin American countries had also nationalized key industries and raw materials prior to that date.[1] However the economic developmental strategies of these nations had, in general, ranked the creation of modern industry above independence from foreign influence, encouraging Latin states to pursue foreign investment at any cost. A turnabout in policy occurred in the early 1970s as influential sectors in these countries came to believe that foreign investment was retarding rather than promoting economic development.

Like most significant historical developments, this turnabout seems to have been caused by a combination of intellectual, materialistic and personal factors. The intellectual ingredient in the new Latin American regulation of foreign economic influence was dependencia theory, developed by social scientists to explain the apparent failure of their countries to follow W.W. Rostow's scenario of stages of economic growth.[2]

Although dependencia theory was initially primarily diagnostic, intellectuals close to the legislative process developed its prescriptive implications into a program for new legal institutions with functions such as the regulation of technology transfer and foreign investment.[3] The role of materialistic and personal factors in the legislative process is more difficult to establish than the influence of ideas. Nonetheless, the coincidence of the change in the policy toward foreign investment with other events permits an inference that these events influenced policy. The election of Chilean President Salvador Allende in 1970 seems to have provided a catalyst in Latin American politics, radically altering the horizon of options available to governments of developing countries and bringing into the mainstream of political discussion a number of alternatives which had not theretofore seemed possible. The rise of the OPEC oil cartel and the successful boycott of autumn 1973 probably gave additional encouragement to policy makers inclined toward nationalistic solutions to economic development problems. The boycott also revealed the vulnerability of the industrialized nations to collective action by third world states. A final factor in the change in policy toward foreign economic influence may have been a change in attitude by businessmen in Latin America. Some observers believe that domestic business leaders began to view their economic interests as allied with autonomous national development which foreign involvement and control were retarding.

In this paper I shall briefly discuss the intellectual antecedents of Mexican legislation regulating transfer of foreign technology. Owing to limitations of space and the interests of the intended audience of this paper, I shall limit this part of the essay to an examination of the legal aspects of economic dependency, especially the critique by Mexican scholars of the role of the international patent system and the influence of transnational corporations on development of indigenous technology. I shall then set out the prescription for action which Mexican academicians drew from their analysis of their predicament before turning to the principal purpose of this paper, examination and criticism of the National Registry of Technology Transfer.

I Dependencia Theory

Prior to the 1970s foreign investment in Mexico was virtually unregulated. Mexican authorities had on many occasions announced their opposition to any regulation, arguing that investment presents complex problems requiring flexible solutions and that the area was not amenable to government control for fear of chilling the climate of investment.[4] The dominant ideologies of economic development supported this *laissez faire* approach to foreign investment, maintaining that Latin America would follow the same pattern of development which the industrialized world had travelled and accepting uncritically the transplantation of foreign firms to Latin soil.[5] Influential Latin American theorists such as Raul Prebisch and Victor L. Urquidi wrote of the importance of cooperation with foreign capital to achieve domestic development.[6]

At least as early as 1971, authors publishing in Mexico began to criticize theories of economic development based on cooperation with international business.[7] One of the most influential of these works, Dependency and Development in Latin America, concluded that Latin nations which had attempted to enter the era of modern industrial production by accepting foreign capital and technology uncritically have advanced "at the expense of the autonomy of the national economic system and of policy decisions for development."[8] The authors wrote:

> Competition in the open market, standards of industrial quality and productivity, size of investment (for example, to install a petrochemical industry), patterns of consumption--all these impose certain forms of organization that affect the overall economy. In this sense, the capital, technology and organization transferred from the external sector create a reordered economy.[9]

Dependencia theorists described this penetration of their local economies as "an assymetrical power relationship" which conditions all aspects of national life: political, economic, technological, cultural and military.[10]

A. Transnational Corporations

Many Mexican analysts believe that the activities of transnational corporations play a fundamental role in conditioning the development of their country. These corporations undertake limited research and development in the host country, preferring to import machinery and technology, from the home office. This technology is, they say, often obsolete, inappropriate for the scale of the local market, the domestic endowment of raw materials, trained labor and environment.[11] Mexican subsidiaries must frequently accept this technology because of the economic power of the home office and pay inflated prices for equipment on which the parent has already taken depreciation. Technology transfers from abroad thus constitute a significant charge against the country's foreign exchange.[12]

Latin American analysts contend that the influence of multinational corporations inhibits the development of native technology and encourages local firms to look abroad for innovation even if indigneous know-how exists. In addition to the subsidiaries of multinationals, which generally must buy technology from the parent on account of the ownership relationship between the two firms, the influence of multinationals affects unaffiliated local firms which supply the subsidiary with intermediate goods. In addition, a typical local firm with no relation to the multinational "will select the technology which, as a function of its particular market situation, will be most remunerative and secure."[13] They have, says one scholar, "a special predilection for that which is of foreign origin."

B. <u>The International Patent System</u>

Transnational corporations import technology into developing countries for the purpose of hoarding know-how as well as for the purpose of exploiting knowledge. Under the auspices of the Paris Convention, an inventor may prevent competitors from adopting technology by obtaining patents throughout the world. Scholars who apply <u>dependencia</u> theory to the predicament of third world technological development argue that the operation of the international patent system hinders rather than encourages innovation. "Since its inception, the convention has favored individual inventors exclusively without concerning itself with facilitating the transfer of technology or avoiding other negative effects implicit in the monopoly created by the patent . . ."[14]

The philosophy of the Paris Convention is the protection of property, not the dissemination of innovation. According to Jaime Alvarez Soberanis, one of Mexico's leading authorities on industrial property, this philosophy has been overtaken by events, by the changing character of the international economy. "The original 'defensive' character of the system has lost, today, its justification." The mission of the patent system should be recast, "promoting and facilitating the transfer of technology to help resolve the problems of poor countries."[15]

The proportion of Mexican patents owned by foreigners indicates that the reservoir of industrial know-how is the patrimony of the developed world. Between 1950 and 1970 92% of the patents registered in Mexico belonged to foreigners.[16] These figures may be repeated throughout the developing world as some observers contend that five-sixths of the patents in those nations are held by foreigners and their subsidiaries.[17] Prior to the 1970s third world nations did not resent this trend nor did their governments consider it hostile to their development. Most Latin American countries based their patent statutes on legislation prevailing in the developed world, without considering these laws to be elements in their strategy of domestic economic development.[18]

Authors in the vein of dependencia theory blame a variety of evil consequences on the concentration of patents in foreign hands. Firms' primary purpose in acquiring these patents is not to exploit them but to prevent others from innovating. One author estimates that 95% of the patents granted by developing countries are never "worked."[19] Transnationals use patents to secure their monopoly in the local market, forcing would-be competitors to innovate around the patent.[20] Patents also permit the foreign firm to gain control over local enterprises by imposing conditions upon licensees of patented technology. The licensor may limit the capacity of the local firm to compete with it by restricting the range of use of the patent, by limiting the territory in which a patented product may be sold or by concessions which allow it to influence managerial decisions of the local firm.[21]

Patents developed in industrial nations may be poorly suited to the needs of poorer states inasmuch as they rely upon raw materials, skills, intermediate components and equipment which are not generally available there. A firm's decision to adopt technology of foreign origin may also entail importing an ensemble of machinery and technicians, further aggravating the foreign exchange problem and leaving local resources idle. Inasmuch as the entourage of accessories for the imported technology is of foreign origin, local commercial research and development and engineering faculties of domestic universities are under-utilized and atrophy. Research and development tends to accumulate in multinationals and within the multinational in the country of the home office.[22]

C. Technological Underdevelopment

Mexican culture has not traditionally placed a high premium on technological research. The arts, social sciences and law have been more prestigious professions than science and have tended to attract the most talented and ambitious students.[23] Absence of interest in research as a profession has tended to retard scientific progress. Moreover, Mexican industry did not develop a demand for scientific and technical personnel. The government has protected domestic industry from competition by imported goods so that

Mexican industrialists have not needed to innovate to maintain their captive markets.[24] Research scientists who seek challenging projects must often immigrate to find employment.[25]

Research institutions which do exist in Mexico are, according to critics, often poorly suited to the country's needs. Scientists are interested in working at the cutting edge of knowledge, viewing themselves as members of an international community of scholars. They have less interest in seeking solutions applicable to domestic problems and direct their research toward foreign audiences. Pure and applied science are widely separated, having little contact or influence on one another. Mechanisms for disseminating knowledge are poorly developed and scientific findings often do not reach those who might apply them.[26]

The absence of a strong tradition of scientific inquiry and the weakness of domestic research and development create a gap in the infrastructure of Mexican industry which, scholars say, imported know-how does not fill. The transnational corporations which import most of the productive technology are interested in profit rather than Mexican development. "The center of technological decisions and the sole source, or at least the principal source, of technology used in the new subsidiary belongs to the parent for decisions regarding technology are adopted with regard to the global strategy and profitability of the whole transnational system. . . . [T]he parent shows little concern for adaptation of the technology to the endowment of factors of production which characterize the transferee country. . ."[27]

The transnational firms, entering the country in the 1950s and quickly dominating the most dynamic industries including metalurgy, food processing, textiles, chemistry and pharmaceuticals, are the only substantial consumers of technology.[28] The traditional elements of Mexican society, such as agriculture and extractive industries, do not significantly participate in the demand for innovation. The goals of research and development are set and the investigation required to carry out the innovation is undertaken outside of Mexico, leaving native industry and domestic universities and laboratories as spectators of their country's technological development.[29]

Lacking an infrastructure of research and development and trained personnel to conduct investigation, relinquishing control over both the supply and the demand for technology which is employed on its native soil, Mexico had fallen into a "technology trap" by the beginning of the 1970s. The term "technology trap," first used in a paper presented to the United Nations Group of Experts of Transfer of Technology in June 1971,[30] refers to a process "removing the innovative capacity of the system to the extent that the modern productive system becomes ever more dependent on foreign know-how".[31] Its consequences include, according to the author of the concept, displacement of services offered by the national system of innovation and frustration of qualified local personnel, distortion of patterns of consumption and creation of employment and income for the highest income group at the expense of the lowest.[32]

Until the early 1970s the Mexican government had encouraged the flow of technology, placing no legal obstacles in the path of foreigners seeking Mexican patents or domestic firms negotiating licenses with owners of know-how. The government's policy implies that it conceived of technology as obeying the laws of entropy, moving from the point of greatest concentration to the point of least density until it achieves homogeneity. If technology followed these laws of physics, the developing world would eventually achieve the same command of know-how as the industrial countries.[33] As social scientists applying dependencia theory to technology began to influence policy makers, the government came to consider that the unhindered movement of technology might be a bane not a boon. Writing in 1972, M.S. Wionczek, one of Mexico's leading scholarly authorities on technology policy, wrote:

> It is only lately that there has been awareness of the fact that the problem ought not be limited to surveillance of the impact these operations have on balance of payments, but should include the adaptation of technologies acquired abroad to the country's requirements, to the domestic availability of production factors other than technology and to priorities defined by a general industrialization strategy.[34]

At least by 1972 scientists and politicians had begun to discuss the amenability of foreign technology to the public interest. Some scientists suggested policies which would make foreign technology licensed to Mexican firms available simultaneously to research organization for study and further adaptation. "If this is not done," Dr. Enrique Leff, coordinator of scientific investigation at the National Autonomous University said, "imported technology will serve only to preserve the competitive capacity of the importer, its monopolistic control over the market and its high rate of profit, and what is more, if there is no research over the transferred technology, dependence on imported know-how will continue."[35]

Other suggestions included new restrictions on permissible terms in licensing agreements, prohibition of clauses which restrict the competitive position of the transferee and creation of a government agency to monitor the provisions of these contracts. These suggestions came upon the heels of recognition that the terms of such contracts have no necessary positive relation to the welfare of the transferee country unless that county has a well defined and coherent policy toward foreign technology and conditions exist to put it into practice.[36] Mexican scholars recognized that technological autarchy is a "utopian pretension" for a country lacking even the rudiments of a scientific infrastructure.[37] They argued instead that purchasers of know-how should investigate alternative sources of technology, achieving greater geographical diversity of supplies.

To attain this diversity of supplies, a number of authors advocate creation of national or international clearing houses for information. The U.N. Council on Trade and Development might, wrote one author, create a central advisory office to "help developing countries formulate and evaluate projects of technology transfer and search for alternative technologies and selection of the most appropriate of them."[38] Alternatively a national information service might assist firms deciding on the most adequate know-how.[39] Some authors favored creation of a multi-purpose national agency which could search for technology relevant to the needs of domestic firms, assess the provisions of licenses, assist in negotiation of agreements, adapt technology of foreign origin to national needs and share information with analagous agencies in other developing countries.[40]

Finally, Mexican authorities also realized the importance of encouraging indigenous technical research. In its letter of transmittal of draft legislation to create the National Registry of Technology Transfer, the Federal Executive noted "the necessity of stimulating and promoting the creation of our own technology as indispensable means for attaining the country's economic independence."[41] Advocates of expansion of national research capacity urged greater federal investment in research and development and an expanded educational system.[42]

II The National Registry of Technology Transfer

A. History of the Law on Control and Registration of the Transfer of Technology

The Mexican government responded to all of the suggestions related here to some extent. During the presidency of Luis Echevarría, Mexico began to coordinate with other developing countries its efforts to improve its firms' bargaining position vis à vis the industrialized countries. Mexico is a leading member of the Group of 77 which has drafted several versions of a proposed Code of Conduct on technology transfer under the auspices of UNCTAD.[43] The government has increased financial aid for technical studies[44] and provided tax incentives to research and development.[45] There is also new legislation on foreign investment[46] and industrial property.[47] These topics are beyond the scope of this paper although I expect to discuss them in a subsequent essay examining technology in the context of Mexican politics.

The Mexican Secretary of Industry and Commerce transmitted to Congress draft legislation on technology transfer on November 3, 1972. This initial draft contained provisions which pertained principally to price controls on technology. The Secretary soon withdrew this proposal, submitting in its place another draft which contained all of the elements later enacted into law. Later that month, the Under Secretary of Industry, Jóse Campillo Sáinz, published a policy statement on behalf of the executive branch in the widely circulated journal Comercio Exterior. Campillo Sáinz responded to conservative critics of the Echevarria administration's proposal:

> It has been said that there is concern because Mexico is changing the rules of the game. To this I reply with all emphasis: Yes, gentlemen, we are changing the rules of the game; we are changing them to make them fit the needs and aspirations of our times. We are changing the rules of the game because we need an economy placed not at the service

of material goods, but at the service of human beings.[48]

The author's tone manifest the self confident and perhaps also the self righteous deportment which leaders from the third world often carried in the early 1970s. "We are certain that the companies that have been working with Mexican firms will understand" the need for regulation, he stated. But, he continued, we can do without those firms who protest our policy for, "happily we live at a time when technology has been developed in a good number of world centers."[49]

Congress debated the draft Law on Control and Registration of the Transfer of Technology in mid December, 1972. A spokesman for PAN, the political party of Mexican business interests, supported the effort to intervene in technology transfers but emphasized that agencies undertaking such intervention "should take care" "to avoid letting this proposed control harm national development." The leader of the PAN delegation noted that technology is not merely a legal problem but also a matter of promoting native Mexican investigation and research.

Ortiz Mendoza, a speaker for PSUM, the socialist party, characterized the draft legislation as fundamentally defensive. Observing that "the basic enemy of development in our country is the penetration of North American imperialism in all its forms in our national life," Ortiz Mendoza avowed that the time had arrived to move to the offense, to begin developing native technology.[50]

Although the Chamber of Deputies unanimously passed the bill and transmitted it to the Senate, some leaders of Mexican elite opinion considered the law too mild. Enrique Leff wrote a letter to the editors of Excelsior exposing what he conceived as an attack by the United States and business interests on Mexican technological independence. Unnamed "representatives of imperialism" had denounced the Mexican project, he said, connecting it thematically with a recent address to the United Nations by Salvador Allende and attacking the "united front" of the Mexican and Chilean people against the interests of business. Leff noted that debate on the draft legislation coincided with the heaviest American bombing of North Vietnam to date. "But this time the coincidence of these two events was not 'pure coincidence.' This is the form in which Mr. Nixon's bombers reverberate in Mexico and in the other

Third World countries which wish to escape underdevelopment."[51] Assembly leaders convinced the deputies, Leff said, that the law merely required registration of technology licenses and that it contained no limitations on their provisions.

Subsequent discussion will show that the law contains both registration requirements and substantive limitations. Other, more moderate observers, agree with Leff, however, that the purposes of the legislation were not extreme. M.S. Wionczek maintains that the law "is not in any sense revolutionary or confiscatory." "It represents the awareness of a country that does not wish to be the object of exploitation in the field of technology and an effort to put things in proper order."[52]

B. <u>The National Registry Of Technology Transfer</u>

The Law on Registration of the Transfer of Technology came into force on December 28, 1972.[53] It has been revised as of January 11, 1982.[54] This statute created the National Registry of Technology Transfer (NRTT), an administrative agency subordinate to the Secretario de Patrimonio y Fomento Industrial. Parties to licenses of the type specified in the law must present them to the Registry for its consideration within sixty days or the contract becomes void. The NRTT has authority to deny registration to any agreement which is not in accord with the provisions of the enabling act.

The 1972 law required registration of the following types of agreements if they were intended to be effective within Mexico:

1) a trademark license, 2) a license of patent or an industrial design, 3) the transfer of know-how through plans, diagrams, models, instructions, formulae, specifications, training of personnel or other methods, 4) technical assistance in any form 5) provision of any services connected with operating or administering a firm.[55] The version of this statute currently in force has expanded the list of transactions which must be submitted for registration and also requires submission for registration agreements which assign a patent or mark, involve the supply of any engineering assistance, authorize the use of a certificate of invention, assign or authorize the use of a trade name, assign literary rights which involve industrial exploitation, relate to computer programs, in-

volve counseling, consulting and supervision by physical or legal persons who are foreigners, or their subsidiaries.[56]

The statute requires the Registry, under the supervision of the Secretary, to register or reject the contract, which must be submitted in Spanish, within ninety days of its receipt.[57] The staff of the Registry is composed of lawyers, economists and engineers. The statute charges them to apply the specific provisions of the law as well as the directives and policy guidelines of the Secretary. This scheme contemplates broad consultation with scientific and technical authorities outside the Registry for the purposes of determining the impact of the contract under consideration upon the Mexican economy. Specifically, the National Council of Science and Technology and the National Polytechnic Institute are charged with rendering advice to the Registry and the Secretary is permitted to consult all foreign and domestic bodies, public or private, which carry out technological development or investigation.[58]

The Secretary's statutory role is the development of an overall policy on technological importation which harmonizes individual licensing agreements with the objectives of Mexican economic independence, industrialization, full employment, balance of payments and the encouragement of indigenous technology. To attain these objectives, the law authorizes the Secretary to direct Mexican firms which are searching for technology, making use of native know-how wherever possible and using foreign information which has already been acquired to the greatest advantage. Where appropriate technology is not already available, however, the Secretary may encourage the search for innovative know-how abroad or enter contracts itself for the development of new industrial processes. Its procedures are intended to protect the Mexican economy by restricting the price which firms may pay for know-how to the lowest cost among appropriate alternative sources of supply available on the world market. The law also urges the Secretary to encourage the export of Mexican technology.[59] Regulations issued by the President in 1982 permit the Secretary and the Registry to evaluate transfer agreements in light of these policies, authorizing the Registry to deny approval to any contract which undermines these objectives even if it does not contain a term specifically prohibited by law.[60]

C. Prohibited Terms in Licensing Agreements

The heart of the statute is the catalogue of terms which may not be included in any agreement submitted for registration.[61] The Secretary may not register an agreement which contains any of these deficiencies:

1. Authorization for the transferor to regulate or intervene directly or indirectly in the management of the transferee. Such interference may consist of reserving the right to appoint certain individuals to management positions, to determine suppliers of materials or components, to require that no shares of stock be sold without approval of the licensor or any other type of control unjustified by the nature of the technology delivered.[62] On the other hand the licensor may supervise quality control where it authorizes the transferee to manufacture under a trademark or in any other case where the licensor might be injured by failure of the Mexican firm to produce according to its standards.[63] The licensor may also reserve the right to examine the accounts of the Mexican factory to verify adequate payment of royalties.[64]

2. An obligation by the transferee to grant-back to the licensor with or without charge the patents, marks, innovations or improvements obtained by the transferee unless there is reciprocity of benefit for the licensee in the exchange of information. The law of 1972 prohibited all compulsory grant-back provisions, irrespective of reciprocity of obligation to share improvements on the part of the licensor.[65] Critics of the original language maintained that the proper vocation of a prohibition on compulsory grant-backs was equality of incentive to innovate for both parties, a purpose which the present provisions seem to further more effectively.[66]

3. Imposition of limitations on investigation and development of the technology by the transferee. Impermissible limitations include any provisions obliging the transferee not to undertake development of new products, processes, equipment, prohibiting it from undertaking its own improvements or adopting those of third parties. In practice, however, the Registry permits clauses which prohibit the licensee from altering products sold under a licensed trademark.[67]

4. Obligation to acquire equipment, tools, parts or raw materials from a specified source where alternative national or international sources of sup-

ply exist. A compulsory tie-in may be permitted in extraordinary cases as an assurance of quality control. Where concern for quality of the product is only a pretext for charging the licensee inflated prices for adjacent goods, however, the clause will be invalid.[68] One study has disclosed that tie-ins of materials in the pharmaceutial industry have involved overpricing in the Mexican industry ranging from 100% to 1000%.[69]

5. Prohibition or limitation on export of goods or services produced by the transferee in a manner contrary to the interests of the country. The Registry will not accept a contract which prohibits all export of a product under the license. Certain export limitations are justifiable in accordance with the industrial property laws of other states and reasonable business practices. The Registry respects the terms of any prior agreement in which the licensor granted exclusive rights to a third party to sell the licensed product in another country. In other cases, exportation of the product to a third country may infringe a valid patent or mark granted by that state. Finally, some nations prohibit the reexport from Mexico or any other country of products manufactured under classified military technology.[70]

6. Prohibition on the use of complementary technology. Such limitations are permitted only if the agreement involves the use of the licensor's trademark or if the restriction is intended to assure the secrecy of the licensor's confidential industrial know-how.[71] Mexican authors note that contractual "tie-outs" are also prohibited by section 3 of the Clayton Act in the United States and by legislation in Japan and the European Community.[72]

7. Obligations to sell to an exclusive client goods produced by the licensee. This provision in the law of 1982 is broader than the corresponding provision of the 1972 statute which only prohibited clauses requiring the transferee to sell exclusively to the transferor of the technology.[73] The Regulations issued by the Secretary in pursuance of this law currently invalidate any contractual requirement that the Mexican firm sell even a portion of the licensed product to a specified buyer.[74] The Regulations permit a sales requirement only if the Registry concludes on the basis of an independent economic study that the purchasing provisions are beneficial to the Mexican firm.[75]

8. An obligation to employ permanently personnel designated by the licensor. The Registry proposed an amendment to this legislation in 1976 which, if adopted by the legislative process, would have further decreased the power of the licensor. The act as amended would have prohibited the foreign firm from designate personnel for any length of time, no matter how brief. The drafters considered that the function which the designated employee performs is more important than the duration of his tenure.[76] The proposed amendment was not adopted and current regulations actually broaden the licensor's authority to designate personnel, excepting licensee firm's which have recently begun operations and those incorporating "technological processes of a totally novel character."[77]

9. Limitations on the volume of production or fixed prices of sale or resale for the production or exportation of the licensee. The Regulations prohibit contractual requirements requiring minimum or maximum volumes of production, minimum payments to the licensor or any authority for the licensor to establish the licensee's resale prices.[78]

Regulations under this section also interpret limitations on the volume of production to include restrictions on the duration of the transferee's use of the technology.[79] Under this interpretation the licensor may not require the Mexican firm to return the technical documentation delivered under the license or to cease producing the licensed product, save in cases of breach of contract by the transferee. The Mexicans regard a technology license as a sale of information. "[K]now-how, once transferred, becomes part of the store of technology of the recipient."[80] "The consequence of clauses [requiring the return of technology] is to extend indefinitely the condition of technological dependency of the transferee and thus of the recipient country."[81]

10. An obligation for the transferee to enter contracts of sale or exclusive representation with the licensor unless relating to export where the licensee accepts it and it is demonstrated to the Secretary's satisfaction that the licensor has command of adequate mechanisms of distribution or enjoys the commercial prestige necessary to undertake sales in more favorable conditions than the transferee. The statute initially prohibited any exclusive representation clause in a technology license on the ground that decisions about sales policy were a prerogative of the

manufacturing firm and not suitable subject matter for a license. The Registry excepted transactions in which the licensor demonstrated its ability to perform the exclusive representation in regulations issued in 1974.[82] A commentator has noted that the Registry's analysis of the sales capacity of the licensor is lax "and even when in some cases dispensing [with the prohibition] would be justified, the problem is that there are no means of adequately investigating the criteria contained in the exception."[83]

11. <u>An obligation for the transferee to protect the secrecy of technical information supplied by the licensor beyond the life of the acts, conventions or contracts or the period established by applicable laws</u>. The Registry permits a secrecy requirement of more than ten years if the technology is protected by unexpired industrial property rights or if secrecy is in the best interest of Mexico.[84]

12. <u>Failure of the licensor to expressly assume responsibility in cases where industrial property rights or third parties are violated</u>. The law of 1972 contained no equivalent provision.

13. <u>Failure of the licensor to guarantee the quality of the results of the technology under contract</u>. This provision, which also had no counterpart in the initial statute, relates to agreements in which the licensor does not assume responsibility "in any form for the deficiencies of the technology." The supplier should undertake liability to the transferee and to third parties for rejected and defective goods, for impossibility to produce goods properly using the technology and for functional problems in factories designed under the technology.[85] The Registry does not expect the licensor to assume liability for defects caused by the licensee's "rejection or open disobedience" to the transferor's instructions.[86]

14. <u>Availability of the technology in Mexico</u>. This provision is substantially more strict than the corresponding article of the 1972 statute. That article provided that a Mexican firm might not purchase foreign technology if the same information were "freely available" from domestic sources.[87] The practice of the Registry interpreted "freely available" to mean technology available without any cost or the need of anyone's permission.[88] Under the 1972 legislation a Mexican firm could not, for example, purchase foreign technology if substantially similar know-how were

available under an expired or invalid domestic patent.[89]

The legislation changed the focus of this article so that it no longer emphasizes savings of expenses. Currently the law encourages enterprises to purchase domestic technology. The Regulations permit a Mexican firm to protest before the Registry a technology license executed by another enterprise, demonstrating that it owns technology appropriate for the latter's needs.[90] The Mexican buyer must then negotiate with the other national firm and demonstrate to the Registry that they are unable to reach agreement or that the technology is not appropriate for its needs.[91]

15. Compensation which bears no relation to the technology acquired or poses an unjustified or excessive burden for the national economy or the acquiring enterprise. Evaluating the compensation for the technology is the Registry's most sensitive and difficult task. One commentator has observed that the Registry cannot perform this task by determining the value of the information in an abstract world market. The relevant value is the worth of the technology to the transferee.[92] In 1974 the Registry published a list of considerations relevant to the value of technology in the agreement.[93] A later section of this paper will discuss criticism, within and without Mexico, of the Registry's performance of this task.[94]

16. Excessive duration of the contract which may not in any case exceed ten years.

The Registry retains authority under this provision to impose an even briefer term on the transaction and to curtail the life of the contract if the technology can be "assimilated" more quickly.[95] Commentators noted that analogous Argentine legislation created a presumption that technology becomes obsolete within five years and limits the agreement's life to that period.[96] "It is a pity that our legislation does not have a provision of this tenor," one author observed.[97] The Registry will also diminish the life span of an agreement which transfers rights to use a patent if rights under that grant will expire in less than a decade.[98]

17. Submission of questions regarding performance or interpretation of the agreement to foreign tribunals. The Registry will countenance provisions submitting to the jurisdiction of private international

arbitration, provided the tribunal applies the substantive law of Mexico in accordance with treaties executed by Mexico.

C. The Registry in Action

The Registry has not released enough information about its procedures to permit careful analysis of its approval process. However, a résumé of the Registry's activities between January 29, 1973 and July 31, 1978 offers an account of the number of agreements reviewed, the proportion rejected, and the grounds on which the government denied registration.[99] During the period in question the Registry considered and rendered opinions on 7,104 agreements and denied registration to 2,179. Many rejected agreements ran afoul of more than one of the provisions of the enabling act.

The most significant ground for denial of registration was excessive cost of the technology. Eighty-four percent of the rejected technological licenses were defective in this respect.[100] The Registry's evaluation of the price of the technology is likely to be more subjective than almost any of the other criteria which it considers. There appears to be no easy definition of the criteria "unjustified and excessive burden" and critics complain that the Registry often accepts or rejects contracts without providing reasoned explanations for its actions. The Registry may issue a terse statement that royalties are "just and reasonable", that services being performed in return are "broad and complete", that personnel providing them are "adequately qualified." Royalties may also be justified on the grounds that the technology "will satisfy national demand," "is very important" or "the industry is very dynamic"[101] Nonetheless, the Registry has developed some criteria for evaluation of the price of technology.

The Registry generally limits compensation for use of a trademark to one percent of sales.[102] The administrative agency apparently selected this figure because it is a percentage commonly agreed to in licenses and because other nation's technology registration agencies apply that percentage.[103] If the licensor of the mark has a majority shareholder position in the licensee, it is not ordinarily entitled to any compensation. The licensor in such cases receives ample benefit from its subsidiary's profitable use of the mark.[104]

The criteria set out by the Registry for evaluation of patent royalties do not take account of number of patents included in the deal. Officials hypothesize that licensors often compel their contracting partners to accept block licenses which include know-how useless to the tranferee along with essential industrial property. Consequently "fair compensation" for a block of patents may be only slightly greater than fair remuneration for one license.[105] The Registry also considers whether the patents have been granted or applications are pending.[106]

In the latter case, the amount of royalties is approved conditionally.

The Registry Criterios relating to patent royalties conclude with the cryptic statement. "In general, royalties for patent rights shall be maintained at the same levels established for trademarks."[107] Presumably this statement indicates the agency's view that parent corporations are not entitled to royalties when they share patents with Mexican subsidiaries. Observers note that the Registry adopts the same policy for transfers of unpatented know-how.[108] Other factors which the agency considers are the age of the technology, evidence that it continues to be economically viable and its novelty as compared to alternative sources.[109]

The availability of alternative sources may be most important in evaluation of compensation for engineering design for, according to Alvarez Soberanis, Mexico has a number of capable engineering firms which are as well able to supply the information under contract as any foreign firm.[110] When the Registry determines that a Mexican firm could supply some of the engineering, it may require the licensing parties to amend the contract so as to share responsibility in this area. In any case the agency considers the volume and quality of anticipated production in determining the value of the engineering.[111]

The enabling act charges the Registry to consider not only the value of the technology when evaluating the compensation but also the burden on the transferee enterprise and the Mexican economy.[112] To fulfill this duty the Registry must employ judgment which is possibly more subjective than that required by the other standards. Alvarez Soberanis writes that the overall burden of the level of compensation can only be evaluated by analyzing the total flow of payments under the agreement, the effect of these payments on the cost of production and efficiency of the firm, the sectoral balance of payments and "other factors belonging to social cost-benefit analysis."[113]

Although excessive price is only one of seventeen grounds on which the Registry may deny effect to an agreement, most of the other provisions do not lend themselves to extended discussion. Application of some provisions is reasonably mechanical, the existence of compulsory grant-backs for example. Other criteria which do require judgment, such as availability of equivalent Mexican technology, have not been a significant basis for denial of registration.[114]

III. Evaluation of the Law on Registration and Control of Technology Transfer

Although the portion of this paper evaluating the performance of the Registry contains more criticism than praise of the system, there should be no inference that the preponderance of opinion is negative. Most observers of the system in action believe that some of its effects are salutary. One scholar who is critical of many of the procedures of the Registry concedes that its mere existence has increased the bargaining power of national firms.[115] The statute has also increased awareness by the Mexican business community of the restrictive commercial practices involved in technology transfer agreements, many of which are illegal under competition laws of the licensors' own countries.[116] The Registry is probably contributing to the development of international standards on commercially restrictive commercial practices. Elimination of these practices from Mexican technology purchase agreements is, by most accounts, the Registry's greatest success.[117]

Criticisms of the registration law belong to one of three classes. Some observers believe that the Registry does not perform its supervisory and evaluative tasks adequately. Other critics maintain that the entire system of regulation impedes the flow of badly needed technology. Finally, some scholars believe that the statutory scheme treats only a sympton rather than the disease of dependency.

One critic complains that the Registry only becomes involved in the transfer process after the parties have struck a deal. "To convert the Registry into a mechanism for regulating the substantive aspects of these operations, its intervention should occur before the execution of the contract, not after."[118] The execution of the contract probably solidifies negotiating positions and the deferred entry of the Registry into the deal may cause exasperation if the parties are satisfied with the arrangement which they have reached.

A random survey of the legal departments of U.S. corporations which this author conducted tends to confirm the statement that the Registry begins its work after the parties have completed theirs. The survey elicited seventeen responses to the question. "Does the Mexican National Registry of Technology ordinarily become involved in negotiations at an early phase or only after the deal is struck"[119] Fourteen respondents stated that they submitted agreements to the Registry only after both parties had reached a complete understanding. One attorney related that his corporation began discussions with the Registry once both firms had reached a "mutually satisfactory basis," i.e. before the deal was consummated. Two firms involved the Registry in the negotiations from an early phase.

Another criticism of the Registry relates to its competence: its ability to evaluate the technology's worth or its availability from other, domestic suppliers,[120] The Registry may be inadequately staffed. The work load is quite heavy. The agency is called upon to review a wide variety of technical procedures. Information about alternative sources is often scarce.

Eleven firms in the author's survey responded to the question, "In your experience, do the officials of the Registry have the technical expertise to judge the value of the technology or its availability from other sources?" Only two attorneys responded with an unqualified "yes." Other affirmative answers included "probably yes" and "only to a limited extent." One respondent stated, "They have the ability to judge the value of technology once it is properly explained. They do not normally have extensive knowledge of other sources." Five respondents were emphatically negative and one replied, "probably not."

The effect of Mexican registration procedures on the flow of technology and the international climate of investment has been warmly debated. As I noted previously, proponents of the law acknowledged that some foreign businesses might be uncomfortable with the new system. These sponsors seemed certain that alternative foreign suppliers would be willing to fill any gaps which this discomfort might cause.[121]

Wionczek noted that Mexican representatives met with foreign businessmen on several occasions in 1972 to discuss the proposed legislation. He relates that these executives found no fault with the law which generally only prohibited conduct already illegal in their own countries.[122] On the other hand, some foreign observers recount a quite adverse reaction to the Registry's activities:

> Although the operation of many of the [Latin American] technology transfer agencies is but a year or two old, the international business community has, in general, actively protested against such legislation, predicting that strict enforcement of such technology transfer laws would virtually stop investment and technology transfer to such countries.[123]

Friends of the technology registration system sometimes offer a related criticism, arguing that the effort is "meritorious" but misguided, because of the nature of the object being regulated. "[I]nternational technology transfer is capricious, temperamental and not subject to certain rules. . . . Its dynamic power is discretionary and lively and it does not allow mechanisms to be imposed on it to transmit it or at least it would be difficult to set them in a regulatory instrument."[124] The military government of Argentina abolished Latin America's oldest registry of technology transfer in 1981, giving a related explanation for the inefficacy of regulation:

> Experience has shown that no one is in a better position than the local businessman himself to select the technology he requires and the trademarks he wishes to use to distinguish his products. The market is the best regulator of the price to be paid by the recipient for such technology or trademarks.[125]

Twelve of seventeen corporate counsel who replied the author's survey responded affirmatively to the question, "Are the Mexican regulations governing technology transfer an impediment to the free flow of information?" One attorney noted that his firm objected principally to the policy of limiting secrecy of the technology to ten years and to the Registry's attempts "to impose terms and conditions to the disadvantage of the licensor." Another attorney observed that the inability to impose export restrictions in the license and prohibition on terms requiring the return of know-how to the licensor at the end of the contract period were most serious. "As a result," he concluded, "the licensor is reluctant to give state of the art technology." The remaining five firms indicated that the regulations had not interfered with transactions which they had undertaken.[126]

A final criticism of the National Registry of Technology Transfer maintains that its activities, no matter how laudable, attack only a small part of the problem of technological dependence. "The central objective of the Registry is to eliminate abuses, but these conditions are a consequence of technological dependence, not its cause."[127] An editorial in Excelsior supports this position noting that, notwithstanding the efforts of the Registry to limit the cost of technology, four billion pesos left Mexico as royalties in 1976.[128] The Registry's activities have had little effect on Mexico's balance of payments.

Mexico will remain technologically dependent, irrespective of its controls on licensing agreements, until it develops a domestic infrastructure of research and development. Cesar Sepúlveda pointed out this problem in a recent treatise on Mexican patent law. Responding to the criticism that industrial property statutes do not adequately protect the rights of Mexican inventors, he rejoined, "in reality there does not exist an appreciable body of Mexican inventions to protect."[129]

Although the Mexican economy has benefited from the removal of many restrictive practices from licensing agreements, the country has not, according to this view, generated any domestic technological capacity. To achieve this capacity Mexico must promote research and development through incentives, formulate a national policy of technology acquisition, establish priorities by sector, educate aspiring scientists and engineers and then employ them.[130]

Authors from other Latin American countries believe that technological dependency, a problem shared by the region, can only be attacked through solutions involving more than one country. They urge the integration of regional technical potential, including cooperation, to overcome the fragmentation of markets, international free exchange of technical information and coordination in the selection and evaluation of technology. Latin nations might also jointly finance research and development.[131]

IV *Conclusion*

I have not intended this paper to be either an evaluation of *dependencia* theory or of the National Registry of Technology Transfer. My purpose has been to show why Mexico created the system of registration for technology licenses, what problems the government was trying to solve. *Dependencia* theory may be either a powerful diagnostic tool or an ideology disconnected from social facts without altering in any way its historic influence on Mexican public policy.

The Registry was the product, however, of a naive interpretation of *dependencia* theory, of an approach which held that the government could cure the predicament of development by regulating contacts with the industrial world. In later years Mexican analysts realized that the achievements of the Registry would be limited to removal of some anticompetitive practices and abuses of economic power and to minimal assistance with the balance of payments. The law did not assist the creation of indigenous technology, the absence of which is the real cause of Mexican dependence.

If the Mexicans are realizing that their technological dependence requires inward-looking remedies, they are not for that reason necessarily readily to abandon their outward-looking solutions. Twelve years of experience with the Registry appears to have removed doubts about the availability of suppliers of foreign technology willing to negotiate through the Registry. In addition, a group of attorneys, civil servants, engineers and economists in Mexico City who either work in the Registry or counsel the firms which are its clientele probably have career interests in maintaining or even expanding this program. To the extent that legislation has altered the registration system since 1972, the effect has been to tighten the controls by adding types of transactions which must be approved by the Registry.[132] The preponderant relevant opinion in Mexico seems to favor retaining the Registry. A limited amount of success by the agency, administrative inertia and absence of intense opposition to its procedures bode well for its survival.

Notes

* Professors Alain Levasseur and Enrique Dahl of this Law Center provided helpful criticism of an earlier draft of this paper.

1. A partial list of Latin American expropriation includes these items. Mexico nationalized oil extraction (1938), American and Foreign Power Company (1960), Asarco Mexicana, S.A. and Industrias Penoles, S.A. (mining companies, early 1960s), Compañía Azufera Mexicana, S.A. de C.V. and Compañía Explotadora del Istmo, S.A. de C.V. (1967). Peru has expropriated International Petroleum Company (1968), Banco Continental (1969), Peruvian Telephone Company (1969), All American Cables and Radio (1969) Cartovio and Paramonga sugar estates of W.R. Grace (1969), Cerro de Pasco Corp. (1973). Bolivia nationalized Standard Oil of New Jersey (1936), tin mines (1952) and Gulf Oil (1969). Other expropriations at the beginning of the 1970s include Chile's nationalization of copper companies and Guyana's expropriation of Demerara Bauxite Company (both in 1971).

2. The Stages of Econmic Growth: A Non-Communist Manifesto (1960).

3. Numerous Latin countries enacted legislation in the early 1970s in response to dependencia theory: Peru, General Law of Industries, Decree Law 18350 (July 1970); Argentina, Law 20.577 (Nov. 7, 1973); Brazil, the Constitution of 1967 prohibits foreigners from owning journalistic concerns including television and radio; Venezuela, as of 1970 foreign banks must have at least 80% national ownership; Mexico, Law to Promote Mexican Investment and to Regulate Foreign Investment, Diario Official Mar. 9, 1973; Andean Community, Common Regime of Treatment of Foreign Capital and of Trademarks, Patents, Licenses and Royalties (Dec. 31, 1970).

4. R. Mendez Silva, El régimen jurídico de las inversiones extrajeras en México (1969) 18-19.

5. After World War II, "it was necessary to pursuade the MNC's, possessors of technology and open credit lines, to establish operations in the separate countries in order to help them develop their own capabilities. At the time, it seemed a wise decision, and a variety of incentives were enacted, granting exemptions from import duties, tax holidays, unlimited profit remittances, and the like in an effort to pur-

suade companies to take the risk of establishing operations. . . . Today, however, it can be seen that this choice led to other unexpected problems, and the new emphasis is on control of foreign direct investment." S. Tancer, *Economic Nationalism in Latin America* (1976) 22.

6. R. Prebisch, *Proposals for the Creation of the Latin American Common Market* (1965), V. Urquidi; *The Challenge of Development in Latin America* (1964) and Free Trade and Economic Integration in Latin America (1968).

7. "The problem of 'technological colonialism' may not be approached as a private matter of 'the spirit of cooperation' of foreign capital for this is already spelled out in the rules of the game of the structure of dependency." Such approaches to development "lose all practical validity." Garcia, A., *El Trimestre Económico* (1971) 731, 746. Also, Furtado, C., *El Trimestre Económico* (1971) 335.

8. Cardoso and Faletto, 162. Cardoso and Faletto were acclaimed as "basic theorists of *dependencia*." J. M. Durand Ponte, *El Perfil de México en 1980* [(1972) 211].

9. *Id*.

10. M. Krieger, Suárez et al. *Autonomía nacional o dependencia: la política científico-tecnológica* (1975) 128.

11. Excelsior Jan. 22, 1977.

12. H. Cuadra *et al*. *Estudios de derecho ecónomico* (1980) 154.

13. E. Amadeo, *La dependencia económica y su relación con la dependencia tecnológica*, in Suarez *supra* no. 10, 141.

14. Jaime Alvarez Soberanis, *La regulación de las invenciones y marcas y de la transferencia tecnológica* (1979) 156.

15. *Id*. 157. Introducing draft patent legislation of 1975, Senator J. Campillo Sainz remarked, "Those elements of bourgeois ideology of the last century which consider patents to be a natural property right and a monopolistic privilege which can be exer-

cised without taking account of the public interest are not acceptable or valid . . . [t]he exercise of their rights should be limited by the interests of the collective and the right of developing countries for economic independence." Quoted in Alvarez Soberanis at 46-47.

16. Gribmont & Rimez, 1977 El Trimestre Económico 771, 825.

17. Alvarez Soberanis, supra, n. 14, 50.

18. M. S. Wionzcek, G.M. Bueno, J.E. Navarrete, La transferencia internacional de tecnología: el caso de México (1974) 265.

19. Alvarez Soberanis, supra n. 14, 50.

20. Id.

21. Dario Abad Arango, El Trimestre Económico (1973) 374, 384.

22. Wionzcek supra, n. 18, 266.

23. Abad Arango, supra, n. 21, 374.

24. Nitsch, La trampa tecnológica y los paises en desarrollo, in M.S. Wionzcek, ed. Comercio de tecnología y subdesarrollo económico (1973), 28.

25. H. Cuadra, supra, n. 12, 154.

26. Abad Arango, supra, n. 21.

27. Wionczek, supra, n. 18, 250.

28. H. Cuadra, supra, n. 12, 152-154.

29. C. Correa, 15 J. of World Trade L. (1981) 388.

30. Nitsch, supra, n. 24, 21.

31. Id., 28.

32. Id., 21.

33. S. J. Patel, 1972 Foro Internacional 15.

34. M. Wionczek and L. María Leal, 1972 Comercio Exterior July, 10, 12.

35. Excelsior, November 30, 1972.

36. Wionczek in Wionczek et al. supra, n. 18 250.

37. B. Sepúlveda and A. Chumacero, La inversión extranjera en Mexico (1973) 112.

38. Patel, supra, n. 33, 25-36.

39. Sepúlveda and Chumacero, supra, n. 37, 112.

40. Wionczek and María Leal, supra, n. 34, 16.

41. 1972 El Trimestre Económico 286.

42. Abad Arango, supra, n. 21, 392.

43. 1972 Comercio Exterior Nov. 7; 11.

44. Id., 12.

45. Excelsior, December 20, 1972.

46. Excelsior, December 27, 1972.

47. Wionczek et al, supra, n. 18, 36.

48. Jose Campillo Sainz, 1972 Comercio Exterior, Nov. 7, 11.

49. Id., 12.

50. Excelsior, Dec. 20, 1972.

51. Excelsior, Dec. 27, 1972.

52. Wionczek, supra n. 18, 36.

53. Ley Sobre el Registro de la Transferencia de Tecnología y el Uso y Explotación de Patentes y Marcas, D.O. 30 Dec. 1972. (Law of 1972), art. 2 a-f.

54. Ley Sobre el Registro de la Transferencia de Tecnología y el Uso y Explotación de Patentes y Marcas, D.O. 11 Jan. 1982. (Law of 1982), art. 2 a-m.

Article 3 excludes from the registration requirement the importation of foreign technology for the purpose of effecting repairs or for the installation of factories and machinery, the supply of designs which are acquired with machinery, assistance in repairs provided pursuant to any agreement which has been registered, instruction or training provided by teaching institutions or enterprises for their employees, exploitation of literary rights in the cinema, publication, etc., agreements of technical cooperation between governments.

55. Supra n. 53, art. 2 a-f.

56. Supra n. 54, art. 2 a-m.

57. Law of 1982, art. 12.

58. Law of 1982, art. 8.

59. Law of 1982, art. 9 (II).

60. Reglamento de la Ley Sobre el Control y registro de la Transferencia de Tecnología y el Uso y Explotación de Patentes y Marcas. (Reglamento 1982) Nov. 25, 1982, Art. 67.

61. Law of 1982, Art. 15.

62. Alvarez Soberanis, supra, n. 14, 531-532.

63. Reglamento 1982, Art. 42 (II).

64. Id. Art. 42 (III).

65. Law of 1972 Art. 7(IV)

66. Alvarez Soberanis, supra, n. 14, 557-558.

67. Id. 564.

68. Alvarez Soberanis, supra, n. 14, 536.

69. B. Sepúlveda and A. Chumacero, supra, n. 37, 110.

70. Alvarez Soberanis, supra, n. 14, 568-569.

71. Reglamento 1982 Art. 51 (1-II)

72. Alvarez Soberanis, supra, n. 14, 538-539.

73. Law of 1972 Art. 7 IX.

74. Reglamento 1982 Art. 52.

75. Id. Art. 53.

76. Alvarez Soberanis, supra, n. 14, 542.

77. Reglamento 1982 Art. 54.

78. Id. Art. 55 (I, IV, VI).

79. Id. Art. 55 (II, III, V).

80. Alvarez Soberanis, supra, n. 14, 548.

81. Id.

82. Resumen de los criterios generales de aplicación de la ley sobre el registro de la transferencia de tecnología y el uso y explotación de patentes y marcas (1974) in Legislación Sobre Propiedad Industrial, Transferencia de Tecnología e Inversiones Extranjeras, Porrua editores (1983) 309, 321.

83. Alvaraz Soberanis, supra, n. 14, 550.

84. Reglamento of 1982, Art. 56.

85. Reglamento of 1982, Art. 58.

86. Reglamento of 1982, Art. 59.

87. Law of 1972, Art. 7, I.

88. Alvarez Soberanis, supra, n. 14, 552 Resumen de los criterios, supra n. 82, 310.

89. Resumen de los criterios, supra, n. 82, 310.

90. Reglamento of 1982, Art. 61.

91. Reglemento of 1982, Art. 62.

92. Alvarez Soberanis, supra, n. 14, 520.

93. Resumen de los criterios, supra, n. 82, 310-315.

94. Infra, nn. 115-132 and accompanying text.

95. Alvarez Soberanis, supra, n. 14, 572. Resumen de los criterios, supra, n. 82, 321.

96. _Id_. 570-571.

97. _Id_.

98. Reglamento of 1982, Art. 65 (II).

99. Alvarez Soberanis, _supra_, n. 14, 667.

100. _Id_.

101. Alejandro Nadel Egea, _Instrumentos de política científica y tecnológica en Mexico_ (1977) 155.

102. Resumen de los criterios, _supra_, n. 82, 312.

103. Alvarez Soberanis, _supra_, n. 14, 524.

104. _Id_., 525-526.

105. Alvarez Soberanis, _supra_, n. 14, 527.

106. Resumen de los criterios, _supra_, n. 82, 313.

107. _Id_.

108. H. Camp and C. Rojas, 8 Lawyer of the Americas (1976) 1, 18.

109. _Id_.

110. Alvarez Soberanis, _supra_, n. 14, 528.

111. Resumen de los criterios, supra, n. 82, 314.

112. Law of 1982 Art. 16 (II).

113. Alvarez Soberanis, _supra_, n. 14, 510.

114. As of July 31, 1978 the agreements considered had contained the following defects:

	Criterion:	Denials(%)
I.	Available technology in Mexico	.41
II.	Level of compensation	84.44
III.	Interference in firm Administration	22.16
IV.	Compulsory grant-back	20.33

V.	Limitations on transferee's research	7.38
VI.	Tie-ins	6.97
VII.	Limits on exports	16.88
VIII.	Restrictions of use of complementary technology	2.20
IX.	Exclusive representation clauses	2.47
X.	Designation of personnel at transferee	.45
XI.	Output or price restrictions	37.81
XII.	Exclusive domestic representation agreements	.50
XIII.	Excessive duration of agreement	37.49
XIV.	Foreign jurisdiction	21.34

115. Nadel Egea, supra n. 91, 152.

116. M. Wionczek, 48 El Trimestre Económico (1981) 45, 63.

117. Id., 64. D. James, 22 Jou. of Inter American Studies (1980) 163, 179.

118. Nadel Egea, supra, n. 101, 160.

119. Although this author assured the confidentiality of respondents to the survey, I will be pleased to discuss the replies in general terms with interested readers.

120. Nadel Egea, supra, n. 101, 156.

121. Supra, n. 49 and accompanying text.

122. Wionczek, supra, n. 18, 36.

123. D. McGlynn, 8 Lawyer of the Americas (1976) 394, 396.

124. C. Sepúlveda, El sistema Mexicano de propiedad industrial (1981) 44.

125. Cited in: Sábato, 1981 Comercio Exterior, 338.

126. I am unable to draw any association between the industry in which the seventeen firms conduct their primary activity and their responses to this question.

127. Nadel Egea, supra, n. 101, 157.

128. Excelsior January 25, 1977.

129. Sepúlveda, supra, n. 124, 107.

130. B. Sepúlveda Amor, Las empresas transnacionales en Mexico (1974) 62-63; Leff, Dependencia científico-tecnológica y desarrollo económico, in Mexico Hoy, Casanova and Florescano eds. (1979) 279.

131. M. Halty et al, supra, n. 10, 309-310.

132. Supra, n. 56.

RÉSUMÉ EN FRANÇAIS

LA SOLUTION MEXICAINE AU PROBLÈME DE LA DÉPENDANCE TECHNOLOGIQUE: OFFICE NATIONAL DE L'ENREGISTREMENT DES TRANSFERTS DE TECHNOLOGIE

L'article qui précède nous présente la théorie de la dependencia, depuis ses origines, comme une critique des relations mexicaines avec le monde industrialisé des années 60, et suggère une politique d'action ainsi que la création d'agences gouvernementales spécialisées dont le principal objectif serait la protection de l'économie nationale. La théorie de la "dependencia" souligne que le Mexique compte énormément sur la technologie importée. Cette dépendance a aggravé le déficit de la balance des paiements, n'a pas permis à la technologie autochtone de se développer et a fait obstacle à l'utilisation des ressources mexicaines en liant la disponibilité de la technologie étrangère à l'emploi d'ingénieurs étrangers, à l'utilisation des matières premières et de leurs composantes.

En 1973, le gouvernement à créé un Office National de l'Enregistrement des Transferts de Technologie en vue de soumettre les licenses étrangères, les contrats d'ingénierie et les accords de concession à une procédure sévère de selection. L'Office d'Enregistrement examine ces transactions pour essayer de déceler les dispositions susceptibles d'avoir un impact négatif sur l'indépendance technologique du Mexique. Les contrats qui violent les dispositions de cette loi et ses règlements d'application se voient dénier l'enregistrement et ne pourraient pas être honorés.

De plus, cet article traite du fonctionnement de cet Office D'Enregistrement et procède à une évaluation du mérite qui lui revient d'avoir réussi à restreindre la dépendance technologique mexicaine. Il évoque aussi les accusations des détracteurs de ce mécanisme qui maintiennent qu'il fait obstruction à l'importation d'une technologie indispensable et ne fait que s'attaquer à un symptôme sans pour autant toucher à la cause fondamentale de cette dépendance.

RESUMEN EN ESPAÑOL

LA SOLUCIÓN MEJICANA AL PROBLEMA DE LA DEPENDENCIA TECNOLÓGICA: EL REGISTRO NACIONAL DE TRANSFERENCIA TECNOLÓGICA

Este artículo presenta la teoría de la dependencia, desde sus orígenes, como una crítica de las relaciones mejicanas con el mundo industrializado de los años 60, y sugiere una política de acción así como la creación de agencias gubernamentales especializadas cuyo principal objetivo sería la protección de la economía nacional. La teoría de la "dependencia" destaca que Méjico cuenta enormemente con tecnología importada. Esta dependencia ha agravado el déficit de la balanza de pagos, ha impedido a la tecnología autóctona desarrollarse y ha obstaculizado la utilización de recursos mejicanos al conectar la disponibilidad de la tecnología extranjera al empleo de ingenieros, de materias primas y de repuestos, también extranjeros.

En 1973 el gobierno creó el Registro Nacional de Transferencia Tecnológica, con el fin de someter las licencias extranjeras, los contratos de ingeniería y los acuerdos de concesión a un procedimiento severo de selección. El Registro examina estas transacciones para detectar las disposiciones susceptibles de tener un impacto negativo en la independencia tecnólogica de Méjico. Los contratos que violen las disposiciones de esta ley y su reglamento de aplicación no son registrados y carecen de fuerza ejecutoria.

Además, el presente artículo trata el funcionamiento de este Registro y procede a una evaluación sobre el mérito que le cabe en la disminución de la dependencia tecnológica mejicana. Se reproducen también las críticas de detractores de este sistema, quienes mantienen que obstruye la importación de una tecnología indispensable y que solamente ataca a un síntoma, pasando por alto la causa fundamental de esta dependencia.

LATIN AMERICAN ANTITRUST LAWS AND THEIR EQUIVALENTS: IMPACT ON REORGANIZATION AND LICENSING BY TRANSNATIONAL ENTERPRISES

Professor Beverly May Carl

The author is a Professor of Law at Southern Methodist University. Specializing in problems of the Third World, she served as editor and contributor to DOING BUSINESS IN MEXICO (Matthew Bender, 1980-83) and authored ECONOMIC INTEGRATION AMONG DEVELOPING NATIONS: LAW AND POLICY (Praeger, in press). After obtaining an LL.M. from Yale Law School, she attended the National University of Chile Law School under a Fulbright Scholarship. During the sixties, she worked for the American Embassy in Rio de Janeiro in the field of private foreign investments.

Extensive publicity has made the informed reader well aware of the foreign debt crisis in Latin America. These countries now owe almost U.S. $400 billion and the interest keeps compounding. Austerity programs demanded as the price for help by the International Monetary Fund have produced economic contraction, including credit shortages, currency devaluations, import restrictions, and business failures.

As private companies in Latin America find themselves unable to repay their overseas loans, they may seek a foreign investor to capitalize the debt in exchange for stock. Or a local company facing bankruptcy may prefer the alternative of refinancing with the creditor taking back equity shares. On the other hand, a straightened company may wish to merge with or sell out to a foreign company. Even healthy firms may find that, with the current lack of credit, they can expand only by bringing in an equity partner from abroad. Finally, Latin America's total debt may be too large for repayment and thus foreign banks may be forced to convert part of their loans into interests in pools of equity shares in various local enterprises.

Achieving an effective corporate restructuring may involve, not only a transfusion of capital, but also perhaps different management personnel and new capital equipment. In addition, a transfer of up-to-date technology may be required to save an ailing concern.

A North American or European lawyer contemplating such reorganization tends to think at once of the antitrust complications which can arise. In Latin America, however, a rather different set of concerns and controls surface. Of greater import will be the foreign investment statutes and technology transfer laws.

Since the Latin American nations follow the civil law system, judicial decisions play a less important role than in common law countries. Rather, the key decisions are those made by the various administrative organs of the host country. Typically, local law will require prior approval by a government agency of new foreign investment or expansion; such approval may also be necessary for licensing agreements, loans, and technical assistance from abroad. Although governments may publish a list of approved investment proposals in an official gazette, usually no such publication is made for applications denied. Thus, it is not always easy to ascertain how these laws and regulations are applied in practise. Some argue this plethora of restrictions impose a barrier which is blocking the flow of equity funds needed to replace international borrowing.

ANTITRUST LAWS

The constitutions and laws of many Latin American states do prohibit monopolies and abuse of economic power.[1] For instance, the Peruvian Constitution contains such a provision, but no implementing legislation has ever been passed and, according to one expert, none is expected in the near future.[2] In most other countries of the region, the anti-monopoly norms have been used primarily to protect consumers against price rises rather than to prevent concentration of economic power.[3]

Brazil. The law of this nation defines abuse of economic power as the domination of national markets or a total or partial elimination of competition.[4] Such "domination" may be brought about through "the association, merger, consolidation, integration or any other form of amalgamation of business."[5] It may also include the formation of an economic group by an association of companies in order to jeopardize the freedom of action of other buyers and sellers.

All acts and agreements between enterprises are subject to prior approval by CADE (the Administrative Board for Economic Defense). Unless they have been so approved, such arrangements or agreements are invalid if their purpose is to "equalize production, stabilize prices, allocate production or distribution, and effect a restriction on distribution to the detriment of other goods of the same or of a similar kind."[6]

Nonetheless, monopolistic activity is only considered "abusive" when prices are raised without justification. As a prominent Brazilian attorney, Jose Pinheiro Neto, has pointed out:

Finally, it is necessary to comment briefly on the problem of amalgamation of business, especially consolidations and mergers. Brazil's economic development has created the need, in many instances, for firms to associate together in groups. Incentives are offered for consolidations and mergers in the interests of the national economy. An Agency attached to the Ministry of Finance has been set up, called the Business Consolidation and Merger Commission (COFIE), which examines applications for amalgamations before submitting them to the Ministry. Hence it seems that one of the examples of abuse of economic power, as described in the Anti-Trust Law, is not punishable provided that it is shown to be in the interests of the national economy.[7]

The Brazilian antitrust laws do not consider growth _per se_ as dangerous. What is suspect are multiple corporations which through giant growth specifically intend to control the market.

Chile. In 1959 Chile was one of the first Latin American nations to enact a comprehensive antitrust law patterned on the United States model.[8] Since, however, it failed to take into account the Chilean realities, this statute was never effectively implemented.[9] In 1979, Chile adopted a new antitrust law[10] which may soon encounter the same problems -- official tendencies to rely on price control mechanisms, direct subsidies to manufacturers, protective tariffs, discriminatory exchange rates favoring importation of primary materials and capital equipment, and cooperation among manufacturers to "protect" themselves. Moreover, Chile's law does permit restriction on free competition when necessary for stability or for growth of national investment.[11]

Argentina. The recent Argentine antitrust law is intended to prevent, rather than just to cure market monopoly by creating a two tier administrative structure charged with enforcing its provisions. The National Commission on Defense of Competition may begin an investigation either on its own initiative or upon complaint of a third party. The Commission may conduct hearings and may recommend negotiated settlements to the Minister of Commerce. Failure to comply with a settlement approved by the Minister of Commerce can result in administrative and criminal sanctions.[12]

Argentine law defines "dominant position" as that held by one who exclusively offers or demands a particular product in the national market. The term also applies where two or more persons agree not to compete with each other, or with a third party.[13] Monopolistic acts included price fixing, limiting distribution rights, fixing resale prices, etc.[14]

Mexico. The Mexican Constitution prohibits "monopolies" and the "cornering of goods" of prime necessity.[15] Nonetheless, the implementing rules, however, seem to focus on the issue of prices rather than on merger policy.[16] Moreover, there is no unified machinery to enforce the rule against monopolies.

Attitudes Toward Competition. A variety of other national laws may tend to debilitate these antitrust rules. For example, Argentina's new law on Industrial Promotion will go so far as to grant a monopoly of a particular market to a given industry, if such company meets the law's requirements and purposes.[17]

In most Latin American nations, a small group of enterprises control the bulk of production. This allows these companies to affect the conduct of other small firms and has provided a wide field for maneuvering through the use of tied purchases and sales agreements, resale price fixing and exclusivity agreements. Expanded diversification and centralization of capital has led to powerful concentrations in industry, trade and finance.

Generally, in Latin America, positions of dominance and monopolistic structure are not per se rejected, but rather are subjected to government control. For example, the integrated industries approach of the Central American Common Market[18] ultimately failed, but its monopolistic character apparently did not concern the organization's leaders. Likewise, the complementarity agreements envisioned under the Latin American Integration Association[19] and the sectoral programs of the Andean Common Market[20] provide significant benefits and preferences to the favored enterprises. Once again, rather than flatly forbidding market concentration, the Latin Americans opt for control and avoidance of abuse.

These nations may have selected different ways of dealing with market power because the orthodox antitrust mechanisms have not been effective in Latin America. The region's typical problems -- inflation, foreign exchange shortages, balance of payments deficits, and unemployment -- have historically not been solved by either a pure market economy or pure state economy. Programs based on credit restrictions, fiscal responsibility, free access to imported capital equipment and materials, free market competition, have traditionally failed. As one observer concludes, "the history of antitrust laws in Latin America is the story of legal measures out of time and place, rendered ineffective by the force and flow of events around them."[21]

On the other hand, the weakness of the existing antitrust structure does not mean transnational enterprises can freely enter any arrangements or build any combinations they might wish. The demands of nationalism, coupled with the need for development, have prompted many Latin American countries to single out foreign enterprises and subject them to certain restrictions of a type American lawyers are accustomed to find under the rubric of "antitrust". South of the border, however, these limitations are more likely to be encountered either in the national laws regulating foreign investment or in those governing the transfer of technology.

FOREIGN INVESTMENT LAWS

Mexico. Any foreign person or Mexican company majority owned by foreigners wishing to merge with or to acquire a Mexican company (including one with a minority foreign participation) must obtain approvals from both the National Foreign Investment Commission and the government agency with jurisdiction over the industry in question.[22]

Moreover, the Foreign Investment Commission has broad discretionary authority where an extraordinary permit (as opposed to an ordinary permit) is required. Extraordinary permits must be obtained for the following transactions:[23]

1. Acquisition of more than 25% of the capital or equity of an already established Mexican corporation by a foreign investor; or the acquisition of more than 49% of the current assets of such corporation; or the leasing to a foreign investor of the essential assets,

where such assets are directly associated with the production activities of a completely owned Mexican corporation;[24]

2. One intends to acquire more than 49% of a yet to be formed Mexican corporation; or more than 34% if such corporation is subject to extraordinary mining concessions (basically deep mining); or more than 40% if the abovementioned corporation invests in petrochemical operations or in the production of spare parts for automobiles, trucks, vans, pick-ups and the like;[25]

3. The opening of a new business by an existing corporation under the jurisdiction of the Foreign Investment Commission. A new business means any technical or physically independent location where a company plans to engage in any industrial, commercial or service activities;[26] or

4. The disposal by any means (including trusts, leases, assignments, etc.) by a foreign investor of more than 49% of the assets of an enterprise subject to the Foreign Investment Act.[27]

An extraordinary permit is also required for any of the following transactions on the stock market:

1. Acquisition of more that 5% of the shares of a company subject to the Foreign Investment Act if the foreign investment in such corporation amounts to between 25% and 49% of the ownership;

2. Acquisition of more than 25% of the shares by a foreign investor in an operating company wholly owned by Mexican nationals;

3. Acquisition of more than 49% of the shares of any enterprise subject to the Foreign Investment Act.[28]

Also requiring an extraordinary permit are transfers between foreign investors or acquisitions from Mexican investors by affiliated foreign investors if the percentage of ownership exceeds certain prescribed minimums (e.g., 3% in a company with less than 33% foreign ownership).[29] In addition, such extraordinary permits are required for capitalization of debt or for creation of a company 100% owned by foreigners.[30]

In applying for an extraordinary permit one must address the following issues:

1. reasons why other alternatives are not preferable or possible;

2. the extent to which the new structure of the foreign investment will

   a. integrate the market;

   b. assist the balance of payments;

   c. create employment;

   d. transfer technology to Mexico or train Mexican technicians;

   e. finance the operation with its own resources;

   f. develop the zone in which the foreign investment will be located;

   g. preserve the socio-cultural values of Mexico and its people.

3. impact of the proposal on national development;

4. methods by which the majority ownership of the project will be transferred to Mexican nationals in the future and to what extent, if at all;

5. legal mechanisms for such transfer of ownership, e.g. sales, concessions, etc.

6. means by which investment will improve Mexico's import-export ratios.[31]

Foreign investors will probably not be allowed to buy into already existing Mexican companies unless such transaction produces a significant contribution to the nation. Such contributions may consist of vitally needed technology, help for the trade imbalance, or an increase in local integration through subcontracting arrangements.[32]

Foreigners are completely prohibited from participating in investments involving oil or hydrocarbons, basic petroleum, nuclear energy, electricity, railroads, telegraph and wireless communication, etc. radio and television, air and marine transport, forest exploitation, gas distribution. On the other hand, the Mexican President recently said the government will close or sell 236 state owned enterprises; this may open additional opportunities for foreign investors.[33]

As for new investments in Mexico, foreigners generally may not acquire stock ownership in excess of the following percentages:

1. up to 49% in mining companies that exploit minerals subject to ordinary mining concessions;

2. up to 34% in mining companies that exploit national mineral reserves, subject to special mining concessions;

3. up to 40% in companies that manufacture secondary products of the petrochemical industry; and

4. up to 40 percent in companies that manufacture automotive parts.

In other cases, foreign ownership is usually limited to 49%. (The foregoing limitations do not apply to the special "maquiladoras" or in-bond program; these projects may be 100% owned by foreigners). In addition, the Foreign Investment Commission may raise or lower those percentages "in the interest of the country's economy."[34]

In July 1983, Mr. Adolfo Hegewisch, Executive Secretary of the Foreign Investment Commission, said the Commission was "willing to [consider] . . . the possibility of foreign investment subscribing 100 percent of the capital in new firms, provided it fulfills certain criteria...."[35] By 1984, the Commission reported having approved majority foreign owned investments by Ford Motor Co., Black & Decker, Caterpillar Tractors and some other firms.[36] Initially a request by IBM involving 100% ownership was rejected, but in July 1985 the project was approved. In return for the concession on the 100% ownership issue, IBM agreed to export 92% of its production and to sell its personal computers within the Mexican market at not more than 15% above world market prices.

The Commission claimed that in 1984, seventy percent of the foreign investment applications were approved. Twenty one percent were rejected and nine percent of the cases are still pending.[37]

ANCOM (The Andean Common Market). Upon forming the Andean Common Market (ANCOM), the member states adopted the Andean Foreign Investment Code (AFIC), which lays down the minimum restrictions its member states must impose on the foreign investor as a condition for doing business in that region. The members -- currently Peru, Colombia, Venezuela, Ecuador and Bolivia--may establish more stringent limitations than those set forth in the Code, but may not apply more liberal norms.[38]

Article 3 prohibits its member states from authorizing direct foreign investment where the purpose is to acquire shares, participations or rights owned by a national of any ANCOM nation. Nevertheless, direct foreign investment in a national enterprise may be permitted if necessary to avoid "imminent bankruptcy", so long as a first option to buy has already been offered to ANCOM nationals. Moreover, in this situation, the acquiring foreigner must agree to place on sale to ANCOM citizens a sufficient number of shares to bring the percentage of local ownership up to 80% within a time period not to exceed 15 years.[39]

Under article 7 a foreign investor may not transfer his shares to another foreigner without prior governmental approval. Moreover, member nations may authorize a foreign investor to buy into a national or mixed enterprise, only if such transaction will increase the capital of the company and only if local shareholders will hold at least 51% of the stock afterwards.[40]

The AFIC divides companies into three types: (a) "foreign" enterprises or those in which foreigners hold more than 49% of the shares; (b) "mixed" enterprises, those in which foreigners hold between 49 and 20 percent of the shares, and (c) "national" enterprises, those in which foreigners hold not more than 20 percent of the stock.[41] A citizen of any ANCOM nation may be treated as a national for the purpose of computing these percentages.[42]

The AFIC prohibits new foreign investments in the field of insurance, commercial banking and other financial institutions in the region.[43] Article 43 provides that only national (80% local) companies may make new investments in domestic transportation services, advertising, television, newspapers, magazines, or domestic market services. Several member countries of ANCOM objected to this last provision as too rigid; thus, in 1976, the Code was amended to permit its member governments to apply different rules when "special circumstances" exist. Venezuela has made a number of exceptions to Article 43.[44]

The most publicized provisions of the AFIC have been its <u>divestment</u> requirements. Foreign enterprises making new investments in the ANDEAN region must agree to transform into a mixed (51% local) or national (80% local) enterprise within 15 years if the project is located in Colombia, Peru, or Venezuela.[45] A 20 year time period is permitted for investments in Ecuador and Bolivia; moreover, for these two nations, that time period does not begin running until two years after production begins.[46] The expansion of an existing investment is treated as new for these purposes.[47]

In the case of Colombia, Peru and Venezuela, the transformation agreement must provide for at least 15 percent local ownership at the time production begins. When one third of the stipulated divestment period has expired, at least 30% of the shares have to be held by nationals. At the end of two thirds of that time period, a minimum of 45 percent of the stock must be in local hands.[48]

For investments in Bolivia and Ecuador, local participation must reach at least 5 percent within three years after production has started. On expiration of one third of the stipulated divestment period, a minimum of 10 percent of the shares have to be locally owned; at the end of two thirds of that time period, a minimum of 35 percent of the stock must be in national hands.[49]

There are some important exceptions to these divestment requirements. Article 34 exempts foreign enterprises which export more than 80 percent of their products outside the ANCOM region.[50] Investments in the tourism sectors are also exempt from the fade-out provisions.[51]

A company will be treated as a "mixed enterprise" if a member state or one of its organs owns a portion of the shares, even if that percentage be less than 51 percent, so long as the state has a determining capacity in the decisions of the enterprise.[52] Hence, a firm owned one third by a private U.S. company, one third by a private Japan concern, and one third by a Peruvian government corporation would be considered "mixed" because the Peruvian partner could play a decisive role.

Reinvestment of profits earned by a foreign enterprise are considered new investment and require prior authorization by the host nation.[53] The Code, however, provides that foreign enterprises may reinvest profits amounting to not more than 7 percent per year without special authorization. Profits above that ceiling may also be invested without special authorization in Portfolio Development Bonds.[54] These are obligations issued by organs of the member governments, by national or mixed enterprises, or by the Andean Development Corporation.[55] Such obligations do not carry the right to participate in technical, financial, administrative or commercial management of the issuing entity.[56] Under Venezuelan domestic law, foreign enterprises that have signed transformation agreements (to divest down to 49 percent in 15 years) may reinvest profits in excess of the 7 percent ceiling without special permission.[57]

<u>Argentina</u>. In dramatic contrast to the Andean Foreign Investment Code stands the new Argentine law.[58] Article 1 of the Argentine Foreign Investments Law grants national treatment to foreign investors, except where specifically provided otherwise by law.

Foreign investments in Argentina are divided into three categories. The first group includes sensitive areas, such as defense and national security, communications, public service, insurance and financial institutions. Foreign investments in these economic sectors must be approved by the "Executive Power" (i.e., the ministerial level).[59]

Where the recipient company has a net worth in excess of U.S. $10 million, such Executive Power approval is also required if the investment would convert a "domestic enterprise of national capital" (at least 51% local ownership or control) into a "domestic enterprise of foreign capital" (more than 49% foreign ownership or control).[60] When such transaction consists of acquiring shares, it is to be approved only "when an evident benefit for the national economy will result therefrom". An exception exists for firms undergoing judicial foreclosure.[61]

Approval of the Executive Power is also a prerequisite to foreigners acquiring a going concern with a net worth in excess of U.S. $10 million. Again such transactions may be approved only if there is an "evident benefit to the national economy" or a situation of judicial foreclosure.[62]

Finally, the Executive Power must approve all foreign investments in excess of U.S. $20 million[63] and any investment in which a foreign state or government is involved.[64] A subsequent regulation added an additional group of industries in which foreign investment requires Executive Power approval; they are metallurgy, aluminum production, mining (except for third class mines).[65] There is no time limit within which the Executive must act on these applications.[66]

A second category of foreign investments may be registered automatically and require no special authorization. This includes:

1. Reinvestments in the same Argentine company of profits derived from properly registered foreign investments;[67]

2. Expansion of existing companies through investment by foreigners in freely convertible foreign currency, provided that the amount does not exceed 30 percent of the registered foreign capital in the enterprise, and provided that the transaction does not convert it to a domestic enterprise of foreign capital (more than 49% foreign);[68]

3. Investments by foreigners exercising preemptive rights to maintain their relative participation equal to or smaller than the one they held previously.[69]

4. Investments in freely convertible foreign currency, not in excess of U.S. $5 million, provided that such transaction does not convert the recipient company into a domestic enterprise of foreign capital (more than 49% foreign).[70]

Investments coming under numbers 1-3 above merit automatic registration even if they would otherwise fall within a category which would require prior approval by the Executive.[71]

A third category of investments requires prior approval of the Undersecretariat of External Investments, the government agency charged with evaluating investment proposals.[72] This group includes those projects which do not fall within the two categories described above. An example would be an investment between U.S. $5 million and U.S. $20 million.

Prior approval of the Undersecretariat is not required to purchase shares on the Argentine stock market, but this office must be notified of any such purchases. Moreover, these acquisitions are void if:

1. The purchase would convert a domestic enterprise into one of foreign capital;

2. An individual foreign purchase exceeds U.S. $2 million or represents more than two percent of the receiving company's capital; or

3. The total foreign investment in the enterprise would exceed 20 percent of the capital.[73]

Capitalization of a foreign debt also requires prior approval of the Undersecretariat. Such approval must be predicated on a finding that commercial and business factors render such capitalization necessary and proper.[74] Loans from a foreign parent to an Argentine subsidiary must be approved by the Central Bank. Loans carrying unusually high interest rates are likely to be rejected.[75]

Brazil. For some years Brazilian nationalists have been complaining about the denationalization of Brazilian industry, i.e. the take over of Brazilian companies by foreign investors. In fact, the percentage of foreign ownership of the Brazilian economy has declined slightly in recent years.[76] Nevertheless, in 1976 these pressures produced the Lehman Amendment to the new Corporation Code. This Amendment requires approval by the Securities Commission (CVM) prior to acquiring a controlling interest in any company whose shares are traded on the stock exchange or over the counter. In addition, any takeover bid must include a simultaneous offer of common shares to the general Brazilian public. Finally, minority shareholders must be offered the same terms for their common shares as those offered to the controlling shareholders.[77]

Brazil does not permit non-residents to invest in Brazilian companies through direct purchases of shares on the Brazilian stock market. Non-residents may, however, make portfolio investments in Brazilian firms through the purchase of shares in special mutual funds (known as Decree Law 1.401 funds), selected and supervised by the Central Bank.[78] These funds nonetheless are circumscribed by a number of restrictions.[79] All shares must be sold outside Brazil and no Brazilian resident, or company, may acquire shares of a Decree Law 1.401 fund. At least 50 percent of the portfolio investments must be reinvested in shares or convertible debentures of open capital (publicly traded) companies controlled by private Brazilian shareholders. There are also tight restrictions on how the remaining 50% of the assets of these funds may be invested. The disappointing amounts of foreign investment entering Brazil through these special funds recently led the government to decrease the holding period for available tax incentives from two year down to 90 days.[80]

Like most countries, Brazil prohibits foreign investments in certain sectors, e.g., communications media and coastal shipping.[81] Corporations controlled directly or indirectly by foreigners must obtain prior approval of the Ministry of Agriculture to purchase rural land for agricultural, livestock, industrial of colonization projects.[82] New foreign investments in insurance companies may not exceed one third of the capital.[83] The Central Bank will not permit foreign interests to control more than one third of the voting stock of leasing or finance companies.[84] Usually the government insists that Brazilians own a majority of the stock in mining projects. In petrochemical projects, the government prefers a three way split among the state, private Brazilian investors and foreign investors.[85]

The most important new restrictions are in the area of computers and software. The Special Secretariat for Informatics (SEI), and the technology transfer agency (INPI) have reserved the mini and micro computer industries to Brazilian owned firms.[86] Brazil has also established a national registry of software to encourage local production and to guard against importation of unnecessary software.[87]

For most economic sectors, Brazilian law does not require foreign investors to take in a local partner. Nevertheless, government agencies urge foreign companies to accept local partners and to increase the percentage of Brazilian content in their products, as a quid pro quo for obtaining certain tax incentives or subsidized financing. An increasing number of tax incentives are being limited to firms majority owned by Brazilian nationals.[88] The Central Bank requires that 70% of all credit extended by banks in Brazil flow to companies controlled by Brazilian nationals.[89] Before 1980, firms majority owned by foreigners could tap the local credit market by selling debentures.[90] This was made more difficult in 1982 when the Securities Commission issued a regulation requiring the input of fresh foreign funds equal to three times the value of the debentures sold on the local securities market by foreign controlled companies.[91]

Chile. In 1976, Chile withdrew from the Andean Common Market, in large part because of disagreement concerning provisions of the Andean Foreign Investment Code. Shortly thereafter, she enacted a new foreign investment law which, aside from a three year waiting period for repatriation of capital, imposes few restrictions on the foreign investor. Approval by the Foreign Investment Committee is required only for the following kinds of investments or technology licensing:

1. those with a total value exceeding U.S. $5 million or its equivalent in other currencies;

2. those relating to sectors of activities customarily reserved to the State or public services;

3. those carried out through the communications media; and

4. those made by a foreign public institution.

As a rule, other foreign investments may simply be authorized pro forma by the Executive Secretary of that Committee.[92]

Paraguay and Uruguay. These two nations have taken an approach similar to that of Chile by enacting liberal legislation. A simplified approval procedure may be used in investments of below U.S. $100,000 in Uruguay. Profits in excess of 20 percent of the capital invested are subject to a 40% withholding tax.[93] Paraguay offers generous tax incentives for "necessary" investments, such as a 50% percent reduction in income taxes for a five year period.[94]

TECHNOLOGY TRANSFER LAWS

A transnational enterprise involved in a reorganization or acquisition may have to include within its planning, patent or trademark licenses, know-how transfers, and technical assistance to the newly created entity. This brings into play a group of norms described in Latin America as technology transfer laws.

Technology imports had imposed a heavy burden on the hard currency resources of poor nations. One study found that payments for technology transfers in a group of developing nations had been growing during the sixties two or three times faster than the growth in the countries' total manufacturing output.[95] In Brazil, payments authorized by the National Industrial Property Institute for royalties and technical assistance fees amounted to $750 million in 1977 alone.[96]

Viewing the previous technology transactions as unduly weighted in favor of the global corporations, several Latin American nations have tried to rectify this imbalance by bringing the government into the negotiating process and by establishing legal perimeters for the contractual terms. Mexico,[97] Brazil,[98] and ANCOM[99] all enacted detailed legislation governing the transfer of technology. The Andean Pack rules establish minimal common standards; a member state may impose additional restrictions.

The principal factors which concerned these nations were the cost of the technology and the time period of the payment obligation; the unbundling of a proposed technology package to permit the individual elements thereof to be procured separately (and hopefully locally); training local personnel; fostering indigenous research and development; as well as controlling the conditions imposed by the supplier, especially the restrictive provisions. Since this paper is focusing on the problems of reorganization of transnational enterprises, the following discussion will stress those aspects of the technology transfer laws which find an echo in our antitrust concepts or those features which relate directly to corporate structure.

While definitions of technology transfer differ, in general the term covers international licensing contracts for patents, know-how and trade marks, as well as technical assistance agreements. Such agreements typically must receive prior approval by the appropriate government agency.

Capitalization of Technology. A company may wish to transfer its industrial property rights in exchange for shares in the foreign enterprise, i.e. to capitalize the intangible technological contribution. The supplier would then receive its earnings on the technology in the forms of dividends rather than royalties. Such alternative can be particularly attractive in Brazil whose law prohibits either royalty payments, or tax deductions therefor, to a foreign enterprise that controls the licensee.[100]

Previously, the laws of both Argentina and Chile prohibited the capitalization of technology. A 1977 Chilean statute changed this rule to permit capitalization of the technology.[101] The Foreign Investment Committee of Chile has 120 days to determine the international market value of such technology; if the Committee does not act within that time limit, the price assigned to the technology is that declared by the investor in his sworn application.[102] Chile does not permit such technological contributions to be amortized or depreciated.[103] Argentine law also now permits capitalization of technology.[104] In contrast, the Andean Foreign Investment Code prohibits capitalization of intangible technological contributions.[105]

Payments to Affiliated Companies. In the ANCOM region, no royalties may be paid where the technology has been transferred to a recipient who is classified as a "foreign enterprise" (over 49% foreign owned), if such company is a subsidiary or affiliate of the supplier. Tax deductions for such payments are also forbidden. Venezuela, however, will treat a company more than 49% owned by foreigners as a mixed enterprise for the purpose of this legal section, if such company has signed a transformation or divestment agreement.[106]

Brazil will not permit payment of royalties for patents or trademarks to a foreign licensor which controls the licensee directly or indirectly.[107] For technical assistance agreements, payments may be remitted to a controlling foreign company for a period not in excess of five years.[108]

Grantback Clauses. Traditionally, licensing contracts often contained a clause requiring the licensee to grant back without compensation any improvements it made in the technology; conversely the licensor was not obligated to transfer to the recipient any improvements made by the supplier. Today, in Brazil, suppliers of unpatented technology (know-how) are required to make their improvements available to the user during the life of the contract; gratuitous grant-back clauses are forbidden.[109]

Mexico will not approve a technology transfer agreement containing a clause requiring the user to grant back to the supplier without compensation any improvements. Nevertheless, clauses which impose reciprocal obligations on both sides are permissible.[110]

In the ANCOM region, grantback clauses are objectionable,[111] but reciprocal grant-back clauses are usually accepted.[112] Brazilian law requires that patent licenses contain a clause stipulating that any improvements made by the recipient belong to it.[113] This, however, merely recognizes that the rights belong to the user and does not prevent the latter from disclosing such knowledge nor does it forbid grantbacks authorizing the supplier to use the improvements, especially if such clauses are non-exclusive.[114]

Limitations on Use. Applications may be rejected in Mexico when the volume of production is limited.[115] The Mexican Regulations prohibit provisions that fix maximum or minimum volumes. Nonetheless, the administration of the law has been flexible. Thus, a contract was approved even though it contained a provision establishing a minimum royalty if the recipient's factory operated at 50 percent of capacity or less during the first two years. The government, in such cases, likes to couple this kind of concession with a ceiling on the volume on which the percentage royalty will be paid.[116]

ANCOM prohibits clauses that restrict the volume or structure of production.[117] Brazil will not permit any limitations on production.[118]

<u>Complementary or Competing Technology</u>. In many industrialized nations, it is illegal to include a contractual provision which prohibits the recipient from acquiring competing or complementary technology from other firms.[119] Such clauses impose a major restraint on competitive freedom. In a few cases, a narrowly drawn restriction may be justified where the supplier has reason to fear the user may pass on trade secrets to a third party furnishing the complementary technology.

In Mexico, an application may be refused if the agreement restricts the use of complementary technology.[120] Such provision may be permitted, though, if the agreement includes authorization to use the supplier's trademark, or if the restriction is considered necessary to preclude disclosure to a competitor of confidential technical information.[121]

ANCOM also prohibits restrictions on the recipient's acquisition of similar technology from other parties.[122] Nevertheless, because the technology recipients are often so dependent upon the supplier for component parts, marketing outlets and good will, economic pressure will often discourage the user from looking elsewhere for complementary technology.

<u>Post Contract Restrictions</u>. Licensing contracts frequently prohibit the use of the technology after expiration of the agreement. This restriction can impose a severe burden on the recipient who has invested substantial time and resources in the particular technical process.

The industrialized nations tend to view technology licenses as "leases"; in contrast, many developing countries wish to treat these transactions as "sales", with no right remaining in the supplier once the agreement has expired. In accord with this sale theory, Peru will not approve a contract where the recipient is required to cease using the technology after the agreement ends.[123] Venezuela prohibits clauses which would restrict the right of the local manufacturer to use the technology, know-how or trademark after the contract is terminated.[124] For patented information, the supplier could look to the Venezuelan Industrial Property Law of 1955 for protection once the agreement has expired. In general, that law does provide adequate safeguards for registered patents,[125] but this will not help in the case of unpatented trade secrets.

Mexican law contemplates denial of approval if the user is required to treat the technology as confidential after the agreement has expired.[126] The regulations, however, provide that a contract may be approved if the technology is protected by industrial property rights that have not yet expired when the agreement terminates, and if the Ministry decides that it is appropriate to impose a confidentiality requirement in light of the advanced nature of the technology.[127]

Brazil proscribes provisions which limit free use of the technology "after the lapse of a period of time considered to be reasonable following the delivery of each of the last item of the information transferred."[128] Five years is usually considered the maximum reasonable time, although in one case a secrecy period of fifteen years was allowed.[129]

Restrictions After Expiration of Industrial Property Rights. Brazil does not allow limitations on the use of information after expiration of a patent.[130] In Venezuela no contract based on a patent or trademark is valid beyond the period of registration for the underlying industrial property rights.[131] Although patents and trademarks which have not been registered in Venezuela may form the basis of a technology transfer agreement, such unregistered rights depend solely on the contract. This may not protect the supplier against infringement by third parties.[132]

No Attack Clauses. Technology transfer contracts often contain a provision forbidding the licensee from contesting the validity of patents or trademarks involved in the agreement or from challenging other industrial property rights of the supplier. Many industrialized nations treat such clauses as illegal under their antitrust laws. Brazil also will not approve a technology transfer contract which prevents the user from contesting the validity of industrial property rights.[133]

Tied Procurement. International technology transfer contracts frequently contain provisions requiring the supplier to buy certain equipment, components or materials from the supplier. At times, such restrictions may be necessary to guaranty the quality of the licensed products, especially in case of an assembly plant. On the other hand, these provisions can give the supplier monopoly control and lead to overpricing. Moreover such clauses preclude the substitution of locally manufactured goods, and thereby inflict a greater outflow of hard currency on the host country.

Mexican law prohibits approval of contracts which require the user to acquire goods from a specified source.[134] On the other hand, there is no objection to a clause obligating the provider to supply equipment, tools, parts or raw materials to the user at the world market price if they are not available in Mexico, so long as the licensee is free to acquire these same items from sources of its own choosing.[135]

ANCOM forbids clauses obligating the recipient to acquire goods or personnel from a specified source.[136] Nevertheless, such tied purchases clauses are permitted in exceptional cases if the price "corresponds to the current market price."[137]

Even after Chile's withdrawal from ANCOM, it was reported in 1978 that her Central Bank was still applying many of the same prohibitions against restrictive agreements. Nonetheless, the trend is toward liberalization. For instance, some tie-in clauses have been permitted on the theory that Chile must meet international marketing standards to increase her exports.[138]

In Brazil, a technology contract may not require the purchase of products from the supplier or from other sources designated by the supplier. The prohibition against sources selected by the supplier applies even to domestic companies.[139]

Price Fixing. Mexico may reject an application if it allows the supplier to set the price on the goods produced under the technology, whether the sales are in the domestic or the international market.[140] Brazil[141] and ANCOM[142] also forbid such clauses.

Restraints on Distribution Channels. Some agreements require the recipient to enter into a distribution contract under which the user will sell his product exclusively to the supplier or to another person designed by the supplier. Mexico may deny an application if the agreement provides the licensee is obligated to sell its goods exclusively through the supplier of the technology or to a customer designated by the supplier.[143] An exception will be made though if the obligation relates exclusively to a specific export market and the provision is beneficial for that market.[144] Registration may also be denied in Mexico if the recipient is required to enter an exclusive sales contract or representational agreements with the supplier, unless exports are involved and the administrative agency has been satisfied that the technology provider has the proper distribution channels necessary to sell the products.[145]

The ANCOM rules will not permit a clause establishing a total or partial purchase option in favor of the technology supplier.[146] Brazil will not allow limitations on marketing or distribution.[147]

Restrictions on Exports. Mexico may reject agreements which impose restrictions on exports "in a manner contrary to the country's interest."[148] Approval is to be denied if the contract absolutely prohibits exports, denies to the recipient the right to export to certain geographical areas in which the provider has not previously granted exclusive rights to third parties, obligates the recipient to export solely through the supplier, requires the prior authorization of the technology provider for exports, or establishes volume limits on exports.[149] On the other hand, approval may be granted despite such export restrictions when the provider has previously granted exclusive licenses to third parties in a limited territory, when the markets in which the user demonstrates export potential are respected; or when the provider reserves to itself its own territory.[150] Any such export restrictions may be imposed only during the life of the contract (and during the effective period of the industrial property right).[151]

The Brazilian regulations also prohibit limitations on exports.[152] In some circumstances, "territorial exclusivity might pass muster, but such provisions are generally disapproved."[153]

Technology agreements in the ANCOM region may not limit exports except upon approval of the individual member state government.[154] Colombia allows restrictions in "exceptional cases", but forbids any limitations on exports to other ANCOM member states.[155] Since Colombia is vigorously encouraging exports, she may permit certain restrictions as a trade-off for higher export goals in markets not off limits. In contrast, Venezuela takes the position that, because of higher costs and structural inefficiencies within her economy, there is little possibility of exporting anywhere; therefore, no reason exists for any restraints.[156]

Research and Development. Mexican law calls for denial of approval, if limitations are imposed on the user's research and development activities.[157] "This . . . standard has been construed extremely broadly." For instance, it has been applied to preclude clauses requiring the user to return technical documentation to the supplier on expiration of the contract, except if the provider's industrial property rights are still in effect.[158]

In 1983 Normative Act No. 64 was promulgated in Brazil to promote the development of technology. The administrative agency involved (INPI) has indicated that in the future it intends to condition approval of technology transfer contracts on the assumption of a formal commitment by the Brazilian licensee to invest in research and development of a similar technology.[159]

Whenever a foreign-controlled Brazilian company wishes to purchase technology from an unrelated foreign firm, the parent company will be required to make an equity investment in its Brazilian subsidiary in an amount equal to the remittances that subsidiary is obligated to pay for the technology. This investment is to be made prior to each respective remittance.[169]

Price. Royalty payments in Brazil are limited to five percent of net sales.[161] Within the ANCOM region, individual member states have developed their own ceilings on royalty remittances. For example, in Colombia, most authorized royalties are in the two to four percent of net sales range.[162] Peruvian approvals average about 5 percent of gross sales.[163]

Mexican law provides that registration of a technology transfer contract may be denied when the compensation "is out of proportion to the acquired technology or constitutes an unjustified or excessive burden for the national economy or for the acquiring company."[164] The question of what is an excessive payment has been the major issue in Mexico. Mexico has now issued regulations setting forth the factors to be considered in determining whether the royalty percentages are reasonable. Such factors include the impact on balance of payments through import savings or export earnings, existence of a corporate relationship between the parties, the extent to which the technology is advanced, etc.[165] In one recent case, the government even authorized a 12 percent royalty for a nuclear energy license.[166]

Duration. Mexican law prohibits technology agreements with "excessively long periods of duration" and states that "in no case shall said period exceed ten compulsory years for the recipient."[167] The Regulations state that approval of a technology contract will be denied when, even though the contract term is less than ten years, the time period is greater than required for the recipient to assimilate the technology.[168] As a practical matter, it appears that the responsible agency has seldom refused to approve a fixed term of ten years. The agency has also approved agreements for indefinite terms such as where the contract is to continue until one of the parties gives termination notice. Likewise, the authorities have approved evergreen contracts for the length of the initial term, plus one additional period.[169]

Venezuela normally limits the contract period to five years, although up to fifteen years may be authorized in "exceptional cases".[170] Colombia restricts technology agreements to not more than three years, but is usually lenient in granting renewals. In the early seventies, Peru was limiting these contracts to a five year period; this rule may, however, have been liberalized in recent times.[171] Contracts which provide for fixed terms, but unlimited renewals, are treated as agreements for an indefinite term in Peru and do not qualify for registration.[172]

Patents in Brazil normally have a life span of fifteen years and those for utility or industrial models, ten years.[173] Royalties may not be remitted abroad until the patent is actually issued in Brazil.[174] Since several years may expire between the time of application and the date of issuance, the beginning of the payment period can be considerably delayed. Moreover, the term of the patent begins running as of the date the application was filed. Once the patent has expired, either in Brazil or in the licensor's home country, no further royalties may be paid, no taxes deducted therefore.[175] The net result of the way in which these various rules intermesh can be a substantial reduction in the duration period of any licensing contract.[176]

If a transaction combines patents and know-how, the latter may be merged with the patents in establishing the time limit for the licensing agreement.[177] Where patents are not involved, Brazil has no statutory norm establishing the maximum time for know-how agreements. Generally, the payment period begins when commercial production starts. The regulations permit payments for know-how for "the period required to transfer all the content of the technology and for the full and complete assimilation thereof by the recipient."[178] The government usually considers five years adequate for this purpose. Technical assistance agreements in Brazil may provide for payment periods up to five years, commencing with commercial production. A five year extension may be granted, if justified.[179] Normally, obtaining an extension calls for proof that new technology has been developed.[180]

Trademark Licenses. Many Latin American nations also regulate the licensing of foreign trademarks. Brazil requires that such agreements be submitted for approval to INPI and prohibits clauses which expressly or impliedly restrict or limit the manufacturing or marketing of the product produced under the license. If a trademark is unregistered or if registration thereof has expired, the licensing agreement also terminates.[181] Tied purchase arrangements and no attack clauses are forbidden.[182] For purposes of tax deductions by the Brazilian recipient, a ceiling of one percent of sales is applied to foreign trademark licenses,[183] and INPI as been using that ceiling to limit royalties for trademarks to one percent of net sales.[184] Payment of trademark royalties is not permitted where the foreign licensor controls the Brazilian licensee directly or indirectly.[185] Finally, Brazil will not approve a technical assistance contract in which the licensee is obligated to use the licensor's trademark.[186]

Under the Mexican Law on Inventions and Trademarks,[187] no foreign mark can be used for a product manufactured in Mexico, unless such mark is "linked" to a trademark registered in Mexico. Both trademarks must be displayed in an equally visible manner.[188] It is hoped that in time this linking system will permit the Mexican manufacturer to achieve greater autonomy and to save on royalties when the foreign mark is no longer needed to market the product. This requirement, nonetheless, has encountered a variety of practical problems and the government has repeatedly postponed the deadline for compliance. Some doubt that the provision will ever be effectively implemented as it now stands.[189]

The Andean Foreign Investment Code provides that licensing agreements for foreign trademarks may not incorporate clauses which limit or forbid exports of goods produced under the trademark, which fix the sale or resale price of the product, which obligate the licensee to pay for an unused trademark, or resale price of the product, or which require the user to employ permanently personnel selected by the licensor. Also, the agreements may not compel the licensee to use raw materials, intermediate goods, or equipment supplied by the licensor or its affiliate companies; in exceptional cases, the recipient nation may authorize such a clause, if the cost of the item does not exceed the world market price.[190] In Colombia, the standard maximum for trademark royalties is one percent of net sales;[191] Peru is allowing 2 percent of gross sales.[192]

Dispute Resolution. Mexican law prohibits clauses submitting disputes to courts of foreign nations, except in cases involving exports of goods made under the technology. Mexico will allow clauses submitting disputes to international arbitration, provided the arbitrator applies substantive Mexican law.[193]

The Andean Code forbids clauses which remove controversies from the courts of the host country.[194] In a few cases, the governments of the ANCOM members have authorized provisions allowing suits to be brought either in the jurisdiction of the supplier or in that of the user; this was believed necessary to obtain jurisdiction over a non-Andean defendant who does not have a legal representative within the Andean region. For the same reason, resort to foreign arbitration may occasionally be permitted; since, however, it is difficult to secure the enforcement of arbitration agreements in these nations, it may be necessary to sue within the Andean territory anyway.[195]

Brazilian regulations are silent on both forum selection clauses and choice of law clauses. Nevertheless, technology suppliers are often pressured to accept Brazilian law as controlling. Since, however, the status of know-how is not clear under existing Brazilian law, it may be possible to persuade the authority to permit the parties to choose the law of another nation to determine some of the legal rights concerning unpatented technology.[196]

Arbitration clauses are unenforceable in Brazil unless and until a submission agreement is signed by the parties _after_ a dispute has arisen.[197] Obviously it is difficult to secure such an accord once the relations between the parties have deteriorated to such an extent.

COMING FULL CIRCLE -- THE ARGENTINE APPROACH

This article began with a discussion of antitrust laws in Latin America and then pointed out that foreign investment laws and technology transfer regimes have become far more important in this region than legislation on competition. Nevertheless, Argentina, one of the early leaders in this movement, has now come full circle.

In 1971 Argentina enacted a technology transfer law circumscribing the right to remit hard currency for royalties and prohibiting "excessive" payments for technology.[198] A 1974 amendment to that legislation[199] imposed additional restrictions, many similar to those detailed above for Brazil, Mexico and ANCOM. Meanwhile, in 1973, Argentina passed a foreign investment law which was heavily influenced by the Andean Foreign Investment Code and contained several comparable provisions.[200]

Then in 1976, a new government began to reverse course with the enactment of a more liberal foreign investment statute.[201] In 1977 a revision of the technology transfer law[202] authorized capitalization of technology, reciprocal grant back clauses, some export restrictions, and a variety of previously prohibited contractual clauses.

The 1980 foreign investment legislation, discussed above, continues this trend toward flexibility. Finally, in 1981 Argentina enacted a new technology transfer law which simply provides for approval of such contracts or arrangements if their terms conform to the standards and normal practices of the free market.[203] The Official Commentary to that statute indicates that, in the future, control of restrictive business practices would be left to the new Law on Competition which had become effective a few months previously.[204]

This antitrust law does prohibit arrangements which limit development of technology or restrict the marketing, production or distribution of goods produced by such technology.[205] But since the law does not follow a per se approach, such marketing arrangements would not be illegal unless they had a negative impact on competition.[206] Similarly, tying arrangements are only punishable if they adversely affect the competitive forces in a particular market or when they result from a dominant position.[207]

That Argentina seems to have lost interest in rigorously screening licensing agreements at the entry stage is further evidenced by the procedures established in the technology transfer law. Failure of the authorized administrative agency to act on an application within ninety days is treated as an approval thereof. If an application is denied, the applicant may appeal to the Secretary of State for Industrial Development. A further appeal to the judicial system is also available.[208]

INTERNATIONAL NORMS

In addition to the plethora of nation-state laws described above, lawyers involved in reorganization of transnational enterprises should also consider the impact of the Guidelines for Multinational Enterprises,[209] adopted by the Organization for Economic Cooperation and Development (the OECD Code) and "The Set of Multilaterally Agreed Equitable Principles for the Control of Restrictive Business Practises,"[210] adopted by the United Nations General Assembly (U.N. Equitable Principles).

Although both documents use voluntary, rather than mandatory language ("should" instead of "shall"), transnational enterprises would be well advised to conform to their terms. First, the OECD Code represents the thinking of the industrialized nations and their multinational corporations. Good public relations would seem to dictate compliance with the standards finally agreed upon by those countries.

Secondly, many of the norms within these international accords may find their way into the national legislation of variously developing nations. Likewise, some of these concepts may eventually achieve the status of customary international law.[211] Finally, blatant disregard of such principles could make a home country government less that eager to press a claim on behalf of such a company if it is expropriated.

The OECD Code calls on multinational enterprises to refrain from actions which would adversely affect competition and includes within such category: anti-competitive acquisitions, anti-competitive abuse of industrial property rights, discriminatory pricing, and limitations on resale or export rights.[212]

The U.N. Equitable Principles direct enterprises to refrain from "abuse of acquisition" or "abuse of a dominant position of market power" where such would "unduly restrain competition" and "have adverse effects on international trade, particularly that of developing countries, and on the economic development of these countries."[213] Acts which should trigger such inquiry include "mergers, takeovers, joint ventures, or other acquisitions of control, whether of a horizontal, vertical or a conglomerate nature."[214] Also questionable are restrictive agreements, such as those which fix resale prices, limit exports,[215] allocate markets or involve collusive tendering.[216]

CONCLUSION

This review seems to indicate that Latin American nations are more interested in applying antitrust laws and equivalent statutes to foreign companies than to their own domestic firms. In view of the small, and often fragile, nature of the local concerns, perhaps this focus on the transnational enterprise is appropriate at the present stage of development. Obviously, if a nation has only one little widget producer struggling to survive, exposure of such a firm to competition, foreign or domestic, is not particularly attractive. On the other hand, some developing nations, like Brazil and Mexico, have now produced their own home grown transnational enterprises. Thus, the time may now be approaching when it would be appropriate to apply antitrust norms more strictly, at least to a few large local companies. Could the new Argentine law on competition herald such a shift in focus?

No summary analysis can answer all the questions a lawyer dealing with a particular corporate reorganization may encounter. Still it is hoped this article will create an awareness of the types of problems which can arise and help identify those subjects requiring further on site investigation in Latin America.

FOOTNOTES

1. Arg. CONST. art. 10 (1853) & Law 22,262 of 1980; Bolivia CONST. art. 134 (1967); Brazil CONST. art. 157 (1967), and Law 4137 of Sept. 10, 1962; Chile CONST. arts. 19-25 (1980) and Decree Law 2.760 of 1979 and Decree Law 211 of 1973; Colombia CONST. art. 31 (1886, amended 1979) and Law 155 of 1959; Costa Rica Law # 18 of June 9, 1915 and Law 2468 of Nov. 13, 1959; Ecuador CONST. art. 45 (1978); El Salvador CONST. art. 142 (1962) and Decree 279 of Mar. 12, 1969, art. 14; Guatemala COM'L. CODE arts. 361, 362 & 663; Honduras CONST. art. 263 (1965) and Decree Law 91 of Nov. 13, 1973 & COM'L. CODE 423; Mexico CONST. art. 4, 5, 28 (1917) & Organic Law of Aug. 31, 1934; Panama CONST. arts. 254, 257 (1972); Paraguay CONST. art. 95 (1967); Peru CONST. arts. 16, 40 (1979) & Law of Jan. 11, 1896; Venezuela CONST. art. 97, 10 (1961).

2. Estudio José Barreda Miller, "Peru", INTER-AMERICAN LAW COMMITTEE OF THE AMERICAN BAR ASSOCIATION, 1 INTER-AMERICAN LEGAL MATERIALS, No. 1, p. 41 (Jan. 1983).

3. German, "Latin American Antitrust", 14 LAW. AM. 1 (1982) and Radway, "Antitrust, Technology Transfers and Joint Ventures in Latin American Development", 15 LAW.AM. 47 (1983).

4. Law 4.137 of Sept. 10, 1962, art. 2-4.

5. Id. art. 2, German, supra note 3, at 16, n. 40.

6. PINHEIRO NETO & CIA, DOING BUSINESS IN BRAZIL (1979), Ch. 20, "Trade Regulations, Anti-Trust and Inflation Measures," at §§20.127, p. 299 [hereinafter cited as "Pinheiro"].

7. Pinheiro, supra note 6, at §§20.129, 130, p. 300.

8. Law 13.305 of April 6, 1959.

9. Furnish, "Chilean Antitrust Law," 19 AM.J. COMP.LAW 464 (1971).

10. Decree Law 2.760 (1979); Decree Law 211, arts. 2,4 (1973).

11. Id.; and German, supra note 3, at 6.

12. Law No. 22.262 of July 1, 1980, arts. 17-31, Legislación Argentina 1980-B, p. 1513; and see Cabanellas & Etzrodt, "The New Argentine Antitrust Law: Competition as an Economic Policy Instrument", 17 J. WORLD TRADE L. 34, 35-36 (1983) [hereafter cited as "Cabanellas"] and German, supra note 3, at 5. This article includes a description of the five cases decided under that new act as of the date of writing.

13. Law 22.262 art. 2 (1980), LEGISLACION ARGENTINA: NACIONAL-PROVINCIAL [1980-B] at p. 1513.

14. Id. arts. 41.

15. Mexico, CONST. art. 28 (1917); Organic Law of Aug. 17, 1934, arts. 3 & 4, and see, Regulations of the Organic Law of the Constitution of Dec. 19, 1931. Both the Spanish original and English translations of these laws appear in Appendices P1 to P6 in 2 SOUTHERN METHODIST UNIVERSITY, DOING BUSINESS IN MEXICO [ed. T. Reiner (1980), B. Carl (1980-83), S. Lefler (1983-84)] hereinafter cited as "SMU").

16. Gonzales Ocampo and Kryzda, "Mexican Antitrust Laws", 1 "SMU", Id. at Ch. 27 (1981).

17. Law 21-608 of 1977, at cited in German, supra note 3 at 9, n. 25.

18. The Central American Common Market (CACM) was formed by Guatemala, El Salvador, Honduras, Nicaragua and Costa Rica in the late 1950's. The current version of that agreement is the General Treaty of Central American Economic Integration (Managua, Nicaragua, 1960), reprinted in INTER-AMERICAN INSTITUTE OF LEGAL STUDIES, INSTRUMENTS RELATING TO THE ECONOMIC INTEGRATION OF LATIN AMERICA 23 (1968).

The CACM adopted the Agreement on the System of Central American Integrated Industries in 1959. Reprinted in Id. at 89; and see subsequent protocols amending that Agreement, pp. 94 through 134. This mechanism was intended to attract new industries to the region by giving them certain benefits on an exclusive basis and by denying competitors equal rights for a period up to ten years. To achieve the status of an "integrated" industry, the company had to negotiate a protocol which would be approved by all five member nations. Once a plant was so designated, its products were to be immediately duty free throughout the region, whereas its competitors would be subject to internal duties for a certain period of time.

In planning for the common external tariff, the integrated industry was to be protected against outside competitors. In addition, it was to enjoy priority in government purchases. CACM was prohibited from granting integrated status to second plant in a country that already had one integrated project until every other member nation had an integrated plant.

In practise, this technique was unsuccessful. As of 1967, only two industries had been designated as integrated: a tire factory in Guatemala and a caustic soda and insecticide plant in Nicaragua. Moreover, the value of the status was blunted when the Executive Council of the CACM approved the establishment of a competing tire plant in Costa Rica. The administrative procedures required for securing this status discouraged many from even trying.

19. Under article 16 of the Latin American Free Trade Association Treaty, the member nations were encouraged to conclude complementation agreements among themselves, under which they might allocate different segments of production of a specific good among several members, and then create an appropriate tariff structure to protect the nation that was assigned a particular component. Treaty Establishing a Free Trade Area and Instituting the Latin American Free Trade Association (Montevideo Treaty, 1960) reprinted in Id. at 207. This scheme could be criticized as amounting to a division of markets and, thus, as uncompetitive. Persons favoring such mechanisms respond that developing areas are too short of resources to engage in inefficient duplication. Not every country can make every item. Thus, it is worthwhile to attain a rational allocation and complementation of the production process.

The concept of complementation was carried over to the new eleven member Latin American Integration Association [LAIA] Convention in articles 8 and 11. Treaty Establishing the Latin American Integration Association (1980), reprinted in 20 INT'L.LEG.MAT'LS. 672 (1981). The first task undertaken by LAIA was to review the complementation agreements previously concluded under the LAFTA Treaty. By the end of 1982, twenty-five former complementation agreements had been updated and approved.

20. Under the Sectorial Program, ANCOM (the Andean Common Market consisting of Peru, Venezuela, Colombia, Ecuador and Bolivia) decides which products within a particular economic sector, such as the metal-working industry, will be reserved for the sectorial program. Then, those items are divided up and assigned among the five member nations. Some assignments are to one member exclusively; in other cases, an assignment may be shared among several members. Cartagena Agreement on Andean Subregional Integration (1969), arts. 37(f), 45(b), 47, 49, & 50, reprinted in 8 INT'L.LEG. MAT'LS. 910 (1969), as amended by Lima Protocol, done Oct. 30, 1976, reprinted in 16 INT'L.LEG.MAT'LS. 235 (1977).

Bolivia and Ecuador, as the poorest members, are to be given special consideration in this process. Once a product has been assigned to a nation, ANCOM creates a special preferential tariffs structure to provide an advantage to the producers in the favored nation. For example, the item from the assigned nation may circulate duty free through the region, while competing manufacturers in other member-nations would be subject to an internal duty.

Technically, such assignments do not create a monopoly because companies in non-favored countries are not prohibited from producing and selling the item throughout the region. Typically, the law establishing the sectorial program will, nonetheless, prohibit non-favored member-states from extending government credit or tax incentives to such competing firms. See, e.g. ANCOM, Decision 146, The Metalworking Sectorial Program, art. 30 (1979). Moreover, the states may not authorize direct foreign investment to produce that good.

21. German, <u>supra</u> note 3, at 18.

22. Amador, "Foreign Investment in Mexico," 52 ANTITRUST L.J. 1017 (1983). The Commission claimed that in 1984, seventy percent of the foreign investment applications were approved. Twenty one percent were rejected and nine percent of the cases are still pending. 2 BNA, INT'L.TRADE REP'R. 133 (Jan. 23, 85).

23. Bugeda Pineiro, "Foreign Investment in Mexico: Procedural Aspects", 1 SMU, <u>supra</u> note 15, Ch. 15A (1984).

24. Law to Promote Mexican Investment and Regulate Foreign Investment, art. 8, March 9, 1973, reprinted in English and Spanish in 2 SMU, supra note 15, Appendices I-1 & I-2. See also, General Resolution of the Foreign Investment Commission, No. 11 of Jan. 15, 1976), as cited in Creel, "Foreign Investment in Mexico: New Rules of the Game?", 1 SMU supra note 15, Ch.15B, §15B.03[5] (1984).

25. Law to Promote Mexican Investment and Regulate Foreign Investment, arts. 5 & 12, supra note 24.

26. General Resolution of the Foreign Investment Commission, No. 8, as cited in Bugeda Pineiro, supra note 23, at §15A.04[3], n. 21.

27. General Resolution of the Foreign Investment Commission, No. 9, as cited in Id., n. 22.

28. General Resolution of the Foreign Investment Commission, No. 10, as cited in Id., n. 23.

29. General Resolution of the Foreign Investment Commission, No. 14, as cited in Id. §15A.04[2], n.9.

30. General Resolution of the Foreign Investment Commission, No. 19, as cited in Id. §15A.04[4], n.26.

31. Bugeda Pineiro, Id. §15A.04[3].

32. Creel, supra note 24, at §15B.04[2].

33. Law to Promote Mexican Investment and Regulate Foreign Investment, arts. 4 & 5, supra note 24 and see Frazier, "Mexico to Cut Outlays and Sell State Concerns," WALL ST.J., Feb. 8, 1985, at 21, col. 1.

34. Id. art. 5. The maquiladora program is described in Fontes Moreno, "Mexican Law on In-Bond Processing Plants," in 1 SMU, supra note 15, Ch. 33; the relevant laws and regulations appear in 2 SMU, Id., Appendices S-1 to S-10.

35. Remarks to the members of the Japanese Economic Community, June 13, 1983, as cited in Creel, supra note 24, at §15B.04[3], n. 16.

36. 2 BNA, INT'L.TRADE REP'R. 133 (Jan. 23, 85).

37. WALL ST.J., July 24, 1985, at 46, col. 2; and see 2 BNA, INT'L.TRADE REP'R. 133 (Jan. 23, 85) and

Junco, "Computer Hungry Mexicans vs. Power-Hungry Bureacrats", WALL ST.J., Mar. 22, 1985, at 23, col. 4; Frazier, "Plans to Expand Plant in Mexico Revised by IBM," WALL ST. J., Mar. 11, 1985, at 29, col. 1; and Frazier, "Mexico Gambles IBM Will Alter Plans for Factory," WALL ST. J., Jan. 21, 1985.

In May 1985, it was announced that the Tandy (Radio Shack) Corporation had entered into a joint venture with a Mexican firm, Computadoras Y Asesoramiento, to produce the Tandy 1000, an IBM compatible personal computer. Jones, "Tandy to Build Computer in Mexico," Dallas Times Herald, May 10, 1985, at B-1, col. 2.

38. Decision 24 of the Commission of the Cartagena Agreement on the Common Regime of Treatment of Foreign Capital and of Trademarks, Patents, Licenses and Royalties, as amended (1976), reprinted in 16 INT'L.LEGAL MAT'LS. 138 1977) [hereafter cited as "AFIC".] The earlier versions of Decision 24, adopted Dec. 31, 1970, are reprinted in 10 INT'L.LEGAL.MAT'LS. 349 (1973). For a detailed list of the national laws enacted by the member states to implement this code, see Schliesser, "Outline of Laws Affecting New Foreign Investment Under Decision 24 in Colombia, Peru and Venezuela, and the Chilean Foreign Investment Statute,", AMERICAN BAR ASSOCIATION, CURRENT LEGAL ASPECTS OF DOING BUSINESS IN LATIN AMERICA 11 (S. Stairs ed., 1981) [hereafter cited as "Stairs"] and Helander, "Legal Framework for Foreign Investment in Latin America", IV AMERICAN BAR ASS'N/AM.LAW. INST., A LAWYER'S GUIDE TO INTERNATIONAL BUSINESS TRANSACTIONS (W.S. Surrey & D. Wallace, 2d ed. 1980) 223, 247.

Under articles 39 and 40 of the Code, member states were not required to apply the divestment provisions to the basic products sector for the first ten years. The term basic products referred primarily to oil and gas, minerals and pipelines. Venezuela, however, has gone beyond the Code by barring foreigners from investing in basic industries, such as petroleum, steel or aluminum. Pine, "Debt-Ridden Nations Impose Many Barriers on Foreign Investment", WALL ST.J., Jan. 21, 1985, at 1, col. 6; and see Ven. Ley Orgánica Que Reserva al Estado la Industria y el Comercio de los Hidrocarburos (Aug. 29, 1975), [1975] GACETA LEGAL No. 405, at 5; and Decreto 580, Por El Cual Se Reserva al Estado La Industria De la Explotación del Mineral de Hierro (Nov. 26, 1974), [1974] GACETA LEGAL No. 384, at 5.

39. APIC, supra note 38, art. 3.

40. Id. art. 4.

41. Id. art. 1.

42. Id.

43. Id. arts. 42 & 43.

44. Id. art. 44, and see Carl & Johnson, "Venezuela and the Andean Common Market," 7 DENVER J.INT'L. L. & POL. 151 (1978).

45. Id. art. 30.

46. Id.

47. Id. art. 1.

48. Id. art. 30.

49. Id.

50. If, however, such firms have not agreed to convert into mixed or national enterprises, their goods will not qualify for duty free treatment when sold in other ANCOM nations.

51. Id. art. 34.

52. Id. art. 36.

53. Id. art. 12.

54. Id. art. 13.

55. Agreement Establishing the Andean Development Corporation, signed Feb. 7, 1968, trans. 8 INT'L. LEGAL MAT'LS. 940 (1969).

56. Decision 24, supra note 38, art. 1.

57. Ven. Decree 2,442 of Nov. 8, 1977, art. 31, GAC. OF. 2,100 Ex (Nov. 15, 1977).

58. Argentine Foreign Investments Law, Law No. 21,382, [1976] C Anales 2071, as amended by Law 22,208, [1980] B Anales 1024 and Decree of June 24, 1980, No. 1062, [1980] C Anales 2585. See also, Dahl, "Argentina's System of Foreign Investments", 6 FORDHAM L.

REV. 33 (1982) and Duggan, "Joint Ventures Under Argentina's New Policy," in Stairs, supra note 38, at 147.

59. Argentine Foreign Investment Law, supra note 58, art. 4(1)(a).

60. Id. arts. 2 and 4(2).

61. Id. art. 4(2)(b).

62. Id. art. 4(3).

63. Id. art. 4(4).

64. Id. art. 4(3).

65. Decree 103 of Jan. 19, 1981, art. 17.

66. Dahl, supra note 58, at 59.

67. Argentine Foreign Investment Law, supra note 58, art. 5(1).

68. Id. art. 5(2).

69. Id.

70. Id. art. 5(3)

71. Id. art. 5(1) & (2).

72. Id. art. 9.

73. Id. art. 7.

74. Decree No. 103 of Jan. 19, 1981, art. 11.

75. Decree No. 103, supra note 65, art. 82; and see Dahl, supra note 58, at 69.

76. Rosenn, "Regulation of Foreign Investment in Brazil: A Critical Analysis", 15 LAW.AM. 307 (1983).

77. Law No. 6,404 of Dec. 15, 1976, art. 254.

78. Decree Law 1.401 of May 7, 1975 and see Rosenn, supra note 76, 347-49.

79. Regulations to Central Bank Res. No. 323 of May 8, 1975, as cited in Rosenn, supra note 76, at 348, n. 184.

80. Id. at 349.

81. Const. arts. 174 and 173 (1967), as amended (1969).

82. Law 5.709 of Oct. 7, 1971, art. 5, §1, as regulated by Decree No. 74.965 of Nov. 26, 1974.

83. Pinheiro, supra note 7, Ch. 18, "Insurance", §18.111.

84. Rosenn, supra note 76, at 343.

85. Id. at 344.

86. Normative Act No. 16 of July 10, 1981 and No. 24 of May 31, 1983. This ban was extended by a Congressional law through 1992. It does not affect main frame computers. Regulations to be issued under this law are expected to include high import tariffs, prohibit against some imports of computers and parts, as well as proscribe joint ventures between Brazilian and foreign firms in this sector. WALL ST.J., Oct. 5, 1984, at 33, c.2.

The United States has requested an Article XXII Consultation under the General Agreement on Tariffs and Trade in the belief that the new Brazilian laws are contrary to Brazil's obligations under GATT. 2 BNA, INT'L. TRADE REP'R. 176 (Jan. 30, 1985).

87. SEI, Normative Act No. 22 of Dec. 2, 1982, as cited in Rosenn, supra note 76, at 345, n. 170.

88. Pinheiro, supra note 6, §§ 4.132-135 & 14.146 et seq.

89. Central Bank Res. No. 656 of Dec. 17, 1980, as cited in Rosenn, supra note 76, at 346, n. 172.

90. Id. at 346.

91. Central Bank Res. No. 755 of Aug. 12, 1982, as cited in Rosenn, supra note 76, at 346, n. 174.

92. Decree Law No. 600, March 18, 1977, arts. 16 & 17, translated in 17 INT'L.LEG.MAT'LS. 134 (1978); and see Wesley, "Chile", AMERICAN BAR ASSOCIATION, TECHNOLOGY TRANSFER: LAWS AND PRACTISE IN LATIN AMERICA 132 (B. Carl ed., 1980 rev.) [hereafter cited as "Carl"]; and Schliesser, "Paper Chase Along the Andes:

The Rules of the Hunt for New Foreign Investment Permits in Venezuela, Colombia, Peru, and Chile", in Stairs, supra note 38, at 1, 10.

93. Uruguay, Decree No. 808/974, Oct. 10, 1974, [97 Second Semester I] Registro Nacional de Leyes y Decretos 988.

94. Paraguay, Law No. 550, Dec. 19, 1975, LA LEY, July-Sept. 1980, at 126.

95. UNCTAD, PROCEEDINGS (3rd Sess., 1973, N.Y.) TD/180, vol. iii, p. 113-116.

96. Nattier, "Brazil", in Carl, supra note 92, at 160.

97. Law on Transfer of Technology, D.OF. Jan. 11, 1982, reprinted in 2 SMU, supra note 15, Appendices J1A & J2A [hereafter cited as "Mex.T.T."].

98. Normative Act No. 15 of the Ministry of Commerce and Industry National Institute of Industrial Property, Sep't. 11, 1975, reprinted in Carl, supra note 92, Appendix [hereafter cited as "Norm. Act 15"].

99. Decision 24, supra note 38. For a discussion of the use of antitrust laws as opposed to technology transfer regimes, see Fikentscher, "Third World Trade Partnership: Supranational Authority vs. National Extraterritorial Antitrust--A Plea for Harmonized Regionalism," 82 MICH.L.Rev. 1489, at 1494 ff. (1984).

100. Profit Remittance Law, Law No. 4.131 of Sep't. 3, 1962, as amend. by Law No. 4.390 of Aug. 29, 1964, art. 14 [hereafter cited as "Prof. Rem. L."] and Brazilian Industrial Property Code, Law No. 5.772 of Dec. 21, 1971, art. 30. DOU-I of Dec. 31, 1971, 35 Lex 1740; see also J. Cerqueira, TRATADO DE PROPRIEDADE INDUSTRIAL (2d ed, 1982).

101. Foreign Investment Statute, Decree Law No. 600, art. 2 (March 18, 1977), transl. in 17 INT'L.LEG. MAT'LS. 134 (1978).

102. Id. art. 2(c).

103. Id.; see also, Wesley, supra note 92, at 134.

104. Law 22.426 of March 12, 1981, art. 11, LEGISLACION ARGENTINA 1981-Ap. 194.

105. AFIC, _supra_ note 38, art. 21.

106. _Id_. and see Venezuela Decree 2.442 of Nov. 8, 1977, art. 69, GAC.OF 2100 Extraordinaria (Nov. 15, 1977).

107. Norm. Act 15, _supra_ note 98, ¶ I-2.2.6(a).

108. Prof. Rem. L., _supra_ note 100, arts. 12 & 14.

109. Nattier, _supra_ note 96, 179 and Norm. Act. 15, _supra_ note 98, at ¶¶ I-4.5.1(c) & I-5.5.1(c) & (d).

110. Mex.T.T., _supra_ note 97, art. 15, § II; and see Hyde, "Regulation of the Transfer of Technology to Mexico," in 1 SMU, _supra_ note 15, at Ch. 30 §§ 30.05[2] (1983).

111. AFIC, _supra_ note 38, art. 21(f).

112. Pate, "The Andean Common Market (Special Focus on Colombia and Venezuela", in Carl, _supra_ note 92, at 59, 94.

113. Norm. Act 15, _supra_ note 98, ¶ I-2.5.1(d).

114. _Id_., ¶ I-4.5.2(b) & I-5.5.2(b), and Nattier, _supra_ note 96, at 179.

115. Mex.T.T., _supra_ note 97, art. 15, § IX; and see, Hyde, "1981 Mexican Technology Transfer of Technology Law," 15 LAW.AM. 37 (1983).

116. Hyde, _supra_ note 110, at § 30.05[9].

117. AFIC, _supra_ note 38, art. 20(c).

118. Norm. Act. 15, _supra_ note 98, ¶¶ I-2.5.2(b), I-3.5.2(c)(i) & I-4.5.2(d)(i).

119. UNCTAD, PREPARATION OF A DRAFT OUTLINE OF A CODE OF CONDUCT ON TRANSFER OF TECHNOLOGY, REPORT OF THE UNCTAD SECRETARIAT, TD/B/C.6/AC.1/2/Supp. 1 (1975). ¶¶ 115-16.

120. Mex.T.T., _supra_ note 97, art. 15, § VI.

121. Hyde, _supra_ note 110, at § 30.05[6].

122. AFIC, _supra_ note 38, art. 20(d).

123. Danino, "Peru", in Carl, supra note 92, at 115, 122.

124. Venezuela, Decree No. 746 of Feb. 11, 1975, art. 1, DERECHO DE LA INTEGRACION, Vol. 11, Mar. 1975. p. 318.

125. Pate, supra note 112, at 98.

126. Mex.T.T., supra note 97, art. 15, § XI.

127. Regulations Under the Law On the Control and Registration of the Transfer of Technology and the Use and Exploitation of Patents, art. 56, D.OF., Nov. 25, 1982, 2 SMU supra note 15, Appendices J3 & J4 [hereafter cited as "Mex.Reg."].

128. Norm. Act 15, supra note 98, ¶¶I-4.5.2(d)(vi) & I-5.5.2(d)(vi).

129. Nattier, supra note 96, at 182; see also, Daniel, "Feeling the Pulse of Brazil's INPI on Technology Transfer and Patent and Trademark License Agreements -- A Glimpse Into Present and Future Trends", in Stairs, supra note 38, at 37.

130. Norm. Act. 15, supra note 98, at ¶ I-2.5.2 (b)(iii).

131. Venezuela, Decree 2442 of Nov. 8, 1977, art. 71, GAC.OF. 2,100 Ex., Nov. 15, 1977, transl. in part in Carl, supra note 92, Appendix D, at 274.

132. Pate, supra note 112, at 73.

133. Norm.Act. 15, supra note 98, ¶¶ii-2.5.2(b)(v) & I-3.5.2(b)(iv) & see also I-3.5.2(b)(v).

134. Mex. T.T., supra note 97, art. 15, § IV.

135. Mex. Reg., supra note 127, 47.

136. AFIC, supra note 38, art. 20(a).

137. Id.

138. Wesley, supra note 92, at 137.

139. Norm.Act 15, supra note 98, ¶¶ I-2.5.2(b)(ii) & I-3.5.2(c)(ii).

140. Mex. T.T., _supra_ note 97, art. 15, § IX.

141. Norm. Act 15, _supra_ note 98, §§I-2.5.2(b)(i); I-3.5.2(b)(i) & I-4.5.2(d)(i).

142. AFIC, _supra_ note 38, art. 20 (b).

143. Mex.T.T., _supra_ note 97, art. 15, § VII.

144. Mex. Reg., _supra_ note 127, art. 53.

145. Mex.T.T., _supra_ note 97, art. 15, § X and see Hyde _supra_ note 110, at § 30.05[10].

146. AFIC, _supra_ note 38, art. 20(e).

147. Norm. Act 15, _supra_ note 98, ¶¶ I-2.5.2(b)(i) & I-3.5.2(b)(i).

148. Mex.T.T., _supra_ note 97, art. 15, § V.

149. Mex. Reg., _supra_ note 127, art. 48.

150. _Id_. art. 49.

151. Hyde, _supra_ note 110, at § 30.05[5].

152. Norm. Act 15, _supra_ note 98, ¶¶I-2.5.2(b)(i); I-3.5.2(c)(i); I-4.5.2(d) & I-5.5.2(d)(i).

153. Rosenn, _supra_ note 76, at 323.

154. AFIC, _supra_ note 38, art. 20.

155. Colombia Decree No. 1.234 of 1972, art. 2(h), transl. in part in Carl, _supra_ note 92, Appendix C at 226.

156. Pate, _supra_ note 112, at 96-97.

157. Mex. T.T., _supra_ note 97, art. 15, § III.

158. Hyde, _supra_ note 110, at § 30.05[3].

159. Rosenn, _supra_ note 76, at 328.

160. _Id._ at 328-9.

161. For tax purposes the Brazilian Ministry of Finance was authorized to set a scale of deductible maximum royalties not exceeding five percent of the

gross sales. Income Tax Law, Law No. 3.470 of Nov. 28, 1958, art. 74. The Ministry's Guideline issued in 1958 established a range from one to five percent, which was believed to reflect the value of the various technologies to Brazil. Portaria 436 of Dec. 30, 1958. The Profits Remittance Law was then interpreted by the Central Bank to prohibit remittances in foreign currency of amounts above the maximum set for tax purposes. Law No. 4,131 of Sep't. 3, 1962, as amend. by Law No. 4.390 of Aug. 29, 1964, art. 11. Previously, these ceilings had applied to "gross" sales, but Normative Act No. 15 changed the base upon which these calculations are made to "net" sales. Supra note 98, § I-2.2.1. See also, "Note, Brazil's Technology Transfer Policies: At Odds with Economic Goals," 4 BOSTON COLLEGE THIRD WORLD L.J. 99 (1983).

162. Pate, supra note 112, at 74.

163. Danino, Id., 115.

164. Mex.T.T. supra note 97, art. 16, § II.

165. Mex.Reg., supra note 127, art. 63.

166. Hyde & Ramirez de la Corte, supra note 110, § 30.06.

167. Mex. T.T., supra note 97, art. 16, § III.

168. Mex. Reg., supra note 127, art. 65.

169. Hyde, supra note 110, § 30.05(16).

170. Venezuela, Decree 2442, supra note 131, art. 65(e).

171. Pate, supra note 112, at 72-73.

172. Danino, supra note 123, at 122.

173. Industrial Property Code, Law No. 5.772 of Dec. 21, 1971, 35 Lex 1740, art. 24.

174. Id. arts. 30(a) and 90(4)(a) and Profits Remittance Law, supra note 100, art. 11.

175. Id.

176. Nattier, supra note 96, at 164.

177. _Id_. at 166.

178. Norm. Act No. 15, _supra_ note 98, at ¶ I-4.2 (h).

179. Profits Remittance Law, _supra_ note 100, art. 12(3).

180. Nattier, _supra_ note 96, at 166.

181. Norm. Act 15, _supra_ note 98, at ¶ I-3.1.1.

182. _Id_. ¶ I-3.5.2(c)(ii) & (iv)..

183. Portaria 436 of Dec. 30, 1958.

184. Norm. Act 15, _supra_ note 98, at ¶ I-3.2.1.

185. _Id_., ¶ I-3.2.4(a).

186. _Id_., ¶ I-4.5.2(d)(iii).

187. Diario Oficial, Dec. 30, 1972, reprinted in 2 SMU, _supra_ note 15, at Appendices K1 & K2.

188. _Id_. art. 127 & 128.

189. Hyde, _supra_ note 110, at § 30.07(3).

190. AFIC, _supra_ note 38, art. 25.

191. Pate, _supra_ note 112, at 74.

192. Danino, _supra_ note 123, at 121.

193. Mex.T.T., _supra_ note 97, art. 16, § IV.

194. AFIC, _supra_ note 38, art. 51.

195. Pate, _supra_ note 112, at 69.

196. Nattier, _supra_ note 96, at 189.

197. Ass'n. of the Bar of New York Comm. on Arb., "The Inter-American Convention on International Commercial Arbitration", 9 LAW.AM. 43 (1977).

198. Law No. 19.231 of 1971; and see Radway & Giacchino, "Argentina", in Carl, _supra_ note 92, at 217, 218.

199. Law No. 20.794, as cited in Id.

200. Law 20.557 of Dec. 6, 1973, [1973] D Anales 3670.

201. Law 21.382 of Aug. 19, 1976, [1976] C Anales 1071.

202. Law No. 21.617 of August 12, 1977, OF.GAZ. Aug. 16, 1977, translated in Carl, supra note 92, Appendix G, at 340; and see Beccar Varela, "Argentina Reverses Trend and Offers Protection for the Supplier of Technology", in Stairs, supra note 38, at 65.

203. Law No. 22.426 of March 12, 1981, Legislacion Argentina 1981-A, p. 194.

204. Law No. 22.262 of July 1, 1980, Legislacion Argentina 1980-B, p. 1513.

205. Id. art. 41(b).

206. Id. art. 1, and see Cabanellas, supra note 12 at 46.

207. Law No. 22.262 of July 1, 1980, art. 1, supra note 203.

208. Law No. 22.426 of March 12, 1981, art. 7, Legislacion Argentina 1981-A, p. 195.

209. Approved June 21, 1976, reprinted in 15 INT'L. LEG.MAT'LS. 967 (1976) [hereafter cited as "OECD Code"].

210. Adopted by the U.N. Gen'l. Assbly. Res. 35/63 (Doc. A/C. 2/35/6 of Oct. 23, 1980); see 19 INT'L. LEGAL MAT'LS. 813 ff. & 1546 (1980). The Latin American nations have also taken the lead in urging adoption of a United Nations Technology Transfer Code, which would incorporate many provisions similar to those contained in the domestic regimes already described. See U.N., CONFERENCE ON AN INTERNATIONAL CODE OF CONDUCT OF TECHNOLOGY, draft of May 6, 1980, reprinted in 19 INT'L. LEGAL MAT'LS. 773 (1980). Progress on this Code has been stymied on the issue of whether it should be voluntary. A similar problem is holding up negotiations on the United Nations Code of Conduct on Transnational Corporations. See draft text (E/1983/17/Rev. 1) in 23 INT'L.LEG.MAT'LS. 626 (1984).

211. See, e.g., article 38 of the Statute of the International Court of Justice, T.S. 993.

212. OECD Code, supra note 209.

213. Supra note 210, § D(4).

214. Supra note 210, § D(4)(c).

215. Supra note 210, § D(4)(d) & D(4)(f)(ii).

216. Supra note 210, § D(3).

RÉSUMÉ EN FRANÇAIS

LÉGISLATIONS ANTITRUST LATINO-AMÉRICAINES ET LEURS ÉQUIVALENTS: EFFET SUR LA RÉORGANISATION ET LES CESSIONS DE BREVET PAR LES MULTINATIONALES

Les pays latino-américains doivent maintenant presque 400 milliards de dollars à l'étranger. En conséquence, les programmes d'austérité exigés par le Fonds Monétaire International ont été à l'origine d'une contraction économique, de restrictions de crédits et de faillites commerciales.

Les sociétés privées latino-américaines, incapables de rembourser leurs dettes à l'étranger, pourraient alors demander à un investisseur étranger de capitaliser les dettes en échange d'actions. En outre lorsqu'une societé locale fait face à la faillite, le meilleur moyen consisterait alors à refinancer la dette en cédant des actions au créancier. Par ailleurs, une société en difficulté aurait le choix de fusionner ou de passer aux mains d'une autre société étrangère. Enfin, même les entreprises qui se portent bien pourraient trouver que, vu la situation difficile du crédit à l'heure actuelle, elles ne prendront de l'essor qu'en faisant appel à un investisseur étranger. Ainsi une restructuration efficace d'une entreprise pourrait nécessiter tant une transfusion de capitaux qu'un transfert de nouvelles technologies. Lorsqu'ils contemplent une réoganisation de société, les juristes d'Europe et des États-Unis pensent tout de suite aux complications que pourrait créer la loi antitrust. Bien que la plupart des pays latino-américains disposent de quelques normes constitutionnelles et législatives sur le pouvoir monopolistique, celles-ci n'ont pas été, en pratique, appliquées d'une manière effective. Lorsqu'elles ont été mise en pratique leur application se limitait surtout à éviter de fixer des prix élevés.

En fait, les lois nationales relatives à l'investissement étranger et au transfert technologique peuvent avoir un plus grand impact sur la réorganisation d'une societé transnationale. D'ordinaire, dans de nombreux pays Latino-américains, l'investisseur étranger se verra limité à une position minoritaire dans la société. Ainsi, par exemple, la législation mexicaine exige normalement que 51% des actions d'une nouvelle société soient entre les mains de nationaux mexicains. Dans le Marché commun andin ou ANCOM (formé du Pérou, du Vénézuela, de la Colombie, de l'Équateur et de la Bolivie), lorsqu'il s'agit d'un nouveau projet, l'investisseur étranger est normalement tenu de se dessaisir des actions au courant d'une période de 15 à 20 années pour qu'à la fin de ce laps de temps, les nationaux puissent en contrôler au moins 51%. Même le Brésil, un pays traditionnellement réceptif aux capitaux étrangers, a commencé à promulguer de sévères restrictions relatives à la propriété dans certains secteurs de l'industrie, comme celui des ordinateurs personnels.

Le Chili, qui se situe à l'autre extrème, n'impose que quelques restrictions aux investissements étrangers. L'Argentine, le Paraguay et l'Uruguay sont aussi généreux dans leur politique.

Les contrats de cession de brevets ou d'assistance technique doivent être, en règle qénérale, approuvés par les autorités administratives du pays hôte. Le Brésil, le Mexique et les pays de l'ANCOM ont promulgué des règles sévères touchant le transfert de technologie, lesquelles normalement limitent le montant des royalties ainsi que la durée de l'accord. De plus, les lois de ces pays prévoient le rejet de tout contrat stipulant des clauses restrictives relatives à la gestion. À titre d'exemple de clauses restrictives prohibées on peut citer: le droit à la rétrocession gratuite des améliorations apportées au brevet; limitations quant à l'utilisation de la technologie par le concessionnaire, interdiction faite au bénéficiaire d'acquérir une technologie complémentaire ou concurrentielle; restrictions du droit d'utiliser la technologie et les droits de proprieté industrielle après expiration du contrat de cession, contrat d'approvisionnement obligatoire; interdiction au concessionnaire de contester les droits de propriété industrielle du fournisseur; clause de fixation de prix des articles produits par la technologie en question, limitations des réseaux de distribution; restrictions relatives à l'exportation; ainsi que de restrictions sur les activités de recherche et de developpement de la part du concessionnaire. Au Brésil, l'investisseur étranger pourrait préférer capitaliser sa technologie étant donné que ce pays ne permet ni le paiement des royalties ni des déductions fiscales à une société étrangère qui contrôle le concessionnaire. En revanche, les contributions technologiques ne peuvent pas faire l'objet d'une capitalisation dans les pays de l'ANCOM. De plus, un concessionnaire de l'ANCOM qui est contrôlé à plus de 49%, n'est pas en droit de verser des royalties à la société étrangère dominante.

Récemment, le Chili et l'Argentine ont procédé à la révision de leur lois sur le transfert de technologie et imposent maintenant moins de restrictions aux fournisseurs étrangers. Par ailleurs, ces deux pays ont été jusqu'à promulguer de nouvelles lois autitrust pour encourager la libre concurrence.

RESUMEN EN ESPAÑOL

LEYES LATINOAMERICANAS DE ANTITRUST Y SUS EQUIVALENTES: IMPACTO EN LA REORGANIZACIÓN Y EL LICENCIAMIENTO DE EMPRESAS TRANSNACIONALES

Las naciones latinoamericanas deben casi 400 billones de dólares al extranjero. Los programas de austeridad resultantes, solicitados por el Fondo Monetario Internacional producen contracción económica, restricción de créditos y quiebras comerciales.

Las empresas latinoamericanas, al verse imposibilitadas de pagar sus deudas en el extranjero pueden buscar un inversor extranjero que asuma la deuda a cambio de acciones. O cuando la empresa local está cercana a la quiebra, la opción preferible sería refinanciar la deuda, otorgando al acreedor acciones de la empresa. Por otra parte, una empresa en dificultades podría desear fusionarse o ser adquirida por una empresa extranjera. Finalmente, aun las empresas en buenas condiciones pueden encontrar que, con la falta de crédito actual, sólo pueden expandirse atrayendo un socio capitalista extranjero. Lograr una reestructuración societaria efectiva puede requerir transfusiones tanto de capital como de nueva tecnología.

Los abogados europeos y estadounidenses al considerar una reestructuración o reorganización, tienden a pensar inmediatamente en complicaciones con la ley de antitrust que pueden presentarse. A pesar de que la mayoría de las naciones latinoamericanas tienen algunas normas constitucionales y/o legislativas referentes al poder monopólico, en la práctica estas normas no han sido efectivamente aplicadas. En la medida en que se las ha aplicado, ha sido con énfasis en evitar la imposición de precios altos.

Las leyes locales de inversiones extranjeras y de transferencia tecnológica pueden tener un impacto más significante en la reorganización de empresas transnacionales. Típicamente, el inversor extranjero se verá limitado a una posición societaria minoritaria en muchos paises latinoamericanos. Por ejemplo, el derecho Mexicano exige normalmente que el 51% de las acciones de una nueva empresa esten en manos de nacionales mexicanos. En el Mercado Común Andino o

ANCOM (formado por Perú, Venezuela, Colombia, Ecuador y Bolivia) un inversor extranjero en un proyecto nuevo normalmente debe desprenderse de las acciones en un período de 15 a 20 años para que, al final de ese lapso, ciudadanos locales puedan controlar al menos un 51% de la empresa. Aun Brasil, que tradicionalmente ha sido muy receptivo de los capitales extranjeros, ha comenzado a colocar severos controles propietarios en ciertos sectores industriales como, por ejemplo, el de las computadoras personales.

Chile, en el otro extremo de esta tendencia, impone pocos controles a los inversores extranjeros. Argentina, Paraguay y Uruguay, también son liberales en el trato que ofrecen.

Contratos sobre licencias o de asistencia tecnológica deben, como norma general, ser aprobados por la autoridad administrativa del pais receptor. Brasil, México, y los paises del ANCOM han promulgado estrictas leyes de transferencia tecnológica, las que normalmente limitan la cantidad de regalías a pagar y la duración del acuerdo. Adicionalmente, las leyes de esos paises disponen que el contrato será rechazado si contiene cláusulas restrictivas de la libre competencia. Cláusulas de este tipo son, por ejemplo, transferencia gratuita a favor del licenciante de las mejoras logradas por el licenciatario, limitaciones al licenciatario en el uso de la tecnología, prohibición de adquirir tecnología suplementaria o competitiva, restricciones en el uso de la tecnología luego de vencido el contrato de licencia o los derechos de propiedad industrial; obligación de procurar ciertos productos; prohibición contra poner en tela de juicio los derechos de propiedad industrial del licenciante; fijación de precios para los artículos producidos por la tecnología en cuestión; restricciones en los canales de distribución; restricciones a las exportaciones; así como limitaciones en las tareas de investigación y de elaboración por parte del licenciatario.

El inversor extranjero en Brasil puede preferir usar su tecnología como un aporte de capital, pues este pais no permite el pago de regalías o deducciones impositivas a favor de una empresa extranjera que controla al licenciatario. En contraste, contribuciones tecnológicas no pueden computarse como aportes de capital en los paises del ANCOM. Más aun, un licenciatario perteneciente al ANCOM no puede pagar regalías a una entidad extranjera, si ésta controla más de un 49% del capital de la primera.

Recientemente Chile y Argentina han revisado sus leyes de transferencia tecnológica de forma tal que ahora son pocas las restricciones impuestas a los licenciantes extranjeros. En vez, estas dos naciones han optado por acentuar la libre competencia y han promulgado nuevas leyes antitrust.

MNE REORGANIZATION AND TECHNOLOGY TRANSFERS:

MEETING CHANGES IN GOVERNMENT REGULATION

Art Dula

Dula, Shields & Egbert, Houston, Texas
Member, International Institute of Space Law
Past Chairman, Science & Technology Section
Chairman-Elect, Aerospace Law Committee
American Bar Association

Multinational enterprises (MNE) prosper according to their ability to respond quickly to their markets. A MNE must plan ahead for changes in its procedure and structures as products, markets and even policies change. One of the concerns in a multinational reorganization involves the intricate patterns of export licensing procedures. These procedures for exporting from the United States are now in a state of change. This poses an additional planning problem for MNE's which intend to change their internal patterns. Planners must leave enough flexibility in their business reorganizations to allow for whatever eventualities occur in technology regulation.

The basic premise of U.S technology transfer is simple. Any "goods" or "data" moved in any way, for any reason, for any length of time, to any person anywhere outside the physical boundaries of the United States is an export. Technology whether in physical, solid things or ideas and information is part of the goods or data and must comply with the export licensing procedures. Sending a U.S.-based engineer to repair a piece of technological equipment offshore Stavanger is probably not an export, provided he takes no tools or documents with him. Sending a copy of a cor rected engineering drawing by satellite transfer to the enterprise's Stavanger office probably is an export within the regulations. The "goods" need not be in a crate with piles of shipping waybills. It needs only to be a movement of goods or data. Even inviting a foreign national to work in one's American laboratory to develop new products or research for new data falls within the general policy statement which controls the export regulations. This is of particular concern when the question of American and foreign patent applications comes up in planning and restructuring. It is the underlying policy and its current strictures which concern us. Let us briefly look at two things - U.S. policy and U.S. regulation.

The basic policy of the U.S. government on technical data movement has shifted in the past four years to emphasize "protection" of technological data. This is at the expense of private commercial interests which need to sell products and research for new information to maintain their market positions in the international field. The basic concern of the policy is "national security". In a cogent article on the results of this policy, Roland W. Schmitt, of General Electric's Research and Development Center, has outlined the problems with this policy. He states, "The proposed new tightening of the Export Administration Regulation to control unclassified technical data exports would require a validated license for millions of routine transactions. This would place a burden of catastrophic proportions on research and technology-based institutions. Technical data involved in sales proposals, the use of foreign consultants, technical discussions, remote computer services, and data bases - all such interactions with people of allied and friendly nations would require government approval. . . . The current impasse centers on a vital issue: whether the gain in security offered by tighter restrictions on trade with allies and neutral parties is worth more to the United States than the economic penalties resulting from lost trade, lost technical contacts with the rest of the world, and lost scientific and engineering creativity, which is at the heart of both our economic and our military strength." (Schmitt, Export Controls: Balancing Technological Innovation and National Security, in Issues in Science and Technology, National Academy of Sciences, Fall 1984, pp. 119-20.) Why is this policy so crucial? Why not just reassure the Department of Commerce that the proposed transfer is for "good" purposes, and that the data and/or goods will not be going to any "bad" end users? This brings us to the regulations by which this policy is implemented. For ease of discussion let us work with a hypothetical transaction. Let us suppose that the American unit of your multinational group wishes to sell submersible vehicles to the People's Republic of China.

DEPARTMENT OF COMMERCE - OFFICE OF EXPORT ADMINISTRATION

The DOC export control program is embodied in the Export Administration Regulations (EAR), and is implemented by a licensing procedure administered by the

Office of Export Administration (OEA). You can contact your local DOC district office for more information.

EXPORT LICENSE

Specific authorization, in the form of an individual validated export license, is required for the export of any controlled commodity or technical data to any destination to which the controls are applicable. The commodities that are subject to controls are specified in the Commodity Control List (15 Code of Federal Regulations (C.F.R.) § 399.1, Supp. No. 1; the technical data controls are set forth in 15 C.F.R. part 379). For purposes of administering this licensing program, the nations of the world have been divided into seven country groups, with varying licensing requirements and policies.

COUNTRY GROUPS

Canada	
Country Group T	North and South America and the nations of the Caribbean (except Cuba)
Country Group V	Western Europe, the Middle East, Africa, noncommunist Asia, Australia, New Zealand, People's Republic of China (with some restrictions)
Country Group Q	Romania
Country Group S	Libya
Country Group W	Poland, Hungary
Country Group Y	Soviet Union, the communist countries of Eastern Europe, Laos, Mongolia
Country Group Z	Cuba, Kampuchea, North Korea, Vietnam

DIVERSION TEST

COUNTRY GROUPS T & V

The vast majority of commodities subject to export controls for national security reasons (generally, the items identified by the code letters "A" and "B" in the Commodity Control List, such as submersible vessels, which are in commodity control group 1418A), require a validated export license for export to any destination, except Canada. The OEA's policy in granting or denying applications for exports of controlled commodities to Country Groups T and V is based on whether there is a significant risk that the commodities will be diverted from their stated destination to a country that is potentially hostile to the United States (i.e., nations in Country Groups Q, S, W, Y and Z).

MILITARY POTENTIAL TEST

COUNTRY GROUPS Q, S, W, Y & Z

In contrast, applications for export of controlled commodities to destinations in Country Groups Q, S, W, and Y are reviewed on the basis of whether the commodities may make a significant contribution to the military potential of the country of destination. The nations of Country Group Z are subject to an absolute embargo.

PEOPLE'S REPUBLIC OF CHINA

In November, 1983, the DOC reclassified the PRC into Country Group "V" for export control purposes, but with some important restrictions.

In implementing the new trade policy, the OEA divided the commodities for which validated license applications are most frequently received into three lists, the "green" list, the "yellow" list, and the "red" list.

Items on the green list, which are identified in various advisory notes to the Commodity Control List, will be subject to the new standard of review and will generally be authorized for export to China. The advisory notes identify those commodities in the following categories for which validated licenses for exports to China will generally be granted: (i) machinery and equipment for the manufacture of electronic equipment; (ii) electronic measuring, calibrating and testing equipment; (iii) electronic test equipment with embedded computers or microprocessors; (iv) integrated circuits and microcircuits; (v) electronic computers and peripherals; (vi) recording and reproducing equipment, including recording media; (vii) oscilloscopes and components.

License applications for exports to China of items on the green list may be approved directly by the OEA, and will not require interagency review by the Department of Defense. It is anticipated that approximately 75 percent of all validated license applications for proposed exports of controlled commodities to China will involve commodities on the green list.

Validated license applications to export items on the yellow and red lists, which involve higher levels of technology and which may be more directly adapted to military uses, will be reviewed both by the OEA and the Department of Defense. The standard will be the non-stringent determination of whether the commodity may make a significant contribution to Chinese military potential. With respect to commodities on the red list (which is classified), license applications will generally be denied.

GENERAL EXPORT LICENSES

The EAR establish a series of general export licenses that permit the export of United States origin commodities to some or all destinations without the necessity of a specific validated export license. Among these general licenses is general license GLV, which permits the export of controlled commodities in limited amounts (generally in values of $1,000 or less) to destinations in Country Groups T and V. The Commodity Control List specifies a general license GLV maximum value for each entry. This value limit is $100, $250, $500 or $1,000, depending upon the particular commodity. Certain commodities, however, which are controlled for nuclear non-proliferation reasons, have a general license GLV value limit of zero for all destinations.

DISTRIBUTION LICENSE

To facilitate multiple export transactions involving commodities for which a validated license is required, the EAR create a series of special licensing procedures which may be utilized, under certain specified conditions and in limited circumstances, in lieu of individual validated export licenses. Of these special licensing procedures, the most important is the distribution license. The distribution license permits the exporter to make repeated exports over a period of one year (subject to renewal for up to two years) of controlled commodities to approved consignees in specified destinations, pursuant to an international marketing program.

China is excluded from the list of eligible countries under the distribution license special licensing procedure. This restriction is consistent with the Office of Export Administration's policy of examining proposed exports of controlled commodities to China on a case-by-case basis.

COCOM

The United States participates in a program of multinational export control, along with Belgium, Canada, Denmark, France, West Germany, Greece, Italy, Japan, Luxembourg, the Netherlands, Norway, Portugal, Turkey and the United Kingdom. This system of multinational controls is administered by an informal Coordinating Committee (COCOM) which reviews proposed exports of multilaterally controlled commodities (i.e., commodities, such as submersible diving systems, identified by the code letter "A" on the Commodity Control List) to consignees in the communist countries of Eastern Europe, the Soviet Union and the People's Republic of China. Thus, even after the Office of Export Administration has determined to grant a validated license for a proposed export of an "A" item to one of these destinations, the license application must be reviewed and approved by COCOM before the validated license will be issued.

Despite the recent Department of Commerce approval procedure changes, COCOM approval requirements for exports to China remain in force. Validated license applications for proposed exports of "A" commodities to China are likely to take considerably longer in processing than similar applications for "A" exports to other Country Group V destinations. United States representatives to COCOM have had a number of discussions with their foreign counterparts about granting favorable consideration to license applications for exports to China.

COMPUTERS & SOFTWARE - SPECIAL DOCUMENTATION

In addition to the normal requirements for an export license, the Export Administration Regulations have established various special documentation requirements for proposed exports of computers to any destination in Country Groups Q, W and Y.

MACHINE TOOLS

The EAR also prescribe additional information that must accompany any application for a proposed export to any destination in Country Groups Q, W and Y, of those machine tools and numerical controls identified in the Commodity Control List. These additional information requirements are generally not applicable for proposed machine tool and numerical controls exports to destinations in Country Group V. The special information requirements for proposed exports of those items have been retained, however, for export to China.

TECHNICAL DATA

The EAR control the export, not only of commodities, but also technical data including all computer software. Most technical data, except those data having certain direct strategic applications, may be exported to destinations in Country Groups T and V (except Afghanistan) under a general license.

Strategic technical data relating to the production and delivery of nuclear weapons, airborne navigation and guidance systems, civil aircraft, and various types of submersible watercraft require a validated export license. Thus, an exporter proposing to export or license its technology to an end-user in a country included in Country Group T or V generally may make the export without a validated export license, although it may be necessary to obtain a letter of assurance from the end-user that neither the technical data nor the direct product thereof will be reexported to a controlled destination.

In contrast, a validated export license has been required for almost all proposed exports of technical data to destinations in Country Group Q, S, W, Y and Z, as well as Afghanistan. A general license may only be utilized for technical data exports to destinations in Country Groups P, Q, W or Y, or to Afghanistan, when it consists of: (a) manuals, instruction sheets or blueprints which are (i) sent as part of a transaction involving, and are directly related to, a commodity licensed for export to the specific destination and consignee, (ii) sent no later than one year after shipment of the commodity, (iii) generally delivered with the commodity, as a matter of established business practice, (iv) necessary for the assembly, installation, maintenance, repair or operation of the commodity, and (v) not related to production, manufacture or construction of the commodity; or (b) technical data supporting an actual quotation, bid or offer to sell a commodity, provided that, (i) the commodity is not identified as an "A" item on the Commodity Control List (i.e., subject to multilateral controls), (ii) the technical data do not disclose the detailed design production, manufacture or means of reconstruction of the quoted commodity or its product.

Current rules modify the broad restriction on the export of technical data to China under general license. They do not, however, bring the requirements for technical data exports to China into full conformance with the requirements for technical data exports to other Country Group V destinations. Although a general license may now be used for some technical data exports to China, it is not available for the export to China of technical data related to any commodity that is controlled for national security, nuclear non-proliferation or crime control reasons. Proposed technical data exports to China are examined on a case-by-case basis.

EXPORT CONTROL TRAINING SEMINARS

The export license application requires very specific information and a good grasp of the export regulations. The Department of Commerce offers introductory and advanced courses on its export administration regulations

The seminar instructors are experienced export licensing and enforcement specialists from the U.S. Department of Commerce in Washington, D.C.

The courses feature an intensive regulatory overview and classroom-style workshop exercises in using and interpreting the EAR (topics include export licensing, shipping tolerances, documentation requirements, export clearances, re-exports, how to fill out export license applications and use the commodity control list, etc.).

Open forum presentations focus on the exporter service functions of the U.S. Department of Commerce, with emphasis on technical data/information transfer licensing, Free World and communist bloc licensing, and export enforcement as well as current major policy and procedural issues.

The instructors will also meet privately with individual attendees to answer questions and discuss their specific export licensing needs and problems.

The advanced course is four days of classroom training in the requirements for compliance with the U.S. export regulations, Standards, and policies. It includes two days of intensive review and discussion of Parts 370, 371, 372, 374 and 376 of the EAR and two days of presentation of Country Policies, Nuclear Distribution Licensing, Technical Data, Agency Referrals, and Export License Application.

Attendance is limited to 50 participants who have completed a two-day "Export Administration Regulations Introductory Course" seminar presented by the Office of Export Administration, U.S. Department of Commerce.

DEPARTMENT OF STATE

Although virtually all non-military exports are regulated by the DOC, including so called "dual use" commodities, export of "submersible vessels having independent capacity to maneuver vertically or horizontally at depths below 1,000 FSW" is controlled by the State Department under category XX(a) of the International Traffic in Arms regulations. These regulations are administered by the Office of Munitions Control, Department of State, Washington, D.C. 20520.

CONCLUSION - SUGGESTIONS

You may well be saying there is no way your client in Europe or South America could possibly do business with American high technology companies, much less join them in forming multinational enterprises. This is not so. American companies and their lawyers are used to doing these transactions through the DOC and doing them successfully. My clients have every intention of competing aggressively in as many high technology markets as they possibly can, and competing within the requirements of government regulation. These particular transactions merely require additional and very careful planning. Management planning and compliance activities can be coordinated worldwide. Your clients and mine are not interested in "good guys and bad buys" but we are interested in transferring technology effectively in the international marketplace. At some points in the marketplace the requirements are extremely strict and the political policies underlying them need careful consideration in structuring transactions. We urge you to proceed with hope and caution.

RÉSUMÉ EN FRANÇAIS

RÉORGANISATION DES MULTINATIONALES ET LES TRANSFERTS DE TECHNOLOGIE: RESPECT DES MODIFICATIONS APPORTÉES À LA RÈGLEMENTATION AMÉRICAINE

Le principe qui gouverne le transfert de technologie en droit nord-américain est simple. Tout "bien" ou "donnée" qui est acquis de quelque manière que ce soit, pour toute raison, pour quelque durée que ce soit, par qui que ce soit en dehors des frontières des États-Unis est considéré comme étant une exportation. Toute technologie quelle que soit sa forme ou sa substance (solide, conceptuelle, telle qu'une idée ou une information) est un bien ou une donnée et devra être soumis aux procédures relatives à l'exportation des brevets. Envoyer un ingénieur opérant aux États-Unis pour aller réparer une pièce d'équipement au large de Stavanger ne sera probablement pas considéré comme étant une exportation, s'il ne prend ni outils ni documents avec lui. En revanche, l'envoi par satellite d'un dessin industriel corrigé à Stavanger sera considéré comme étant une exportation d'après la règlementation sur l'exportation. Les "biens" ne doivent pas nécessairement être en caisse accompagnés d'une pile de lettres de voiture. Il ne suffit en fait que d'un déplacement de biens ou de données. Le fait d'inviter un étranger à travailler dans un laboratoire américain en vue de produire de nouveaux articles ou y faire de la recherche de données est défini par les règles de la politique générale qui détermine la règlementation de l'exportation. Cela devient très important lorsqu'il est question de la mise en application de brevets étrangers et américains au moment de la prise de décision de planification et de restructuration.

L'orientation de la politique de base du gouvernement américain relative au déplacement des données techniques a tendance depuis quatre années à mettre l'accent sur la "protection" des données technologiques. Ceci se fait au détriment des intérêts privés, lesquels ont besoin de vendre des produits et de la recherche en échange de nouvelles données en vue de maintenir leurs positions sur le marché international. Le souci majeur de cette politique est "la sécurité nationale". Toute donnée technique reliée à des projets de vente, toute utilisation de consultants étrangers, toute discussion technique, tout service d'informatique éloigné ou relié à une banque de données, qu'ils aient lieu avec des pays alliés ou amis, ces échanges nécessiteront l'approbation du gouvernement

L'impasse actuelle gravite autour d'une question d'une importance capitale: est-ce que le bénéfice qu'on pourrait en retirer du point de vue de la sécurité en imposant des restrictions au commerce avec nos alliés et les parties neutres est plus avantageux pour les États-Unis que l'impact économique négatif qui résulterait de la détérioration du commerce, la rupture de contacts techniques avec le reste du monde, la perte de créativité dans les domaines de la science et de l'ingénierie, qui sont à la base de notre puissance économique et militaire?

L'article traite d'une transaction hypothétique spécifique concernant la vente d'un véhicule submersible à la République populaire de Chine par une multinationale américaine.

RESUMEN EN ESPAÑOL

REORGANIZACIÓN DE EMPRESAS MULTINACIONALES Y TRANSFERENCIA TECHNOLÓGICA: CUMPLIMIENTO CON LOS CAMBIOS EN LAS REGULACIONES GUBERNAMENTALES

El principio que rige la transferencia tecnológica en el derecho norteamericano es bien simple. Todo "bien" o "información" que se adquiere, de cualquier manera que sea, por cualquier duración, por quien sea, fuera de las fronteras de los Estados Unidos, se considera una exportación. Toda tecnología, cualquiera sea su forma o su sustancia (sólida, conceptual, como una idea o dato) es un bien o una información y deberá ser sometido a los procedimientos relativos a la exportación de patentes. El envío de un ingeniero que trabaja en los Estados Unidos para ir a reparar una pieza de una maquinaria en la costa de Stavanger, probablemente no será considerado como una exportación, si el ingeniero no lleva consigo herramientas ni documentos. Contrariamente, el envío por satélite a Stavager de un diseño industrial corregido, será considerado como una exportación según los reglamentos aplicables. Los "bienes" no necesariamente deben estar embalados y acompañados por una pila de documentos comerciales. El mero desp azamiento de bienes o de información es suficiente. El hecho de invitar a un extranjero a trabajar en un laboratiorio norteamericano con vistas a producir nuevos artículos o a investigar información allí disponible, cae dentro de la política general aplicable al control de exportaciones. Esto resulta muy importante cuando se trata de planear y de reestructurar patentes americanas y extranjeras.

La orientación de la política básica del gobierno americano relativa al desplazamiento de información técnica tiende, desde hace cuatro años, a acentuar la "protección" de la información tecnológica. Esto se hace en detrimento de intereses privados, los que tienen necesidad de vender los productos y la investigación a cambio de nueva información, con vistas a mantener sus posiciones en el mercado internacional. La mayor preocupación de esta política es la "seguridad nacional". Toda información técnica relativa a proyectos de venta, toda utilización de consultores extranjeros, toda discusión técnica, todo servicio de informática alejado de o unido a un banco de datos, aunque sea con paises aliados o amigos, tales intercambios necesitrarían la aprobación del gobierno.

La situación actual gravita alrededor de una pregunta crucial: ¿el beneficio producido por la seguridad resultante al imponer restricciones al comercio con nuestros aliados y paises neutrales, es más ventajoso para los Estados Unidos que el impacto económico negativo, resultante de la deteriorización del comercio, la ruptura de contactos tecnológicos con el resto del mundo, la pérdida de creatividad en el campo de la ciencia y de la ingeniería, que forman la base de nuestra potencia económica y militar?

El cuerpo de este artículo trata sobre una transacción hipotética, la venta de un submarino a la República Popular China por una empresa multinactional americana. Se mencionan además una reglamentación específicia, ministerios y ciertas personas.

CHAPTER III

TAXATION

LATIN AMERICA

UNITED STATES

FRANCE

TAX ASPECTS OF MULTINATIONAL REORGANIZATIONS: THE LATIN AMERICAN PERSPECTIVE

Sergio A. Leiseca and Paul D. Slocomb

Mr. Leiseca is a partner in the Chicago office of Baker & McKenzie. He has 14 years' practice in international matters, with emphasis on Latin American foreign investment, tax, technology transfer, commercial and corporate law. His J.D. degree is from Tulane University School of Law where he was a member of the Law Review.

Mr. Slocomb is a partner in the Chicago office of Baker & McKenzie. He has 13 years' practice in international matters, with emphasis on Latin American foreign investment, tax, technology transfer, commercial and corporate law. His J.D. degree is from Harvard Law School.

I. Introduction

A. General

The introductory comments elsewhere in this volume regarding foreign investment aspects of multinational reorganizations in Latin America emphasize lack of uniformity. The lack of uniformity pervades foreign investment legislation more than tax legislation. That is not to say that tax laws in Latin America are uniform, but they do share many common features. What can be stated, and is true almost universally in Latin America, is that tax laws do not contain specific rules regarding reorganizations. While there are a few notable exceptions (e.g., Argentina), tax issues in reorganization almost always must be analyzed by reference to more general rules and principles embodied in the applicable tax law.

In the reorganization context one may tend to think principally of income tax laws. But, in some Latin American countries with respect to some kinds of reorganization, other taxes play a much more significant role. Such other taxes may include stock transfer taxes, real estate transfer taxes, sales taxes, turnover taxes, value added taxes and stamp taxes, not to mention charges not really of a tax nature, such as notaries' and registration fees. As is the case with our foreign investment discussion, we cannot in this chapter be exhaustive with respect to all taxes, all countries or, for that matter, any single country. Again, our focus will be not encyclopedic treatment, but rather a roadmap. Our emphasis will be income taxes, but we will mention the potential impact of other taxes where appropriate.

B. Income Tax Laws

Some introductory comments regarding concepts generally embodied in Latin American income tax legislation will help focus our discussion.

1. Reorganization Rules

As noted earlier, the income tax legislation of few Latin American jurisdictions specifically addresses reorganizations. Odd as it may seem to one familiar with, e.g., United States income tax legislation, there may be no specific provisions with respect to tax-free mergers, with respect to liquidations, or with respect to redemptions. One usually must apply the more general rules applicable to, e.g., dividends and stock and asset transfers.

2. Source of Income - Territoriality

Most Latin American countries tax on a territorial basis -- both foreign and local taxpayers are taxed only on their local source income. Definitions of local source income vary, but in general it is income derived from activities conducted (sometimes only habitually conducted) in and from the exploitation of assets located in the local country.

3. Arms-Length Standards

The income tax legislation of most Latin American countries does not include provisions comparable to Section 482 of the United States Internal Revenue Code, fixing an arms-length standard for transactions between related parties. Such arms-length standards as do appear may be quite limited in scope. Furthermore, in those countries having provisions setting arms-length standards, there often is relatively little precedent for their application by local tax authorities.

4. Substance Over Form

Few Latin American countries have legislation or judicial precedent for viewing transactions in accordance with their underlying substance, rather than in accordance with their form. Those countries that do have a basis for the application of such principles (e.g., the "economic reality" provisions of Argentina's tax procedure code) often have little experience in applying the principles.

5. Debt vs. Equity

Consistently with the rare application of substance over form principles, it is unusual in Latin American countries for debt to be recharacterized as equity for income tax purposes.

6. Basis of Shares

The basis of shares of stock typically is historical cost, stated in local currency. Sometimes there are indexing provisions to step up the basis to keep pace with inflation or devaluation of the local currency. The indexing sometimes is not automatic, but requires affirmative action on the part of the shareholding taxpayer. It is important to note that the tax basis, as stated in local currency and converted to foreign currency at current exchange rates, may be vastly different from the basis in foreign currency used to determine the foreign-income tax liability of a foreign shareholder of the local company. Also note that a single shareholder may have different bases in different shares, depending on when, how, and for what amount they were acquired. Indeed some stock, for example stock-dividend stock, may have zero basis, rather than a positive basis resulting from reallocation of the basis in shares existing prior to the issuance of the stock dividend.

7. Net Operating Losses

In some Latin American countries there is no provision for deduction of net operating losses in earlier or later years. If deductions are allowed, the right to deduct generally is not transferable. If one wishes to use an existing net operating loss, it is better to keep the company intact and not try to transfer the deduction.

8. Tax Treatment of Limitadas

The limitada, or limited liability company, is a form of company that exists in most Latin American jurisdictions. It normally, but not always, is taxed locally in the same way as a corporation. But depending upon the provisions of the limitada's articles, its foreign shareholder for its own tax purposes in its country of incorporation may be able to treat the limitada as a partnership.

The limitada is in fact a kind of hybrid between a corporation and a partnership. The equity owners ("quotaholders") of the limitada generally have limited liability, but in some Latin American countries the general rule of limited liability can be changed by provisions of the articles of the limitada. A limitada need not, and often does not, have centralized management. Rather it is equally managed by all of its quotaholders. The quotaholders' quotas in the *limitada* generally are not freely transferable. And while a limitada may be dissolved by the death or dissolution of a quotaholder, that is not necessarily the rule. However, even if it is the rule it may be altered through an articles provision. Those familiar with the rules for characterization of foreign entities as corporations or partnerships for United States income tax purposes will recognize that, by appropriately drafting the articles of a *limitada*, it may be qualified as a partnership for United States income tax purposes. Such characterization may offer significant advantages to the foreign quotaholders of the local *limitada*.

9. Taxes as "Income" Taxes

Again of particular interest to United States investors, it is not always clear that Latin American taxes are creditable "income" taxes for United States purposes. Questions frequently arise as to the creditability of, *e.g.*, excess remittance taxes discussed in the foreign investment chapter of this volume, "presumed" income taxes based on percentages of net worth, and the like.

II. Issues

Tax issues depend on the kind of reorganization. The kind of reorganization depends on the motive. For discussion of reasons for reorganizing in Latin America, see the chapter in this volume discussing foreign investment considerations. Hereinafter we identify and discuss income tax issues in the context of the same kinds of reorganizations discussed in that chapter.

A. Amendment of Purpose Clause

An amendment of the purpose clause of a local company does not generate any income tax liability. There may be registration and notarial fees but they, in most instances, will be modest.

B. "Transformation"

A "transformation" of a local company from one form of corporate organzation to another usually involves just an amendment of the articles. In most countries, no income tax liability should attach, unless, for example, the old form is taxed like a corporation and the new form like a partnership. The more typical consequences, usually rather insignificant, are registration and notarial fees.

C. Increase in Capital

Increase in the capital of a local subsidiary generally does not give rise to income tax liability, but in some countries share issuance premiums are taxable to the local company. The basis of pre-existing and newly-issued shares should be considered carefully. It may depend on the kind of capital increase.

Apart from income tax considerations, these may be capital registration taxes, sometimes substantial, as well as filing and notarial fees.

D. Merger

Tax-free mergers are permitted by specific tax legislation in only a few Latin American countries. In those countries there may be post-merger conditions including, e.g., continuity of business and a holding period. Elsewhere, where the tax law is silent, the corporate law may permit mergers, and a practice may have developed allowing mergers without income tax consequence, perhaps on the theory that a merger from an income tax point of view is much like an original incorporation. In yet other countries, uncertainty regarding the tax status of mergers may require restructuring a transaction to achieve the same result through a combination of, e.g., sale of assets at tax basis, followed by contribution of sale proceeds to the surviving company in exchange for stock, followed by the liquidation (or the maintenance) of the resulting shareholding company.

While income tax issues generally can be satisfactorily resolved, other taxes may have a more significant bearing. There may be significant real estate transfer taxes, personal property transfer taxes, and sales or value added taxes, as well as registration and notarial fees.

E. Split-Up or Spin-Off

As in the case of merger, a few tax laws in Latin America specifically permit tax-free split-ups or spin-offs, often with post-transaction conditions. In countries without specific rules, the transaction may have to be restructured to achieve the same result through a combination of, _e.g._, establishment of a new company to purchase assets at tax basis, followed by a partial liquidation of the original company and distribution of the sale proceeds received.

As in the case of merger, there may be significant real estate transfer taxes, personal property transfer taxes, and sales or value added taxes, as well as registration and notarial fees.

F. Capital Reduction, Liquidation, Redemption

In the case of capital reduction, liquidation and redemption, income tax issues predominate. There are not always clear rules. In general a capital reduction will not attract income tax. A liquidation, complete or partial, often will attract dividend treatment and result in income tax exposure. Redemptions generally will be treated as sales or exchanges and may result in local tax liability significantly different from that which would apply to, _e.g._, a partial liquidation. But there are important exceptions to these general rules.

In some countries, reinvestment of earnings avoids some income taxes at the time of reinvestment. The price that is paid is the possibility of higher income taxes at the time of a later capital reduction or liquidation. Thus, planning for a capital reduction or liquidation often requires a close look at the capitalization history of the local company.

Liquidation may trigger excess remittance taxes. Such taxes, if imposed, generally apply not only to excess amounts of annual dividends, but also to proceeds of liquidation.

If redemption is contemplated, the tax basis of the particular shares being redeemed must be carefully investigated. As noted earlier, some shares may have zero tax basis or, in any event, a lower tax basis than others.

G. Stock Transfers

Tax rules regarding share transfers vary widely from country to country in Latin America. In some countries the source of income on a share transfer is determined by the situs of the transfer of the shares. In others, the source is determined by the situs of incorporation of the company that issued the shares.

This can present problems if, for example, a tax credit in the country of incorporation of the shareholder depends on source of income, and that country considers the source to be that of the situs of the share transfer. Assume a shareholder in non-Latin American country X sells shares of a company organized in Latin American country Y. Assume the share transfer takes place in country X. The income tax law of country Y may nonetheless tax the transaction. If the tax credit available in country X depends upon foreign source of the income, and if country X determines the source of income by reference to the situs of the transaction, the shareholder in country X will pay country Y tax without being able to credit it in country X.

When planning share transfers it is crucial to remember that the basis of the shares for local income tax purposes may not be the same as the basis for income tax purposes in the shareholder's country. If the local basis is lower, the effective rate of local tax imposed on the transfer may be so high as to prevent full crediting of the local taxes in the shareholder's country.

In some Latin American countries there is no income tax on share transfers, but a stock transfer tax may apply. Even with respect to stock transfer taxes, the situs of the share transfer may be determinative of the applicability of the tax.

H. Sale of Assets

Because of the general absence of clear income tax rules regarding tax-free reorganizations, assets sales assume considerable importance in Latin American tax planning practice. Most, if not all, reorganizations can be documented as a series of sales of shares (discussed above) and sales of assets. As noted earlier, the substance over form or step transaction doctrine generally does not apply in Latin American countries. This is often a happy coincidence for, e.g., a United States shareholder. In the United States, transactions most often are characterized for income tax purposes in accordance with their overall substance, rather than their form. Intervening steps to reach an end result are often ignored. Thus, a series of sales of stock and assets in a Latin American country may, for United States tax purposes, simply be viewed as a tax-free merger, split-up, or whatever.

The common use of assets sales in Latin America is also encouraged by the general absence of arms-length rules for transactions between related parties. Reorganizations are often accomplished through assets sales at prices equal to the tax basis of the assets.

III. Examples

A. Assumed Structure

Assume that a United States multinational enterprise ("USM") owns a United States holding company ("USH"), which in turn owns a company organized in a Latin American country ("LA1"). Further assume that USM directly (not through USH) owns a second company organized in the same Latin American country ("LA2"). We will use this structure to illustrate the tax aspects of mergers and divestitures, two of the more common forms of reorganization in Latin America.

B. Merger

USM may wish to have LA1 and LA2 merge. In some Latin American countries there will be clear provisions in the tax legislation permitting tax-free merger. This will be true, for example, in Argentina. In other Latin American countries (Venezuela as an example) there are no tax-free reorganization provisions in the income tax law. In these countries, USM would consider having LA1 or LA2 sell all of its assets, subject to all of its liabilities, to the other of the two companies. It likely would want to do so at the tax basis of the underlying assets. But depending upon the tax status of the company to survive the "merger", and applicable local income tax law, pricing might be lower or higher to, e.g., generate losses or absorb losses while at the same time upping the basis of the assets transferred for future tax purposes. In any event, if one but not both of LA1 and LA2 has losses that can be carried forward, it likely will be advantageous to have that company survive the merger.

The most significant tax aspects of the transaction would not likely be income taxes but other taxes. The asset transfers could generate liability under real estate transfer taxes, personal property transfer taxes, sales taxes, and value added taxes, and also might result in substantial charges for registration and notarial fees.

C. Divestiture

Now assume USM wishes to dispose of all of its interests in the Latin American country in question. It may consider selling to, *e.g.*, an unrelated United States company ("USCO"), or to an unrelated company organized in the Latin American country in question and owned by nationals of the country ("LATCO").

If USH has no interest other than its interest in LA1, no local tax generally would be incurred upon sale by USM of its shares in USH to USCO. USM might, however, incur local income tax liability upon a sale of its shares in LA2 to USCO. That would depend upon the source rules of the local country.

If USM sold its shares in LA2 to LATCO, local income tax liability most often would be incurred, but even LATCO's status as a local company owned by local nationals would not necessarily make its purchase of those shares local source income.

The divestiture might also be accomplished by sale of assets followed by liquidation. This approach could increase the burden of local taxes, and that increased burden might not be fully creditable in the United States.

IV. Conclusion

The effect of local tax legislation on reorganizations in Latin America varies considerably from country to country. Some general patterns can be identified. But, as in the case of foreign investment legislation, there is no substitute for careful planning of the structure of the original investment and careful examination of the tax legislation and alternative approaches to reorganization when a change must be made.

RÉSUMÉ EN FRANÇAIS

LES ASPECTS FISCAUX RELATIFS AUX RÉORGANISATIONS DES MULTINATIONALES: LA PERSPECTIVE LATINO-AMÉRICAINE

En Amérique Latine, les lois fiscales ne contiennent généralement pas de règles précises concernant les réorganisations. Les lois relatives à l'impôt sur le revenu ont parfois moins d'importance que d'autres lois fiscales comme celles qui ont trait aux transferts d'actions, aux transferts d'immeubles, aux ventes, à la valeur ajoutée et aux timbres fiscaux et vignettes´sans compter d'autres frais qui ne sont pas de nature fiscale tels que les honoraires notariaux et les frais d'enregistrement.

Bien que les lois latino-américaines relatives à l'impôt sur le revenu ne soient pas uniformes, il existe néanmoins quelques importants principes qui sont d'habitude similaires. Les lois relatives à l'impôt sur le revenu sont typiquement territoriales, en ce sens qu'elles ne touchent que le revenu de source locale. Le modèle des transactions habituelles entre des entreprises vraiment indépendantes (arm's length standards") n'existe que rarement, et lorsqu'il est suivi, son application est sporadique. D'ordinaire, la forme prime sur le fond. La dette est rarement recaractérisée comme participation. Le coût des actions est naturellement déterminé en monnaie locale. Ce coût peut être vraiment différent du coût historique en monnaie étrangère qu'on applique souvent pour des motifs fiscaux dans le pays même de l'actionnaire étranger. Ce coût pourrait aussi varier pour les différentes actions que détient un simple actionnaire. Bien que les pertes opérationnelles nettes soient déductibles, elles ne sont pas généralement transférables d'une société à l'autre. Une entité peut être imposée comme une société anonyme ("corporation") dans le pays hôte, mais serait traitée comme une société collective ("partnership") dans le pays de l'actionnaire étranger. Un impôt sur le revenu dans le pays hôte peut ne pas être considéré comme un impôt sur le revenu pour déterminer le crédit fiscal étranger ("Foreign tax credit") disponible à l'actionnaire étranger dans son propre pays.

Les aspects fiscaux relatifs à une réorganisation dépendent de la nature de la réorganisation. Dans le cas où la réorganisation n'exige qu'une modification du statut social de la société locale, l'impôt sur le revenu ne sera pas normalement appliqué. Par contre, si la réorganisation implique une augmentation de capital, l'impôt sur le revenu ne sera normalement pas appliqué, mais la répercussion sur le coût des actions peut être imprévisible.

Si la réorganisation se présente sous forme de fusion, la législation ou la pratique locale peuvent l'accepter sans pour autant assumer les retombées fiscales quant à l'impôt sur le revenu. Toutefois, dans certains pays, pour atténuer les retombées fiscales, il est parfois nécéssaire de restructurer la transaction sous forme, par exemple, d'une vente d'actifs suivie d'une contribution en échange d'actions et d'une liquidation.

Si la réorganisation se fait sous forme de scission, la législation de certains pays permet qu'il y soit procédé sans supporter les conséquences en matière d'impôt sur le revenu. Dans certains autres pays, il est nécéssaire de restructurer la transaction en établissant, par exemple, une nouvelle société suivie d'une liquidation partielle et une distribution du produit de la vente. Dans le cas où la réorganisation nécessite une réduction de capital, une liquidation ou un rachat, les règles d'impôt sur le revenu peuvent s'avérer complexes. En effet, il est possible qu'il n'y ait pas de prélèvement d'impôt sur le revenu, comme il se peut qu'on applique à cette situation le traitement correspondant aux dividendes, à une vente ou à une permutation.

Si la réorganisation nécessite un transfert d'actions, les règles en vigueur dans les pays hôtes relatives à la source du revenu détermineront l'impôt sur le revenu qui s'y applique. Ces mêmes règles, et le coût des actions, peuvent différer de celles qu'on retrouve dans le pays de l'actionnaire étranger, ce qui pourrait compliquer la planification du crédit d'impôt étranger ("foreign tax credit"). Dans certains pays les transferts d'actions sont d'ailleurs assujettis à un impôt spécial, au lieu de l'impôt sur le revenu traditionnel.

En Amérique latine, les réorganisations sont souvent structurées de façon à inclure les ventes d'actifs et installations pour un montant égal au coût fiscal des actifs. Cet aspect est dû à l'absence de primauté de la forme de "step transactions" et des règles sur les opérations normales entre des entreprises indépendantes ("arm's length standards").

RESUMEN EN ESPAÑOL

ASPECTOS IMPOSITIVOS DE REORGANIZACIONES MULTINACIONALES: LA PERSPECTIVA LATINOAMERICANA

Las leyes impositivas en Latinoamérica generalmente no tienen reglas específicas para las reorganizaciones. Las leyes de impuesto a las rentas a veces tienen menor importancia que otras leyes impositivas, incluyendo las leyes de impuesto a la transferencia de acciones, a la transferencia de inmuebles, a las ventas, al valor agregado y el impuesto de sellos; y también que otros costos no impositivos, tales como honorarios notariales y aranceles de registro.

Mientras las leyes de impuesto a las rentas latinoamericanas no son uniformes, existen algunos importantes principios que suelen ser similares. Las leyes de impuesto a las rentas son típicamente territoriales en cuanto a su alcance--ellas comprenden sólo rentas de fuente local. El parámetro de operaciones normales entre empresas no vinculadas ("arm's length standards") raramente existe--y si existe, usualmente el mismo es sólo esporádicamente aplicado. Normalmente, la forma prima sobre la substancia. La deuda es raramente recaracterizada como participación. El costo de las acciones está, naturalmente, determinado en moneda local. Este puede ser muy diferente del costo histórico en moneda extranjera, a menudo usada por motivos impositivos en el propio pais del accionista extranjero. Tal costo puede también ser diferente para diferentes acciones poseídas por un simple accionista. Las pérdidas operativas netas, si es que fueren deducibles, generalmente no pueden ser transferidas de una compañía a otra. Una entidad puede ser gravada como una sociedad anónima ("corporation") en el país local, pero tratada como una sociedad colectiva ("partnership") en el país del accionista extranjero. Un impuesto a las rentas en el país local puede no ser considerado como un impuesto a las rentas a efectos de determinar el crédito por impuesto externo ("foreign tax credit") a disposición del accionista extranjero en su propio país.

Los aspectos impositivos de una reorganización dependen de la clase de reorganización. Si la reorganización sólo requiere una modificación del

Estatuto Social de la compañia local, el impuesto a las rentas normalmente no será aplicado. Si la reorganización requiere un aumento de capital, el impuesto a las rentas no será normalmente aplicable, pero el efecto sobre el costo de las acciones puede ser imprevisible.

Si la reorganización adopta la forma de una fusión, la legislación o práctica local puede permitir su procedencia sin responsabilidad impositiva en cuanto al impuesto a las rentas. Pero en algunos países, a fines de reducir la responsabilidad impositiva, puede ser necesario reestructurar la transacción bajo la forma de, por ejemplo, una venta de activos seguida por una contribución a cambio de acciones y una liquidación.

Si la organización adopta la forma de una escisión, la legislación local en algunos países permitirá su procedencia sin responsabilidad en cuanto al impuesto a las rentas. En otros países puede ser necesario reestructurar la transacción bajo la forma de, por ejemplo, el establecimento de una nueva compañía seguida por una liquidación parcial y distribución del producto de la venta.

Si la reorganización requiere una reducción de capital, liquidación o rescate de acciones, las reglas del impuesto a las rentas pueden no ser claras. Puede no haber impuesto a las rentas o puede caber el tratamiento correspondiente a dividendos o puede caber el tratamiento correspondiente a una venta o permuta.

Si la reorganización requiere la transferencia de acciones, las reglas de los países locales sobre la fuente de la renta determinarán la incidencia del impuesto a las rentas. Las mismas reglas y el costo de las acciones pueden diferir de aquellas del propio país del accionista extranjero, las cuales pueden complicar la planificación del crédito por impuesto extranjero ("foreign tax credit"). En algunos países, las transferencias de acciones están sujetas a impuestos especiales, en lugar del normal impuesto a las rentas.

Las reorganizaciones en Latinoamérica a menudo están estructuradas para incluir las ventas de activos e instalaciones por un monto igual al costo impositivo de los activos. Esto es propiciado por la ausencia de primacía de la substancia sobre la forma de "step transactions" y de reglas sobre operaciones normales entre empresas no vinculadas ("arm's length standards").

TAX ASPECTS OF INTERNATIONAL REORGANIZATIONS AND LIQUIDATIONS: THE UNITED STATES

Hugh J. Ault

The author is Professor of Law at Boston College Law School. He has written extensively in the field of taxation, with particular emphasis on United States International Taxation. He has lectured extensively on international tax topics both in the United States and abroad. He is co-author of a leading treatise on United States taxation.[1]

I. Introduction

International reorganizations and liquidations have two distinctive characteristics. First, property is often entering one tax jurisdiction and leaving another tax jurisdiction. Second, there is typically a change in the relation between the shareholders and the corporate organizations which are holding the assets in question. These special characteristics of international reorganizations and liquidations have required a series of special tax rules to ensure that the transfer of assets and change in shareholder relationship does not result in inappropriate tax consequences, leading to either undertaxation or overtaxation. The purpose of this paper is to describe those rules in the context of United States international taxation. In order to understand the specific United States rules dealing with international reorganizations and liquidations, it is first necessary to review briefly some of the basic principles of United States international taxation. Thereafter, the implications of these principles for international reorganizations and liquidations will be examined.

II. General Overview of United States International Tax Principles[1]

1. Worldwide Taxation

In principle, the United States taxes the worldwide income of its citizens and residents. A corporation is treated as a United States resident if it is organized in the United States; the management and control of the corporation is irrelevant to the determination of its taxable status. Correspondingly, if a corporation is organized outside the United States, it is treated as a foreign corporation, regardless of the fact that it may have its management and control in the United States.

2. Foreign Tax Credit

In order to accommodate the claims of source jurisdictions on income of United States citizens and residents arising abroad, the United States grants a credit for foreign income taxes imposed on foreign income. Through the mechanism of the credit, the United States, as the country of residence, cedes its taxing jurisdiction to the country of source. This is only true, however, where the income subject to foreign tax is viewed, from the perspective of the United States, as constituting foreign source income. If the foreign taxing jurisdiction asserts a source-based tax on income which is deemed, under United States principles, to be from United States sources, the foreign tax credit provides no relief from double taxation.

3. Deferral of Tax on Foreign Corporate Earnings

The logical conclusion of the principles discussed so far is that the foreign source income of a corporation organized abroad would not be subject to United States taxation when the income was earned. The United States tax would be deferred until the foreign corporation distributed the income to its United States shareholders as a dividend. Beginning in 1962, however, the United States began to tax the United States shareholders of United States-controlled foreign corporations on certain types of transactions. In general, so-called "base company" income from transactions with related parties and passive income were taxed directly to the United States shareholders. Of particular importance in the context of foreign liquidations and reorganizations, certain capital gains from the disposition of assets of a foreign corporation are included in the category of "tainted" income which could result in direct taxation to the United States shareholder.

4. Conversion of Ordinary Income into Capital Gains

Under normal United States tax principles, gain from the disposition of the shares of stock of a corporation are given preferential capital gains treatment, even where that gain in effect represents an increase in the value of the shares due to the undistributed corporate earnings. Thus, if no special rules applied, the United States shareholder in a foreign corporation could defer United States tax on the income as it was being earned currently (because it was being earned in a foreign corporation) and did not constitute "tainted" income as discussed above) and could then realize preferential capital gains on the sale of the shares. On the other hand, if the foreign earnings had been distributed as a dividend, they would have been taxable at ordinary rates.

In order to prevent the so-called "conversion" of potential dividend income into capital gain on the disposition of the shares of stock of a foreign corporation, special provisions require that the gain, to the extent of the undistributed earnings of the foreign corporation, must be treated as ordinary income rather than as preferential capital gains when realized by a United States shareholder in the foreign corporation. This provision only applies in the case of a ten percent or greater United States shareholder in a foreign corporation in which over 50% of the stock is held by United States persons (a "controlled foreign corporation".) It is of particular importance in the context of foreign reorganizations and liquidations since it is necessary to have special rules for situations in which, as a result of the reorganization, the taxpayer would be able to avoid the application of this principle.

5. Reorganization and Liquidation Principles

The United States tax rules dealing with liquidations and reorganizations are enormously complex. In very general terms, a transfer of assets in a reorganization results in no gain or loss to either the transferor corporation or the transferee corporation. The transferee corporation inherits the tax "basis" or cost of the transferor corporation in the assets. Similarly, if the shareholder exchanges shares in a corporation for shares of a second corporation in a reorganization transaction, no gain or loss is recognized on the share transaction and the shareholder retains as his basis for the new shares the basis which he had for the old shares. As a simple example, suppose that Corporation B is merged with Corporation A and Corporation A is the surviving corporation. The Corporation B assets will have been transferred to Corporation A and the old Corporation B shareholders will now be shareholders in Corporation A. Such a transaction would qualify as a tax-free reorganization with the tax results described above.

Corporate liquidations are subject to a different set of rules. Two points distinguish the

American liquidation rules from those of most other countries. In the first place, the corporation distributing its assets in liquidation in general realizes no gain should the assets which are distributed in liquidation have a fair market value in excess of their tax basis. The appreciation in the assets distributed in liquidation simply escapes tax at the corporate level. Second, in general, no attempt is made to tax the accumulated but undistributed profits of the corporation as a dividend to the shareholders. The entire liquidation transaction is treated as a capital gain from the point of view of the shareholder with gain being measured as the difference between his tax basis in the stock and the fair market value of the proceeds received. The shareholder in turn receives a new tax basis for the assets received in the liquidation equal to their fair market value. A special rule applies in the case of the liquidation of corporate subsidiaries. If a corporate shareholder owns at least 80% of the shares of a subsidiary, the liquidation of the subsidiary is tax-free to the corporate shareholder. Just as in the reorganization context, the shareholder inherits the subsidiary's basis in the underlying assets distributed in the liquidation.

Similar principles apply in the tax treatment of the formation of a corporation. In general terms, the transfer of property to a corporation in exchange for a controlling (80%) interest in the corporation does not require the recognition of gain or loss. The tax basis of the transferred assets carries over to the corporate transferee and the contributing shareholder has a basis in the stock of the corporation equal to the basis of the assets which were transferred to the corporation.

III. Outbound Transactions

1. General

If the principles described above were applied to reorganizations, liquidations, and corporate formations which involved a transfer of assets outside the United States taxing jurisdiction, it would be possible to avoid the United States tax on any appreciation in the assets transferred. For example, suppose a United States person transferred appreciated property to a foreign corporation in a transaction which qualified as a reorganization. After the transfer, the property would be held by a foreign corporation and, unless the special provisions concerning "tainted" income were applicable, the foreign corporation could dispose of the assets with no United States tax. A number of complex rules have been developed to limit the ability of the United States taxpayer to transfer appreciated assets outside of the jurisdiction without a current recognition of gain.

2. Basic Structure

Section 367(a) of the Internal Revenue Code provides that, where property is being transferred outside of the United States, the transferee foreign corporation will not be treated as a corporation (a precondition for the various non-recognition provisions described above) unless the taxpayer includes in income the gain attributable to certain types of assets.

Changes made by the Tax Reform Act of 1984 modified substantially the structure of Section 367. Under prior law, the taxpayer was required to obtain an advance ruling from the Internal Revenue Service that the purpose of the transfer of the assets abroad was not "tax avoidance". While the test was formulated in terms of a subjective determination of purpose, in fact the Internal Revenue Service had developed guidelines which utilize objective standards. Under the 1984 changes, the requirement that the taxpayer obtain a ruling with respect to the "outbound" reorganization or formation transaction was eliminated. Instead, the objective tests which the Internal Revenue Service had developed in its guidelines were made part of the statute and directly applicable to outbound transfers. More technically, Section 367 in principle makes all outbound transfers taxable. However, a series of exceptions are then made which, in effect, give tax-free treatment in a number of situations.

(a) Active Trade or Business. In general, gains will not be recognized on a transfer of property to a foreign corporation for use by such corporation in the active conduct of a trade or business outside the United States. However, the "active trade or business" exception does not apply to a number of specific types of assets. In particular, inventory, accounts receivable, foreign currency, and certain leased property are not covered by the exception. Thus, outbound transactions involving those types of property will result in the current recognition of gain. The basic theory here is that the gain attributable to assets which are likely to be sold, such as inventory, or collected, such as installment obligations or accounts receivable, should not be allowed to escape the United States taxing jurisdiction through the transfer to a foreign corporation. General business assets, such as machinery, equipment, etc., which will be used in the active trade or business can be transferred on a tax-free basis. But assets which are in the ordinary course of events likely to be disposed of or collected by the foreign corporation are not entitled to non-recognition treatment, despite the fact that they will be utilized in an active trade or business. Special rules apply for stock and securities and intangibles.

(b) Stock and Securities. Under prior law, the outbound transfer of stock or securities was in general not permitted. The Internal Revenue Service was concerned that stock or securities could be easily disposed of after they had left the United States taxing jurisdiction and accordingly was not willing to grant favorable rulings to such transfers. The 1984 amendments to Section 367 did not specifically deal with the treatment of stock and securities. However, the legislative history of the section indicates that stock and securities may qualify under the active trade or business exception. A typical case would be the transfer of stock which was to be used to insure a source of raw materials for the foreign transferee company. In addition, the legislative history indicates that regulations will provide for the tax-free transfer of the stock of an 80%-owned foreign corporation to a transferee foreign corporation which is organized in the same country. This will enable a United States corporation which has two "brother-sister" corporations in the same jurisdiction to transfer, on a tax-free basis, the stock of one of the subsidiaries to the other, thus creating a "parent-subsidiary" relationship in the foreign jurisdiction without a current imposition of United States tax.

The legislative history also indicates that the Internal Revenue Service will issue regulations whereby tax will not be imposed on the transfer of stock and securities which are not registered or traded and which represent a substantial interest in the corporation, provided that the United States transferor agrees that the stock or securities will not be disposed of by the foreign corporate transferee for a substantial period following the year of the transfer. If, despite such an agreement, the shares are disposed of, the United States transferor would be taxed on any income or gain from the disposition as if the disposition made by the foreign corporation had taken place in the year of the original transfer at fair market value. In addition, an interest charge would be added to the tax for the period between the initial transfer and the subsequent disposition.

(c) Transfers of Intangible Assets. Under prior law, the Internal Revenue Service guidelines required that outbound transfers of United States patents, trademarks, and similar intangibles could not be made on a tax-free basis if the assets were to be used in a foreign business producing goods for sale or consumption in the United States. In other circumstances, however, transfers of intangibles for use in connection with a foreign trade or business were permitted. The 1984 changes in Section 367 substantially reduce the circumstances in which transfers of intangibles can be made in a tax-free basis.

Intangibles are excepted from the class of assets which can be transferred for use in connection with an active trade or business. Thus, the fact that the intangible is being used in an active business will not entitle it to be transferred on a tax-free basis. In recognition of the fact that it is extremely difficult to value intangibles, no current tax is imposed on the transfer of an intangible in a corporate formation or reorganization transaction. Rather, the U.S. transferor will be deemed to receive a "reasonable" royalty over the life of the transferred intangible. In effect, the transaction is treated as if the United States person had entered into a licensing agreement with the foreign corporate transferee which provided for reasonable periodic royalties. However, the deemed royalty which is created under Section 367 by virtue of an outbound transfer of the intangibles is treated as United States source income. This has important implications for the foreign tax credit since the treatment of the royalties as United States source income will, in general terms, reduce the availability of the foreign tax credit for United States taxpayers. It is expected that in practice actual license agreements will be entered into rather than transfers which would be subject to the deemed license rules of Section 367. Actual licenses would generate foreign source income and be more beneficial from a foreign tax credit point of view.

A special rule applies if the transferred intangible is disposed of by the foreign corporate transferee. In that case, the United States transferor will be treated as having received a payment at the time the foreign transferee corporation disposes of the intangible. Similarly, if the United States person disposes of the stock in the foreign corporation to which the patent or other intangible was transferred, a portion of the sales price on the stock attributable to the value of the patent will be taxed as ordinary income and will be treated as income from United States sources.

The restrictive rules on the tax-free transfer of intangibles abroad were enacted because of Congressional concern with situations in which United States persons were deducting the developmental costs of the intangibles against United States source income. Then, at the point at which the intangible was developed and would begin to be profitable, the intangible would be transferred to a foreign corporation, thereby avoiding the United States tax on the income.

The statute has a very wide definition of "intangible," including patents, formulae, know-how, copyrights, tradenames and franchises. Systems and studies will constitute intangible property if they have a substantial value independent of the services of any individual. The legislative history indicates that goodwill and going concern value developed by branch operations abroad will not be treated as intangibles for purposes of Section 367. Thus, it would be possible to incorporate a successful foreign branch which had no actual intangibles and only operating assets without any current recognition of gain. Regulations will have to be issued demarcating the exact extent of the goodwill/going concern value exception to the intangibles rule.

3. <u>Outbound Liquidating Transactions</u>

As indicated above, a liquidating distribution of appreciated property by a United States corporation does not generally result in the recognition of gain or loss at the corporate level. As a result, prior to 1984, it was possible for a foreign parent corporation to liquidate a United States subsidiary and take the position that neither it nor the subsidiary recognized any gain or loss on the liquidating transaction. The foreign corporate parent would not be subject to tax since it had not received a dividend distribution from the United States subsidiary, and its gain on the difference between the assets which it received and its basis in the stock of the subsidiary would be a capital gain which did not arise in the conduct of a trade or business carried on by the foreign corporation in the United States. The United States subsidiary would escape tax because of the general rule that liquidating distributions do not result in income to the distributing corporation. Changes made in Section 367 in 1984 prevent this result. Under Section 367(e), a domestic corporation is required to recognize gain on liquidating distributions of appreciated property to foreign persons. Regulations will be issued under this Section which will provide that gains shall be recognized under principles similar to those involved in outbound transfers by United States persons generally described above.

4. Incorporation of Loss Branch

Since the United States taxes on a worldwide basis, technically, the transfer of a foreign branch to a foreign corporation in exchange for shares of the corporation constitutes an outbound transaction as the assets transferred are leaving the United States taxing jursdiction. Under prior law, the Internal Revenue Service had attempted to require that the taxpayer include in income the amount of any losses which branch operations had generated as a condition for the tax-free incorporation of the other assets in the branch. This position had been rejected by some court decisions and the 1984 changes to Section 367 adopt the Internal Revenue Service policy as a matter of statutory law. In general, if a foreign branch which has been operating at a loss is incorporated, gain will be recognized in an amount equal to the excess of the losses incurred by the foreign branch before the transfer over the taxable income derived by the foreign branch in any taxable year after the loss including the year of the transfer. Any gain on incorporation of the foreign branch which is required to be recognized under this rule will have a character determined with reference to the character of the previously incurred losses. It should be noted that the branch loss rule applies where the losses have been offset against foreign source income and not against United States source income. A special provision, Section 904(f), deals with this latter situation.

5. Partnerships

Under prior law, the transfer of partnership interests in the context of corporate formation or reorganizations was not clear. Under one analysis, the transfer of the partnership interest could be viewed as similar to the transfer of the share of stock. Alternatively, the transfer of a partnership interest could be seen as a transfer of the partner's pro rata interest in the underlying assets owned by the partnership. As a general rule, Section 367, after the 1984 changes, treats the transfer of a partnership interest as a transfer of the underlying assets. Thus, if the assets are to be used in the active conduct of a trade or business abroad, the outbound transfer of the partnership interest could be made on a tax-free basis. However, the legislative history indicates that limited partnership interest will be treated as shares of stock rather than as pro rata share of the underlying assets. This will make it more difficult for transfers of limited partnership interests to qualify under the active trade or business exception.

6. Procedural Requirements

As indicated above, it is no longer necessary for a taxpayer to receive a ruling from the Internal Revenue Service concerning the treatment of the outbound formation, liquidation or reorganization transaction. However, the United States person who transfers property to a foreign corporation in an outbound transaction is required to furnish to the Internal Revenue Service certain information, the exact nature of which is to be determined in regulations. Failure to comply with the notification requirement will result in a penalty equal to 25% of the amount of the gain realized on the exchange. In addition, failure to give notice extends the statute of limitations for purposes of taxes imposed on the exchange.

7. Effective Dates

The 1984 changes in the treatment of outbound transactions described above are in general effective for transfers made after January 1, 1985. There is a special rule for transfers of intangibles made after June 6, 1984 and before January 1, 1985, which, in effect, makes the new restrictive legislation applicable to such transfers.

IV. Inbound Transfers

The rules relating to inbound transactions are substantially less complicated than those applicable to outbound transfers. Since property is coming into, rather than leaving, the taxing jurisdiction, the concern with amounts escaping the tax base is not present. The principal concern in connection with inbound transfers is to insure that foreign profits which have been accumulated abroad are not converted into capital gains or allowed to escape tax altogether. In general, if the inbound transaction involves the liquidation of a foreign corporation, the United States shareholder will be required to treat as ordinary income (rather than as preferentially taxed capital gain) the amount of gain recognized which is attributable to earnings and profits which have been accumulated by the foreign corporation during the period that the United States person was a shareholder of the corporation. Thus, for example, suppose that the United States shareholder in a controlled foreign corporation has a tax cost of 100 for his shares. He receives a liquidating distribution of 140 and his share of the earnings and profits of the foreign corporation, which have been accumulated abroad without United States tax, is 25. In those circumstances, the United States shareholder would include 25 of the gain as ordinary income and the remaining 15 as capital gain. If the shareholder was a corporation, a foreign tax credit would be available for the foreign corporate level taxes paid on the amount included as ordinary income.

A special rule applies with respect to the liquidation of corporate subsidiaries. As indicated above, in general, the liquidation of a corporate subsidiary is tax-free. However, if the subsidiary is foreign, the liquidation will not be tax-free unless the United States shareholder agrees to include in income as a dividend its share of the accumulated but untaxed earnings of the foreign corporation. If the taxpayer so agrees, the remainder of the liquidation is on a tax-free basis. If the shareholder does not so agree, the liquidation is treated as taxable and the rule described above converting the gain on the transaction from capital gain to ordinary income is applicable. Which of these two methods of repatriating foreign profits is most advantageous depends on a number of variables, including the total amount of gain to be recognized, the amount of foreign profits, and foreign corporate level taxes which may have been imposed on such profits.

V. Wholly Foreign Transactions

1. General

Where reorganization and liquidation transactions involve only foreign corporations, there is by definition no movement of property outside the United States jurisdiction. On the other hand, the United States does have an interest in insuring that wholly foreign transactions do not result in the United States "losing" its tax claim on foreign earnings and profits which have arisen during the period in which a United States person has had a direct or indirect interest in the foreign corporation. As indicated above, the United States shareholder is in general taxed at ordinary income rates on the foreign earnings and profits when those profits are realized, and the provisions in this area are intended to insure that this tax cannot be avoided through a foreign reorganization.

This problem is illustrated in the following example. Suppose A, a U.S. person, is the sole shareholder of FC, a foreign corporation. FC has accumulated 1,000 of earnings on which no United States tax has been paid. FC is acquired by FP, a foreign, publicly-held corporation, in a transaction in which all of the assets of FC are transferred to FP and A receives 1% of the stock in FP in exchange for his FC stock as the result of the reorganization. If no special rules applied, the reorganization would be tax-free both to FC and to A. Since A now holds only 1% of the stock in FP, the special rules converting his gain on the sale of the shares from capital gain to ordinary income would no longer be applicable to a subsequent disposition of the FP shares. Those rules only apply to sales of shares by 10% or greater U.S. shareholders in a foreign corporation which is controlled by United States shareholder, neither of which condition is now present.

Situations of this type are dealt with in extensive regulations which have been issued under Section 367(b). The regulations apply two techniques. In some situations, the United States shareholder is required to include in income at the time of the reorganization the amount which would have been taxable to him as a dividend if a distribution had been made prior to the reorganization. In other cases, a mechanism is provided under which tax can be deferred as long as it is insured that the earnings will subsequently be taxed.

2. Current Inclusion Situations

In general, where a 10% or greater United States shareholder in a United States-controlled foreign corporation receives, in a reorganization transaction, stock of a foreign corporation which is not a controlled foreign corporation, then the United States shareholder must include in gross income his share of the post-1962 earnings and profits of the corporation attributable to the stock exchanged. Current gain recognition is required in this circumstance since, as indicated above, if gain was not recognized currently there would be no basis for imposing a tax on the subsequent disposition of the shares received in the reorganization exchange. This is due to the fact that the basic rule for taxing deferred earnings as ordinary income on the disposition of the shares of the stock only applies (a) if the disposing shareholder is a 10% or greater shareholder in the corporation and (b) the corporation itself is a controlled foreign corporation (or was a controlled foreign corporation any time in the past five years). In all situations in which these conditions are not met, the only way to insure that the earnings on which United States tax has been deferred will be properly taxed is to impose the tax at the time of the reorganization transaction.

3. Preservation of Earnings and Profits and Deficits.

In circumstances in which the stock received in the reorganization transaction is stock of a controlled foreign corporation and the recipient United States shareholder has a 10% or greater interest so that he will be taxed on disposition of the stock, it is still necessary to make an appropriate adjustment to earnings and profits to reflect the amounts which would have been taxed if the acquired corporation had been disposed of. In general, the regulations under Section 367 require that the earnings and profits referable to the shares exchanged be attributed to the shares received. This preserves the potential taxability of the earnings and profits of the acquired corporation. Thus, if the United States shareholder disposes of the stock of the acquiring corporation in a later transaction, he must, in effect, pay tax at ordinary rates on the portion of gain attributable to the earnings and profits of the acquired corporation which were attributed to the stock of the acquiring corporation. For example, assume that A owns all of the stock in F, a controlled foreign corporation. The assets of F are acquired by X, an unrelated foreign corporation which is a controlled foreign corporation, in a reorganization transaction and A receives X stock in exchange for his F Stock. The regulations under Section 367 require that F's earnings be attributed to the X stock which is received in the reorganization. If A subsequently sells the stock in X he will be taxed at ordinary rates on the amount of the F corporation earnings which were attributed to X stock.

Where lower tier reorganizations are involved which do not directly affect the interest of the United States shareholder, similar principles are applied to insure that the tax will be obtained on the earnings and profits of the lower tier corporation when the stock of the upper tier corporation is disposed of. Thus, suppose, for example, that A, a United States shareholder, owns all of the stock of F1 which in turn owns all of the stock of F2. F2 owns all of the stock of F3. If F2 transfers the stock of F3 in a reorganization transaction with an unrelated foreign corporation, appropriate adjustments will be made in the earnings and profits account of F2 to preserve the earnings of F3 on which United States tax has been deferred, so that those earnings can subsequently be taxed to A.

4. Procedural Requirements

There is no requirement that the taxpayer obtain a ruling with respect to the tax consequences of a reorganization involving only foreign corporations. However, the taxpayer is required to file a notification with his United States tax return describing the transaction which has been undertaken and calculating the various earnings and profits amounts and their attribution as described above. In addition, if the transaction is of a type which requires a current inclusion of an earnings and profits amount, such amount must be included or else the whole transaction will be treated as a taxable transaction.

It is important to note that the notification requirement must be satisfied even though the transaction is one on which no current tax is payable by the United States shareholder because the attribution of the earnings and profits preserves the earnings and profits for subsequent taxation. If the notification is not filed with the United States shareholder's tax return, then the Section 367 regulations have not been complied with and the foreign corporation will not be entitled to non-recognition treatment. This is especially important because the transfer of stock in a transaction which does not qualify as a reorganization would constitute "tainted" income which would be subject to current tax at the shareholder level under the provisions described in Section II.3. In the example given above, if the proper notification was not filed with A's tax return, all of the appreciation in the stock in F3 would have to be realized currently by A.

VI. Conclusion

While the technical rules described above are somewhat complex, their underlying philosophy is relatively straightforward. In the case of outbound transactions, limitations must be placed on the ability of the taxpayer to transfer assets outside the United States taxing jurisdiction without recognition of gain. In some countries this problem is solved by having a general rule that all outbound transactions result in immediate gain recognition. Rather than taking this approach, the United States has tried to distinguish between appropriate and inappropriate transfers. It allows the transfer of assets which will be used in an active trade or business to remain on a tax-free basis despite the fact that the assets are being transferred outside the United States taxing jurisdiction. Only assets which are likely to be sold or collected immediately are subject to immediate taxation. In this context, the transfer of intangibles represents a special problem and has required a special solution.

With respect to non-outbound transactions, the basic concern is to insure that the United States taxpayer will remain subject to potential ordinary income tax on amounts of foreign earnings on which United States tax has been deferred at the time of the reorganization transaction. If at all possible, no current recognition of income is required and various mechanisms are used to preserve the earnings and profit amount so that it may be taxed at a later date. If the preservation of the earnings and profits amount is not possible, for example, in the situation in which the stock in the acquiring corporation is not stock in a foreign controlled corporation, then current taxation is required.

FOOTNOTE

1. For a general discussion of the United States international tax system, *see* McDaniel and Ault, *Introduction to United States International Taxation* (Kluwer 1980). A French edition is also available, *Introduction à la Fiscalité Internationale Américaine* (Kluwer 1981).

RÉSUMÉ EN FRANÇAIS

LES ASPECTS FISCAUX DES RÉORGANISATIONS ET DES LIQUIDATIONS INTERNATIONALES: L'APPROCHE DES ÉTATS-UNIS

Lorsqu'il y a réorganisation et liquidation internationale, il est souvent question de transfert de biens d'une juridiction fiscale à une autre. De plus, souvent les intérêts que détient l'actionnaire dans la société en réorganisation changent et, par contrecoup, il en est de même de la nature des droits des actionnaires. Par exemple, une fusion de la société X du pays X avec la société Y du pays Y, sachant que la société du pays Y est celle qui demeure opérationnelle, signifiera que l'actif qui était auparavant soumis à l'impôt du pays X sera dorénavant soumis à celui du pays Y. De la même façon, les actionnaires du pays X détiennent alors des actions de la société Y, laquelle est une société étrangère à leur égard.

Les États-Unis appliquent un grand nombre de dispositions fiscales complexes à ces opérations. Le rapport présenté ici, traite d'abord des principes généraux de la fiscalité internationale nord-américaine ainsi que des dispositions internes relatives aux réorganisations et aux liquidations. Les aspects internationaux d'une réorganisation et d'une liquidation sont ensuite examinés. En général, si la formation, la liquidation ou la réorganisation implique le transfert d'actif en dehors de la juridiction fiscale des États-Unis, ce transfert est assujetti à l'impôt et toute appréciation de la valeur de l'actif en question devrait être reconnue même si l'existence de certaines dispositions auraient permis, en temps normal, d'exonérer cette transaction d'impôt. Toutefois, il y a un certain nombre d'exceptions à cette règle de base. Généralement, le profit ne sera pas reconnu au cours d'un transfert d'un bien à une société étrangère si le bien en question est utilisé par la société comme moyen d'exploitation de son activité commerciale ordinaire à l'extérieur des États-Unis. Toutefois, cette règle ne s'applique pas aux transferts d'actions ou de valeurs puisqu'il est fort possible que ces actifs soient vendus par la société étrangère afin d'échapper à l'impôt américain. De même, les transferts d'actifs incorporels comme les licences etc., sont aussi imposables au moment de leur execution. Le cédant américain est présumé recevoir une royaltie raisonnable couvrant la durée de vie de l'actif incorporel. En fait, la transaction est traitée comme si la personne résidante aux États-Unis avait conclu un contrat de licence avec la société cessionnaire étrangère. Par ailleurs, il existe des règles spéciales applicables à l'actif transféré qui était utilisé dans une filiale étrangère dont les opérations étaient déficitaires.

Différents principes entrent en jeu lorsque la réorganisation implique des transferts vers les États-Unis plutôt qu´à partir des États-Unis. Dans ces circonstances, des règles précises sont appliquées pour que les impôts sur les profits qui ont été accumulés à l´étranger par la société qui effectue le transfert de ses biens aux États-Unis soient acquittés par les actionnaires Américains.

Enfin, lorsque les transactions de réorganisation et de liquidation ne concernent que les sociétés étrangères, il n'y a, par définition, ni entrée ni sortie de biens des États-Unis. Il serait toutefois préférable de prévoir d'autres règles pour ce cas en particulier de façon à ce que les États-Unis puissent s'assurer le droit d'imposer les actionnaires américains dont les intérêts au sein de la société en réorganisation ont changés. Par exemple, la réorganisation pourrait avoir pour conséquence que la société ne serait plus soumise au contrôle des actionnaires américains si leurs intérêts dans la société absorbante tombaient au dessous d'un certain niveau. Pour ce cas, en particulier, il existe des règles spéciales selon lesquelles, s'il y a disposition d'actions acquises au cours de la transaction relative à la réorganisation, les actionnaires américains seront imposés de la même façon qu'ils l'auraient été si la société étrangère était encore sous le contrôle des États-Unis.

RESUMEN EN ESPAÑOL

ASPECTOS FISCALES DE REORGANIZACIONES Y DE LIQUIDACIONES INTERNATIONALES: LOS ESTADOS UNIDOS

Cuando se realizan reorganizaciones y liquidaciones internationales, frecuentemente se trata de la transferencia de bienes de una jurisdicción a otra. Además, los intereses de los accionistas interesados en la reorganización suelen cambiar, cambiando consecuentemente la naturaleza de los derechos accionarios. Por ejemplo, la fusión de una sociedad X, de un país X, con una sociedad Y, de un país Y, sabiendo que la sociedad del país Y es la que permanecerá operativa, significa que el activo que antes se encontraba sometido a los impuestos del país X quedará ahora sometido a las normas del país Y. De igual manera, los accionistas del país X poseen ahora acciones de la empresa Y, que para ellos es una empresa extranjera.

Los Estados Unidos ofrecen un gran número de disposiciones fiscales complejas aplicables a estas operaciones. El presente informe comienza por tratar los principios generales de tasación internacional norteamericana, así como las disposiciones internas relativas a reorganizaciones y liquidaciones. Luego trata los aspectos internacionales de reorganizaciones y de liquidaciones. En general si la formación, la liquidación o la reorganización implican la transferencia del activo fuera de la jurisdicción fiscal de los Estados Unidos, tal transferencia queda sujeta a impuesto y la apreciación del valor del activo en cuestión deberá ser reconocida, aun ante la existencia de ciertas disposiciones que en transacciones normales hubieran resultado en la exención del impuesto. De todos modos existen ciertas excepciones a esta regla básica. En general el impuesto no será aplicable a la transferencia de un bien a otra empresa extranjera, si el bien en cuestión es utilizado por la empresa como un medio de explotación de su actividad comercial ordinaria en el exterior de los Estados Unidos. Sin embargo, esta regla no se aplica a la transferencia de acciones o de valores, dado que es muy posible que tales activos sean vendidos por la sociedad extranjera con el fin de evitar el impuesto americano. Igualmente, la transferencia de activos incorporales como licencias, etc., son también imponibles al momento de su transferencia. Se presume que el cedente americano recibe una regalía razonable que cubre la duración del activo incorporal. En efecto, la transacción se trata como si la persona residente en los Estados Unidos hubiese concluído un contrato de licencia con la empresa cesionaria extranjera. Además, existen reglas especiales aplicables al activo transferido que ha sido utilizado en una filial extranjera cuyas operaciones han sido deficitarias.

Diferentes principios entran en juego cuando la reorganización implica la transferencia hacia los Estados Unidos antes que desde los Estados Unidos. En estas circunstancias hay normas especiales para que los impuestos sobre las ganancias que han sido acumulados en el extranjero, por la empresa que transfiere sus bienes a los Estados Unidos, sean pagados por los accionistas americanos.

Finalmente, cuando las transacciones de reorganización y de liquidación sólo conciernen a empresas extranjeras, no hay, por definición, ni entrada a, ni salida de bienes de los Estados Unidos. Sería siempre preferible prever otras reglas para casos particulares para que los Estados Unidos puedan tasar a los accionistas americanos cuyos intereses en el seno de la sociedad han cambiado. Por ejemplo, la reorganización podría tener como consecuencia que la sociedad no quede ya sometida al control de los accionistas americanos si sus intereses en la sociedad fusionante caen por debajo de un cierto nivel. Para este caso en particular, existen reglas especiales por las cuales, ante la disposición de acciones adquiridas en el curso de la transacción relativa a la reorganización, los accionistas americanos quedan sujetos a impuesto de la misma manera que si la sociedad extranjera estuviese sujeta al control de los Estados Unidos.

UNITED STATES INCOME TAX AND REORGANIZATION POLICIES APPLICABLE TO MULTINATIONAL ENTERPRISES

Stanley Siegel

The author is Professor of Law at the University of California, Los Angeles, where he teaches courses in Business Associations, Income Taxation and Accounting. He is the author of texts on Enterprise Organization and Accounting and Financial Disclosure, as well as numerous articles and reviews. Professor Siegel was the draftsman of the Michigan Business Corporation act. He holds a B.S. from New York University and a J.D. degree from Harvard. Professor Siegel is also a Certified Public Accountant.

Throughout this paper, the principles of taxation are illustrated with respect to corporations, since most multinational enterprises (MNE) will use the corporate form. Some of the principles also apply in whole or in part to other forms, such as partnerships and unincorporated joint ventures. However, since the U.S. Internal Revenue Code (IRC) treats corporations and partnerships quite differently, the rules may vary substantially when a MNE uses other than the corporate form.

I. Principles of Income Taxation Applicable to United States Based Multinational Enterprises:

A. Taxation of United States Source Income:

1. In general, all income of a U.S. corporation, from whatever source derived, is subject to taxation. IRC § 61(a). The items of includible gross income (with a few exceptions) are the same for all taxpayers. These include such items as compensation for services, gross income from business, interest, royalties, rents and the like.

2. In general, taxable income is calculated by subtracting from gross income, as broadly defined in IRC § 61(a), a series of defined deductions, as provided in IRC §§ 161-196, 241-250. These deductions include ordinary and necessary trade and business expenses -- IRC § 162 -- as well as a list of specifically detailed and delimited deductions, such as interest (§ 163), certain taxes (§ 164), and depreciation (§§ 167-169). Certain expenditures are specifically disallowed as deductions, such as capital expenditures (§ 263). See generally IRC §§ 264-280G).

3. The income tax is therefore imposed on taxable income, which can generally be defined as gross income less deductions. Because of complexities in tax policy, taxable income is rarely the same as net income

for accounting purposes. The tax rate is progressive for the smallest of corporations; under IRC § 11, the corporation's taxable income is taxed as follows:

15% of the first $25,000;
18% of the next $25,000;
30% of the next $25,000;
40% of the next $25,000;
46% of all in excess of $100,000.

However, corporations with taxable income in excess of $1 million are effectively taxed at a flat rate of 46%.

4. Capital gains -- gains from the sale of capital assets and certain property used in the trade or business (IRC §§ 1221, 1231) are taxed under IRC §1201(a) at an alternate rate of 28% of the net capital gain.

B. <u>Taxation of Foreign Source Income</u>:

1. Generally, citizens of the U.S., including domestic corporations, are taxed on their worldwide income under IRC § 61(a). With respect to corporations, the principal exception to this rule concerns Foreign Sales Corporations (FSC), discussed under III(B), below. Special rules also govern domestic corporations that derive income from sources within United States possessions.

2. In computing taxable income and paying the required income tax, United States dollar amounts must be used. Neither the Internal Revenue Code nor the IRS regulations specify the method of conversion, but a variety of methods have been accepted. These include methods based on individual transactions and methods based on conversion of the ultimate profit or loss figure for the period.

The exchange rate is also not prescribed, but in general when a currency transfer takes place the actual rate governs. See Rev.Rul. 64-307, 1964-2 Cum.Bul. 163.

3. For tax purposes, foreign currencies are treated as property. See Rev.Rul. 74-7, 1974-1 Cum.Bul. 198. As a result, gains or losses on foreign currencies will be treated like other items of income or expense.

4. In 1981, the Treasury Department made proposals with respect to foreign exchange gains and

losses. See Ann. 81-4, 1981-2 IRB 37. For commentaries on these proposals, see ABA Section of Taxation, Report on the US Treasury Department Discussion Draft on Taxing Foreign Exchange Gains and Losses, 36 Tax L.Rev. 425 (1981); Newman, Tax Consequences of Foreign Currency Transactions, 36 Tax Lawyer 223 (1983).

C. The Foreign Tax Credit:

1. The foreign tax credit (IRC §§ 901-908) was designed to mitigate the double-tax effects of a U.S. corporation paying tax on its foreign-source income while simultaneously paying U.S. taxes on the same income. In general, it provides a credit, or offset, against the U.S. income tax payable, based on the amount of foreign tax paid or accrued for the year.

2. The credit is available to domestic corporations, citizens and resident aliens. Usually, no credit would be available to foreign corporations, since they pay no U.S. tax on foreign source income. However, when U.S. tax is payable by virtue of realization of foreign income "effectively connected" with the conduct of a trade or business within the U.S., then foreign income taxes allocable to that income -- except taxes payable to the corporation's home country -- will qualify for the credit (IRC § 906). [The foreign source rules, including the "effectively connected" concept, are discussed at II(B), below.]

3. The foreign tax credit is elective, and may be elected from year to year. An alternative to taking the foreign tax credit is to take a deduction for foreign taxes paid under IRC § 164(a)(3). The credit and the deduction are mutually exclusive: if the taxpayer elects to take advantage of the foreign tax credit to any extent, it is denied all deductions for income, war profits or excess profits taxes imposed by any foreign country for that year. See IRC § 275(a)(4) In most circumstances, the foreign tax credit will be more advantageous, since it directly reduces taxes dollar-for-dollar, rather than reducing taxable income. The credit will therefore usually be worth approximately twice the deduction.

4. In order to qualify for the credit, the amount paid must be an income, war profits or excess profits tax imposed by a foreign country or a U.S. possession. Interpretive problems have arisen concerning the meaning of "tax" and the nature of the tax. The IRS has taken the position that the tax must be the

substantial equivalent of the income tax imposed in the United States in order to qualify for the credit. See Rev.Rul. 78-61, 1978-1 Cum.Bul. 221.

5. The foreign tax credit is available only to the extent of the U.S. tax that would be allocable to the foreign-source income of the taxpayer. IRC § 904(a). Any unused credit is carried back 2 years and carried forward 5 years to offset the tax payable in those years, subject to the same allocation limits.

6. In order to avoid a host of potential abuses, separate allocation rules are applicable to certain interest income and dividends from a DISC or FSC. IRC § 904(d).

7. A form of indirect foreign tax credit is available by virtue of IRC § 902, which provides for a foreign tax credit on dividends received by a U.S. corporation which owns at least 10% of the voting stock of a foreign corporation. In operation, § 902 effectively treats the recipient U.S. corporation as though it had paid any foreign taxes allocable to the earnings thereby distributed by the foreign corporation. Within certain limitations, similar rules are applicable to second and lower-tier foreign corporations.

II. Principles of Income Taxation Applicable to Foreign Based Multinational Enterprises:

A. Taxation of United States Source Income:

1. The basic tax structure calls for three levels of taxation:

(i) Dividends, interest, royalties and other fixed or determinable annual or periodic income from U.S. sources are subject to a withholding tax at a flat rate of 30%, without any deduction for costs or other expenses involved in obtaining such income. IRC § 881(a)(1). Certain items are excluded from this category, including nontaxable income (e.g., interest on municipal bonds) and interest on domestic bank and insurance deposits (which are categorized as foreign-source income). Also excluded from this category is "effectively connected" income, discussed below. The 1984 Tax Reform Act repeals this tax as to newly-issued obligations, as noted below.

(ii) Capital gains, with certain exceptions, are effectively excluded from taxation. However, "effectively connected" gross income will be taxed under IRC § 882, as discussed below. Also taxed, under very complex provisions designed to deal with various tax-avoidance schemes, are gains or losses from the disposition of U.S. real property interests. IRC § 897.

(iii) A foreign corporation engaged in a trade or business in the U.S. during the taxable year is taxed on its taxable income "which is effectively connected with the conduct of a trade or business within the United States," on the same basis -- and at the same tax rates -- as a U.S. corporation. IRC § 882.

2. The 1984 Tax Reform Act added IRC § 881(c), which repeals the 30% withholding tax as to "portfolio interest" with respect to portfolio obligations issued after July 18, 1984. As noted below, this tax had already been reduced or eliminated with respect to some nations by means of bilateral tax treaties. "Portfolio interest" is defined essentially to include interest paid on obligations the beneficial owner of which is -- under stated procedures -assured of not being a U.S. person.

3. The concept of "trade or business within the United States" is not clearly defined in the IRC or the Regulations. Ordinarily, the test will be whether the profit-oriented activities are sufficiently regular, substantial and continuous. In the case of a MNE -- as contrasted with a foreign individual -- the line is often easily drawn. The "effectively connected" test is elaborated in IRC § 864(c), which sets forth various criteria including the following:

(i) As to capital gains, or periodic income, the factors to be considered are whether the income, gain or loss is derived from assets used or held in the conduct of a trade or business; or the activities of such trade or business were a material factor in the realization of the income, gain or loss.

(ii) All other income, gain or loss from sources within the U.S. is treated as effectively connected with the conduct of a trade or business within the U.S.

(iii) Detailed criteria are set forth in IRC § 864(c)(4) to determine when foreign-source income is "effectively connected." See II(B), below.

4. The U.S. has entered into bilateral tax treaties with many nations, the terms of which affect -- in varying ways --the tax results noted above. These treaties, pursuant to the U.S. Constitution, take precedence over all prior statutes. See also IRC § 894. Although the treaty terms vary widely, many reduce the tax payable on dividends (often to 15%, and reduced further to 5% on intercorporate dividends); provide residence nation taxation of interest, royalties and capital gains; and provide taxation of business net income by the host nation only if the corporation maintains a permanent establishment therein. See U.S. Department of Treasury, Model Income Tax Treaty (May 17, 1977), 1 CCH Tax Treaties, Par. 153.

B. Calculation and Taxation of Foreign Source Income:

1. Income is characterized as foreign-source or domestic-source, for a variety of purposes. IRC §§ 861-864 prescribe rules for characterization of gross income. Domestic-source taxable income is determined by deducting the following items from domestic-source gross income, pursuant to IRC § 861(b):

(i) Expenses, losses and other deductions "properly apportioned or allocated thereto," and

(ii) "A ratable part" of any expenses, losses and other deductions that cannot be definitely allocated to an item or class of gross income. Similar rules are prescribed for foreign-source taxable income in IRC § 862(b), and for income partly from domestic and partly from foreign sources in IRC § 863(b). Treasury regulations further implement each of these sections.

2. The source allocation rules embody different tests for a variety of different forms of gross income, and provide general rules for unspecified income items. Illustrative of the specified items are the following:

(i) Interest: In general, the residence of the obligor governs, irrespective of the location of payment of the interest or of the transaction giving rise to the debt. IRC § 861(a)(1). However, interest on bank deposits or on insurance proceeds received by a foreign corporation is foreign-source income unless it is "effectively connected" with the corporation's U.S. trade or business.

(ii) Dividends: Dividends paid by a domestic corporation are domestic-source income. IRC § 861(a)(2). An exception to this rule is a domestic corporation that derives less than 20% of its gross income from domestic sources during the preceding three-year period. Also excepted are DISC's and FSC's, discussed in III(B) below. With respect to a foreign corporation, if 50% or more of its gross income for the preceding three years was "effectively connected with the conduct of a trade or business within the United States," the dividends are allocated pro rata between domestic and foreign-source income.

(iii) Personal services: Compensation for labor and services rendered in the United States is domestic-source income; compensation for labor and services rendered outside the U.S. is foreign-source income. IRC § 861(a)(3). To the extent services are rendered within and without the U.S., an allocation must be made based on appropriate factors. E.g., Rev.Rul. 76-66, 1976-1 Cum.Bul. 189; Rev.Rul. 77-167, 1977-1 Cum.Bul. 239.

(iv) Sales of personal property: In general, the place of sale governs. Thus if the property was purchased outside the U.S. and sold within the U.S., the income is domestic-source. See IRC § 861(a) (6). Correspondingly, if the property was purchased within the U.S. and sold outside the U.S., the income is deemed foreign-source. See IRC § 862(a)(6). This issue has been greatly clouded by tax-avoidance devices, and has been heavily litigated.

(v) Other items: Apart from the specific rules in IRC §§ 861, 862, there are few general guidelines. Where the IRC does not specify, the IRS generally looks to situs of property or activities that resulted in the income. See Rev.Rul. 73-252, 1973-1 Cum.Bul. 337. See also IRC § 863(a).

3. The problem of allocation of gross income from manufacturing and other mixed sources is addressed by IRC § 863(b) and the regulations thereunder. Often, the problem arises from manufacture of goods within the U.S. and sale of the goods outside of the U.S.; similar problems arise when the manufacturing

process is divided between domestic and foreign operations. The IRC allows for allocation of the taxable income in accordance with processes or formulas of general apportionment prescribed by the IRS. These include (under the regulations) allocation by independent factory price; by allocation one-half to place of sale and the remaining half by reference to the value of taxpayer's domestic and foreign property; or by allocation pursuant to taxpayer records satisfactory to the IRS.

4. Foreign-source income is deemed "effectively connected" with a U.S. trade or business, and is therefore subject to U.S. taxation, in only a sharply limited set of circumstances, as set forth in IRC § 864(c)(4). The corporation must have an office or other fixed place of business within the U.S. to which such income, gain or loss is attributable; and, in addition, the income, gain or loss must be in one of three categories:

(i) Rents or royalties for the use of trademarks, patents, copyrights or similar properties derived in the active conduct of the trade or business;

(ii) Dividends, interest or capital gains derived from the active conduct of a banking or financing business within the U.S.; or

(iii) Profits from the sale of stock in trade, unless sold for foreign use and a foreign office of the taxpayer participated materially in the sale.

The above rules are aimed primarily at tax-abuse and tax-haven transactions, intended to avoid U.S. taxation.

III. Special Problems Posed by Certain Corporate Structures:

A. The Controlled Foreign Corporations (CFC):

1. As noted above, the foreign-source income of a foreign corporation is not subject to U.S. income taxes except to the extent that it is "effectively connected" with the conduct of a U.S. trade or business. This fact offers substantial tax-planning potential. A domestic corporation doing business abroad might consider organizing a foreign subsidiary, with the result that the income thereof would not be

subject to U.S. taxation until such time as it is distributed to the U.S. parent company in the form of dividends. This arrangement would be particularly advantageous if the foreign subsidiary were incorporated in a country with no taxes on income or low taxes thereon.

2. Subpart F of the IRC, §§ 951-964, is primarily concerned with the use of controlled foreign corporations as devices to avoid or defer the imposition of U.S. taxes on income. A controlled foreign corporation (CFC) is defined as a foreign corporation more than 50% of whose voting power is owned by U.S. shareholders on any day of the taxable year. IRC § 957(a). Such a shareholder, to be included in the definition, must own 10% or more of the corporation's voting power.

3. To the extent that a CFC has "Subpart F income" or increases in earnings invested in U.S. property during the taxable year, such income is taxed pro rata to the U.S. shareholders when earned, irrespective of the date of distribution. In other words, the ability to defer income is lost. The definitions of both forms of income are essentially directed to preventing the use of CFC's as tax havens.

4. Subpart F income is defined in IRC §§ 952, 954 primarily to include foreign base company income -- the use of corporations established in foreign tax-haven jurisdictions to avoid current payment of taxes both to the U.S. and to foreign countries. As an example, goods manufactured in the U.S. are sold to a CFC based in a tax-haven nation, which CFC, in turn, resells the goods to another foreign corporation. Adjustment of the sales prices between the controlled companies results in income being recognized primarily by the tax-haven corporation, with resultant deferral or avoidance of tax on a substantial portion of the income. In this case, the income would be categorized as Subpart F income (profit realized on sale of goods purchased from a related person, where the goods were neither produced nor consumed in the CFC country).

B. The Foreign Sales Corporation (FSC) [Formerly the Domestic International Sales Corporation - DISC]:

1. The concept of the DISC was originally created to provide incentive for United States exports by allowing deferral of tax for certain foreign sales

activities. A portion of the income of a qualified DISC would be taxed solely to its shareholders and only when actually distributed. IRC §§ 991-997. Among the qualifications for DISC treatment -- apart from a DISC election -- were the requirements that 95% of the gross receipts be qualified export receipts (receipts from sale of U.S. produced property for consumption outside the U.S.) and 95% of the DISC assets be qualified export assets (sales and packaging assets, receivables and working capital). Since the DISC provisions were enacted, they have been the subject of dispute by some of the members of GATT, who have argued that they constitute an illegal export subsidy. The new FSC provisions are in response to the GATT objections.

2. The Tax Reform Act of 1984 replaces the DISC with the Foreign Sales Corporation (FSC). In general, a FSC will be exempt from federal income tax, and dividends received therefrom by a domestic corporation attributable to certain foreign trade income will be subject to a 100% dividends received deduction. As a result, no tax will be imposed at the corporate level on such foreign trade income. See IRC §§ 921-927.

3. In order to qualify for FSC treatment, the FSC will be required to be a foreign corporation, have a foreign presence, have economic substance, and perform the activities related to its export income outside the U.S. customs territory. The exempt foreign trade income is treated as foreign-source income which is not "effectively connected" with the conduct of a trade or business within the U.S.

GENERAL REFERENCES

1. B. Bittker, Federal Income Taxation of Income, Estates and Gifts (Little, Brown & Co., 1981, with supplements), Chapters 65-70.

2. Research Institute of America, Complete Analysis of the '84 Tax Reform Act (1984), pp. 547-631.

3. Bureau of National Affairs, BNA Tax Management Portfolios (various) on Foreign Income Taxation.

RÉSUMÉ EN FRANÇAIS

L'IMPÔT AMÉRICAIN SUR LE REVENU ET PRINCIPES DE RESTRUCTURATION APPLICABLES AUX MULTINATIONALES

L'article qui précède présente les grands principes de la législation fédérale américaine relative à l'impôt sur le revenu dans leur application aux multinationales. Les multinationales opérant aux États-Unis sont imposées comme le serait une société américaine: tout revenu, quelle que soit sa source, est imposable. Généralement, le revenu imposable est calculé en effectuant certaines déductions du revenu brut. Les principes applicables au calcul du revenu imposable sont similaires, mais non identiques, à ceux employés pour déterminer le revenu net en comptabilité financière.

Aux États-Unis, les sociétés, comme tout citoyen, sont tenues de payer des impôt sur leurs revenus de toute provenance. Les revenus doivent être convertis en dollars américains selon différents moyens de conversion. Les problèmes inhérents à la possibilité d'une imposition multiple du revenu de source étrangère sont, dans une certaine mesure, mitigés par le crédit d'impôt étranger. Ce crédit contrebalance les impôts payables par les sociétés aux États-Unis, compte tenu du montant de l'impôt payé à l'étranger ou accumulé pendant l'année. Le crédit d'impôt étranger n'est offert qu'aux sociétés américaines et il est facultatif: une société a le choix de déduire l'impôt de source étrangère de son revenu imposable. En règle générale, il est préférable de choisir l'option du crédit d'impôt étranger à celle de la déduction. Les sociétés domiciliées à l'étranger sont assujetties à trois niveaux d'imposition; i) 30% d'impôt à la source sur les dividendes, les intérêts, les royalties et autres revenus périodiques fixes de sources américaines; ii) le revenu "qui est intimement relié à l'exploitation d'un commerce à l'intérieur des États-Unis" est imposable comme le serait le revenu perçu par une société américaine; iii) les plus-values en capital, qui ne sont pas généralement assujetties à l'impôt, pourraient l'être si elles étaient considérées comme étant un revenu brut "intimement relié" ou, dans des circonstances complexes, si elles représentaient des gains provenant de la disposition de biens aux États-Unis. Le TAX REFORM ACT de 1984 a annulé les 30% d'impôt à la source sur "les intérêts en portefeuille" pour ce qui est des obligations en portefeuille émises après le 18 juillet 1984.

Le concept "d'un commerce ou d'une entreprise à l'intérieur des États-Unis" n'est pas défini avec précision. En général, il faudrait déterminer si les activités à but lucratif sont assez régulières, importantes et continues à l'intérieur des États-Unis. Ce pays est partie à un grand nombre de traités bilatéraux de double imposition, dont les dispositions affectent de façons différentes les règles d'impôt que nous venons de citer. D'une façon générale, ce genre de traités prévoient: 1) une réduction de l'impôt payable sur les dividendes; 2) les critères de détermination du pays de résidence pour autoriser à payer les intérêts, les royalties et les plus-values; et 3) l'imposition du revenu net d'une activité commerciale n'est imposable par le pays hôte que si la société y maintient une résidence permanente.

Dans la mesure où une société étrangère est assujettie à l'impôt des États-Unis elle n'est imposée que sur son "revenu de source étrangère," lequel est calculé en suivant différentes règles pour chaque catégorie de revenus. Ainsi, par exemple, en matière d'intérêts, la source de revenu est considérée comme étant la résidence du débiteur. Lorsqu'il s'agit de revenu personnel découlant d'un service, la source est celle du lieu où les services ont été rendus. Les problèmes de la détermination de la source sont mentionnés dans le Code des impôts (Internal Revenue Code, section 863(b)) et dans la règlementation d'application.

Il existe des règles d'impôt précises relatives aux "Controlled Foreign Corporations" (sociétés appartenant en majorité à des étrangers), Internal Revenue Code section 951-964, et aux "Foreign Sales Corporations" (société de droit américain dont le but social est la promotion des ventes à l'étranger), Internal Revenue Code section 921-927.

RESUMEN EN ESPAÑOL

IMPUESTO AMERICANO A LOS RÉDITOS Y PRINCIPIOS DE REESTRUCTURACIÓN APLICABLES A LAS MULTINACIONALES

Este artículo presenta los principios más importantes de la legislación federal americana sobre el impuesto a los réditos aplicable a las multinacionales. Las multinacionales que operan en los Estados Unidos tributan de la misma manera que una empresa americana: todo rédito, cualquiera sea su fuente, está sujeto a impuesto. Generalmente el rédito imponible se calcula efectuando ciertas deducciones al rédito bruto. Los principios aplicables al cálculo del rédito imponible son similares, mas no idénticos, a aquéllos empleados en determinar el rédito neto en contabilidad financiera.

En los Estados Unidos las empresas, como todo ciudadano, deben pagar impuestos sobre sus réditos sin distinción en cuanto a origen. Los réditos deben ser convertidos en dólares según diferentes medios de conversión. Los problemas inherentes a la posibilidad de una imposición múltiple sobre réditos de fuente extranjera, son mitigados en cierta manera por el crédito sobre impuestos extranjeros. Este crédito compensa los impuestos a pagar por las empresas a los Estados Unidos, teniendo en cuenta el monto del impuesto pagado en el extranjero o acumulado durante el año. El crédito por impuesto extranjero sólo se ofrece a empresas americanas y es facultativo: una empresa tiene la opción de deducir el impuesto de fuente extranjera de su rédito imponible. Como regla general, es preferible elegir la opción de crédito por impuesto extranjero antes que la opción de deducción. Las empresas domiciliadas en el extranjero están sujetas a tres niveles de imposición; i) 30% de impuesto en la fuente sobre los dividendos, intereses, regalías y otros réditos periódicos fijos de fuente americana; ii) el rédito "que está íntimamente ligado a la explotación de un comercio en el interior de los Estados Unidos" es imponible como lo sería el rédito percibido por una empresa americana; iii) la plusvalía en capital, que normalemente no se halla sujeta a impuesto, podría estarlo si se la considera como un rédito bruto "íntimamente ligado" o, en ciertos casos complejos, si representa ganancias provenientes de la disposición de intereses y bienes en los Estados Unidos. EL TAX REFORM ACT de 1984 ha anualdo el 30% de impuesto en la fuente sobre "los intereses en cartera" en lo que respecta a las obligaciones en cartera emitidas luego de julio 18 de 1984.

El concepto de "un comercio o una empresa en el interior de los Estados Unidos" no está definido con precisión. En general, haría falta determinar si las actividades con fines de lucro son suficientemente regulares, importantes y continuas en el interior de los Estados Unidos. Este país es parte de un gran número de tratados bilaterales sobre doble imposición, cuyas disposiciones afectan en forma diferente las reglas impositivas que hemos citado. En forma general, esta clase de tratados contempla: 1) una reducción del impuesto pagable sobre los dividendos; 2) criterios sobre la deteminación del país de residencia para autorizar el pago de intereses, regalías y plus valía; y 3) la imposición del rédito neto de una actividad comercial no es una facultad del país receptor, a no ser que la empresa mantenga allí una residencia permanente.

En la medida en que una empresa extranjera se encuentre sujeta a impuestos de Estados Unidos, la misma sólo tributa sobre su "rédito de fuente extranjera", el que se calcula siguiendo las diferentes reglas correspondientes a cada categoría de rédito. De tal forma, por ejemplo, en materia de intereses la fuente del rédito se considera la residencia del deudor. Cuando se trata del rédito personal originado en la prestación de un servicio, la fuente es aquélla donde tales servicios han sido prestados. Los problemas de la determinación de la fuente se mencionan en el Código de Réditos interno, o Código impositivo (Internal Revenue Code, section 863 (b)) y en su decreto reglamentario.

Existen reglas impositivas precisas relativas a las "Controlled Foreign Corporations" (empresas con mayoría perteneciente a extranjeros), Internal Revenue Code section 951-964, y a las "Foreign Sales Corporations" (empresas americanas cuyo objeto social es la promoción de ventas en el extranjero), Internal Revenue Code section 921-927.

THE FRENCH TAX SYSTEM

Jean-François Serval

At the age of 23, Mr. J. F. SERVAL was the youngest ever graduated French Expert-Comptable. He was listed as a professional when he reached the minimum legal age of 25. He joined Cabinet Constantin, a French C.P.A. firm, as a partner in 1971. Under his supervision, the firm in which he is one of the two principal partners rapidly expanded, becoming the auditor of some of the most important and prestigious French companies. He established throughout Europe a network of branches and correspondents for Cabinet Constantin. In 1982, after years of approaches and studies of the U.S. market anticipating the resurgence of the American economy, he reactivated the New York office of Leon Constantin and Co., which had become dormant after the death of Leon Constantin in 1973. He now shares his time between the U.S. and France and is responsible for all the international operations of Leon Constantin and Co.

GENERAL STRUCTURE OF THE FRENCH TAX SYSTEM

Introduction

The French tax system is basically a national one. All French residents are subject to the same taxes on their income, their property and their transactions. The only exceptions to this general rule are those applying to Corsica and to certain overseas territories (the French "Departments d'Outre-Mer" and Territoires d'Outre Mer).

All residents are considered equal when subject to taxation; French law makes no distinction between French nationals and foreigners residing in France. Taxes in France may be divided into two broad categories: direct taxes (for the most part, income taxes) and indirect taxes (value added tax or VAT).

The French tax system derives its definition and its specification from the General Tax Code ("Code Général des Impôts" or "C.G.I."). The principal taxes levied are the following:

- The personal income tax (Impôt sur le Revenu des Personnes Physiques" or "I.R.P.P.") Article 1, C.G.I.
- The corporate profit tax ("Impôt sur les Sociétés" or "I.S.") Article 206, C.G.I.
- The value added tax (VAT), Article 256-263, C.G.I. which is a tax levied on final consumption through a collection at each level of production.

Taken together, these three taxes account for 70% of all French tax receipts, the VAT representing 40%, the personal income tax and corporate tax representing

20% and 10% respectively. Each is collected according to uniform rates within France by the various administrative subdivisions of the Ministry of Finance. In addition, the tax base is always determined according to a uniform set of rules.

In accordance with the law passed on December 30, 1981, a fourth tax known as the wealth tax ("Impôt sur les Grandes Fortunes" or "I.G.F.") Article 885A to 885, C.G.I., has been added to the three aforementioned taxes. This tax subjects French residents to additional taxes according to the value of their estates and other personal holdings and regardless of whether these holdings are situated in France or abroad.

Over and above these principal taxes, there exist taxes on the transfer of certain assets. These transfers can take the form of non-monetary transfers (inheritance, succession or donation of wealth) or transfers made at a certain price (sale of buildings, commercial papers, etc.). This category also includes various other taxes which, although collected by state agents, are destined for localities: professional tax, real estate tax, residence tax, etc.

Social charges on salaries are not perceived as taxes in France and are collected by special entities (URSSAF) which have a separate status from the other authorities responsible for the collection of taxes and also by private institutions. The large majority of social charges is paid by the employer, the rest being taken out of the salary of the employee.

I. PERSONAL INCOME TAX

1. General Information

The personal income tax is a progressive tax which, upon declaration, applies to the income of all individuals physically residing in France, regardless of both the source and of the nature of the income. The basis of the tax is the family unit, the income of each family member being included in one single declaration. Couples legally married may not file separate income tax returns unless they are physically separated. The children of a married couple, however, do have the right to do so. Dependent children of legal age (between 18 and 25 years) who maintain their student status are generally included in the same tax return as their parents, unless the student status is dropped or the children begin earning a permanent income, in which case separate returns are usually filed.

The personal income tax is collected by the French administration, the amount to be paid being determined according to the return filed by the tax payer. Taxes computed on a given year's income are paid in three parts during the following year, one-third in February, one-third in May and the balance, including any adjustments, during the period between September and December. If need be, a taxpayer may request that his payments be automatically withdrawn from an account on a monthly basis.

2. Determination of Taxable Revenue

Taxable income is determined by adding the various possible types of income. Each type will be presented here separately.

a) Salaried persons are entitled to a 10% deduction for professional expenses without a justification up to a limit of 57,840 FF (gross salary minus 10% deduction); on the net having a limit of 523,000 FF which is adjusted every year, a 20% deduction is automatically applied. This does not apply to persons paid by a corporation in which they have more than a 35% interest nor to persons salaried in certain other professions to whom special rules of deductions apply which reduce or increase them (like salesmen who are entitled to extra special deduction or 30%)

The two following examples show how it is proceeded:

Example one

Mr. Jacob is employed as a senior officer by a firm with a salary of 700,000 FF (equivalent to 100,000 USD). He gets no reimbursement from his employer for professional expenses. The taxable income in the salary category is determined thereafter:

.	Salary................................	700,000
.	Deduction for professional expenses 10% = 70,000 but limited to...........	57,840
		642,160

.	20% on net = 168,431 but bases are limited to 523,000 (20% x 523,000).....	104,600
.	Net taxable salary.....................	737,560

Example two

Mr. Durand is employed by a firm as a salesman. Due to his salesman status he is allowed a 30% extra deduction for professional expenses. This additional deduction granted to certain professions is limited to 50,000 FF. His 1985 salary is 380,000 FF (equivalent 55,000 USD). He received 40,000 FF as reimbursement of justified travel expenses from his employer:

.	Salary + reimbursement.................	420,000
.	10% ordinary deduction.................	42,000
.	Difference.............................	378,000
.	Extra-deduction for salesmen (30%) 378,000 x 30% = 113,400 but limited to.....................................	50,000
.	20% on net.............................	65,600
.	Net taxable salary.....................	262,400

b) Non-commercial income or income earned by persons not linked to an employer. This category includes revenues of doctors, lawyers, accountants, writers, etc. This type of income is determined on a cash-basis method of accounting.

c) Industrial and commercial profits. This item includes profits stemming from any industrial or commercial activity, whether operated directly or by means of an intermediary such as a corporation whose partners are directly tax-eligible (the French form of the partnership, limited family partnership, etc). The net profit generated by this category of revenue is determined by the accrual method of accounting (see II.1.).

d) Real estate incomes are those generated by the rental of real estate. The incomes taxed are calculated according to the cash-receipts accounting method. Deductions include management fees, interest charges or other debts incurred upon acquisition of real estate, the construction and maintenance of buildings and, under certain conditions applying to residential buildings, expenses incurred to improve a property or to bring it into conformance with safety or sanitary living standards (includes elevators, fire exits, waste disposal, etc). An automatic deduction of 15% of gross income for urban buildings and 10% for agricultural buildings is also granted. These deductions are meant to replace the amortization of real estate and administration expenses, neither of which are deductible from real estate income. It is important to note that there can be no offsetting between other categories of revenue and deficit derived from the ownership of real property. Such a deficit can only be carried forward for five years and be offset against profits in this same category over the same period. Nevertheless, this drastic rule does not apply to historical monuments, regulated rehabilitation programs, etc.

e) Agricultural profits. This includes profits generated both by farmers and by persons directly or indirectly involved in the exploitation of rural property.

f) Unearned income. This includes income derived from dividends of corporate stock or from interest revenue realized from loans or from other assets such as money accounts, bond holdings or certificates of deposit. All capital gains income is taxable, withholding tax and "avoir fiscal" (a tax credit equal to 50% of dividends received from French companies) included. However, for certain types of income, the taxpayer may opt for a withholding to be paid by the debtor of the income (a corporation; a bank, etc). These withholdings are set at fixed rates according to the type of revenue involved:

- at a 26% rate for bond coupons
- at a 46% rate for income received from certificates of deposit and current accounts
- at a 33% rate for certain other financial assets.

Dividends from corporate stock are not taxable below a level of 5000 FF, since a maximum deduction of 5000 FF is allowable on each declaration.

g) Capital gains on the sale of property are subject to taxation, although the taxable base is adjusted according to the duration of ownership of the property and on the basis of the original purchase price, as corrected by an inflation index.

One will note that the sale of a principal residence in France is tax-exempt when the duration of ownership surpassed ten years or when the sale is carried out for family reasons.

h) Capital gains realized from the sale of corporate securities equaling or exceeding 25% of a corporation's capital are taxed separately. Such profits are normally taxed at a flat rate of 16% with no adjustments.

3. Territoriality

All income of a French resident is taxable in accordance with the General Tax Code, regardless of the country of origin of the income. If and when an international tax treaty attributes any income to another contracting country the revenue is nevertheless added to the resident's taxable French income for the purpose of calculating the progressivity of the tax still to be paid in France. A tax credit equal to the tax paid on foreign-earned income is accorded to French residents.

Income earned in France by persons not domiciled in such country remains taxable according to a unique set of terms most of which are governed by the various international tax treaties (see Annex A). When a non-resident maintains one or more residences in France, he is tax-eligible, either because of revenues earned in France or for lack of a signed international treaty with his country of citizenship. If no income is earned by this individual, he is taxed in France on a tax-base equal to three times the annual rental value of his residence(s).

4. Calculation of the Personal Income Tax

Very few expenses are deductible from the taxable income which is derived from the addition of the different categories of revenue not previously submitted to a flat tax rate, (see above). With the exception of deductions concerning annuities and subsistence allowances, deductions granted for interest charges on loans designed to finance a principal residence or for energy-saving materials, life-insurance charges, donations given to recognized charities, etc. are limited according to specific conditions and contractual agreements.

In order to apply the progressive tax schedule, the taxable income which results from the addition of the various categories of revenue and the deduction of the deficit (except from real estate) is divided by a coefficient which varies with the family situation of the taxpayer (the family quotient method). Married couples divide their total income by two and by an additional half-unit for each dependent child, the third child representing a whole unit. A family of five, for example, would divide its total income by four.

Single or divorced taxpayers are granted a half- unit divisional point for each dependent under their care, a whole unit being accorded for the first dependent. Surviving spouses with dependents are treated in the same manner as married couples with children.

Once the appropriate divisions have been calculated, the tax to be applied is determined in accordance with the official schedules. The amount is then remultiplied by the same number of units used in the division. The resultant sum represents the total tax deemed to be owed (see annex B). The net amount to be paid is determined after deducting tax credits resulting from foreign taxation (see above, I.3) or from unearned income (see above, I.2.f. "avoir fiscal").

One final note on the family-quotient method. The tax advantages afforded parents with dependent children is limited to an annual level. In 1985, for example, the maximum tax savings resulting from the family- quotient rule was set at 10,520 FF.

II. CORPORATE TAXES

1. General Principles

Income taxes are levied on every sort of corporation in France. A uniform rate of 50% applies to all ordinary corporate income, which is calculated in accordance with stipulations laid down by the General Tax Code for industrial and commercial profits (B.I.C.-BENEFICES INDUSTRIELS ET COMMERCIAUX). The principle lying behind the determination of the taxable net profit is the accrual method, in which revenue is recorded when earned, expenses are recorded when incurred, and other changes in the condition of an organization are recognized as they occur. All expenses deemed necessary for the administration of a corporation are tax-deductible.

In order to encourage capitalization of profits, the 1986 budget reduces the normal corporate income tax rate from 50% to 45% for fiscal years starting January 1, 1986 for all retained earnings that occurred in 1986 and in following years. If distributed in the following years, these retained earnings will be subjected to a penalty equal to the difference of taxation between 50% and 45%.

A special system of decreasing amortization (l'amortissement dégressif) is designed to encourage investment by permitting the rapid depreciation of equipment and machinery. The duration of the depreciation corresponds to the expected lifetime of the equipment purchased.

2. <u>The Principle of Corporate Autonomy</u>

Unless a special authorization is given by the Ministry of Finance, each corporate entity is taxed separately, the system of consolidated taxation being a rare exception in France. Likewise, the partners of a corporation are never subject to taxation on the profits of such a corporation, whether or not a personal holding is involved, as long as a dividend is not distributed.

In addition, for the fiscal years starting after December 31, 1985, the dividends placed in a special reserve as retained earnings and not distributed give a tax credit of 10% to the mother company.

3. <u>Parent Companies and their Affiliates</u>

As a rule, the consolidation of accounts does not exist for the purposes of taxation. To avoid double taxation among groups of companies, a special system which exonerates most of the dividends paid between the corporations of the group has been created. When a corporation subject to taxation receives a dividend from an affiliate, whether French or foreign, in which it holds a 10% interest (or more), 95% of the income received is tax-exempt, all tax credits included; only the remaining 5% is considered as a taxable base.

4. Territoriality

The territoriality of the corporate income tax allows the exclusion from the tax base of all operations not carried in France. This principle distinguishes the corporate income tax from that imposed on individuals. No tax credit exists for taxes paid abroad on a foreign branch or affiliate.

5. Profits from the Sale of Assets

For that part not corresponding to amortizations deducted from fiscal results, profits earned from the sale of property obtained more than two years before are taxed only at a 15% rate, rather than the normal rate of 50%.

At the same time, in order to benefit from this reduced rate, the profits realized ought not be distributed to the corporation's associates. If such is not the case, a rate corresponding to the difference between the reduced rate and the norm is applied.

6. System of a Favored Tax Treatment

Newly formed corporations and enterprises having two-thirds of their investments engaged in building and equipment eligible for declining amortization are tax-exempt during the first 35 months in existence. During a second period of twenty-four months, their profits receive a 50% reduction before being subject to normal corporate taxes (or, as the case may be, to taxes corresponding to the B.I.C. category in individual returns).

7. Mechanism designed to prevent the double-taxation of individuals.

In order to avoid a second taxation of corporate profits when, in the form of dividends, they are distributed to individual shareholders, a tax credit (l'avoir fiscal) calculated on the annual tax due and equal to 50% of the dividends received from French corporations is accorded to these individuals. This credit, therefore, represents one-half of the tax already collected at this level. This "avoir fiscal," representing in effect a tax reimbursement, is added to the net dividend distributed to an individual which is itself taxable under the category of personal income (see above).

Example: An individual receiving a French dividend of 100 FF adds 50 FF (l'avoir fiscal) to his declarable income. The sum of 150 FF is taxable as personal income but the avoir fiscal of 50 FF is subtracted from total tax due at year's end.

III. TREATMENT OF FISCAL DEFICITS

Deficits incurred by industrial and commercial enterprises may be carried forward only during the five years following their occurrence. However, that portion of the deficits corresponding to amortizations may be carried forward indefinitely.

In the case of taxation of individual income, certain forms of income cannot be set off against annual deficits or profits. Losses incurred from real estate investments may be carried forward during five years and deducted from future profits, but they may not be deducted from profits earned from other income sources in a given year.

French law makes no provision for the carry-back of fiscal deficits. For enterprises subject to corporate tax, waiver of this principle has nevertheless been accorded for those fiscal years starting with January, 1984. At their option companies may request the carry-back of a deficit to the three preceding years provided one or more of these years has been profit-making and that the corresponding taxes have been paid.

In order to benefit from this clause, corporations must have realized, during the course of the three years, a net investment in amortizable property equal to or greater than any amortization actually practiced during the period. The tax credit resulting from a deficit carry-back constitutes an asset which can be used as a payment for any tax due during the ten years following the realization of the deficit. If not applied as payment, the credit is reimbursable at the end of the ten year period.

IV. THE VALUE ADDED TAX SYSTEM (V.A.T.)

1. General description of the VAT system

VAT has been generalized in France since January, 1968. At the same time, 8 other countries of the European Economic Community (EEC), (Germany, Belgium, United Kingdom, Italy, Netherlands and Luxemburg) began progressively to adopt a VAT system.

In 1977, with the application of the Sixth European Directive, VAT was adopted permanently by all EEC countries even though the rates were different in each country.

VAT is a tax on consumption, applied and collected on all goods and services which are consumed or used. This tax must be paid at each stage of production. However, through a complex system, the tax is neutral on the production process and is only borne by the final consumer.

The following example will explain how the system of the VAT works :

	Producer	Wholesaler	Retailer	Total
Purchase price		118.60	177.90(*)	
Sale price	100	150	200 VAT rate	
	18.60%	18.60%	18.60%	
VAT due	18.60	27.90	37.20	83.70
VAT credits		(18.60)	(27.90)	46.50
VAT paid to the collecting Agency	18.60	9.30	9.30	37.20

- (*) Purchase price includes the VAT paid to the supplier -Each seller (producer, wholesaler, retailer) has to collect the VAT on the sale price and has to remit the amount to the governmental agency. Nevertheless, each purchaser, if he is not the final consumer, will get a tax credit for the VAT paid on his purchase of goods used in his production. Therefore, in the above example, the governmental agency will have collected 37.2 - (200.0) x 18,6% - and the consumer will have paid it in its entirety.

From an economic point of view, the sum of the added values has been taxed and therefore the Gross National Product of France can easily be determined by adding all the VAT returns.

2. Applications

Generally speaking, all transactions on products, goods and services which are produced, consumed or utilized in France, i.e., France, Monaco, Corsica and overseas territories, are taxable. But some goods or services, well defined by law, are exempt from VAT.

a) All sales made by manufacturers, artisans, wholesalers, dealers, and shopkeepers are taxable. However, some transactions and services (for example, medical services, exports, insurance other than life, sales of second hand goods, etc.), are exempt. Passive income (interest, dividends) is also exempt.

All invoices have to show on one line the cost of the product delivered or the service rendered before VAT ("prix hors taxes"). On a second line appears the percentage of VAT and its amounts, and the total of both figures is the sale price ("prix toutes taxes comprises"). If the VAT does not appear on the invoice, the tax is still due by the seller, but the purchaser is not allowed to take credit for it. (see IV.4.)

b) Some associations like sports, religious or political associations are normally exempt from the VAT. Nevertheless, if they enter into transactions which are also conducted by for-profit corporations, they will be subject to VAT for that type of transaction.

c) The above rules apply to transactions conducted within a country of the EEC. For international transactions, the general rule is as follows (France will be taken as the reference country) :

i) Goods and services imported are taxable when these goods or services are consumed or transformed in France, and they are not taxable if the goods are in temporary transit in the country (See IV.6). A VAT form, called Form C1 has to be filled out with the French customs when the goods are imported and customs authorities are responsible for the collection of the tax.

ii) Goods and services exported are, most of the time, exempt from VAT in the exporting country. Nevertheless, these goods or services will be subject to VAT in the importing country if it participates in the system. For example, exports will be exempt from French VAT but are taxable in Italy or Belgium.

For services rendered in the EEC, the place of residence is used to determine which country will collect the VAT. For services billed to a non-EEC customer but rendered in the EEC, the place of service is used to determine if the EEC VAT is applicable or if the exemption for exports is to be granted.

d. Grants and subsidies related to the normal course of business, i.e., supply discounts and credit notes are subject to VAT by the receiving corporation like any other transactions, even if given by a U.S. corporation to a French company. Therefore, the U.S. corporation's agent will have to apply for a refund of the VAT which was previously paid at customs clearance and which belongs to the U.S. corporation.

If the grant or subsidy has a finanical cause (grant to a French subsidiary because of heavy losses), it is exempt from the VAT.

This distinction is very important because for the first type of transaction, the U.S. corporation will have to labor through a formal administrative procedure in order to obtain a refund of the VAT (see IV.4). In the second type of transaction no tax is involved.

3. Computation and rates

. Computation

It is very important to know when VAT is due since it has a big impact on cash flow (See IV.5). There are three situations, as follows:

a) Sales of products and goods

VAT is due at the time of delivery. Practically speaking, each corporation totals, at the end of each month, its sales and the amount of VAT to be collected from its customers and remits this amount after having deducted its potential credits (See IV.4 infra).

b) Services

For services and real estate transactions, VAT is due when the agencies or corporations are paid by their customers (cash basis). This solution avoids paying VAT in advance.

c) Imports

For improved goods, VAT is due at the time of customs clearance.

. Rates

At the present time, there are four (4) VAT rates used in France:

A rate of 5.5% is applied to agricultural goods and products, and food for human consumption (meat, bread, etc.), except drinks and spirits (18,60%).

A rate of 7% is applied to books, newspapers, medical prescriptions, hotel services, and passenger transportation.

A rate of 33,3% applies to luxury goods (furs, perfumes, tobacco, jewelry, caviar) cars, motorcycles, tape recorders, and cameras.

Lastly, a rate of 18,60% applies to all goods and services which are not taxed at 5.5%, 7%, or 33.3%.

4. VAT credits

Manufacturers, shopkeepers or any other traders that are not final consumers are entitled to a credit for VAT paid to their suppliers of goods or services. Generally, companies can deduct VAT paid on investments. The credit is deducted from the VAT payment made to the governmental agency in the same month that it is paid to the supplier. Purchases and current expenditures are deducted from the VAT payment to the governmental agency the month following the purchase from the supplier.

VAT paid on products and services which are personally consumed by employees cannot be taken as a credit (restaurants, hotels, passenger cars, gasoline, etc.).

5. Payment of VAT

Every month, companies must file a VAT form

CA3/CA4 and pay the amount of VAT due less allowable credits. The form can be described in this way :

VAT due on sales of goods + VAT collected on sales of services	A	Month N
VAT credits on investments	B	Month N
VAT credits on purchases and current expenditures	C	Month N-1
Amount to be deposited:		A - (B+C)

If a mistake is discovered, an amended VAT return can be filed by the taxpayer up to December 31 of the second year after the original filing. From the point of view of the taxing authorities, the prescriptive period is four years.

Since companies have to pay the VAT computed on sales the same month as invoices are issued and get credit for their purchases (other than investments) only the following month, they are actually providing financial asssistance to the Treasury Department.

Due to the same time lag, and when a company has a low added value to its products or when it is building its stocks, this company can easily have a VAT credit due from the Treasury Department. In that case, a reimbursement can be asked from the administration. Foreign businesses are, in that respect, to be treated as French entities and are eligible for those refunds if the credit exceeds a given amount during a complete three-month period (See IV.6.c).

6. VAT and international trade

a) Exports (CGI articles 262, 263 & 275)

As mentioned previously (2.c), exports from France to another country are exempt from VAT. Therefore, exporting companies never show a VAT tax on their invoices to foreign customers. In addition, and in order to prevent these exporting companies from constantly claiming refunds from the Treasury Department, they are allowed, with the prior authorization of the tax authority, to purchase a given volume of goods (based on export percentage) from their suppliers without paying VAT. The supplier will receive an exemption certificate and will not charge the VAT tax to its customer up to the stated amount. This special process is called "Achats en suspension de taxes".

b) Imports

As stated above (2.c), imports of goods and products consumed in France are subject to the VAT tax. Nevertheless, imports which are only made for a limited period of time can be exempt from VAT. This system is applicable to corporations which import goods and, without transforming them, re-export them within 6 months. This is called "Transit Temporaire", and the goods remain either in a "Free trade Zone" or in a container sealed by customs.

c) Foreign Corporations

A permanent establishment in France of a foreign corporation is treated, for VAT purposes, just as a French taxpayer, i.e., it is subject to VAT. The same rule applies to foreign corporations which have no permanent establishment in France and deliver goods or perform services in France. These corporations will have to designate a tax correspondent who will be responsible for complying with the tax regulations and formalities, file the required returns and make the appropriate deposits on behalf of the foreign business.

V. TAXATION OF INCOME AND PROFITS EARNED OR PRESUMED EARNED BY NON-RESIDENTS OF FRANCE.

1. Distribution of Profits by foreign corporations.

Article 115 of the C.G.I. states the following:

"Profits generated in France by foreign corporations are assumed to be distributed each fiscal year to associates having neither a residence nor a head office in France."

Accepting as true the presumption set forth in the preceding article, the profits earned by foreign companies are in principle subject to a withholding tax of 25%, a withholding which affects every dividend distribution to non-residents. However, this presumption being seldom upheld, and because of the complex set of international conventions tying France to the majority of foreign nations, the 25% tax applies but only very rarely. The foreign company can always prove that its profit distribution has been limited or that the distribution was made uniquely to French residents or to residents of countries with whom France has entered into tax treaties.

2. <u>Withholding taxes applicable to income earned by non-residents</u>.

When they are distributed by a resident of France, (whether within the French territory or overseas) to a nonresident, profits and other incomes are subject to an automatic tax mechanism called a withholding tax. The principal categories of withholdings are the following:

a) <u>Dividends</u>.

Articles 119 bis and 187.1 of the General Tax Code call for a 25% withholding on the gross amount of dividends from stock or from shares of entities <u>or</u> corporations whose centers of operation are located in France. This 25% tax is often limited by the various international tax treaties. Between France and the United States, for example, the rate is normally reduced to 15% or 5%, depending on whether the American corporation possesses less than or more than 10% of the capital of the French company.

b) <u>Interest from assets or loans</u>.

International treaties often reduce or negate withholding taxes on this type of income when distributed to persons not domiciled in France. When a treaty does not apply, the withholding rates are the following:

. on income collected from bonds 25%

. on income collected from nominal certificates of deposit, other deposits and current accounts 45%

. on anonymous certificates of deposit 50%

When interest income from one of the aforementioned categories is distributed to an American resident by a French resident (be it an individual or a corporate entity), the income is normally exempt from withholding taxes in France.

c) Salaries.

Salaries paid by a debtor residing in France and received by a non-resident are subject to a progressive withholding tax of either 10%, 15%, or 25%.

d) Occasional supplementary income (royalties, professional fees, real estate revenue, profits from the sale of property, etc.)

Income falling under this category is, except where otherwise stipulated by international tax treaties, subject to a withholding tax of 33 1/3%.

3. Foreign controlled companies owning real estate.

Since January 1983 the Tax Code stipulates that persons maintaining their center of business outside France but who are the rightful owners, whether directly or indirectly, of one or more buildings (or shares of ownership in buildings or real estate partnerships) are taxed at the yearly rate of 3% of the value of their property or shares.

Only individuals or corporations maintaining their head office in a country having signed tax and administrative assistance agreements with France may escape paying this 3% tax. In addition, the exemption requires that the company file an annual declaration with the French authorities stating the location and official value of their buildings, the identity of all shareholders and the number of shares or stocks owned by each member.

VI. THE STRUGGLE AGAINST FRAUD AND TAX EVASION

Because of the territorial nature of the French tax system, the legislation must resort to mechanisms which foster, if and when necessary, the struggle against the transfer of revenues (profits, most likely) from France to legal entities or individuals situated abroad. Various texts allow the French examiners to track down and rectify the accounting and fiscal results of enterprises located within the national territory.

1. Article 57 of the C.G.I. stipulates:

"For the purpose of establishing the personal income tax due from enterprises under the control of or possessing control of enterprises situated outside France, the profits indirectly transferred to these foreign enterprises, be it by way of price adjustment of sales or purchases or any other method, are incorporated into the accounting results of the entity located in France. The process works in the same manner with regards to enterprises under control of any enterprise as to a particular group possessing control of enterprises situated outside France."

For lack of detailed methods needed to carry out the aforementioned adjustment, the taxable revenues are determined by means of comparison to those of similar enterprises carrying out operations deemed normal. In addition, a presumption is created allowing the (French) administration to rectify stated results when two (or more) enterprises, one situated in France, the other abroad, are tied together by some sort of common interest, whatever its form may be (Article 263.1.4. of the C.G.I. and decree 64.223, 11 March, 1964). This common interest may take the form of a 50% (or more) share of the capital of an affiliate. It could take the form of a contractual relationship or even be implicit from the transactions entered into between the two corporations concerned.

In order to apply Article 57, the administration must be able to prove the existence of an abnormal profit discrepancy in favor of a foreign-situated enterprise. The only workable method capable of accomplishing this task is a difficult one; it involves comparing the transactions of companies independent from one another, yet engaged in a type of international trade similar to that of the corporation under investigation.

2. Immaterial Transfers: Tax Evasion in Disguise

The Federal Republic of Germany, Belgium and France have all adopted severe measures designed to prevent the transfer of fiscal results by means of purely financial methods, both within the network of a company owning multiple enterprises in a given national territory and between such enterprises and their affiliates situated in nations applying a tax system less severe than the system in question. In France, the device allowing an examiner to repress such transfers is provided by Article 238A of the C.G.I. which reads:

"Interest, pensions, and other revenues from securities, assets, deposits and guarantees, fees for the sale or purchase of exploitation licenses, patents, brand names, manufacturing processes or formulas, or other analogous rights or remunerations paid to or due by an individual or incorporated person domiciled or established in France to other such persons domiciled or established in a foreign state or other territory situated outside of France and benefitting from privileged tax treatment, may not be declared as deductible expenses from a taxable base unless the debtor in question is able to prove that the expenses correspond to operations actually in existence and are not of abnormal or exaggerated character.

For the application of the preceding paragraph, persons are regarded as being subject to favorable tax treatment in the state or territory under consideration if they are not tax-eligible or if they are taxed on profits or income at notably lower rates than those existing in France."

This text gives significant powers of redress to the administration inasmuch as interest payments, fees for services rendered, etc., often change hands for the profit of individuals or corporations situated in tax havens or in Switzerland. A company need not possess ties of dependence with a foreign company or affiliate to be investigated. The administration defines "tax haven" as existing if and when the foreign tax paid by a beneficiary is less than two- thirds of the amount that would have had to have been paid on the same income in France.

3. <u>International Transaction bearing on services rendered in France</u>.

In certain service industries, notably in those operating outside of industrialized and often heavily- taxed territories (e.g., petroleum exploration) or in those in which often intangible services have been rendered (engineering, accounting, banking services, etc.), it is clearly to a company's advantage to create business entities in countries with a less burdensome tax system than their own. In order to control transfers on account of services rendered in their territories to countries with more lenient tax systems, the principal nations of the E.E.C. have all taken action of some sort. In France, Article 155A of the C.G.I. addresses the problem in the following manner:

"Notwithstanding any contrary device, sums received by a corporation or other individual entity having an operational center outside France, as remuneration for services rendered by one or more persons domiciled in France, are taxable in the name of the latter:

a) if these French residents have control, whether direct or indirect, of the corporations or entities involved;

b) if these French residents fail to prove that the corporations or entities involved are engaged in industries or commercial activities other than the services in question;

c) or if the corporations or entities involved maintain their center of business in a country not bound to France by a double-taxation Treaty".

4. <u>Other mechanisms designed to fight tax evasion</u>.

In order to face this problem, the administration has at its disposal two standard mechanisms.

One mechanism, provided for by Article 39 of the C.G.I., allows the examiner to claim, under judicial control, that a transaction is abnormal because it does not enter into the normal type of decisions that a corporate executive would have ordered. In this case, upon verification and judicial authorization, the expense or loss taken can be reintegrated into the taxable result. This process is subject to a very strict appraisal both by a judicial official and, above all, by the Conseil d'Etat. As a result, an abundant and elaborate jurisprudence has developed in an attempt to define the exact meaning and character of an "abnormal" administrative act.

The second mechanism is provided for by Article 1649.5B of the C.G.I., which concerns realizations or transfers of profits or their revenues by the taxpayer in question under cover of a contract which misstates the reality of the operations being carried out. Although an examiner can easily claim that such a situation is an obvious abuse of the law, the administration often encounters problems when trying to prove and punish such violations, because of the restrictive procedure imposed by law. It requires detailed proof of all claims made before a judge or a special advisory committee. Nevertheless, the difficulty involved in proving and prosecuting such transfers do not make them any less tolerable nor acceptable in the eyes of the administration.

ANNEX A

INCOME TAX CONVENTIONS AND AGREEMENTS BINDING FRANCE TO OTHER COUNTRIES

Below is a list of the countries party to a treaty with France for the purpose of avoiding double taxation. The date of signature of the treaty (and, when necessary, the date of the additional agreement modifying it) and the targeted taxes, are indicated as well.

Abbreviations

AA: Additional Agreement
A: Arrangement
II: Investment Income
IT: Income Tax
RR: Registration Rights
ST: Succession Tax
WT: Wealth Tax

COUNTRY	DATE OF CONVENTION (and additional agreement when relevant)	TAXES
Algeria	May 17, 1982	IT-ST-RR
Argentina	April 4, 1979	IT-WT
Australia	April 13, 1976	IT
Austria	October 8, 1959 AA of October 30, 1970	IT-WT-ST
Belgium	March 10, 1964 AA of February 15, 1971	IT
	January 20, 1950	ST
Benin (ex. Dahomey)	February 27, 1975	IT-ST-RR
Brazil	September 10, 1971	IT
Burkina Faso (ex. Upper-Volta)	August 11, 1965 AA of June 3, 1971	IT-ST-RR
Cameroon	October 21, 1976	IT-ST-RR
Canada	May 2, 1975	IT-WT
Central African Republic	December 13, 1969	IT-ST-RR
China	May 30, 1984	IT
Comores and Mayotte	March 27 and June 8, 1970	IT-ST-RR
Cyprus	December 18, 1981	IT
Czechoslovakia	June 1, 1973	IT
Denmark	February 8, 1957	IT-WT
Egypt	June 19, 1980	IT
Federal Republic of Germany	July 21, 1959	IR-IF
Finland	September 11, 1970	IT-WT
	August 26, 1958	ST

COUNTRY	DATE OF CONVENTION (and additional agreement when relevant)	TAXES
French-Polynesia	March 28 and May 28, 1957	II
Gabon	April 21, 1966 AA of January 23, 1973	IT-ST-RR
Greece	August 21, 1963	IT
Hungary	April 28, 1980	IT-WT
India	March 26, 1969	IT
Indonesia	September 14, 1979	IT-WT
Iran	November 7, 1973	IT
Ireland	March 21, 1968	IT
Israel	August 20, 1963	IT
Italy	October 29, 1958	IT-WT
Ivory Coast	April 6, 1966	IT-ST-RR
Japan	November 27, 1964 AA of March 10, 1981	IT
Jordan	May 28, 1984 (1)	IT
Kuwait	February 7, 1982	IT-ST
Lebanon	July 24, 1962	IT-ST
Luxemburg	April 1, 1958 AA of September 8, 1970	IT-WT
Madagascar	July 22, 1983	IT
Malaysia	April 24, 1975	IT
Mali	September 22, 1972	IT-ST-RR
Malta	Agreement of July 25, 1977	IT-WT
Mauritius	December 11, 1980	IT-WT

COUNTRY	DATE OF CONVENTION (and additional agreement when relevant)	TAXES
Mauritania	November 15, 1967	IT-WT-RR
Monaco	May 18, 1963 AA of June 25, 1969	(2)
	April 1, 1950	ST
Morocco	May 29, 1970	IT-WT-RR
Netherlands	March 16, 1973	IT-WT
New Caledonia	March 31 and May 5, 1983	IT-ST-RR
New Zealand	November 30, 1979	IT
Niger	June 1, 1965 AA of February 16, 1973	IT-ST-RR
Norway	December 19, 1980	IT-WT
Pakistan	July 22, 1966	IT
Philippines	January 9, 1976	IT
Poland	June 20, 1975	IT
Portugal	January 14, 1971	IT
Rumania	September 27, 1974	IT
Saudi Arabia	February 18, 1982	IT-ST
Senegal	March 29, 1974	IT-ST-RR
Singapore	September 9, 1974	IT
South Korea	June 19, 1979	IT
Spain	June 27, 1973	IT-WT
Sri-Lanka (ex. Ceylon)	September 17, 1981	IT
Sweden	December 24, 1936	IT
	Numerous agreements; in particular of March 9,	IT

COUNTRY	DATE OF CONVENTION (and additional agreement when relevant)	TAXES
	1971 and September 19, 1936	ST
Switzerland	September 9, 1966 AA of December 3, 1969	IT-WT
	AA of April 11, 1983 (1)	ST
Thailand	December 27, 1974	IT
Togo	November 24, 1971	IT-ST-RR
Tunisia	May 28, 1973	IT
United Kingdom	May 22, 1968 AA of February 10, 1971 and May 14, 1973	IT
	June 21, 1963	ST
United States	July 28, 1967 AA of October 12, 1970 and November 24, 1978	IT-ST
Yugoslavia	March 28, 1974	IT
Malawi Zambia and Zimbabwe (ex. Rhodesia)	December 14, 1950	IT

(1) Agreement not ratified yet

(2) Special fiscal agreement

The following table includes those countries whose nationals are entitled to the same benefits available to French citizens.

Such system, which classifies foreign nationals as French nationals, is found, according to each country, in a general convention for the purpose of avoiding double taxation or in a special convention and, sometimes, in a particular agreement.

<u>List of the countries concerned</u>:

Algeria
Andorra
Argentina
Austria
Belgium
Benin
Bolivia
Brazil
Burkina Faso
Cameroon
Canada
Central African Republic
Chile
Colombia
Comores
Congo
Cyprus
Czechoslovakia
Costa Rica
Cuba
Denmark
Dominican Republic
Ecuador
Egypt
Federal Republic of Germany
Finland
Gabon
Greece
Guatemala
Haiti
Honduras
Hungary
India
Indonesia
Iran
Ireland
Israel
Italy
Ivory Coast
Japan
Lebanon
Liberia
Luxemburg
Madagascar
Malawi
Malaysia
Mali
Malta
Mauritius
Mauritania
Mexico
Monaco
Morocco
Netherlands
New Zealand
Nicaragua
Niger
Norway
Pakistan
Panama
Paraguay
Peru
Philippines
Poland
Portugal
Rumania
Senegal
Singapore
South Korea
Spain
Sri Lanka
Sweden
Switzerland
Syria
Thailand
Togo
Tunisia
Turkey
United Kingdom
United States
Venezuela
West Germany
Yugoslavia
Zaire
Zambia
Zimbabwe (ex. Rhodesia)

ANNEX B

INCOME TAX (IT)

TAXABLE REVENUE (one unit)				RATE %
Not greater than	F 14,820			0
Situated between	F 14,820	and	F 15,490	5
Situated between	F 15,490	and	F 18,370	10
Situated between	F 18,370	and	F 29,050	15
Situated between	F 29,050	and	F 37,340	20
Situated between	F 37,340	and	F 46,920	25
Situated between	F 46,920	and	F 56,770	30
Situated between	F 56,770	and	F 65,500	35
Situated between	F 65,500	and	F 109,140	40
Situated between	F 109,140	and	F 150,100	45
Situated between	F 150,100	and	F 177,550	50
Situated between	F 177,550	and	F 201,970	55
Situated between	F 201,970	and	F 228,920	60
Beyond	F 228,920			65

35% on the fraction situated between F 59,950 and F 69,170
40% on the fraction situated between F 69,170 and F 115,250
45% on the fraction situated between F 115,250 and F 158,510
50% on the fraction situated between F 158,510 and F 187,490
55% on the fraction situated between F 187,490 and F 213,280
60% on the fraction situated between F 213,280 and F 241,740
65% on the fraction superior to F 241,740

Once the amount of tax corresponding to each unit revenue is determined, the gross total amount of tax is obtained following this formula:

GROSS TAX = Tax corresponding to each unit X number of units

RÉSUMÉ EN FRANÇAIS

LE RÉGIME FISCAL FRANÇAIS

L'auteur analyse le régime de la fiscalité française applicable aux multiples aspects de la réorganisation des multinationales. Ces aspects sont examinés sous des titres différents.

Dans un aperçu général de la fiscalité française, l'auteur rappelle deux grands principes: celui de l'égalité devant l'impôt et celui de la division des impôts directs et impôts indirects. Les trois principaux impôts sont l'impôt sur le revenu, l'impôt sur les sociétés et la taxe sur la valeur ajoutée. A ces trois impôts traditionnels il a été ajouté un impôt sur les grandes fortunes en 1981. Parmi les impôts subsidiaires il faut citer l'impôt foncier, la taxe professionnelle etc...

Le deuxième titre traite de l'impôt sur le revenu. L'impôt sur le revenu est basé sur l'unité familiale; il est progressif et payé sous forme de tiers provisionnels. Le calcul de l'impôt varie selon la nature des revenus: salaires, professions libérales, bénéfices commerciaux etc... Le fisc français applique le principe de la territorialité des revenus tout en tenant compte de l'existence possible de traités de double imposition.

Les impôts sur les sociétés sont examinés dans une troisième partie. Le taux uniforme de l'impôt sur les revenus des sociétés est de 50%, et le principe applicable ici est celui de la territorialité du régime fiscal applicable aux pertes et déficits encourus tant par les personnes que par les sociétés. L'auteur consacre une longue quatrieme partie à l'analyse de la taxe sur la valeur ajoutée (T.V.A.)

Appliquée en France depuis 1968, la TVA a été étendue progressivement à d'autres pays membres du marché commun. Une directive (la sixième) des communautés tente d'apporter une certaine uniformité au régime de la TVA au sein du marché commun. Le taux de la TVA varie selon l'objet de la transaction (biens, services, importations) et admet des exceptions.

Dans une cinquième partie l'auteur se penche sur le problème de l'imposition des revenus et profits perçus par des non-résidents. L'auteur bâtit son analyse sur l'article 115 du code général des impôts qui stipule que les profits perçus en France par des sociétés étrangères sont présumés être distribués à des non-résidents. Toutefois les articles 119 bis et 187-1 prevoient des retenues d'impôt à la source sur les profits.

Enfin, sous un sixième titre, l'auteur étudie les mesures prises contre les tentatives de fraude fiscale. Les moyens mis à la disposition de l'administration des finances sont les articles 57, 238A, 155A, 39 et 1649.5B du code général des impôts.

RESUMEN EN ESPAÑOL

EL RÉGIMEN FISCAL FRANCES

El autor analiza el régimen fiscal francés aplicable a varios aspectos de la reorganización de multinacionales. Estos aspectos son examinados bajo diversos títulos.

Describiendo en lineas generales el sistema francés, el autor destaca dos grandes principios: el de la igualdad ante los impuestos y el de la división entre impuestos directos e indirectos. Los tres impuestos principales son el impuesto a los réditos, el impuesto a las sociedades y el impuesto al valor agregado. A estos tres impuestos tradicionales se agregó, en 1981, el impuesto a las grandes fortunas. Entre los impuestos secundarios puede citarse el impuesto a la propiedad inmueble, el impuesto profesional, etc...

El segundo título trata sobre el impuesto a los réditos. El impuesto a los réditos esta basado sobre la unidad familiar; es progresivo y se paga por tercios en forma provisoria. El cálculo del impuesto varía según la naturaleza del rédito: salarios, profesiones liberales, beneficios comerciales, etc... El fisco francés aplica el principio de territorialidad de réditos, aunque teniendo el cuenta la posible existencia de tratados sobre doble imposición.

La tercera parte examina el impuesto a las sociedades. La tasa uniforme del impuesto a los réditos societarios es del 50%, y el principio aquí aplicable es el de la territorialidad del régimen fiscal respecto de pérdidas y déficits sufridos tanto por personas físicas como por empresas. El autor dedica una extensa cuarta sección al análisis del impuesto al valor agregado (IVA).

Aplicado en Francia desde 1968 el IVA se ha extendido progresivamente a otros países miembros del mercado común. Una directiva (la sexta) de la comunidad trata de aportar una cierta uniformidad al sistema del IVA en el seno del mercado común. La tasa del IVA varía según el objeto de la transacción (bienes, servicios, importaciones) y admite excepciones.

En una quinta sección el autor aborda los problemas del impuesto a los réditos y ganancias percibidas por los no-residentes. El autor construye su hipótesis sobre el artículo 115 del código general de impuestos, que establece que los beneficios percibidos en Francia por empresas extranjeras se presumen como distribuídos entre no-residentes. Aunque los artículos 119 bis y 187-71 preven retenciones impositivas en la fuente de tales beneficios.

Finalmente, bajo el sexto título, el autor estudia las medidas tomadas contra las tentativas de fraude fiscal. Los medios puestos a disposición de la administración son los artículos 57, 238A, 155A, 39 y 1649.5B del código general de impuestos.

CHAPTER IV

COLLECTIVE BARGAINING

LATIN AMERICA

CANADA

EUROPE

MULTINATIONAL ENTERPRISES AND COLLECTIVE BARGAINING FROM A LATIN AMERICAN PERSPECTIVE

Carlos E. Alfaro

The author has practiced law in Buenos Aires for several years. Since 1982, he has been in charge of the New York representative office of Allende & Brea, an Argentine law firm. He has also taught government contracts at a private (Catholic University) and a public (State University) law school. He has published several articles in Argentina for Jurisprudencia Argentina and La Ley as well as for the newspapers La Prensa and El Cronista Comercial on constitutional, regulatory, trade and labor matters. He is a member of the Inter-American Affairs Committee of the City Bar Association of New York and Director of the Argentine American Chamber of Commerce in U.S.A.

1. History, Politics and Economy

As a preliminary statement I should point out that this is one of those legal matters in which political issues, social values, and history are deeply related and mixed with the legal questions involved. Therefore, instead of giving a detailed explanation of the specific procedural legal labor-related regulations that a multi-national enterprise faces in Latin America in a reorganization process, I will analyze which are, in my opinion and to the best of my knowledge, the real underlying conflicting issues that a multinational enterprise (MNE) should be aware of in Latin American countries.

For many years the general assumption had been that the activities of a multinational enterprise in Latin America always create a frictional political situation with the local forces (unions, political parties, the army, the church, and other important institutions) because, among other things, "the interest of a MNE was always in direct conflict with the national interest of the country." Exploitation, loss of independence and sovereignty were the common issues that generally appeared when discussing this problem.

In my belief, this is no longer a valid assumption. All statistics presently gathered show that, to the contrary, the impact of a foreign investment and/or the activities of a MNE in a foreign country are beneficial and not detrimental to the development of the economy as well as to the social conditions of the same.

In effect, if we look at those statistics, we will see that:

First, the investment and the activities of multinational enterprises have an important impact on the level of production of the country and, consequently, reduce unemployment.

Second, it has also been proven that the quality of the works and level of the wages provided by these companies are higher than those of the national local companies.

Third, it is also true that MNE are usually the companies that comply better with the local union industrial-relations system and government regulations.

That is why, nowadays, almost all the countries in the world, no matter which kind of ideology is in power, accept and heavily promote foreign investment as a necessary tool for their economic development and the improvement of the standard of living of their population. Spain, with the Socialists in government, China, Saudi Arabia and France, are very clear examples which prove the above - mentioned point. The truth is that there are very few cases of a negative impact of the MNE's activities in a country other than for political reasons.

Consequently, we should focus our analysis on the real problem involved in the relation MNE-labor forces in a Latin American country. Due to these and other facts, I believe that the problem rests, not specifically on the economic effect that a foreign activity, operation or investment has in the economy of a country, but on a question of political power and influence, especially in those countries where the labor movement is organized in centralized, powerful unions.

2. Multinational Enterprises and the Unions. Struggle for Power. Special Interests

Unions are a source of incredible political influence, and many labor demands are guided towards achieving that end. Sometimes, workers' vindication of rights are only a pretext to exercise political pressure. This becomes evident if we realize that MNE offer union leaders the best scenario for their political careers, and an excellent opportunity to exercise their power.

The recognition of this problem, specifically of the different special interests involved, is crucial for a MNE wanting to achieve its economic goals without suffering undue interference.

In effect, when these special interests are acknowledged by the MNE, the resulting panorama is that of a quiet and peaceful relationship because:

First, the relations between the MNE and a centralized powerful union are conducted through well-established official and unofficial channels, making such communications much easier than in other cases. Both parties know the rules of the game, who makes the decisions and why. There is an implicit agreement for an open dialogue and, consequently, they avoid unnecessary confrontations that spring from the lack of an appropriate level of communication.

Second, MNE are aware that they should comply with the basic governmental requirements on industrial regulations, social benefits and labor matters. Therefore, they are also ready to make more concessions than the minimum legal standards, provided of course that production costs remain reasonable.

Third, the unions know that dealing with big, foreign companies gives them a political and social leverage, which they lack with local companies, a leverage that they can exploit politically.

3. <u>Decision-Making Power. Potential Conflicting Issues</u>

So far, we have focused on normal operations and activities, and day-to-day decisions. But there are other types of corporate decisions, mainly institutional ones, that could still create big problems for the MNE in their relations with the labor forces, even in the above situation. For example: the decision to reduce the production of the company may lead to layoffs, to stay or not in the country, to reorganize the company, mergers, splitting, etc. Why would such decisions be challenged by the unions? Because of several factors and among them:

1) The labor leaders fear losing their representation, which is the base of their political power.

2) The centralized structure of the decision-making power of a MNE, in such cases, precludes any dialogue with the unions.

In effect, in such situations, the unions and labor leaders are directly affected because we are talking about losing jobs, and that means losing votes and, consequently, losing power. It is here that the real problem between the unions and the MNE surfaces, mainly because the labor leaders have to, not only negotiate the rights of the workers, but also their own political future. And what happens? When they go to the company to discuss these issues, they discover that the ordinary communication channels described above, between them and the companies, do not work in these cases.

The kind of decisions mentioned above are not made by the local managers of the corporation because the decision-making power of a MNE is a centralized one. Those are important policy decisions, institutional ones, that are made at the home offices. Furthermore, they are made, sometimes, disregarding the real economic facts of a particular country. That is why we can see companies pulling out of a country during an economic recovery, or establishing there during periods of crisis.

Unions are aware of these facts and, consequently, the dialogue with the local corporate officers is disturbed by the fact that, in these cases, the officers of the subsidiary simply obey orders from abroad. Ultimately, there are no channels left for a dialogue. If a multinational enterprise does not take adequate care of this problem, the unions will resort to other means in order to protect themselves, or to receive an adequate compensation for the damage to their interest as a result of such decisions. There are typical situations in which the unions do not have any other recourse than raising the issue of foreign interference with internal affairs of a country in order to get the attention of the government and of public opinion. Unions are forced to exploit the situation in order to compensate for the loss. For example, Ford Motors in Argentina decided, in 1985, to reduce the number of employees in its local manufacturing plant, in the outskirts of Buenos Aires. One of the layoffs included 30 union representatives. As a result, the plant was immediately occupied by workers who challenged the decision and looked upon it as an interference, by the I.M.F. and other "powerful foreign institutions," with Argentina's internal affairs.

4. Negotiation Techniques

Negotiation techniques are, consequently, one of the most important issues to be considered in order to avoid any kind of problems. I will mention two clear and different cases that took place in Argentina.

The first one is that of Swift Corporation, one of the largest meat-packing concerns in Argentina, owned by Deltec International. The company was losing money, and had heavy loans to repay. Europe was not buying any more Argentina meat, and Deltec had to take a decision about the future of the company. The circumstances at that time were: a large, powerful and aggressive union, a product essential to the people and the internal economy of the country, the government pressing for local participation in foreign companies and a period of social and political unrest in the country. Furthermore, although Swift was losing money, Deltec had other profitable subsidiaries in Argentina which, although legally unrelated, undoubtedly formed part of the same economic group. In reaching a solution, the group decided to follow the principle of the lower cost possible and ended up in a bankruptcy procedure. The company tried to avoid any dialogue with the unions and the government that could force them to negotiate the terms of their decision.

The issue of national interest and foreign interference with Argentine social and economic life was raised by the unions, getting the attention, not only of the politicians and the government, but also of the judges in charge of the matter. Finally, the courts extended the bankruptcy of Swift Corporation to the subsidiaries and related companies of the Deltec Group in Argentina and worldwide. What was viewed as simple and easy ended up in one of the most complicated cases, resulting in the loss of a large amount of money and, worse than that, damaging the reputation of the group in Argentina and all Latin America.

In the second case, General Motors decided to cease its operations of manufacturing cars in Argentina. Here, although the political situation was more favorable, the company carried on the closing of the plant in an orderly way, taking appropriate care, first, of the governmental reaction, then the rights of the workers, and, finally, the interests of the unions in such a way that everyone was offered adequate compensation for the loss suffered. General Motors offered to their workers more than what labor law required, but eased in this way the process of leaving the country. It avoided a political confrontation that could have damaged the company in other countries and forever in Argentina.

The above overview and recommendations can also be applied to cases where MNE only reduce their operations in a particular country or, in cases of merger, transformation, or splitting of their subsidiaries. A typical situation is the case where a MNE is acquired by another multi-national corporation, ending up with two subsidiaries in a particular country. The reorganization process that follows, in almost all the cases, imply a reduction of activities and personnel, with the consequent crisis potential.

5. Legal Framework. Rules of Public Order

In the same view, a MNE should also be aware, in a reorganization process, of the so-called rules of "public order" as seen in Latin America.

A rule is of public order because it regulates matters which are considered, by the State, of such importance that they deserve a special kind of protection. The rights granted by these laws cannot be altered by the parties to an agreement, and the private sector is bound by them.

This kind of laws exists in almost all the Latin American countries for the protection of workers. The reason is that workers are generally considered the weak side of the labor relationship and, consequently, stronger protection than that given by the normal rules is considered necessary.

A clear example can be found in the Labor Contract Law of Argentina, No. 20.744, which establishes the rights of workers. Article 1 stipulates an order of priorities. This article says that all workers, labor contracts, and labor relations are governed by the following regulations (of law No. 20.744) and only in the order listed below :

a) this law

b) professional charters

c) collective bargaining agreements

d) mutual agreement of the parties

e) usages and custom

You can clearly see that the will of the parties is in the fourth place in the above enumeration, and collective bargaining is in the third place, after the law and the professional charters.

This means that only more favorable conditions than those contemplated in the law can be established by the parties, individually or in a collective bargaining (Article 8); and that conditions less favorable to the worker, or contrary to those established by law, are considered null and void (Article 7).

Furthermore, Article 9 states:

"In case of doubt, as to the application of legal or conventional rules, the one most favorable to the worker shall prevail,...Should a doubt arise on the interpretation or scope of the law, the judges or the authority in charge of its application shall decide on the manner most favorable to the worker."

Another example of the public order rank of the law is given by Article 12. It reads:

"Any mutual agreement which suppresses or reduces the rights envisaged in this law, collective bargaining agreements, or professional charters, shall be declared null and void." Another example, still, is given by Article 13, which says:

"The clauses of labor contracts which, to the detriment of workers, modify imperative rules established by law, or by collective bargainig agreements, are null and shall be substituted as a matter of law."

The above rules establish a very special legal framework in which the freedom of the parties to enter into an agreement is curtailed, notwithstanding that it is a right guaranteed by the Constitution.

These rules must be taken into account by a MNE in a reorganization process because it always happens that, as a consequence of them, either the labor contract is terminated or it is transferred to another company. Both situations clearly jeopardize the economic situation of the worker and his rights. These rules of public order, consequently, establish a special protection for workers.

In a reorganization process a MNE will face certain unavoidable restrictions, or obligations that should inevitably be fulfilled, and responsibilities that cannot be waived.

For example, Title XI of the Labor Contract Law establishes that:

a) "In the event of a transfer of the establishment for any reason, all the obligations arising, at the time of transfer, from the labor contract between the transferor and the worker, shall pass to the successor or acquirer, as well as any obligation arising from said transfer. The labor contract, in such cases, shall continue with the successor or acquirer and the worker shall maintain the length of service acquired with the transferee and all the rights derived from it." (Article 225)

b) "The tranferor and the acquirer of an establishment shall be jointly responsible with regard to obligations arising from the labor contract at the time of the transfer which might affect the labor relationship." (Article 228)

c) "The transfer of personnel to another establishment shall be subject to the express consent, in writing, of the worker. Even when such has been given, the transferor and the transferee shall be held jointly responsible for the obligations arising from the work relationship duly transferred" (Article 229)

These regulations not only establish a limitation to the action of a MNE, but also clearly affect the price and conditions of a deal between two companies, and should be carefully considered when establishing the terms of the agreement.

6. <u>Collective Bargaining</u>

In the case of collective bargaining, a MNE should understand that the above rules of public order are only the basis from which the workers start to bargain for special rights and, consequently, they should offer to give more, especially when dealing with labor leaders and representatives belonging to well-organized and politically strong unions.

Furthermore, the law grants certain kinds of protection and rights to workers who perform any kind of public activity on behalf of the unions, or in the government; for example:

a) Those workers who, on account of their holding of official posts at the national, provincial or municipal level, stop performing their duties, shall not lose their jobs and can request reinstatement. The period of time during which the workers have held office, as mentioned above, shall be considered as time worked to calculate their working period in order to determine the benefits to which they would have been entitled had they actually rendered their services all the time. (Article 215).

b) In the event of dismissal or failure to reinstate a worker coming under the above provisions, he shall be able to claim the payment of the corresponding indemnity. For the purposes of calculating said indemnity, the time during which his job was maintained shall be computed in the working period (Article 216)

Coming back to my previous statement, you can now clearly appreciate why I stress the importance of the channels of communication in order to avoid conflicting situations that could disrupt a normal process of re-organization.

I will now briefly summarize the specific procedure for collective bargaining.

Collective Bargaining is ruled by a statute which is also considered of public order, in the sense and within the scope already described (Law 14.250). The law, as frequently happens, does not define collective bargaining, but in the discussions carried out in Congress before its approval, the consensus was that the consequences and the nature of the matters involved in a collective bargaining were of such importance that the State could not leave it to the free will of the parties involved.

Those parliamentary discussions describe a collective bargaining as one carried out only between the most representative labor union and the most representative employers' union.

The system established by the statute is a very simple one and follows these principles:

a) Only unions recognized and authorized to act, as such, by the Government, can legally participate in a collective bargaining.

b) A collective bargaining has to be approved by the Ministry of Labor to become effective.

c) When it is approved, it is mandatory for all workers and companies, irrespective of their participation in the agreement.

d) Contributions or dues established in a collective bargaining in favor of the union that was involved in the negotiations are mandatory for all workers, irrespective of their affiliation to it. As it can be clearly seen, the law establishes a system that reaffirms the need to have an open and fluid system of communication between the MNE and the unions.

I have merely referred to the Argentine legislation but the nature of the principles I have described are generally included in the legislation of all the other Latin American countries.

7. Conclusion

The message that, as a conclusion, I want to convey to you is that, if a MNE wants to avoid conflicting and potentially damaging situations to its subsidiaries as a consequence of their relations with labor forces in Latin America, the officers in charge should:

a) Establish a fluid system of communication with the labor leaders and the unions

b) Recognize the real interests involved

c) Take into account the economic, social and political reality of the circumstances surrounding the operations of the company

d) Seek the cooperation of the Government before taking any decision

e) Comply with the laws of public order.

There is a very simple unwritten rule that everyone understands in America, which is the following: if you want to protect your interests, you must first know which those are and, second, avoid harming the interests of others. The same principle is to be applied in Latin America, especially when dealing with unions and the labor forces in general. The labor movements of Latin America have become not only politically but economically powerful. They can no longer be ignored or destroyed. We should acknowledge that reality. Modern times are characterized by dialogue, agreements and pacts. Political stability and social economic progress demand nothing less.

RÉSUMÉ EN FRANÇAIS

LES MULTINATIONALES ET LES CONVENTIONS COLLECTIVES DE TRAVAIL D'UN POINT DE VUE LATINO-AMÉRICAIN

Les règles en vigueur et les problèmes d'ordre juridique émanant de la relation entre les Multinationales et les conventions collectives de travail en Amérique Latine ne peuvent être analysés correctement qu'à la lumière des valeurs politiques, sociales et économiques de chaque pays et région, de l'évolution historique et du contexte actuel du mouvement ouvrier. Dans ce sens, et en accord avec les statistiques de la majorité des pays de la région, nous pouvons affirmer comme postulat a priori que:

1) Les activités d'une multinationale sont bénéfiques et non pas défavorables, comme l'affirment certains idéologues, pour le progrès social, économique et politique d'un pays (par exemple, elles augmentent le niveau de la production, le nombre d'employés et améliorent les conditions d'emploi ainsi que les salaires).

2) L'existence dans les pays latino-américains de mouvements ouvriers organisés sous la tutelle de syndicats ayant une grande influence politique, ne veut pas nécessairement dire qu'il se trouve des intérêts contraires à ceux des multinationales représentant une source permanente de conflits possibles.

En fait, les multinationales sont celles qui offrent les meilleures conditions de travail mais aussi celles qui proposent aux syndicats et aux leaders ouvriers le cadre le plus adéquat à la progression de leurs activités et de leur carrière politique. Il est plus probable qu'un conflit entre une multinationale et un syndicat naisse à cause du déni des intérêts particuliers de ce dernier que pour des revendications salariales.

3) Que ce soit pour des raisons de prestige ou parce qu'elles font l'objet d'un contrôle sévère, les multinationales sont parmi les entreprises qui observent avec beaucoup plus d'attention la règlementation gouvernementale.

4) Un dialogue ouvert entre les représentants des multinationales et les syndicats permet d'assurer une

stabilité et une continuité dans les programmes de production.

Ainsi, les conflits les plus graves naissent lorsqu'une des règles susmentionnées est violée, notamment dans le cas où l'on ne reconnaît pas les interêts particuliers des diverses parties en question. C'est souvent le cas quand la réorganisation d'une multinationale cause la fermeture d'une usine, ce qui entraîne la suppression de la base ouvrière qui donne son pouvoir, sa représentativité politique et salariale à un syndicat.

En pareils cas, la structure du pouvoir décisionnel d'une multinationale (lequel est centralisé) met un terme au dialogue des deux parties. Puisque les décisions sont généralement prises par les maisons mères, les responsables de la filiale en question ne peuvent rien changer.

Si la multinationale ne compense pas adéquatement chacun des intérêts affectés, les ouvriers et leurs leaders ont souvent recours à d'autres types d'arguments (souveraineté, impérialisme, grève, etc.) en vue de réparer les torts causés sans se préoccuper de la bonne image ni du nom de la multinationale dans la région.

L'intervention du gouvernement et une technique de négociation adéquate visant à reconnaître et à compenser les parties touchées par le conflit deviennent alors indispensables.

Cela dit, lors de ces négociations, il serait important de tenir compte des normes d'ordre public, en faveur de l'ouvrier et des syndicats, qui imposent une série d'obligations et de conditions requises qui doivent être observées sine qua non.

En conséquence, pour éviter toute situation susceptible de créer des conflits, il serait important, dans toute procédure de réorganisation d'une multinationale en Amérique Latine, de tenir compte des points suivants:

a) Établir un système fluide de communication avec les syndicats et les leaders ouvriers;

b) Reconnaître et individualiser les véritables intérêts en jeu de façon à rétablir l'équation des intérêts affectés par le biais d'une technique de négociation adéquate;

c) Tenir compte des circonstances politiques, sociales et économiques qui entourent l'opération;

d) Demander la coopération et la complaisance du gouvernement;

e) Respecter les lois d'ordre public.

Il existe une règle non écrite selon laquelle le meilleur moyen de protéger ses propres intérêts est de respecter et non pas de dénigrer les intérêts des autres. Cela dit, les mouvements ouvriers sont une réalité politique et économique dont la puissance ne peut être ni ignorée ni anéantie. À notre époque, il est nécéssaire d'établir un dialogue, de faire des compromis et de s'entendre. Le progrès économique et la stabilité politique, nécéssaires à la consécration et à la survie de tout système démocratique, libre et juste, passent par les mêmes critères d'entente.

RESUMEN EN ESPAÑOL

EMPRESAS MULTINACIONALES Y CONVENCIONES COLECTIVAS DE TRABAJO DESDE UN PUNTO DE VISTA LATINOAMERICANO

Las regulaciones vigentes y los problemas legales que surgen de la relación entre Empresas Multinacionales y Convenciones Colectivas de Trabajo en Latinoamérica no pueden ser analizadas correctamente sino a la luz de los valores políticos, sociales y económicos de cada país y región, la evolución histórica y las circunstancias presentes del movimiento obrero.

En este sentido, de acuerdo con las estadísticas de la mayoría de los países del área, afirmamos como postulado apriorístico que:

1) Las actividades de una multinacional son beneficiosas y no perjudiciales como muchos ideólogos afirman, para el progreso social, económico y político de un país (por ejemplo,) elevan el nivel de producción, de mano de obra empleada, de condiciones de empleo y de salarios).

2) La existencia en los países latinoamericanos de movimientos obreros organizados en sindicatos con gran influencia política, no implica necesariamente la existencia de intereses contrapuestos con los de las EM como una permanente fuente potencial de conflictos.

En efecto, las multinacionales no sólo son las que ofrecen mejores condiciones laborales, sino que proporcionan a los sindicatos y líderes obreros el escenario más apropiado para el desarrollo de sus actividades y carrera política. Es más probable que se origine un conflicto entre una multinacional y un sindicato por no reconocerse la existencia de estos intereses particulares que por reivindicaciones salariales.

3) Las multinacionales, ya sea por prestigio o por estar más controladas, son las que mejor cumplen con las regulaciones gubernamentales.

4) Un diálogo abierto entre los funcionarios locales de las multinacionales y los sindicatos asegura estabilidad y continuidad en los programas de producción.

Por lo tanto, los conflictos más graves se producen cuando se quiebra alguna de las reglas arriba mencionadas, especialmente cuando no se reconocen los intereses particulares de las diversas partes interesadas. Ello ocurre frecuentemente en el caso de una reorganización de empresa que da lugar al cierre de una fábrica o planta, lo que ocasiona despidos y más importante aún la supresión de la base obrera que da poder y representatividad política y laboral a un sindicato.

En estos casos, la estructura del poder de decisión de una multinacional (que es centralizada) hace que se interrumpa todo diálogo, ya que este tipo de decisiones son adoptadas en las casas matrices, independientemente de las circunstancias locales, y, en consecuencia, los funcionarios de la subsidiaria poco o nada pueden decidir.

Si la multinacional no compensa adecuadamente cada uno de los intereses afectados, los obreros y sus líderes recurrirán a otro tipo de argumentos (soberanía, imperialismo, huelgas, etc.) para compensar el daño causado a la imagen y nombre de la multinacional en la región.

El beneplácito del gobierno y una adecuada técnica de negociación donde se reconozcan y compensen los intereses afectados, se impone como una necesidad imperiosa.

Ahora bien, en estas negociaciones deben tenerse en cuenta las normas de orden público, que imponen en favor del obrero y de los sindicatos una serie de obligaciones y requisitos que deben cumplirse necesariamente.

En consecuencia, para evitar una potencial situación de conflicto, en todo proceso de reorganización de una multinacional en Latino América, ésta debe:

a) Establecer un sistema fluído de comunicación con los sindicatos y líderes obreros.

b) Reconocer e individualizar los reales intereses en juego, de forma tal de poder restablecer la ecuación de intereses afectada, através de una técnica de negociación adecuada.

c) Tomar en cuenta las circunstancias políticas, sociales y económicas que rodean la operación.

d) Buscar la cooperación o complacencia del gobierno.

e) Cumplir con las leyes de orden público.

Existe una regla no escrita que dice que para proteger los intereses propios, se debe respetar y no avasallar los intereses de los demás. En este sentido los movimientos obreros son una realidad política y económica poderosa, que no puede ser ignorada o destruída. Los tiempos modernos requieren diálogo, acuerdos, compromisos. El progreso económico y la estabilidad política, necesarias para la consagración y perdurabilidad de un sistema democrático, libre y justo, así lo requieren.

MULTINATIONAL ENTERPRISES AND COLLECTIVE BARGAINING IN A REORGANIZATION PROCESS

Translated By Syma Solovitch

HENRI GRONDIN
[Biographical paragraph]

There are two elements which are essential to any enterprise: capital and labor. Up until now, the speakers at this seminar have addressed themselves to the corporate and fiscal aspects of multinational enterprises (MNE). The purpose of this paper is to define the labor-related problems encountered by multinationals and, more specifically, to examine the Canadian approach to these problems, from which the other panelists may draw appropriate comparisons with their own systems.

Before engaging in a discussion of wage negotiations, however, it is first necessary to define the context within which these negotiations are conducted. In Canada, labor law essentially follows the American model, although an attempt is being made to introduce original concepts and concepts based upon or inspired by European theories. The Canadian system is based upon two fundamental principles: freedom of association and the exclusive right of representation.

FREEDOM OF ASSOCIATION

Freedom of association is, first and foremost, a right which is guaranteed by all of the labor laws in effect in Canada; it is a rule of public order and, as such, cannot be denied or discarded by the insertion of special clauses within an agreement.

Thus, an employer who obstructs the formation of a union or finances or somehow controls a union shall incur severe sanctions. Furthermore, an employer cannot dismiss or penalize in any way (through disciplinary measures or harassment) an employee who is affiliated with a union. If an employee accuses his employer of resorting to any of these tactics, the employer must prove to the administrative court that his actions were based upon reasonable grounds and were in no way related to or prompted by the employee's union affiliation. If he fails to convince the court of this, the employee shall be reinstated or restored to his former position and the court may impose a fine upon the employer.

EXCLUSIVE RIGHT OF REPRESENTATION

Although every worker has the right to join any association of his choice, every union does not necessarily have the right to represent and negotiate on behalf of its members. Only an "accredited" union can represent its members and must act on behalf of all of the employees. This is called the exclusive right of representation. In order to be accredited, a union must represent the absolute majority of the employees of either the entire enterprise or of a part of the enterprise (a collective bargaining unit).

These units are generally defined by a quasi-judicial body, made up of 1 to 3 members. The community of interests of the employees, which serve to determine the limits of these collective bargaining units, is identified according to certain criteria enumerated by the courts: namely, the similarity of function and qualification, the similarity of the terms and conditions of employment, the similarity of the determination of wages, the interdependence of functions and the possibility of transfer from one category of employment to another. Thus, office workers and shop workers generally belong to different units or categories of employment.

In addition to the community of interests of the employees, one must also take into consideration the workers' desire to form or not to form a distinct group and, more importantly, the physical structure of the enterprise.

The employer may contest the description of this unit, which has a significant influence over the accreditation of a labor union since the latter must represent, as decided by the administrative court, the absolute majority of the employees of the collective bargaining unit.

The accredited labor union acquires both rights and obligations: first, it has the right to represent its members and all of the employees within the collective bargaining unit. Second, it has the right, at least in the province of Quebec, to have the employer collect union fees (or their equivalent) from its members and from all of the employees within the bargaining unit, regardless of whether or not they are affiliated with the particular union. In return, the labor union has the obligation to negotiate a collective labor agreement whose application shall extend to all of the employees of the collective bargaining unit. The union must also protect and defend the rights and interests of its members and of all the other employees within the collective bargaining unit, including members of rival unions and non-union workers.

In the event that the labor union fails to fulfill its obligations, Canadian law allows the injured employee to bring an action for damages against the accredited union and, in certain provinces, force the union to defend his grievances before the court.

FEDERAL AND PROVINCIAL LEGISLATION APPLICABLE TO CANADIAN FIRMS AND FOREIGN-OWNED ENTERPRISES OPERATING IN CANADA

Canada has a federal government and, as such, is able to pass labor-related laws at both the federal and provincial levels. The question often arises, therefore, as to whether an enterprise is subject to the federal or provincial laws of Canada. This question is settled, not by the will of the parties but, rather, by the very nature of the enterprise. According to the general rule, an enterprise falls within the jurisdiction of the province in which its operations are carried out. The country or province in which its corporate headquarters are based is irrelevant to the applicable rule of law. Certain enterprises are exempt from provincial legislation and fall within federal jurisdiction: these enterprises are, as a rule, in the area of communications (radio, television, telephone, air, interprovincial transport--whether by road, railway or sea). Certain areas of communication are not always as easy to define and these grey areas are hotly debated before the courts whose decisions complete the broad and often vague provisions of the Canadian constitution.

Yet, we must remember that the principles are the same and that only the modalities distingusish the various laws, although certain transactions may be prohibited under federal legislation and permitted under provincial laws, and vice versa. Before establishing a subsidiary branch in Canada, a MNE must first examine the labor laws to which it shall be subject.

ACCREDITATION TO MULTINATIONAL ENTERPRISES

A MNE with Canadian subsidiaries does not have any more rights than a Canadian- based company and is subject to the labor laws of each province in which it operates. Up until now, the laws have made no distinction between large and small companies or between Canadian- and foreign-owned firms--with one exception: the Parliament of Nova Scotia has restricted the Michelin factories to one collective bargaining unit to represent all of its Nova Scotia factories, notwithstanding the fact that the general legislation in effect would not have allowed this. However, this is an isolated case and the chances of it repeating itself are very slim.

Although only 28% of Canada's labor force belong to a union, the multinational which establishes a subsidiary branch in Canada will, 99 times out of 100, become unionized, at least for a percentage of its employees.

We have seen that unionization occurs both at the factory level and, within the factory, at the level of each collective bargaining unit. The multinational corporation may therefore have to negotiate with several unions, which may very well have different ideologies regarding trade agreements. This is, moreover, why Michelin chose the province of Nova Scotia to impose the above-mentioned restriction.

A distinction must be drawn between the multinational which operates large factories (which are almost automatically unionized) and the multinational which owns small- and medium- sized corporations which are related to one another only by virtue of capital and in which unionization is not as widespread and where there might not exist a collective agreement. Nevertheless, the enterprise is required to conform to all labor laws imposing certain minimum standards, as we shall later see.

If a group of employees requests the right to represent all of the other employees, the employer, as we have seen, may contest the description of their unit but, in accordance with most Canadian laws, he cannot contest the representative nature of the association: in other words, whether the union represents the absolute majority of the employees is left to the discretion of the administrative court, which may either grant or deny accreditation.

If the court grants accreditation, the enterprise must negotiate in good faith with the accredited union. Yet, even in the absence of an accredited union, the employees are protected to some extent by certain laws throughout Canada which guarantee a minimum wage and certain minimum social security benefits, which vary from province to province. Moreover, the government imposes minimum monetary standards upon certain corporations in order to protect free competition with other unionized enterprises (This is known as being governed by a "decree"). The employee maintains a certain margin within which to exercise his control, although this control is subject to the control of the State or defined by those agreements concluded with an accredited union.

TRANSFER OF ACCREDITATION

A multinational which purchases a Canadian firm shall be subject to and bound by any collective labor agreement in effect prior to the transaction. Moreover, any union formerly accredited shall continue to represent all of the employees of the firm. This holds true, not only in cases where the shares of the enterprise are transferred but, also, where its assets are sold. These civil law rules were introduced into Canada in order to protect the rights of the workers guaranteed under Canada's "social democracy."

Moreover, in the province of Quebec, the courts have decreed that an employee who has been dismissed by his former employer and who has successfully contested such dismissal shall be reinstated by the new employer. This demonstrates, not only that the collective rights of the workers shall be transferred in the sale of the enterprise but, also, that certain individual rights shall be transferred as well.

It is therefore of the utmost importance that a multinational examine the nature of the rights of the desired enterprise before purchasing it. It should also examine past labor relations problems in order to determine the probability of a future conflict arising. Lastly, it should examine any collective labor agreement currently in effect in order to determine whether the wages are competitive.

Naturally, there are many grey areas in the transfer of accreditation from one enterprise to another, enabling legal scholars to hypothesize and set forth their theories and allowing jurists to argue before the administrative courts and, often, to appeal to the highest authorities within the civil courts.

WITHDRAWAL OR CHANGE OF ACCREDITATION

The accredited union has an exclusive right of representation which shall remain effective until the collective bargaining agreement expires, at which time the employees may choose to either join another union or resign without joining any union. Upon request, the administrative court shall determine whether the union still exists and, if so, whether it represents the majority of employees. At this time, the court can either grant accreditation to another union or revoke accreditation entirely.

WAGE NEGOTIATIONS

As we have seen, in the absence of an accredited union, there is total freedom to contract, provided the minimum wage and social security benefits are observed. Individual contracts may vary from one employee to another although, in large corporations, the employer tends to adopt a general policy of remuneration in order to avoid conflicts between employees.

Where an accredited union exists, negotiations must be carried out in good faith in order to arrive at a collective labor agreement. A party who fails to fulfill this obligation may incur a fine.

A union may be accredited in several of an employer's establishments, especially in cases of multinationals. Often the parties prefer to negotiate one collective bargaining agreement which shall be applied in all of the employer's establishments. When these establishments are located in more than one province, the laws of each province must be taken into account. This is often the case in large industrial sectors, such as the automobile industry and paper manufacturing. Sometimes an agreement may be reached whereby a union and several employers are grouped together in the same industry.

In the event that the union and employer are unable to agree upon a labor contract, the employees have the right to strike and the employer has the right to lock out, except in certain sectors which provide an essential public service. These rights, to strike and lock out, can be exercised only after giving prior notice, as provided by law. In the area of public services, the employees must give notice before the strike begins. Moreover, in a province such as Quebec, recourse to strike breakers is prohibited.

However, it should be noted that at all times the parties may, by mutual consent, waive the right to strike or lock out and voluntarily refer their dispute to a conciliation board. As an exception, in the case of a first collective labor agreement in the province of Quebec, one of the two parties may have the dispute brought before an arbitration board whose decision shall be final and binding.

GOVERNMENT INTERVENTION IN THE SETTLEMENT OF INDUSTRIAL DISPUTES

Before a strike begins, the government usually intervenes by sending a conciliator to settle the dispute. The government also intervenes during the dispute by sending a mediator (a highly-distinguished conciliator). In the area of public services, the dispute may be settled by the legislature who imposes a special law; up until now, however, this has never occurred in private enterprises.

SUBSTANCE OF COLLECTIVE BARGAINING AGREEMENTS

In Canada, the only restriction placed upon collective bargaining agreements is that nothing can be inserted in an agreement which is contrary to the rules of public order. However, many laws and regulations impose the insertion of certain clauses or influence the substance of these clauses. Therefore, laws relating to the language of labor, the obligation to grant maternity leave and to contribute to unemployment benefit plans, health insurance plans and pension plans are equally important factors to be considered in collective labor agreements. These agreements, therefore, include certain rules for the application of such plans and often add considerably to the minimum benefits guaranteed under the law. Certain laws, such as those which impose French as the official language of labor in Quebec, or the hiring of a certain percentage of handicapped employees require the parties to agree upon these matters.

Wages, therefore, are not the only important aspect considered in collective agreements. The granting of fringe benefits often account for more than twenty percent of salaries. Moreover, certain standard clauses often play a major role in determining the total cost of labor. I am referring in particular to those clauses which relate to job security, notice of dismissal and job descriptions.

Therefore, this freedom to conclude collective labor agreements, in principle absolute, is significantly limited by the legislature which, in addition to imposing rules and regulations, intervenes in the actual substance of the provisions of collective labor agreements.

Wages depend upon supply and demand and vary a great deal from industry to industry and from one region of the country to another in order to account for various factors as, for example, isolation and cost of transport.

The term of a collective bargain can be no less than one year and no more than three years. A collective bargain must be written and, in Quebec, must be in French.

Therefore, a multinational enterprise which establishes a subsidiary branch in Canada has no way of knowing in advance exactly how much it will spend on labor, since it cannot be certain as to whether or not it will be unionized, or as to the exact terms and conditions of employment which shall be in effect in its Canadian firm. However, by consulting specialists in these areas, the enterprise could estimate and provide for the approximate costs of labor in its operational budgets.

EFFECTS OF COLLECTIVE BARGAINING AGREEMENTS

The collective bargaining agreement binds both employer and employee. In other words, the employer cannot pay his employees less than what has been agreed upon. Moreover, by virtue of a certain court decision, it has been established that the employer cannot pay his employees any more than what has been agreed upon without the prior consent of the accredited union. This proceeds from the fundamental principle according to which the accredited union is granted the exclusive right to represent the employees.

EXECUTIVES

Everything that has been mentioned up until now has applied to employees in the strict sense of the term. A distinction must be drawn at this time between company employees and executives. The latter are not governed by the majority of labor laws which apply to employees. The relationships between employers and executives are governed by general rules.

A fundamental question is often raised, in this regard, as to whether multinationals can import their own executives into Canada in order to replace those executives already in office. The multinational must first verify with the immigration authorities whether it has the right to bring foreigners into Canada in order to fill managerial positions. The enterprise must show its need for these particular executives, whose equivalents cannot be found within Canada.

Moreover, those executives already serving cannot be dismissed without first being paid considerable compensation, which may, in certain cases, correspond to the equivalent of up to two years' wages, taking into consideration the seniority and age of the employee and his difficulty in finding a similar or equivalent position. In Quebec, there exists a provision whereby an executive who has served the same employer more than five years and who has been dismissed without just and sufficient cause, has the right to demand to keep his position. In these cases, negotiations must be held in order to reach an agreement as to the amount of compensation to be paid (which is often higher than the amount provided by law).

CONCLUSION

In short, the element of labor is becoming increasingly important in the operation and development of an enterprise and requires, on the part of its leaders, much clearness and flexibility in order to assure a productive work force at competitive rates. Too often, decisions to establish subsidiaries in a foreign country are made on the political level and fail to take into account the available human resources.

I hope that this short exposé will bring to light an additional aspect which I consider very important in all international transactions carried out by multinational enterprises.

RÉSUMÉ EN FRANÇAIS

MULTINATIONALES ET CONVENTIONS COLLECTIVES DANS LE PROCESSUS DE RÉORGANISATION DES ENTREPRISES: LA PERSPECTIVE CANADIENNE

Au Canada, le droit relatif au travail est essentiellement du type américain, même si on assiste à des tentatives d'insérer certains concepts originaux ou inspirés de la théorie européenne.

Toute multinationale intéressée à venir s'établir au Canada a donc intérêt à connaître les principales lignes directrices du cadre juridique dans lequel elle aura à évoluer.

Liberté d'association

La liberté d'association est un droit qui est garanti par toutes les législations du travail en vigueur dans le pays et qui est aussi d'ordre public, en ce sens qu'on ne peut le mettre de côté par des conventions particulières.

Ainsi, il est interdit à l'employeur de s'immiscer dans la formation d'un syndicat, de le financer, de le contrôler de quelque façon que ce soit: des pénalités sévères sont prévues.

De plus, il est aussi interdit à l'employeur de congédier, ou même de pénaliser par des mesures disciplinaires ou du harassement, les salariés qui ont des activités syndicales.

Monopole de représentation

Chaque salarié a droit d'appartenir à l'association de son choix, mais seul un syndicat accrédité peut représenter l'ensemble des salariés auprès de l'employeur: c'est ce qu'on appelle le monopole de représentation.

Pour être accrédité, un syndicat doit représenter la majorité absolue des salariés de toute une entreprise ou, encore, d'une partie de cette entreprise que l'on appellera alors unité de négociation.

Le syndicat accrédité acquiert des droits et des obligations: représentation équitable de tous ses membres et des salariés compris dans l'unité, salariés membres ou non du syndicat, etc.. Il est tenu de remplir les obligations que la loi lui impose sous peine de sanction.

Lois applicables

La première question à se poser face à un système confédéral comme le Canada est celle-ci: l'entreprise sera-t-elle sujette aux lois fédérales ou aux lois d'une des provinces?

Cette question est tranchée en fonction de la nature même de l'entreprise. La règle générale c'est que chaque entreprise tombe sous la juridiction des lois de la province où le travail s'effectue. Le lieu du siège social de l'entreprise n'entre nullement en ligne de compte ici. Toutefois, indépendamment du lieu où elles feront affaires, certaines entreprises échapperont à la juridiction des provinces et tomberont sous la juridiction fédérale: entreprise de communications, de transport inter-provincial, de téléphone, etc..

Accréditation auprès des multinationales

Au Canada une multinationale n'aura pas plus de droit qu'une entreprise locale. Elle devra se conformer aux législations du travail en vigueur dans chacun des endroits où elle aura des travailleurs.

En général la syndicalisation s'opère au niveau de chaque usine et, même à l'intérieur de chaque usine, au niveau de chaque unité de négociation. Une multinationale peut avoir à négocier avec plusieurs syndicats différents.

Transfert de l'accréditation

Il faut se rappeler que si une multinationale décide d'acheter une entreprise déjà existante au Canada, elle doit s'attendre à ce que tout le régime syndical suive l'entreprise dans la transaction.

Négociation

S'il y a un syndicat accrédité, la négociation doit se faire de bonne foi et avec diligence dans le but de conclure une convention collective de travail. En cas d'impossibilité de s'entendre sur un contrat de travail, le droit de grève existe tout comme d'ailleurs le droit au lock-out. Ces droits de grève et de lockout sont cependant réglementés, en ce sens qu'ils ne peuvent être utilisés avant certains délais prévus par la loi.

Contenu et effets de la convention collective

Le contenu de la convention collective au Canada n'est pas limité, cependant on ne peut rien y inscrire qui irait à l'encontre de l'ordre public.

Quant aux salaires, ils dépendent de l'offre et de la demande; ils varient beaucoup d'une industrie à une autre et aussi d'une région à une autre du pays, pour tenir compte de divers facteurs comme, par exemple, l'isolement et le coût du transport.

Les cadres

La Multinationale doit vérifier auprès des services de l'immigration, la possibilité de faire admettre au Canada des personnes étrangères pour occuper des postes de cadre.

Ces cadres ne sont pas régis par la majorité des lois du travail applicables aux salariés de l'entreprise et leurs relations avec l'employeur demeurent régies par les lois générales.

Conclusion

Trop souvent les décisions relatives à l'implantation de multinationales dans un pays sont prises au niveau politique sans se soucier des conditions relatives aux ressources humaines.

RESUMEN EN ESPAÑOL

MULTINACIONALES Y CONVENCIONES COLECTIVAS EN EL PROCESO DE REORGANIZACIÓN EMPRESARIAL

En Canadá, el derecho relativo al trabajo es esencialmente de tipo americano, aun cuando se presencian tentativas de inyectar ciertos conceptos originales o inspirados en doctrinas europeas.

Toda multinacional interesada en establecerse en Canadá, debe interesarse por conocer las principales lineas directivas del marco jurídico dentro del cual se desarrollará.

Libertad de asociación

La liberad de asociación es un derecho garantizado por, todas las legislaciones laborales vigentes en el pais, y que es también de orden público, en el sentido de que no puede derogarse por convenciones particulares.

De este modo, está prohibido al empleador inmiscuirse en la formación de un sindicato, financiarlo, controlarlo de modo alguno: severas penalidades están previstas.

Además, también se halla prohibido para el empleador despedir o aun penalizar con medidas disciplinarias, o trato desfavorable, a los empleados que desempeñan tareas sindicales.

Monopolio de representación

Cada empleado tiene el derecho de pertenecer a una asociación de su elección, pero sólo un sindicato acreditado puede representar el conjunto de empleados ante el empleador: es lo que se llama monopolio de representación.

Para ser acreditado, un sindicato debe representar la mayoría absoluta de empleados, de toda una empresa o aun de una parte de esta empresa, lo que se llama unidad de negociación.

El sindicato acreditado adquiere derechos y obligaciones: representación de todos los miembros y empleados comprendidos en la unidad, percepción de una cuota sindical de los empleados miembros o no del sindicato, etc... Debe cumplir las obligaciones que la ley le impone, bajo pena de sanción.

Jurisdicción

La primera pregunta en un sistema federal como Canadá es la siguiente: ¿la empresa está sujeta a las leyes federales o a las leyes de una de las provincias?

La respuesta se halla en la naturaleza misma de la empresa. La regla general es que cada empresa queda sujeta a la jurisdicción de las leyes de la provincia donde se efectua el trabajo. El lugar del domicilio social de la empresa no se tiene para nada en cuenta en este caso. De todas maneras, independientemente del lugar donde se administra, ciertas empresas desbordarán la jurisdicción provincial y caerán en la jurisdicción federal: empresas de communicaciones, de transporte interprovincial, de teléfonos, etc...

Acreditación de multinacionales

Una multinacional no tendrá mejores derechos que una empresa canadiense. Deberá respetar la legislación laboral vigente en cada uno de los lugares donde tenga empleados.

En general, el sindicalismo opera a nivel de cada empresa y aun en el interior de cada empresa, a nivel de cada unidad de negociación. Una multinacional puede tener que negociar con varios sindicatos diferentes.

Transferencia de la acreditación

Debe recordarse que si una multinacional decide comprar una empresa ya existente en Canadá, debe aceptar que todo el régimen sindical continue luego de la transferencia.

Negociación

Si hay un sindicato acreditado, la negociación debe hacerse de buena fe y diligentemente, con el fin de concluir una convención colectiva de trabajo. Si no se llega a un acuerdo sobre el contrato de trabajo, el derecho de huelga existe al igual que el derecho de lock-out. Tales derechos de huelga y de lock-out se hallan, sin embargo, reglamentados en el sentido que no pueden ser utilizados antes de ciertos plazos previstos por la ley.

Contenido y efecto de la convención colectiva

El contenido de la convención colectiva en Canadá no está limitado, pero nada puede acordarse contra el orden público.

En cuanto a salarios, dependen de la oferta y de la demanda. Estos varían mucho de una industria a otra y también de una región del pais a otra, para acomodarse a los diversos factores, como por ejemplo, el aislamiento y el costo del transporte.

Los cuadros

La multinacional debe verificar ante las autoridades de inmigración, la posibilidad de hacer admitir al país a extranjeros para cubrir vacantes en los cuadros.

Los cuadros no estan regidos por la mayoría de las leyes laborales aplicables a los trabajadores de la empresa, y sus relaciones con el empleador quedan sujetas a leyes generales.

Conclusión

Con demasiada frecuencia, las decisiones para el establecimiento de una multinacional en un país son tomadas a un nivel político, sin preocupaciones sobre las condiciones relativas a los recursos humanos.

Me atrevo a esperar que esta breve exposición pueda agregar un aspecto, que considero muy importante, en toda transacción empresarial a nivel internacional.

COLLECTIVE BARGAINING: THE EUROPEAN PERSPECTIVE

FRANÇOISE GENOT-DELBECQUE
Fiduciaire de France
France

Multinational enterprises and their subsidiaries operate in very diverse countries throughout the world, whether in countries with elaborate legal systems or in others where legal dispositions are practically non-existent.

Governments of developing countries and union organisations representing workers have realised the possible danger to their nation and to their people resulting from arbitrary, powerful economic actions which could undermine the sovereignty of States and have a negative influence on the standard of living and the social well-being of the people.

It was only after 1968 that a movement was launched to try to regulate labor relations, throughout the world, between multinational enterprises and their employees. This movement was pursued until 1977 by international authorities, such as the Organisation for Economic Cooperation and Development (OECD) and the International Labour Organisation (ILO). Shortly thereafter the international economic crisis stopped such movement.

Experience shows that even if multinational operations are controlled by a supranational decision-making center, contacts with the employees' representatives are made in each country under the domestic legislation of the country concerned. As illustrations, we could mention the case of two multinationals which called on my services when making choices affecting the situation of a subsidiary's employees. The decision-making organs of the multinationals were never concerned about following any supranational directive or giving information to local parties about what was happening elsewhere in other countries.

In one instance, during reorganisation proceedings, it was decided to close an English factory and to continue production in France because the English procedure for economic dismissals was easier and there was no risk of a refusal by the State or the administration. By contrast, in France, the dismissal procedure governed by the collective agreement for the relevant industry would have consisted of a preparatory phase of about six months, plus about one month for the government to reach a decision. At the end of these seven months there still would have been no guarantee that the State would authorize the dismissals in a politically protected zone, namely the Lille Region where Mr. Mauroy, Prime Minister of France at the time, would undoubtedly have opposed such a large-scale operation.

On the English side, the union representatives of the employees requested no information concerning the situation of the multinational on a world-wide level.

I would dare say that, whenever reorganisation of a group doing business in various European countries has been necessary, each country has handled the problem solely with respect to the subsidiary falling under its jurisdiction. No information is usually given concerning the situation of the multinational throughout the world. It must be stressed that, in France, in the case of a Japanese multinational, the very powerful unions represented in the subsidiary never appeared very concerned by what was happening beyond their own frontiers.

I. <u>Multinationals and international regulation of collective bargaining</u>.

We will attempt to ascertain, first, what positive attempts have been made at an international level to implement rules of conduct governing the collective bargaining process when a multinational embarks upon an operation of reorganisation.

A. <u>The first attempt at establishing a code of conduct was made by the OECD which, in 1976, issued a declaration setting out guidelines for multinational enterprises</u>.

1: <u>The aims of this declaration are</u>:

- to guarantee multinational enterprises the same treatment within a territory as that reserved for national enterprises,

- to try to ensure that multinationals respect the laws of each country where they operate,

- to try to develop the positive aspects which multinational actions could have on social development,
- to see that employment is brought to a maximum level in each country where a multinational operates.

This declaration of 21st June 1976 was not meant to undermine multinational activities. Actually it states that:

"The common aim of the Member countries is to encourage the positive contributions which multinational enterprises can make to economic and social progress and to minimise and resolve the difficulties to which their various operations may give rise. In view of the multinational structure of such enterprises, this aim will be furthered by co-operation among the OECD countries where the headquarters of most of the multinational enterprises are established and where a substantial part of the their activities is located."

Though recognizing the positive aspect of the activity of multinational enterprises, the first article of the guidelines states that "the advances made by multinational enterprises in organising their operations beyond the national framework may lead to abuse of concentrations of economic power and to conflicts with national policy objectives."

The guidelines which address many of the issues relating to a multinational enterprise's responses to structural changes, which can be a source of concern to governments, mean to lay down standards for the activities of multinational enterprises in the different member countries with regard to the specific aspects of employment and industrial relations.

2: Compliance with the laws of the country in which the subsidiary is situated

Article 1 of the section entitled "Employment and Industrial Relations" provides that enterprises should operate within the framework of the law, regulations and prevailing labour relations and employment practices in each country.

3: Non obstruction of employees representative organisations

Multinational enterprises should:

1. "respect the right of their employees to be represented by trade unions and other bona fide organisations of employees, and engage in constructive negotiations, either individually or through employer's associations, with such employees' organisations with a view to reaching agreements on employment conditions, which should include provisions for dealing with disputes arising over the interpretation of such agreements, and for ensuring mutually respected rights and responsibilities;

2. Provide such facilities to representatives of the employees as may be necessary to assist in the development of effective collective agreements."

4: Disclosure of information

Enterprises should "provide to representatives of employees information which is needed for meaningful negotiations on conditions of employment."

It is clear that, in order to carry out negotiations, the representatives of each party to those negotiations must have the necessary information at their disposal. The OECD document frequently emphasizes this need for increasing the information provided, but does not specify the content of such information. The only specification given is in article 3:

"Enterprises should provide to representatives of employees where this accords with local law and practice, information which enables them to obtain a true and fair view of the performance of the entity or, where appropriate, the enterprise as a whole."

It is interesting to note that the OECD recommendation is not limited to the entity in the country where the negotiations are held but extends "where appropriate, [to] the enterprise as a whole", which should enable the employees' unions to have an exact idea of their enterprise's situation in the world context of the group and to enable them to understand the choices made by the general management.

5: <u>Context of bona fide negotiations</u>

It is recommended not to threaten to use the possibility of transferring all or part of an operating unit from the country concerned, nor to transfer employees from an enterprise's component entities in other countries, in order to influence unfairly those negotiations or to hinder the exercise of a right to organise.

6: <u>Reorganisation operations</u>

As far as reorganisation operations are concerned, it is no longer collective bargaining which is recommended. Instead, enterprises should "provide reasonable notice of such changes to representatives of the employees and, where appropriate, to the relevant governmental authorities and <u>cooperate</u> with the employees' representatives and appropriate governmental authorities so as to mitigate to the maximum extent practicable adverse effects."

7: <u>Scope of application</u>

- in OECD countries

- and multinational enterprises

A precise legal definition of multinational enterprises is not required for the purposes of the guidelines. These usually refer to companies or other entities whose ownership is private, state or mixed, established in different countries and, so linked, that one or more of them may be able to exercise a significant influence over the activities of others and, in particular, to share knowledge and resources with the others.

These guidelines also apply to operations resulting from specific agreements not necessarily involving any participation in capital.

8: Observance of guidelines

Observance of the guidelines is voluntary and not legally enforceable. However, they should help to ensure that the operations of these enterprises are in harmony with the national policies of the countries where they operate and to strengthen the basis of mutual confidence between enterprises and states.

B. The International Labour Organisation issued a tripartite declaration in 1977 to develop what had been achieved by the OECD

The preliminary exposé of the "Tripartite declaration of principles concerning multinational enterprises and social policy, adopted by the governing body of the International Labour Office on 16 November 1977", reiterates the intentions of the OECD declaration but seems more aimed at improving the situation in developing countries. It, too, is concerned with ensuring that multinationals operate in accordance with the laws of the countries in which they carry out their activities and respect international regulations.

In the section entitled "Employment", multinational enterprises are recommended to "give priority to employment, occupational development, promotion and advancement of nationals of the host country at all levels in co-operation, as appropriate, with respresentatives of the workers and governmental authorities."

This declaration, although very similar to the OECD Guidelines, is much more detailed with regard to "changes in operations", including those resulting from mergers, take-overs or transfers of production.

C. The 1981 Recommendation n° 163 of the ILO attempts to organise industrial relations by promoting collective bargaining.

1: The parties to collective bargaining are defined as follows:

- on the employers' side: the employers' representatives and independent organisations,

- on the employees' side: the workers' representatives and independent organisations.

The recommendation stipulates that the criteria for representation be objective and drawn up before the negotiations but after consultation with employers' and employees' organisations.

2: It is recommended to develop collective bargaining at all levels, that is:

- the company
- the subsidiary
- the industry
- the branch of activity
- the regional or national levels.

3: It is also recommended to take measures to ensure that those taking part in the negotiations receive a suitable training at all levels and that they are really empowered to lead and conclude the negotiations. Furthermore, measures must be taken so that the parties can have access to the information necessary for them to be able to negotiate in full knowledge of the facts.

D. In the domain of industrial relations, there are two other ILO Recommendations, 129 and 130 issued June 28 and June 29, 1967 respectively, which concern communications between management and labor within a company and the examination of complaints made in the company, and the way to settle them. Every government's attention is drawn to the need to establish an atmosphere of mutual understanding and trust in the company, to stimulate company efficiency and favor the workers' aspirations by distributing the information relating to different aspects of company life and social conditions of workers.

E. Amongst all the international recommendations, the United Nations Organisation (UN) Code of Conduct is still in the preliminary studies stage.

The main problem is defining its scope of application.

The Eastern bloc countries do not want their companies abroad to be subject to the forthcoming Code of Conduct, and claim that their companies cannot be considered as multinational enterprises because they are under state control.

In any case, it is certain that the document currently being drafted will remain vague and will not create a real right for workers' representatives to negotiate at any time.

There is talk of distributing information to the workers' representatives of each country, so that they may have an exact idea of the results at a national level or, if need be, at the level of the whole enterprise.

Consultation procedures in matters of mutual interest should be developed by the management of multinational enterprises together with the unions or other representatives of the workers.

Appropriate precautions must be taken to ensure that the information given remains confidential so as not to cause any damage to the parties concerned.

One may speculate that this document will go no further than those already referred to. It will merely reflect the principles enshrined in the OECD guidelines, as was done by the ILO Tripartite Declaration.

F. EEC Regulations

The European Economic Community has tackled the problems in a manner slightly different from the angle taken by international organisations.

The creation of a unified market presupposes reducing the differences between the employment regulations of the various countries. To ensure that enterprises operating in several EEC countries did not choose to invest or divest according to the particular domestic regulations of the various countries, it was essential to bring some uniformity to the national legislations - The Council of the EEC therefore issued several directives to try to solve the existing problems.

The directives have been issued in accordance with articles 100 and 101 of the Treaty of Rome. Article 100 states that:

"The Council shall, acting unanimously on a proposal from the Commission, issue directives for the approximation of such provisions laid down by law, regulation or administrative action in Member States as directly affect the establishment or functioning of the common market.

Three directives are particularly relevant to our topic: they deal with collective dismissals, vested rights of employees and mergers.

1: Council Directive of 17 February 1975 on the approximation of the laws of the Member States relating to collective dismissals.

The Council's aim in drawing up such a directive was to eliminate the differences existing, in this respect, among the various common market countries. These differences do "create disparities in the conditions of competition which influence the decisions of national or multinational enterprises with regard to the distribution of their operations." These disparities were considered by the Council as "having an adverse effect on social progress" and as being "prejudicial to balanced overall and regional development within the Community."

The Directive states that employers contemplating collective dismissals should begin consultations with the workers' representatives with a view to reaching an agreement. "These consultations shall, at least, cover ways and means of avoiding collective redundancies or reducing the number of workers affected, and mitigating the consequences.

To enable the workers' representatives to make constructive proposals, the employer shall supply them with all relevant information and shall, in any event, give in writing the reasons for the redundancies, the number of workers to be made redundant, the number of workers normally employed and the period over which the redundancies are to be effected."

It is worth pointing out that this directive merely details the consultation procedure, states that the consultation must take place before the public authorities are notified of the decision taken and that, eventually, there is no obligation to reach an agreement. The consequence is that workers cannot prevent the dismissals once the decision has been made by the management.

The actual implementation of this directive by the respective EEC members is far from being uniform. Thus, although France has passed legislation on the matter, the French statute nevertheless stipulates that no dismissal for economic reasons can be carried out without prior authorization from the administrative authorities.

This French legislation is far more restrictive than English statutes which merely reenact the Directive in its original provisions.

2: Council Directive of 14 February 1977 on the approximation of the laws of the Member States relating to the safeguarding of employees' rights in the event of transfers of enterprises, businesses or parts of business.

This Directive provides for the automatic transfer of all employment agreements from the transferor to the transferee, and the observance for at least 12 months of the terms and conditions agreed in the collective agreement effective in the transferor's company before the transfer.

With respect to the collective bargaining process, the Directive provides for a period of time, before the transfer is carried out, during which the transferor must give information relating to the measures envisaged to the workers' representatives. In addition there must be consultation with the workers' representatives with a view to reaching an agreement.

3: Council Directive of 9 October 1978 on the subject of mergers carried out on the territory of one Member State

This Directive reiterates the guidelines of the Directive regulating company transfers and confirms, in the case of mergers, the procedures of information and consultation applicable for transfers.

4: The Vredeling Directive

The aim of the Vredeling Directive, which is still in draft form, is to bring into line the laws and practices of the various EEC countries with regard to information disclosed to and consultation with the workers.

Because of the many differences still existing between the laws and practices of the member countries, there can be differences in the treatment of workers in one single enterprise. There are such differences with respect to the type of information supplied to the workers.

Some measures are being considered to do away with such differences. The supply of information to workers would be developed and increased both in multinational enterprises, regardless of the location of their decision centre, and in enterprises with complex structure having their decision centre situated in the same country as the entity concerned.

This Directive would apply to multinational enterprises employing at least 1,000 workers in one or more subsidiaries situated in the common market and employing at least 100 workers in the subsidiary involved. In all cases the management of the subsidiary would be responsible for supplying information to the workers.

If the management of the subsidiary does not supply the information provided for by the Directive, or is unable to do so, the workers should allow the management of the subsidiary 30 days to obtain and communicate the relevant information. If at the end of the 30-day period no information has been communicated, the Directive provides for the workers direct access to the decision centre of the dominant entity.

However, the Directive recognizes to the management of subsidiaries responsible for supplying information to the workers, the right to withhold any information which it deems confidential. It is obvious that a provision of this nature greatly restricts the workers' right to be informed of the enterprise's activities and plans.

Where operations of reorganisation are concerned, the Directive provides for communication of the information to the workers and the implementation of consultation and negotiation proceedings.

Such proceedings must take place, in particular, in the following instances:

- the closing down or transfer of a company or of a substantial part of a company,

- reorganisation or expansion operations or major changes of activity,

- major changes of organisation,

- rationalization plans and changes in work methods.

When such measures of reorganisation are contemplated, the information to be disclosed to the workers should address:

- the reasons behind the measures contemplated,
- the economic, financial and social consequences of such measures for the workers concerned,

- the actions contemplated in regard to the workers.

Because of the mandatory delays attached to the different phases of the proceedings, the implementation of this Directive would result in the suspension of any decision concerning reorganisation for a period of at least 30 days, which is the time granted to the workers' representatives for giving their opinion following receipt of the relevant information. However, it is to be noted that it is not compulsory for any agreement to be signed with the workers' representatives in order for reorganisation operations to be carried out.

The one original characteristic of the Vredeling Directive in comparison to the existing international documents on the subject of informing and consulting workers, is that it provides for sanctions in the event of non observance of the provisions contained therein: "The Member States should provide for appropriate sanctions in the event of violation of the obligation stipulated in the present article." No specifications have been given in the original text as to what these sanctions should be. In France, all violations of regulations governing labour relations are criminally sanctioned. If an employer neglects his obligation to negotiate annually on wage matters with the trade unions active in the enterprise, he will be exposed to criminal sanctions such as large fines or, even, a prison sentence.

II. A practical evaluation of the rules and regulations issued by international organizations.

1. The relevance of these texts

Many of the texts considered above, as well as others, merely give recommendations which are not legally enforceable. In addition they use an ambiguous terminology. The result is that many of them are inefficient. Even if they are integrated into a domestic legislation, the majority of the terms they use are very vague and give rise to different interpretations which may be contested.

Many unions have raised several complaints of violation of the OECD guidelines but their complaints, most often, fell on dead ears. As an illustration we will report a case related to us by Mr. Tapiola, Secretary of the Trade Union Advisory Committee (TUAC):

A multinational enterprise took over a Swedish company specialising in the domain of health care. Its main line of business was the manufacture and sale of intravenous therapy products and 85% of the output was exported from Sweden. Since the take over by the multinational group, the headquarters of which were located in London, the Swedish company has been included in the parent company's corporate planning and all the decisions concerning the localization of production have ultimately been decided by the corporation's executive management in London.

When certain changes in production became necessary, it was contemplated to transfer production to another sister company located in the United States. It was obvious that such a change in production would affect (or influence) the volume of production of the Swedish company.

Negotiations between the employees' representatives and management of the Swedish company took place according to Swedish regulations. The minutes of these negotiations stated that decisions on the localization of production had been taken by the groups's central management in London. At the time, reference was made by the employees' representatives to the OECD Guidelines for Multinational Enterprises as they felt that the group's future structure of production threatened their jobs.

In application of these guidelines the unions requested negotiations between the employees and the representatives of management who were in a position to decide on the future localization of production, meaning the central management in London. The parent company replied that the negotiations should be conducted with the management of the Swedish subsidiary. The Swedish employers' confederation had expressed its opinion on the basis of §9 of the Guidelines, stating that the negotiations should be held with the Swedish company and the central management in Sweden, and that there was no obligation for the parent company to negotiate on its overall financial plans and world-wide strategy. Faced with such a refusal by the parent company, the trade unions made a formal request to the Swedish Ministry of Industry asking for access to the real decision makers.

The representative of the Swedish Ministry of Industry gave an interpretation similar to that of the unions. He referred to the OECD's Review report adopted in June 1979 which states:

> ". . . The purpose of §9 was to lay stress on the access of employee representatives to the management representatives who are authorized to take decisions on the matter under negotiation. This is the key consideration and the management of a multinational enterprise should see that it is observed in the circumstances of each case.
>
> . . . Parent companies, therefore, are expected to take the necessary organisational steps to enable their subsidiaries to observe the guidelines, inter alia, by providing them with adequate information and ensuring that their representatives carrying out negotiations at the national or local level have sufficient authority to take decisions on the matters under negotiations."

In the meantime, negotiations at the Swedish level had been initiated in accordance with local regulations. However the management of the local subsidiary, instead of presenting the decision to develop production outside Sweden as a decision of the group's central management in London, stated that the decision had been taken by the Swedish management which had acknowledged that further expansion in Sweden was not desirable due to lack of facilities and labor as well as high labor costs. Although these negotiations ended without agreement, management representatives stated that they had fulfilled their obligations under domestic law.

The British government which had been contacted by the Swedish government, concluded that the parent company and its subsidiary had acted in accordance with the OECD Guidelines. The Swedish Employers' Confederation welcomed the British government's interpretation which pointed out that the difficulty of interpretation resided in determining in each case where the decision-making power lay. "Decisions are mainly the result of a long process in which several parties are involved and play different roles at different times." According to the British authorities, the problem with §9 of the "Employment and Industrial Relations" section of the OECD Guidelines, is that it presupposes that one can ascertain clearly where the decision making power lies.

At that point in the negotiations the Swedish unions decided to consult the TUAC and ask for clarification from the OECD.

After examining the case, the TUAC concluded that the employees' representatives had not been able to negotiate with the real decision makers and it proceeded to submit the case to the Committee for International Investment and Multinational Enterprises (CIME). The Levy's group (a working group named after its chairman which was set up by the CIME to examine all issues raised in relation to the Guidelines) clarified §9 of the "Employment and Industrial Relations" section by stating that the choice of the level at which the negotiations should take place remains in the hands of the multinational enterprise. The same group noted that labor relations practices in the country where negotiations have been initiated are prevailing and that the choice of the level at which the negotiation must be handled depends on a series of factors which it undertook to enumerate.

All in all, and as a result of these various interpretations by the OECD bodies, the situation has not really been clarified. The union representatives considered that the obligation to negotiate with management representatives having sufficient powers to conduct meaningful negotiations had not been fulfilled and the employers' representatives considered that the company had fulfilled all its obligations.

Concerning the EEC Directives, there are other problems due to differences between national legislations which lead to disparities between the EEC countries. For instance, the 1975 Directive concerning collective redundancies has not been applied uniformly in all EEC countries. It was stipulated that the Member States should bring their laws and practices in line with the provisions of the Directive, unless their legislation already provided more favorable conditions for the workers. In the case of France, before the Directive was issued, there existed statutes and regulations which prohibited redundancies for economic reasons unless prior authorization was obtained from the relevant authorities. These statutes and regulations distorted the rules of conduct between the Member States because, in most common-market countries, the enterprises take the final decision even if they have to give reasonable notice and seek solutions by means of negotiations to reduce the harmful effects of the redundancies. This extra special protection afforded to French employees risks having a damaging effect on investments in France and on employees in other Member States where shut-downs or reorganization operations will be decided mainly on the ground of the lower costs and shorter time involved.

2. The Unions' position

The unions have pointed out that the OECD Guidelines adopted in 1976, the UN Code of Conduct and the ILO Tripartite Declaration are all very similar documents and can be considered together in one lump judgment. By and large the Unions are most disappointed with the lack of binding force of these texts and their failure to be implemented.

These unions consider that what has already been achieved is insufficient because the documents in existence have not enabled them to participate effectively in negotiations on matters affecting them, and to oppose reorganisation operations.

For instance, with respect to the kind of information to be given to the workers, no guarantee exists as to the quality of this information when there is a certain degree of discretion involved as it is the employer who decides whether such information is too confidential or not to be disclosed.

As far as consultations and negotiations are concerned, they never enable the workers to question the grounds for the decision itself. In order for negotiations to be meaningful, access must be open to the actual decision-making power, and the exact structure of the capital of the multinational enterprise involved must be known. As long as no document forces multinational enterprises to give information on these two points, the unions will never be certain that they are faced with the representatives of the actual decision-making power.

These problems are compounded by the fact that the unions are currently worried about the anti-union attitude in a large part of the business world. They are disappointed that the Member States of the OECD have not acknowledged that the anti-union policies aimed at preventing employees from organising themselves constitute an obstacle to the implementation of the international regulations. They firmly believe that the application of these texts depends entirely on cooperation between the business world, the governments and the unions. Yet, the unions represented in the TUAC, despite their desire to see more binding instruments developed, do not consider that the time is ripe to implement such documents. They speculate that the economic crisis and recession will change the structures of multinationals and complex-structured enterprises in a way which cannot be foreseen. They believe that the documents to be implemented cannot be decided upon for another five years as the structures of enterprises will not become stable before that time. They also believe that it is unrealistic, at a time when changes must be brought about rapidly, to bring in measures likely to interfere with such changes.

3. The employers' position.

The position of the employers has been widely spread by the Business and Industry Advisory Committee (BIAC).

The employers represented by the BIAC, believe that the "soft law" approach of the guidelines is in keeping with the spirit of free enterprise and seems perfectly suited to facilitating the necessary and rapid adaptation to economic changes. In a report on the OECD Guidelines, the BIAC stated that it "was pleased that following extensive discussions on the subject of changes in operations, the OECD Committee recognized that management should be guided by the special circumstances of each case in determining whether it is possible to provide employees with notice prior to taking a final decision on a change of operations."

In this same report "BIAC welcomed the positive efforts made by Member governments to coordinate their attitude towards international investment and multinational enterprises and, in particular, OECD's explicit recognition of the positive contribution made by international investment to economic and social progress. BIAC expressed confidence that the Guidelines would be followed by individual enterprises, welcoming the fact that the Guidelines sought to eliminate discrimination between national and multinational and between state-owned and private enterprises. BIAC hoped that Guidelines on disclosure of information would add to the public understanding of multinational operations, but drew attention to the difficulty and cost of assembling all the figures, particularly for widely spread enterprises in countries where the recommendations of the Guidelines went beyond current practice. Moreover, BIAC again pointed out that comparisons of information from different enterprises in areas where conditions were widely dissimilar could be misleading and might confuse rather than enlighten."

Employers constantly emphasize the difficulties which stand in the way of direct access to the central decision-making power whenever a decision is taken by management outside the subsidiary involved. They claim that such a policy cannot be implemented in groups with numerous subsidiaries spread throughout the world. They reaffirm that contacts must be made at the level of the management of the subsidiary involved. Any other solution would deprive the local management of its authority and its credibility.

UNICE (Union of the Industries of the European Community) is of the opinion that the European directives are not effectively applied. It is opposed to the setting up of a uniform framework because it will not take into account the specific practices existing in matters of labor relations at a European level. UNICE also believes that binding provisions for complex structured enterprises or multinationals would be unfavorable to multinational enterprises and would threaten their competitiveness in relation to companies with a simple structure. The latter are more flexible and capable of adapting themselves quickly to the new operational requirements imposed by economic changes.

As far as the confidentiality provision is concerned, UNICE believes that it is ill-advised to let the workers' representatives, or a local court, decide what information likely to be distributed must be kept confidential. It also maintains that it is inopportune to introduce into labor relations a certain lack of flexibility which does not fit in with the decision-making procedures in complex-structured enterprises.

In consultation and negotiation matters, the employers consider that the management should have the last say. In other words, decisions relating to reorganisation remain its prerogative even if the workers' and their representatives' wishes are taken into account. While discussing reorganisation plans, they consider that negotiations must be held with the workers on matters such as planning the operations, searching for solutions more acceptable or less prejudicial to the workers (for example, looking for a buyer for an establishment which is about to be closed down) and other ways and means likely to soften the consequences of these decisions for those directly affected (for example, compensation schemes, training courses or assistance in finding another job, etc.).

Conclusion

Is there any particular reason why multinational enterprises should be controlled and why their subsidiaries should be under the obligation to consult and negotiate with the personnel?

An affirmative answer to these questions would be justified if one could establish that multinational enterprises have an adverse impact on employment and on the personal social well being of their employees.

A special OECD report published in 1983 provides some answers to these questions. It discloses that, since the 1970s, direct foreign investment has become far more dynamic than national investment. Even if the reasons for a foreign local investment are not always clear, it appears that the results on employment in multinational enterprises are usually the same or even better than those of the national enterprises. The specific characteristics of multinational enterprises enable them to avoid certain difficulties or drastically reduce their impact when carrying out a successful reorganisation operation.

It cannot be said that multinationals have had more of a negative effect than national enterprises on the employment front. We can only note that, when faced with changes, the workers of multinational enterprises felt that, when reorganisation plans were announced, the decisions had already been made at a level higher than that of the local company or subsidiary and that they had no opportunity of suggesting any modifications to the plan already decided upon by the group's management.

Another question which must be addressed is whether it is appropriate to develop the collective bargaining process within the framework of an operation of reorganization or restructuring. Ideally the answer ought to be yes, as it is normal to involve all concerned parties in the negotiation phase of situations which affect them directly.

Yet, the problem is one of knowing whether this is a realistic approach as well as one of defining what must be understood by collective bargaining. Should negotiations take place before the decision is made, or should they serve only to define the way in which the decision ought to be implemented? Obviously a decision based on a political choice has to be made at this point: how far can the employees' representatives be allowed to challenge the authority of the company's management body?

To allow French labor unions to be deeply involved in the negotiation process would, most likely, lead to a stalemate situation. In a recent instance, French unions, and the CGT in particular, were involved in a take over and reorganisation scheme. It required harmonizing the vested rights of the employees in order to smooth out the differences between the various plants of the company and avoid unnecessary costs. The new management denounced the existing vested rights and proceeded to start negotiations with the workers' representative to draft a more realistic company agreement. The unions were advised, in writing, of the start of these negotiations which were to be based on the proposals they had been asked to make.

The position of the French unions represented in the company consisted in saying that the law states that, in the event of denunciation of vested rights, these rights will continue to apply for twelve months following a three-month notice period starting from the date of the letter of denunciation. Therefore, in this case the rights ought to continue to apply for fifteen months and the Unions refused to negotiate on any other preliminary issue, positing that the management's proposals did not interest them. Every time the management would summon the unions to the negotiation table, the unions would claim that the correct procedure had not been followed and used this as a pretext for avoiding any further discussion.

Keeping this example in mind, it is clear that for the term "collective bargaining" to have its full significance in France, mentalities will have to change drastically.

RÉSUMÉ EN FRANÇAIS

LES MULTINATIONALES ET L'EMPLOI

Dans quelle mesure la politique commerciale et financière d'une société multinationale est elle dictée, ou inspirée, par des considérations humaines portant sur l'emploi et le bien être social de ses employés?

Dans cet article l'auteur combine une analyse théorique des dispositions législatives et réglementaires promulguées aussi bien par des gouvernements nationaux que par un certain nombre d'organisations internationales à une étude de cas pratiques de quelques sociétés multinationales sur lesquels l'auteur a été appelé à travailler.

Les premières tentatives de règlementer les activités des multinationales, du point de vue des relations du travail, datent de la fin des années 1960 pour culminer vers la fin de la décennie suivante avec l'intervention de l'OCDE et de l'OIT.

En 1976 l'OCDE adopta une sorte de guide de bonne conduite des multinationales. Le guide les invitait à respecter un certain nombre de règles qui visaient à encourager les contributions positives des multinationales au développement économique et social des pays membres tout en s'efforçant de minimiser les difficultés que ces contributions pouvaient engendrer. L'accent était mis sur la nécessité de partager toutes les informations nécessaires à une bonne conduite des relations entre les employés et leur employeur.

L'OIT devait étendre les efforts de l'OCDE aux relations des multinationales avec les pays en voie de développement. Puis en 1981 l'OIT tentait de fournir un cadre de règles destinées à promouvoir des négociations collectives entre les employeurs et les représentants des employés.

L'auteur fait ensuite une analyse relativement détaillée des dispositions règlementaires au sein de la Communauté Européenne, se penchant en particulier sur la directive Vredeling qui tente d'apporter une certaine uniformité entre les législations nationales portant sur les consultations entre employeurs et employés et les droits de ces derniers d'être informés.

Dans la deuxième partie de son rapport l'auteur cherche à tirer quelques conclusions pratiques sur la prolifération de tous les textes adoptés par ces organisations internationales.

Un cas pratique fort illustratif des problèmes soulevés par les activités des multinationales dans leurs rapports avec leurs employés est le cas d'une multinationale anglaise qui prit le contrôle d'une société suédoise.

Peut-être la crise économique qui étreint le monde est-elle responsable du non respect des dispositions prises par les organisations internationales. Il est certain que, dans les conditions actuelles, les syndicats sont un peu sur une position de repli attendant des jours meilleurs pour faire valoir leur point de vue.

En règle générale on ne peut pas dire que les multinationales aient eu un effet négatif plus marqué que les sociétés de statut national sur la situation de l'emploi. Ce qu'on peut affirmer, par contre, c'est que les employés des multinationales considèrent que les plans de réorganisation d'une multinationale sont décidés à l'échelon de la direction internationale sans que les syndicats nationaux aient l'ocasion de faire valoir leurs positions. Cela est particulièrement vrai lorsque les syndicats sont "politisés" comme ils le sont en France.

RESUMEN EN ESPAÑOL

LAS MULTINACIONALES Y EL EMPLEO

En qué medida la política comercial y financiera de una empresa multinacional está dictada, o inspirada, por consideraciones humanas referentes al empleo y al bienestar social de sus trabajadores?

En este artículo el autor combina un análisis teórico de las disposiciones legislativas y reglamentarias promulgadas, tanto por gobiernos nacionales como por un cierto número de organizaciones internacionales, junto con el estudio de casos prácticos de algunas empresas multinacionales, en los cuales el autor ha intervenido profesionalmente.

Las primeras tentativas de reglamentar la actividad de las multinacionales, desde el punto de vista de las relaciones laborales, comienzan al fin de la década de 1960 para culminar diez años mas tarde con la intervención de la OCDE y de la OIT.

En 1976 la OCDE adoptó una especie de criterios de buena conducta para las multinacionales. La OECD invitó a las multinacionales a seguir un cierto número de reglas con el fin de fomentar las contribuciones positivas de las multinacionales al desarrollo económico y social de paises miembros, esforzándose al mismo tiempo por minimizar las dificultades que tales contribuciones pudiesen acarrear. El énfasis estaba puesto en la necesidad de compartir toda la información necesaria para la buena conducción de relaciones entre empleados y empleador.

La OIT debía extender los esfuerzos de la OECD a las relaciones de las multinacionales con países en vías de desarrollo. Luego, en 1981, la OIT trató de crear un conjunto de normas destinadas a promover la negociación colectiva entre los empleadores y los representantes de los empleados.

El autor hace luego un análisis relativamente detallado de las disposiciones reglamentarias en el seno de la Comunidad Europea, contemplando en particular la directiva Vredeling, que trata de aportar una cierta uniformidad a las legislaciones nacionales referentes a las consultas entre empleadores y empleados y el derecho de estos últimos a ser informados.

En la segunda parte de su presentación el autor trata de extraer algunas conclusiones práticas de la proliferación de todos los textos adoptados por estos organismos internacionales.

Un caso práctico, altamente ilustrativo de los problemas creados por la actividad de las multinacionales en sus laborales, es el caso de una multinacional inglesa que tomó control de una empresa sueca.

Quizás la crisis económica que sufre el mundo sea responsable por la falta de observación de las disposiciones tomadas por organismos internacionales. Ciertamente, en las condiciones actuales, los sindicatos se encuentran un poco en una posición de retirada, esperando la llegada de tiempos mejores para hacer valer sus puntos de vista.

Como regla general no puede decirse que las multinacionales hayan tenido un efecto negativo más marcado que las empresas nacionales sobre la situación laboral. Lo que puede afirmarse, en cambio, es que los empleados de las multinacionales consideran que los planes de reorganización de una multinacional son decididos al nivel de dirección internacional, sin que los sindicatos nacionales tengan la ocasión de hacer valer sus puntos de vista. Esto es particularmente cierto cuando los sindicatos estan "politizados", como en Francia.

CHAPTER V

PURCHASE AND SALE OF SECURITIES

LATIN AMERICA

UNITED STATES

EUROPE

SECURITIES: PROBLEMS IN SELLING SECURITIES IN LATIN AMERICAN PRIVATE AND PUBLIC MARKETS

Ricardo J. Diez

Licenciado en Derecho, 1970, Universidad Nacional Autónoma de México. Admitted to Bar in all of the Courts of México and the Courts of the State of New York, U.S.A. Associate: Santamarina & Steta (Mexico City) 1971-1978. Curtis, Mallet-Prevost, Colt & Mosle (New York) 1978 to present. Member of the American Bar Association, the New York State Bar Association and the Association of the Bar of the City of New York. Specializing in Latin American Law with regard to international financings, oil contracts, commercial transactions, taxation, corporate, foreign investment and transfer of technology.

The securities markets in major Latin American jurisdictions such as Mexico, Argentina, Venezuela, Colombia, Chile and Perú are regulated by special legislation dealing specifically with the offer, issuance and sale of securities.[1]

Generally, the abovesaid legislation deals with the public offer and sale of the securities indicated therein, which include stocks, bonds and commercial paper, among others.

As to the private offer and sale of securities in Latin America, such transactions are governed by the Commercial Codes and laws deriving therefrom.

A multinational enterprise with interests in Latin American countries seeking to trade publicly in securities or to pursue other kinds of reorganization should, at the outset, analyze the scope and limitations imposed by local legislations on the trading of securities. In this regard, a distinction should be drawn between the public offer and sale of securities issued by companies existing under the laws of the Latin American jurisdiction involved and the offer and sale of securities issued by companies existing under the laws of a foreign jurisdiction.

While most legislation is not precise on the issue, it appears that the intent is the regulation of the public offer and sale of the securities issued by companies incorporated and existing under the laws of the Latin American country in question. In Mexico, for instance, while the Ley del Mercado de Valores is not entirely clear on this issue, we find that under the requirements for the registration and approval by the Comisión Nacional de Valores of the securities to be offered and sold there is language which clearly reflects that such registrations and approvals are meant for securities issued by local companies.[2]

By contrast, in Venezuela the Comisión Nacional de Valores has the authority to authorize the public offer within Venezuelan territory of "stocks and other securities issued by international organizations, governments and foreign institutions, corporations domiciled abroad and any other persons assimilated therein provided [that] it is convenient to the national interest and the favorable prior opinion of the National Executive through the Ministry of the Treasury [has been obtained]" (Article 10, Paragraph 2 of the Venezuelan Ley del Mercado de Capitales.) (Our translation.)

In practice, however, it must be mentioned that the securities sold and traded in the Latin American markets are for the most part securities issued by local companies.

For this purpose, the Comisiones de Valores (Securities Commissions) of the various Latin American jurisdictions have the primary function of enforcing the legislation dealing with the public offer and sale of securities. Accordingly, they have the authority, among other things, to approve and register the securities offered to the public, and to analyze the financial and commercial situation as well as other aspects of the issuers of the securities. In addition, the Comisiones de Valores have the power to make routine inspections and in some instances the authority to suspend the operations of an issuer or of appointing receivers or trustees to administrate the business of issuers.

Multinational corporations with a presence in Latin America during the last 25 years have witnessed that the evolution of some of the securities markets (and their stock exchanges) in Latin America has been spectacular. In some jurisdictions, such as Mexico, the authorities have primarily encouraged the growth of the stock exchange[3] by eliminating over-the-counter and third market activities and by granting important income tax incentives.[4] While in the near past such growth appears to have halted due to the present economic crisis existing in the area, it is generally believed that such slowdown is temporary. In fact, the stock exchange in Mexico has shown considerable activity during 1984.

As noted above, the private offer and sale of securities in Latin America is basically governed by private law, namely, the Commercial Codes as well as specific laws on business organizations, if any.

Transfers of stocks, bonds or commercial paper is generally carried out by means of private contracts and in some cases by complying with some other legal requirements such as proper endorsements and/or delivery of the instruments (e.g. commercial paper or bearer shares) and registrations entered in the Stockholders Registry Books in the case of nominative stock.

Multinational companies doing business in Latin America have also witnessed that legislation on foreign investments plays an important role in the private and public sales of securities in those jurisdictions where such legislation has been enacted.

As you are probably aware, beginning in the late sixties, all through the seventies and in the early eighties, a wave of economic nationalism swept over Latin America. With the notable exception of Chile and Venezuela, this wave of economic nationalism did not lead to outright expropriation of foreign-owned business but rather to the institution of legal restrictions, on the inflow of foreign capital, its direction, supervision and subsequent outflow. Although many Latin American countries previously had legal provisions affecting foreign investment dispersed throughout their laws, it was not until the enactment of Mexico's Foreign Investment Law and the Andean Common Market adoption of Decision 24 (presently the Andean Common Market is composed of Venezuela, Colombia, Ecuador, Peru and Bolivia) that countries in the area began to elaborate unified laws and regulations involving standards applicable to foreign investments.

Under the typical foreign investment legislation, investment in certain areas is restricted to either the State or local citizens. For instance, certain "basic industries" are generally reserved for investment by either State-owned enterprises or locally owned companies.

Mexico reserves to State-owned enterprises such sectors as petroleum, basic petrochemicals, railroads, electricity, nuclear energy, postal, telegraph and radio-telegraph communications and others established by specific laws, such as coining money and the issue of currency; and to Mexicans or enterprises wholly owned by Mexicans: radio and television stations, passenger and freight road transport, national air and maritime transport, exploitation of timber resources, distribution of gas, insurance, bonding, and investment companies, and petrochemicals other than basic.

Venezuela and other Andean Pact countries exclude some of the above areas from foreign investment and, in addition, exclude internal marketing of goods and certain professional services.

As to areas not specifically excluded to foreign investment, the immediate question is whether the foreign investor can have 100% equity ownership and, if so, for how long. Countries with legislation on foreign investment deal with this question in different ways.

In Mexico, foreign investors may, as a general rule, subscribe for up to 49% of the capital of a new business organization. However, the Law on Foreign Investments allows the Foreign Investment Commission to permit foreign ownership in an enterprise in excess of 49% and up to 100% if, for instance, the proposed investment: is labor intensive; will result in the employment and training of Mexican technicians and administrative personnel; will have a positive effect on the balance of payments (e.g. the primary purpose of the venture being the export of goods); will contribute to the development of more backward areas of the country; and will bring needed high technology into Mexico.[5] While in the seventies and early eighties most new investments flowing into Mexico were made on a 49-51% basis (49% foreign), due to the present economic crisis the authorities have indicated that they will be more receptive to foreign ownership of up to 100% of the equity ownership of a Mexican venture.

As to investments in the Andean Pact countries in areas not specifically restricted to local investment, the basic characteristic for approval is that the foreign investors agree to sell a specified portion of their equity position over a period of time.[6]

Because of the divestment requirement, and for other reasons as well, some Latin American countries are interested in developing and revitalizing their local stock markets as a possible vehicle for spreading foreign ownership interest among a broader spectrum of local investors.[7] However, a reservation has been expressed by some that using stock markets as vehicles to divesting may lead to a dispersal of the 51% local ownership over such a broad group of people that local control may not be attained in view of the 49% foreign interest.

Aside from divestment considerations where the local stock markets can play a significant role, foreign investors may find the stock market a practical vehicle for the acquisition of interest in existing local companies. In this regard, however, let me note at the outset that it is a recurrent feature of the laws regulating foreign investment in Latin America that the displacement of local capital by foreign capital is generally discouraged. Accordingly, it is often found that buying into an existing locally owned company is not a very easy proposition. For instance, Mexico requires government authorization for the acquisition by a foreigner of 25% or more of the stock of an existing company, or 49% of its fixed assets.[8] Such authorization is in practice difficult to obtain and is required for acquisitions made on the Mexican stock exchange of more than 5% of the equity of the local issuer. If the acquisition represents less than 5% of the equity, no prior approval is required provided that such acquisition, when added to prior acquisitions, does not exceed 25% of the equity of the company in question.[9] If an acquisition is made on the exchange in violation of the foregoing and registration with the National Registry of Foreign Investments is later denied, the sale must be undone.[10]

Exceptions to this policy have been made but only in cases in which the Mexican company already had some foreign ownership, or where the company was in financial difficulty and the new investor would inject new and needed capital.

Venezuela is equally strict in this area. It is virtually impossible for a foreign investor to buy into an existing company at least majority-owned by Venezuelan parties. Approval of such acquisitions are seldom granted and then only in cases where the existing company would otherwise go into bankruptcy, thus aggravating the country's unemployment situation, and provided the capital of the existing company would be increased so that after the acquisition by the foreign investor the company would still retain its status as a national company, which under current laws is defined as one in which local investors own at least 80% of the capital.

As a general rule, in Argentina the approval of the Executive Power for the acquisition of the equity of locally-owned companies is required in cases where the acquired company's net worth exceeds US$20,000,000. Foreign acquisitions of local companies with a net worth of between US$5,000,000 and US$20,000,000 still require authorization from the Secretariat of Foreign Investment within the Ministry of the Economy. Investments of up to US$5,000,000 do not require authorization as long as the investment does not turn the local company into a domestic enterprise of foreign capital (e.g. 49% or more of the equity is owned directly or indirectly by persons domiciled outside of Argentina).

By not requiring approval in certain instances and by shifting the authorization process in other cases to the ministerial level, the authors of the relatively recent Argentine Foreign Investment Law intended the process to be more open, less cumbersome and presumably faster. It should be noted that denationalization (i.e. foreign acquisition of locally-owned enterprises) was prohibited outright under the pre-1976 Argentinian Law on Foreign Investments. Current rules, therefore, represent a substantial liberalization.

Nevertheless, the Law still distinguishes between a new foreign investment that results from a capital increase of the acquired company and the acquisition of existing shares from their local owners. The Law requires that in order for government approval to be granted for a foreigner's acquisition of existing shares from a local investor, it must be shown that a clear benefit to the national economy will result from such acquisition. Of course, the infusion of new capital into the acquired company will certainly be a positive feature of the proposed acquisition.

Note that one of the most significant features of the 1976 Argentine Foreign Investments Law, as amended, has been the opening of the Argentine stock market for acquisition by foreign investors of listed stock. Acquisitions by foreign investors on the stock exchange need not be approved by nor registered with any government institution, provided, however, (i) that the acquisitions do not convert the company into a domestic enterprise of foreign capital, (ii) holdings by any one foreign investor do not exceed US$2,000,000 or 2% of the capital of any local company, and (iii) total foreign purchases in a local company do not exceed 20% of its capital.

Finally, a word in connection with the conversion of obligations of Latin American companies into equity of such companies is in order. As all of you know, the economies in Latin America are passing through difficult times and companies therein are in many instances on the verge of bankruptcy.

Creditors of such companies (e.g. lenders, owners of commercial paper, or suppliers) with matured or defaulted credits have a three-fold alternative: (i) sue for collection, (ii) refinance the debt, or (iii) convert the debt into equity.

With regard to the first alternative, foreign creditors (aside from problems of obtaining jurisdiction in forums different from the Latin American jurisdictions of the debtor companies) should take into account before deciding on suing that, if they obtain a judgment against a Latin American debtor but cannot locate sufficient assets in the country where the action is brought, they must undertake an expensive and time consuming "exequatur" proceeding in order to enforce the foreign judgment in the debtor's jurisdiction.

Bringing their actions in the courts of the debtor's own country would, in many instances, mean a long, expensive and difficult litigation. In addition, a foreign creditor who ultimately prevails in a collection action will, in many of those countries, encounter difficulties in converting the judgment monies into foreign "hard" currencies due to exchange control regulations existing in most Latin American jurisdictions and the practical fact that sometimes no foreign currencies are obtainable due to the scarcity of such currencies in the country in question.

If refinancing is chosen, local bankruptcy laws must be taken into account. The bankruptcy rules of Latin American jurisdictions generally provide that certain transactions of the debtor are void or voidable if they occurred during a certain period preceding the declaration of the debtor's bankruptcy (período de sospecha). The length of the período de sospecha varies from jurisdiction to jurisdiction. While in Chile the period may not exceed one year, in Argentina and Venezuela it is two years. In Mexico, as in Italy, the bankruptcy declaration is made retroactive by a date fixed by the judge.[11]

Generally, gratuitous acts or transfers without sufficient consideration, prepayments of debts, payments in kind of money debts, the granting of mortgages, pledges or other security interests to secure obligations where such securities were not originally contracted, and other payments or agreements, where the payees or other parties knew at the time of payment or agreement that the debtor had generally suspended payments of its obligations, are void or voidable under the bankruptcy laws in Latin America. Depending on the country, if a refinancing agreement is executed within the "período de sospecha," and a security interest is obtained on the debtor's property, the same may be void and voidable. The debtor's interest obligation may be unenforceable, payments received by the foreign creditor under the refinancing agreement may be held to have been for the account of all the debtor's creditors and required to be refunded to the receiver in the bankruptcy proceedings. The foreign creditor's claim for the refinanced obligation will rank only with those of the debtor's unsecured creditors and at any rate will rank well below the amounts owed to the workers and employees and tax obligations.

Considering the above, the conversion of credits into equity may, in many instances, seem to be the best solution for all the interested parties. A conversion into equity in some cases might help the ailing company to survive the bankruptcy. The workers and employees would retain their jobs, the local authorities would look favorably on the saving of local companies through this vehicle, and the creditors may be able to recover more in the medium or long term.

In practice, conversion of debt into equity is opposed by local owners of companies in bad financial situations and also by some groups of persons, both in the public and private sectors, who oppose the denationalization process.

Aside from the legal principles limiting foreign investments quoted above, the philosophy which promoted the enactment of such principles under the laws on foreign investments in the area is now probably stronger. Nevertheless, the drastic reduction of inflow of capital via new financings into the economies of the area, together with factors such as population growing and the entrance of millions of persons into the working force every year, makes it indispensable not only to maintain afloat the existing business but to allow the inflow of new direct foreign investment.

While the outcome of this process is uncertain at this time, I believe it will be very interesting to follow.

FOOTNOTES

1 In Mexico, the Ley del Mercado de Valores published in the Official Daily of January 2, 1975; Argentina, Ley de Oferta Pública de Valores, Bolsas o Mercados de Comercio y Mercado de Valores, No. 17,811 published in the Official Bulletin of July 22, 1968; Venezuela, Ley del Mercado de Capitales, Decree No. 882 of April 29, 1975; Colombia, Law No. 32 of May 17, 1979; Chile, Ley del Mercado de Valores, No. 18,045, of October 31, 1981; and Perú, Ley Normativa del Mercado Bursátil of June 12, 1981.

2 See Instructivo para Solicitar la Inscripción de Acciones en la Sección de Valores del Registro Nacional de Valores e Intermediarios.

3 Although Mexico had three operating stock exchanges, located in the major cities of Mexico City, Guadalajara and Monterrey, since January 1975 all trading of securities takes place in Mexico City in a centralized stock exchange known as Bolsa Mexicana de Valores.

4 Taxes on capital gains on the transfer by individuals of stocks through the stock exchange have been virtually nonexistent.

5 The above criteria are typical and illustrative of the kinds of factors which governments in Latin American countries other than México take into consideration when called upon to approve proposed new foreign investments.

6 Such period is generally between 10 and 15 years.

7 Alexander C. Hoagland, Jr., in Company Formation in México at J-31 states, for instance, that "the stock market may be utilized in the disinvestment process in several ways: (1) a public offering of the share capital required to be Mexicanized; (ii) an offering of the shares placed privately with local investors and/or several credit institutions; (iii) a combination of (i) and (ii); (iv) setting up a trust with a Mexican credit institution covering the Mexicanized portion of the share capital at least until a public and/or private offering can be effected successfully; this requires prior Foreign Investment Commission approval."

8 *See* General Resolution No. 5 of the National Commission of Foreign Investments of July 25, 1984.

9 *See* General Resolutions No. 4 and No. 8 of the National Commission of Foreign Investments as reenacted on July 25, 1984.

10 Under Article 39 of the Regulations of the National Registry of Foreign Investments enacted on December 8, 1981, foreign investors acquiring stock of Mexican corporations through the stock exchange have the option of either registering the investment individually with the Registry on Foreign Investments, or of depositing the stock with INDEVAL (*Instituto de Depósito de Valores*) and registering the acquired stock on the stock exchange through INDEVAL. Such deposit shall operate as a provisional registration with the National Registry on Foreign Investments, which in turn shall make a final registration upon its certifying that such acquisitions have been made pursuant to the law on Foreign Investments and the General Resolutions of the National Commission on Foreign Investments.

11 The judge may also modify such date, extending or shortening the term (Articles 15, Par. IX, and 118 of the Mexican Bankruptcy Law).

RÉSUMÉ EN FRANÇAIS

VALEURS: PROBLÈMES DE LA VENTE DES VALEURS SUR LES MARCHÉS PUBLICS ET PRIVÉS D'AMÉRIQUE LATINE

En Amérique latine, l'offre et la vente publique de valeurs sont régies par la législation spéciale promulguée à cet effet. L'offre et la vente privée de valeurs sont principalement déterminées par les Codes de commerce (Códigos de Commercio) et les lois qui en découlent.

Bien que la législation portant sur l'offre et la vente publique de valeurs manque de clarté, elle est généralement interprétée dans le sens d'une intention de réglementer la circulation des valeurs émises par des sociétés constituées sous les lois du pays latino-américain en question. Le Vénézuela, dont la Commission nationale des valeurs (Comisión Nacional de valores) peut autoriser l'offre publique de valeurs émises par des entités et entreprises étrangères, fait exception. En tout état de cause, la plupart des valeurs en circulation sur les marchés publics d'Amérique latine sont des valeurs émises par des sociétés locales.

En Amérique latine, les Commissions de valeurs ont principalement pour tâche d'approuver et d'enregister les valeurs destinées à être offertes au public, et d'analyser la situation financière et commerciale des sociétés émettrices ou de désigner des vérificateurs (interventores) de l'administration de celles-ci.

La croissance des marchés de valeurs latino-américains a généralement été spectaculaire. Dans certaines juridictions, comme celle du Mexique, les autorités ont accéléré cette croissance par des exemptions fiscales et l'élimination de fait de marchés de valeurs parallèles. Bien que la croissance des marchés de valeurs latino-américains ait été freinée du fait de la présente crise économique, on estime généralement qu'elle devrait reprendre dans un proche avenir.

Le transfert privé des valeurs s'effectue par contrats privés; il doit aussi satisfaire certaines exigences juridiques telles que, dans le cas des actions nominatives, les avals et les inscriptions aux registres des actionnaires de la société émettrice.

La législation réglementant les investissements étrangers est déterminante sur les marchés de valeurs, particulièrement au Mexique et dans les pays membres du Pacte Andin (Pacto Andino) (actuellement le Vénézuela, la Colombie, le Pérou, l'Equateur et la Bolivie). En général, cette législation restreint la participation des investisseurs étrangers dans certains secteurs économiques, comme par exemple le pétrole, les produits pétrochimiques de base, les chemins de fer, l'électricité, l'énergie nucléaire, les communications télégraphiques ou radio-télégraphiques, etc. Dans d'autres cas, elle limite l'investissement dans certains domaines ou activités aux investisseurs locaux; c'est le cas notamment des stations de radio et de télévision, du transport national aérien, maritime, et routier de passagers, de la distribution du gaz, des assurances, etc. Dans les secteurs où la législation sur les investissements étrangers n'exclut pas la participation d'un investisseur étranger, la règle générale est que l'investissement ne doit pas dépasser 49% du capital de l'entreprise. On admet certaines exceptions à cette règle générale lorsque l'investissement projeté aura des effets positifs sur l'économie du pays.

D'autre part, cette législation comporte des règles prévoyant la nationalisation des entreprises tenues par des investisseurs étrangers. Dans ce domaine, les marchés publics de valeurs jouent un rôle important dans le processus de nationalisation des entreprises.

Pour les investisseurs étrangers qui acquièrent des valeurs, les marchés publics remplissent une fonction importante. Au Mexique par exemple, les investisseurs étrangers peuvent acheter des actions de sociétés mexicaines par le truchement de la bourse lorsque ces actions ne dépassent pas 5% du capital-actions de la société qui les émet, à condition que toutes les acquisitions ne dépassent pas 25% dudit capital. De même en Argentine, l'acquisition de valeurs en bourse par des investisseurs étrangers ne nécessite l'approbation d'aucune autorité, à condition que l'acquisition ne transforme pas la société émettrice en une société locale à capital étranger, que les valeurs détenues par tout investisseur étranger n'excèdent pas 2 millions de dollars ou 2% du capital-actions, et que la totalité des acquisitions réalisées par des étrangers dans une société locale n'excède pas 20% du capital-actions de celle-ci.

En Amérique latine, plusieurs entreprises de la région se trouvent au bord de la faillite en raison de la crise économique actuelle. Les créanciers de ces entreprises peuvent procéder de trois façons différentes: (i) intenter un procès, (ii) refinancer les dettes ou (iii) capitaliser celles-ci. Dans plus d'un cas, la dernière opération paraît convenir le mieux pour protéger les intérêts des parties en cause (créanciers, débiteurs, employés et ouvriers des débiteurs et gouvernments locaux). Cependant, cette manière d'agir soulève l'opposition de certains groupements locaux. Malgré cela, la diminution drastique de l'afflux des capitaux par de nouveaux financements dans les économies de la région, ajoutée à d'autres facteurs tels que l'explosion démographique et la croissance des marchés du travail, rendent indispensables non seulement le renflouement des affaires en cours au moyen de la capitalisation des passifs, mais aussi l'assentiment à l'afflux de nouveaux investissements étrangers.

Bien que le résultat de ce processus soit encore incertain, il promet d'être intéressant.

RESUMEN EN ESPAÑOL

VALORES: PROBLEMAS EN LA VENTA DE VALORES EN LOS MERCADOS PUBLICOS Y PRIVADOS LATINOAMERICANOS

La oferta y venta pública de valores en Latinoamérica se rige por legislación especial promulgada para tal efecto. A su vez, la oferta y venta privada de valores se rige fundamentalmente por los Códigos de Comercio y las leyes que se derivan de los mismos.

Aunque la legislación no es precisa en relación a la oferta y venta pública de valores, la misma generalmente se interpreta en el sentido de que su intento es reglar la circulación de valores emitidos por compañías constituídas y existentes bajo las leyes del país latino-americano en cuestión. Una excepción a este caso es Venezuela, país en el cual la Comisión Nacional de Valores puede autorizar la oferta pública dentro del territorio venezolano de valores de entidades y empresas extranjeras. En cualquier caso, la mayoría de los valores en circulación en los mercados públicos Latinoamericanos son valores emitidos por compañías locales.

En Latinoamérica las Comisiones de Valores tienen fundamentalmente la función de aprobar y registrar los valores que van a ofrecerse al público y de analizar la situación financiera y comercial de los emisores de valores. En algunos casos, dichas Comisiones tienen incluso la autoridad de suspender las operaciones de los emisores o de nombrar interventores en la administración de los mismos.

El crecimiento de los mercados de valores Latino-americanos ha sido generalmente espectacular. En algunos han impulsado dicho crecimiento mediante exenciones fiscales y la virtual eliminación de mercados paralelos de valores. Aunque el crecimiento de los mercados de valores en Latinoamérica se ha visto recientemente menoscabado debido a la presente crisis económica, en general se cree que el mismo se reanudará en un futuro cercano.

La transferencia privada de valores se lleva a cabo mediante contratos privados y cumpliendo con ciertos requisitos legales, tales como endosos y registros en los libros de registro de acciones de la sociedad emisora en el caso de acciones nominativas.

La legislación sobre inversiones extranjeras tiene un impacto fundamental en los mercados de valores especialmente en México y en los países miembros del Pacto Andino. (Actualmente, Venezuela, Colombia, Perú, Ecuador y Bolivia). Dicha legislación restringe en general la participación de inversionistas extranjeros en ciertas áreas de la economía, como por ejemplo el petróleo, los productos petroquímicos básicos, los ferrocarriles, la electricidad, la energía nuclear, las communicaciones telegráficas y radiotelegráficas, etc. En otros casos dicha legislación limita la inversión en ciertos campos o actividades a inversionistas locales, como por ejemplo, en estaciones de radio televisión, transporte nacional de pasajeros aéreo, marítimo y terrestre, distribución de gas, seguros, etc. En áreas en las que la legislación sobre inversiones extranjeras no excluye la participación del inversionista extranjero, la regla general es de que dicha participación no puede exceder del 49% del capital de la empresa. Sin embargo, se admiten excepciones a esta regla general cuando la inversión en cuestión va a tener efectos positivos en la economía del país.

Existen por otro lado bajo esta legislación reglas para la nacionalización de las empresas, propiedad de inversionistas extranjeros. En este aspecto los mercados públicos de valores juegan un papel importante en el proceso de nacionalización de empresas.

Dichos mercados públicos juegan asimismo un papel importante en la adquisición de valores por parte de inversionistas extranjeros. Por ejemplo, en México los inversionistas extranjeros pueden comprar acciones de compañías mexicanas a través de la bolsa de valores cuando las mismas no exceden del 5% del capital de la sociedad emisora y siempre y cuando la totalidad de dichas adquisiciones no excedan del 25% de dicho capital. En forma similar, en Argentina no se requiere ninguna aprobación de autoridad alguna en la adquisición de valores en la bolsa de valores por inversionistas extranjeros siempre y cuando la adquisición no convierta a la emisora en cuestión en una empresa doméstica de capital extranjero, las tenencias de cualquier inversionista extranjero no excedan de 2 millones de dólares o del 2% del capital social y la totalidad de las adquisiciones por extranjeros en la compañía local no excedan del 20% de su capital.

Con motivo de la crísis económica actual diversas empresas locales en Latinoamérica se encuentran al borde de la quiebra. Los acreedores de dichas empresas tienen una triple alternativa: (i) demandar, (ii) refinanciar los adeudos o (iii) capitalizar los adeudos. En no pocos casos la última alternativa parecería ser la más conveniente en la protección de los intereses de las partes involucradas. (Acreedores, duedores, empleados y obreros de los deudores y gobiernos locales). Sin embargo esta alternativa encuentra oposición en ciertos grupos locales. No obstante lo anterior, la reducción drástica de la afluencia de capitales vía nuevos financiamientos en las economías de la zona, conjuntamente con factores tales como la explosión demográfica y el crecimiento de los mercados de trabajo, hacen indispensables no únicamente el mantener a flote los negocios existentes mediante capitalización de pasivos, sino permitir la afluencia de nuevas inversiones extranjeras.

Aunque el desenlace de este proceso todavía es incierto, el mismo se antoja interesante de observar.

APPLICATION OF U.S. SECURITIES LAWS TO THE PURCHASE AND SALE IN THE U.S.

Allan S. Mostoff, Esq.

The author is a partner at the law firm of Dechert, Price & Rhoads. Mr. Mostoff's practice largely involves advising and counseling mutual funds, investment banking houses, banks, institutional investors and some international representation. He was formerly with the Securities and Exchange Commission as Director of the Division of Investment Management Regulation and Director of the Office of Policy Studies.

Multinational enterprises operating or planning to operate in the United States are likely to encounter the U.S. securities laws in a variety of contexts. This paper will focus on two of the most frequent situations, namely, the offering of securities in the United States by foreign issuers and the acquisitions of U.S. companies by foreign enterprises.

I. Securities Offerings in the United States by Foreign Issuers

Offerings of foreign securities in the United States come within the purview of the U.S. Securities and Exchange Commission ("SEC" or the "Commission"). Under the federal securities laws, the SEC's primary mandate is that of investor protection. Although the statutes do not generally distinguish between domestic and foreign private issuers selling their securities in the United States, in administering the requirements of the statutes the SEC has made certain adjustments to accommodate differences in laws and in business and accounting customs pertaining to foreign private issuers.

Of the various laws administered by the SEC, three are of particular concern to the foreign issuers wishing to offer their securities in the United States.[1] These are the Securities Act of 1933 ("Securities Act"), the Securities Exchange Act of 1934 ("Exchange Act") and Trust Indenture Act of 1939 ("Trust Indenture Act").

The Securities Act deals primarily with public offerings by issuers and their controlling persons. It sets general disclosure and anti-fraud standards and requires that securities be registered prior to their offer for sale, unless one of a number of specific exemptions applies.

The Exchange Act governs secondary market trading in securities but also expands on the Securities Act's disclosure requirements by requiring, among other features, continuous reporting for issuers whose securities are publicly traded in the United States.[2]

The Trust Indenture Act sets special requirements for debt securities which are supplemental to those required by the Securities Act. Procedures under this statute are integrated with Securities Act registration.

A. Foreign Private Issuers

1. Securities Act Requirements

The requirements of the Securities Act are, in general, the same for foreign as for domestic private issuers. Therefore, foreign private issuers proposing to offer their securities in the U.S. must register the securities with the SEC unless they qualify for one of the exemptions described below.

a. Registration

As in the case of U.S. issuers, registration under the Securities Act by foreign issuers involves the disclosure of information about the securities being registered, the issuer's business and management, risk factors, the trading market for the issuer's securities, its financial condition and financial statements.

Three forms are available for registration by foreign private issuers under the Securities Act -- Forms F-1, F-2 and F-3 -- which differ in the extensiveness of information required. Form F-1 is the most extensive and must be used by all foreign private issuers that are not eligible to use either Form F-3 or Form F-2. Form F-3, designed for the most widely known issuers[3], is the briefest, providing for significant incorporation by reference from periodic reports filed pursuant to the Exchange Act. Form F-2, for moderately well-known issuers, permits incorporation by reference but also requires delivery of reports to which reference is made.[4] In addition to the type of issuer involved, eligibility for use of each of these forms depends upon the nature of the offering. For example, Form F-3 may be used by eligible issuers for primary offerings for cash, offerings or non-convertible investment grade debt securities, secondary offerings, rights offerings, re-investment plans and conversions or warrants.

In each case, the registration form must be signed by the issuer, its management and by the issuer's authorized representative in the United States.

One area of special concern for foreign private issuers registering securities in the United States is the financial statements which must be included in the registration statement. Differences between U.S. accounting and auditing practices may present special problems in providing the required financial statements. For example, accounting practices may differ with respect to:

- -- requirements for and policies concerning consolidated statements;
- -- methods for valuing inventories, investments and fixed assets;
- -- accounting for contingencies and estimated liabilities;
- -- accounting for stock dividends;
- -- accounting in cases of mergers and acquisitions;
- -- requirements for statements of sources and applications of funds; and
- -- standards regarding the timing and recognition of income.

The SEC permits foreign issuers the option of preparing required financial statements in accordance with U.S. generally accepted accounting principles ("GAAP") and the SEC's Regulation S-X, or in accordance with applicable foreign principles provided a reconciliation is made from foreign to U.S. practices of net income and principal balance sheet items. In each case, however, the format of presentation must be substantially the same as the format required by U.S. standards. Certain relaxations in required disclosures (including industry segment and geographic net profit information) are made for offerings of non-convertible investment grade securities, secondary offerings for widely-held issuers, rights offerings, re-investment plans, conversions and warrants. All other offerings involve the full disclosure required by U.S. standards.

U.S. and foreign auditing practices also may differ significantly. The practices employed in confirming receivables and for observing physical inventories represent two major areas of variation. A third difference is the U.S. requirement that auditors be fully "independent", while foreign auditors may even be shareholders of the issuers they audit. Notwithstanding these differences, the SEC generally requires that foreign issuers conform to the same auditing standards as U.S. issuers. Thus foreign issuers should alert their auditors well in advance of any planned U.S. offering.

Rule 415 under the Securities Act is of particular interest to many issuers. That rule provides for the registration of certain securities to be offered or sold on a delayed or continuous basis in the future (so called "shelf registration"). Securities which may be registered pursuant to this rule include those qualified for registration on Forms F-3 and S-3, the equivalent form for widely distributed securities of well-known domestic issuers. Other categories include securities to be issued in conversions, securities underlying exercisable options, warrants or rights, securities offered pursuant to regular re-investment plans, securities represented by American Depositary Receipts ("ADRs"), mortgage related securities and securities issued in business combinations. Specific additional conditions are applicable to registrations of certain of the qualified types of securities. For example, in the case of securities qualified for registration on Forms F-3 or S-3, only an amount expected to be sold within two years may be registered.

b. Exemptions from Registration

Several exemptions are available from the registration requirements for certain types of securities or for certain types of transactions in securities. None of these exemptions is specifically applicable to foreign issuers but any may be relied upon by a foreign issuer which meets the exemption requirements. Those which are likely to be of interest to foreign issuers are described below. It should also be noted that these exemptions remove only the registration requirement. Issuers relying on them are still subject to the general anti-fraud provisions.

Sections 3(b) and 4(2) of the Securities Act provide exemptions from registration for limited and non-public offerings. Regulation D (Rules 501-506) under the Securities Act is the most widely used means of complying with these exemptions. Conditions under Regulation D involve generally the size of the offering and the type and number of purchasers.[5] These conditions apply only to offerings in the U.S. and are not generally affected by offerings -- even simultaneous offerings -- made entirely outside the U.S.

Although the "safe harbor" aspects of Regulation D make it the most commonly relied on exemption for private placements and limited offerings, an issuer may also prefer to rely on judicial and administrative rulings construing Section 4(2). Under the SEC's administrative rulings, the following factors are relevant to the applicability of the private placement exemption: the number of offerees, the relationship of the offerees to each other, the relationship of the offerees to the issuer, the number of shares offered, and the manner of making the offering. The exemption is not available unless the offerees or their representatives are sophisticated enough not to need the protection of registration and the exemption will not be satisfied merely by providing offerees with information which would be required in a registration statement.

Securities sold pursuant to Regulation D or otherwise pursuant to the Section 4(2) exemption cannot be resold unless an exemption applies to the resale, or they are first registered. In this respect, the SEC has promulgated Rule 144 as one means of permissible resales without registration. The rule has a number of conditions, including mandatory holding periods and current Exchange Act reporting by the issuer, though a recent amendment eliminates the latter requirement for sales by non-affiliates.

2. Exchange Act Requirements

The Exchange Act contains periodic disclosure and anti-fraud requirements for issuers of securities traded in the U.S. after their initial distribution. While foreign issuers subject to the terms of the statute must, in general, satisfy the periodic reporting requirements, there have been considerably more specific accommodations made for foreign issuers under the Exchange Act than under the Securities Act.

a. Registration

Any issuer with securities listed on a U.S. stock exchange must register the securities pursuant to

Section 12(b) of the Exchange Act. Any other issuer with assets of over $3 million on the last day of its most recent fiscal year, and an outstanding class of equity securities held of record by 500 or more persons, must register the securities under Section 12(g). This latter registration may be terminated (a) when the number of shareholders of the class falls below 300 or (b) when the number of such shareholders falls below 500 and the issuer's assets have not exceeded $3,000,000 at the end of each of the three latest fiscal years. Section 15(d) of the Exchange Act, in turn, requires that issuers of securities which have not been registered under either Section 12(b) or Section 12(g), but which have been registered under the Securities Act in connection with their public offerings, comply with periodic reporting requirements similar to those for companies registered under Section 12. This requirement is suspended for domestic issuers for any year during which the number of security holders and assets of the issuer are below the limits noted above, and for foreign issuers if the class of securities has fewer than 300 resident U.S. shareholders. In each case, qualification for termination must be certified to the SEC on Form 15.

The SEC has provided special registration, annual, report and periodic reporting forms -- Forms 20-F and 6-K -- for most foreign issuers.[6]

Form 20-F is an integrated registration annual report form which calls for narrative disclosure somewhat less extensive than the comparable forms for domestic issuers (Forms 10 and 10-K). It requires information describing the issuer's business, property and management, legal proceedings, the nature of the trading market for the issuer's securities, exchange controls and taxation, selected financial information and financial statements, management's discussion and analysis, securities to be registered, defaults and changes in security.

The specific disclosure is less than would be required for domestic issuers in several notable respects. For example, specific reporting of profits by business segment is not required in the case of an annual report, nor is information on salaries of officers and directors on an individualized basis required unless the issuer already publishes such information. The financial statements filed with Form 20-F, when used as an annual report or, as part of the integrated disclosure system, for offerings of non-convertible investment grade debt securities on Form F-3, secondary offerings of widely-held issuers, re-investment plans, conversions and warrants, do not require full U.S. GAAP and Regulation S-X disclosures, which include full industry and geographic segment information. These disclosures are required, however, when the form is used for other public offering purposes.

The required information must be provided in the initial registration on Form 20-F, and restated annually (within six months of the end of the issuer's fiscal year), again by use of Form 20-F.

Form 6-K[7] requires the prompt furnishing (not filing)[8] of material information which the issuer (i) is required to make public in its country of domicile or organization pursuant to the laws thereof, (ii) has publicly filed with a foreign stock exchange or (iii) has distributed to its securities holders. As most recently amended, Form 6-K also requires English translations, versions or summaries only of information distributed to security holders and of material press releases. Other types of information need be furnished only if English translations, versions or summaries are prepared by the issuer.

b. Exemptions

Rule 3a12-3 exempts certain foreign private issuers from the proxy rules under Section 14 and exempts managements of foreign private issuers from the insider trading limitations and other provisions of Section 16. A "foreign private issuer" for this purpose does not include one (a) more than 50 percent of the outstanding voting securities of which are held by U.S. residents and (b) a majority of the executive officers or directors of which are U.S. citizens or residents, or more than 50 percent of the assets of which are in the U.S., or the business of which is administered principally in the U.S.

Rule 12g3-2 generally exempts the securities of foreign private issuers entirely from the registration provisions of Section 12(g) if the class of securities is held by fewer than 300 U.S. residents or such issuers annually furnish (not file) to the SEC material information which is provided to their own government, to foreign stock exchanges or to shareholders. A recently-adopted amendment makes this exemption unavailable for over-the-counter securities listed in the NASDAQ quotation system unless they have been continually so listed since October 5, 1983 and the issuer has been continually in compliance with the information furnishing requirements.[9] For Canadian issuers, this latter "grandfathering" provision expires January 2, 1986 and Canadian issuers may then no longer rely on this exemption. An issuer which, through issuance of its stock, acquires another issuer subject to the periodic reporting requirements of Section 13(a) of the Exchange Act also would not be exempt, if proposed changes are adopted.[10]

c. Stock Exchange Requirements

While a foreign issuer ordinarily must meet the listing standards and comply with reporting and other requirements (e.g. proxy solicitation requirements) of any U.S. exchange on which it wishes to be listed, certain exchanges provide alternative criteria for foreign issuers.

Listing standards for the New York Stock Exchange, for example, generally require than an issuer have 2,000 U.S. holders of 100 or more shares and have at least 1 million shares publicly held in the U.S. and $16 million dollars worth of shares publicly held in the U.S. The NYSE does, however, make available an alternative set of standards for foreign issuers which cannot meet the regular standards.

A foreign issuer may thus list its securities if it meets the following numerical standards on a world wide basis: 5,000 round lot shareholders, 2.5 million publicly held shares outstanding worth over $100 million, tangible assets of at least $100 million, and at least $25 million of pre-tax income in each of the latest 3 years, with cumulative pre-tax income over the three year period of at least $100 million. Where an issuer cannot demonstrate that it meets the 5,000 round lot shareholder test, it is required to obtain a NYSE member sponsor as to depth and liquidity of the market for the issuer's securities, and the Exchange staff itself must be satisfied as to liquidity.

Certain non-numerical NYSE standards, which apply to U.S. and foreign issuers, also may be relaxed for the latter. These standards concern shareholder voting rights, outside directors, financial reporting, free share distributions or stock dividends and corporate relationships with insiders.

The American Stock Exchange also provides an alternative set of standards for foreign issuers.

Trust Indenture Act Requirements

The Trust Indenture Act sets special requirements for debt securities publicly offered in the U.S. These are generally supplemental to registration requirements under the Securities Act. This statute sets requirements regarding the trustee's eligibility and duties, establishes procedures in event of defaults, and requires reporting both to security holders and to the SEC. Of particular interest to foreign borrowers is the requirement that at least one trustee be a U.S. corporation which is authorized to exercise trust powers and which is subject to supervision by a U.S. or state authority.

Exemptions under the Trust Indenture Act are generally co-extensive with those under the Securities Act, but do not include exemptions for exchange offers and reorganizations. The Trust Indenture Act contains certain additional small offering exemptions. Section 304(d) gives the SEC authority to exempt securities of foreign issuers from one or more of the Act's requirements but this power is not often used.

B. Foreign Government Issuers

Foreign governmental securities are also subject to registration under the Securities Act. However, in registering under the Securities Act, foreign governmental issuers are governed by Schedule B rather than Schedule A of the Securities Act. The information required or otherwise provided generally includes a description of the government and its role in the economy and such economic and financial factors as natural resources, population, gross domestic product, balance of trade and payments, fiscal and monetary policies, inflation rates, employment, debt payments, debt payment experience and schedules of historical and budgeted receipts and expenditures.

By interpretive release,[11] the SEC has also made available to foreign governments that have registered securities under the Securities Act within the previous five years (so-called "seasoned issuers"), and have not defaulted on any principal or interest, a shelf registration procedure for delayed offerings. The procedure is similar to Rule 415 for which foreign governments are ineligible. Using this procedure, an eligible foreign government may register an amount of securities expected to be sold within two years. The procedure involves filing a registration statement including a prospectus which contains general political, economic and statistical information, as well as Schedule B information. At the time of the offering, a basic prospectus may be furnished and pricing and other information may be provided by supplements or by sticker. If a foreign government issuer does not meet the seasoned issuer criteria it cannot use a shelf registration and the standard registration procedure is ordinarily followed.

Foreign governments, subdivisions and instrumentalities are specifically exempted from the Trust Indenture Act and from the financial statement requirements of Regulation S-X.

II. Acquisitions of U.S. Concerns by Foreign Issuers

Foreign issuers may acquire securities of U.S. companies in a number of fashions, such as through mergers, exchange offers, tender offers, open market purchases and privately negotiated transactions. Depending on the context, one or more securities laws may apply.

A. Registration Requirements

If an exchange of securities is involved, such as in direct exchange offers or merger transactions, the foreign issuer's securities must be registered under the Securities Act, unless an exemption is available. The Securities Act registration requirements outlined above will then apply.

Effective July 1, 1985, the SEC adopted a new registration form, Form F-4, to be used to register securities under the Securities Act in connection with business combinations involving foreign private registrants. Form F-4 is available only to foreign private issuers eligible to use Form 20-F and corresponds to Form S-4 for business combinations involving domestic concerns and foreign issuers (mostly Canadian) not eligible to use Form 20-F. Form F-4 may be used for certain reclassifications, statutory mergers and consolidations, transfers of assets, mergers in which a vote or consent of the security holder is not required by applicable law, exchange offers for securities of the issuer or another person, and public reoffering of securities acquired pursuant to the above provisions.

Form F-4 adheres to the philosophy underlying integrated disclosure and permits incorporation of information by reference to the same extent as Forms F-1, F-2, and F-3. This recognizes the fact that investment decisions made in the context of business combinations are similar to those made in the purchase or sale of securities in the primary or secondary markets. However, the SEC believes there also are significant differences, most notably the "non-volitional" aspects of business combinations and the possibility that an investor's inaction may give rise to a change in security ownership. Accordingly, the SEC has adopted certain additional provisions.

Specifically, the prospectus must contain an expanded summary item in the front of the prospectus designed to clarify the transactions for investors. Further, if the prospectus to be used will incorporate information by reference, then it must be sent to shareholders at least twenty days before their final decision concerning the proposed business combination must be made, with incorporated information to be provided on request from a U.S. location. Alternatively, to avoid the twenty-day time period, the registrant may provide the information, which would be furnished on Form F-1.

In cash mergers or other cash purchases of stock from a U.S. company, no registration is required. However, depending on the nature of the transaction, and generally in the case of mergers, the U.S. company may be required to prepare a proxy statement or information statement to its shareholders. The disclosures required with respect to the foreign acquisition depend on the circumstances of the case, but normally are less than for a registration statement under the Securities Act.

In all securities acquisitions, regardless of whether registration is required, the anti-fraud provisions of the federal securities laws are applicable. They prohibit deception or manipulation and can result in criminal as well as civil penalties.

B. Beneficial Ownership Reporting Rules

Once an investor owns more than five percent of a class of equity security, the beneficial ownership reporting provisions of the Exchange Act will apply. Persons or organizations beneficially owning more than 5% of a class of equity security registered under Section 12 of the Exchange Act (generally, listed or other publicly traded securities), or of stock of an insurance company or closed-end investment company, must make reports concerning their ownership of the securities to the issuer, pertinent securities exchanges and the SEC.[12] The rules are designed to provide issuers, investors and regulators with information concerning holders of substantial amounts of securities indicating, particularly, whether these holders exercise, or intend to exercise, control over the issuer.

The beneficial ownership disclosure rules are complex but their general outlines are as follows:

A "beneficial owner" is one who has or shares, directly or indirectly

a) "voting power", including the power to vote or direct the voting of the securities, or

b) "investment power", including the power to dispose of or direct the disposition of the securities.

The beneficial ownership rules apply only with respect to the voting equity securities described above, not to non-convertible debt securities.

The rules require aggregation of all securities under a person's direct or indirect control. For example, securities held in various trust accounts over which a bank has voting or investment power must be aggregated to determine whether more than 5% of a security is beneficially owned by the bank.

The rules require, similarly, attribution of ownership by subsidiaries to their parents. If seven subsidiaries each own 1% or more of a given security, for example, the parent would be required to report. A single subsidiary would report only if it beneficially owned over 5%.

All the above principles apply equally to foreign entities and subsidiaries owning the described types of equity securities.

The rules require a report on Schedule 13D to the issuer, applicable exchanges and to the SEC within 10 days after a person becomes beneficial owner of over 5% of a security. Certain types of institutional investors which do not intend to exercise control over issuers are eligible to file only annually, on Schedule 13G, with respect to equity securities of which they own over 5% as of the last day of the year. However, this annual reporting provision is only available to certain entities, such as broker-dealers or investment advisers that have registered with the SEC. It is also not available for reports on holdings of several institutions if one of those institutions is ineligible. However, under Rule 13d-1(b)(ii)(G), a parent holding company can report on Form 13G provided a non-qualifying subsidiary (e.g., a foreign subsidiary) owns not more than one percent of the security.

C. <u>Tender Offer Rules</u>

Section 14(d) of the Exchange Act makes it unlawful for any person, foreign or domestic, "to make a tender offer for, or a request or invitation for tenders of," any class of equity security registered under Section 12 or any equity security issued by a closed-end investment company or for certain equity securities of insurance companies, if, as a result, that person would directly or indirectly be the owner of more than 5 percent of such class of security unless that person, at the time of publication or distribution of the tender offer, has filed with the Commission the information specified in Section 13(d) as well as such other information as Commission rules require.

The Commission, pursuant to this mandate, has promulgated Regulation 14D and Schedule 14D-1, which are in addition to Regulation 13D-G and Schedules 13D and 13G promulgated under Sections 13(d) and 13(g) relating to acquisitions and ownership of certain equity securities of over five percent. Regulation 14D provides for the filing of specific information on Schedule 14D-1 concerning the identity and background of the person making the tender offer; citizenship; past relationships, transactions or negotiations with the subject company; source and amount of funds or other consideration for the purchase of the securities; purpose of the tender offer and plans and proposals of the bidder; interest in the securities of the subject company; contracts, arrangements, understandings or relationships with respect to the subject company's securities and certain other material information which may be applicable to the tender offer, including the financial statements of the bidder. The rules are designed to obtain disclosure of material information for the benefit of security holders so that they can make an informed decision whether to tender their securities, hold them or sell them in the open market.

Additional rules impose specific filing, delivery and disclosure requirements, optional dissemination provisions, stringent provisions on the use of inside information, and additional substantive regulatory protections with respect to certain tender offers.

FOOTNOTES

1. In addition to these federal laws, foreign issuers must comply with the requirements of any state in which they plan to offer their securities. The state statutes, generally referred to as the blue-sky law, vary considerably and it is difficult to generalize as to their requirements. Most states do provide an exemption from registration for securities listed on a major U.S. stock exchange. However, even if an exemption is available, state anti-fraud rules still generally apply.

2. The Exchange Act also provides the basic authority for the SEC's beneficial ownership reporting requirements and regulation of tender offers which are discussed below.

3. Form F-3 may be used by an issuer and its majority-owned subsidiaries which, together with predecessors:

> 1. has a class of securities registered under the Exchange Act or is subject to its reporting requirements and which is eligible to and has, in fact, filed annual reports on Form 20-F (the integrated registration annual report form for foreign private issuers);
>
> 2. has been required to file and has filed Exchange Act reports for 36 months preceding the filing of Form F-3 -- in a timely fashion during the preceding 12 months;
>
> 3. has not (including subsidiaries) failed to pay a preferred stock sinking fund installment or dividend or defaulted materially on a loan or long-term lease; and
>
> 4. has at least $300 million of voting stock held by non-affiliates (except in the case of registrations of non-convertible investment grade debt securities to be offered for cash).

4. Form F-2 may be used by issuers which meet criteria 1, 2 and 3 for Form F-3. Criterion 2 need not be met by an issuer which has filed its latest Form 20-F and

1. of which at least $300 million of its voting stock is held by non-affiliates, or non-convertible investment grade securities are being registered; and

2. at least one, and the latest required, Form 20-F has been filed.

5. Rules 504 and 505 govern U.S. offerings of not more than $500,000 and $5,000,000, respectively, while Rule 506 is applicable to offerings made to no more than 35 purchasers (other than certain specified types of institutional, sophisticated or wealthy investors).

6. Forms 20-F and 6-K generally are not available for use by Canadian issuers which have had Securities Act registration statements during the previous year or which list securities on a U.S. exchange, or have merged with United States companies.

7. Rules 13a-11(b) and 13a-13(b) exempt foreign issuers from filing interim reports on Forms 8-K and 10-Q. Rule 13a-16 requires them, instead, to file Form 6-K. <u>Cf</u>. <u>also</u> Rules 15d-11, 15d-13 and 15d-16.

8. The difference results in a reduced liability standard.

9. Release No. 33-6493, October 6, 1983.

10. <u>See</u> Release No. 33-6433. Oct. 28, 1982.

11. Release No. 33-6424. Sept. 2, 1982 and Release No. 33-6499, effective Dec. 31, 1983, confirming the 1982 position. <u>See</u> also Release No. 33-6240, Sept. 10, 1980.

12. <u>See</u> Section 13(d) and 13(g) of the Exchange Act and rules under these sections.

RÉSUMÉ EN FRANÇAIS

APPLICATION DES LOIS AMÉRICAINES SUR LES TITRES ET OFFRES DE TITRES AUX ETATS-UNIS

Aux États-Unis, les ventes de titres par des émetteurs étrangers sont règlementées par la U.S. Securities and Exchange Commission "SEC" suivant les mêmes règles générales que l'on applique aux émétteurs établis aux États-Unis, bien que certains ajustements aient été apportés pour tenir compte des différences dans la législation en général, dans les coutumes et pratiques des affaires et dans les principes de comptabilité.

Les émetteurs privés étrangers ayant l'intention de placer des titres aux États-Unis sont tenus d'enregistrer ces titres conformément au Securities Act de 1933 ("Securities"), à moins qu'ils en soient exemptés. Le Securities Act prévoit des critères relatifs à la divulgation d'informations ainsi que des normes contre la fraude. Selon la notoriété de l'émetteur, un formulaire (F-1, F-2, F-3) devra être utilisé pour procéder à l'enregistrement. Il est particulièrement important de concilier l'information financière avec les exigences américaines et de respecter les critères de vérification et de contrôle prévus par la législation américaine. Conformément aux articles 3(b), 4(2) du Securities Act et du règlement D, certaines émissions à diffusion restreinte peuvent bénéficier de l'exemption relative à l'enregistrement.

Les émetteurs gouvernementaux étrangers sont assujetis aux exigences d'enregistrement prévus par le Securities Act, tout en étant soumis à des conditions différentes de celles qui sont imposées aux émetteurs privés étrangers.

Le Securities Exchange Act de 1934 ("Exchange Act") régit les marchés secondaires de titres aux États-Unis et contient des exigences additionnelles ayant trait à l'enregistrement, à l'information et au rapport périodique. D'après la loi susmentionnée, les émetteurs dont les titres figurent sur la cote d'un marché financier américain ou les émetteurs qui ont des actifs de plus de trois millions de dollars, dont une catégorie de participations appartient au moins à 500 personnes sont tenus d'enregistrer leur titres. De même, les sociétés émettrices dont les titres ont été enregistrés en accord avec le Securities Act doivent aussi respecter les exigences du Exchange Act quant au rapport périodique. Ces exigences ne s'appliquent pas aux sociétés émettrices étrangères dont les actifs baissent à moins de trois millions de dollars et dont aucune catégorie de titres n'est détenue par au moins 300 actionnaires Américains. Il existe des formulaires réservés à cet usage que les émetteurs privés étrangers peuvent se procurer pour présenter leurs rapports annuels spéciaux et périodiques (les formulaires 20-F et 6-K). Par ailleurs, certains émetteurs étrangers pourraient peut être bénéficier de la Règle 12g3.2 relative à "la divulgation d'informations" pour être exemptés de l'enregistrement conformément à cette loi.

Les sociétés émettrices étrangères privées qui veulent faire inscrire leurs titres à la cote d'un marché financier américain doivent satisfaire aux exigences du marché en question. Les états dans lesquels des titres seront placés pourraient aussi imposer leurs propres conditions.

Lorsqu'il s'agit d'offrir des titres d'emprunt, le Trust Indenture Act impose certaines autres exigences ayant trait à la sélection et aux obligations du fiduciaire, à la procédure par défaut et aux normes concernant les rapports à produire.

Dans le cas où une société émettrice étrangère fait l'acquisition ou est partie à une fusion avec une entreprise américaine et que la transaction en question nécessite une opération d'échange relative aux titres de l'émetteur étranger, ces titres doivent être enregistrés sur le formulaire F-4.

Tout investisseur, y compris l'investisseur étranger, qui est propriétaire véritable de 5% ou plus d'une catégorie de titres de participation enregistrée selon l'article 12 du Exchange Act (généralement inscrits à la cote ou sous forme de titres négociés en public) est tenu de faire des rapports concernant ladite propriété à la société émettrice, la SEC et les autres marchés de valeurs mobilières. D'autres normes relatives à l'information s'appliquent aux offres publiques d'achat.

RESUMEN EN ESPAÑOL

APLICACIÓN DEL DERECHO AMERICANO A LA COMPRA Y VENTA DE VALORES EN AMERICA

En los Estados Unidos, la venta de valores por emisores extranjeros está reglamentada por la U.S. Securities and Exchange Commission "SEC" siguiendo las mismas reglas generales aplicalbes a los emisores establecidos en los Estados Unidos, aunque ciertas modificaciones han sido introducidas para tener en cuenta las diferencias en la legislación general y en los principios contables.

Los emisores privados extranjeros que desean negociar sus valores en los Estados Unidos deben registrar tales valores de acuerdo con el Securities Act de 1933 ("Securities"), a no ser que se encuentren exentos. El Securities Act preve criterios relativos para la divulgación de información, al igual que normas contra el fraude. Según la notoriedad del emisor, un formulario (F-1, F-2, F-3) deberá ser utilizado para proceder al registro. Es especialmente importante conciliar la información financiera con los requisitos norteamericanos y respetar los criterios de verificación y de control previstos por la legislación norteamericana. Según los artículos 3 (b), 4 (2) del Securities Act y del reglamento D, ciertas emisiones de difusión restringida pueden ser exentas de registro.

Los emisores gubernamentales extranjeros estan sujetos a las mismas exigencias de registro previstas por el Securities Act, quedando al mismo tiempo sometidos a condiciones diferentes de aquéllas impuestas a los emisores privados extranjeros.

El Securities Exchange Act de 1934 ("Exchange Act") rige los mercados de valores secundarios en Estados Unidos e incluye requisitos adicionales referentes al registro, a la información y a los informes periódicos. Según esta ley, los emisores cuyos valores son cotizados en un mercado financiero americano o los emisores con un activo superior a tres millones de dólares y una clase de tenedores de tales valores de no menos de 500 personas, deben registrar sus valores. Igualmente, las sociedades emisoras cuyos valores han sido registrados de acuerdo con el Securities Act deben también cumplir con los requisitos del Exchange Act en cuanto a los informes periódicos.

Estos requisitos no se aplican a las sociedades emisoras extranjeras con activos inferiores a los tres millones de dólares y donde ninguna categoría de valores se encuentra en poder de por lo menos 300 accionistas americanos. Existen formularios reservados para este uso que los emisores privados extranjeros pueden obtener para presentar sus informes anuales especiales y periódicos (formularios 20-F y 6-K). Además, ciertos emisores extranjeros podrían quizas beneficiarse de la Regla 12g3.2 relativa a "la divulgación de información" para ser exentos de registro conforme a tal ley.

Las sociedades emisoras extranjeras privadas que desean inscribir sus valores para su cotización en un mercado financiero americano, deben satisfacer los requisitos del mercado en cuestión. Los estados donde tales valores sean colocados podrán también imponer sus propios requisitos.

Tratándose del ofrecimiento de títulos de deuda, el Trust Indenture Act establece ciertos requisitos adicionales relativos a la selección y a las obligaciones del fiduciario, al procedimento en caso de falta de pago y a las normas concernientes a los informes a producir.

En el caso que una sociedad emisora extranjera adquiera o forme parte de una fusión con una empresa americana, y que la transacción del caso requiera una operación de cambio relativa a valores del emisor extranjero, tales valores deben ser registrados en un formulario F-4.

Todo inversor, incluso el extranjero, propietario de un 5% o mas de una categoría de valores de más participación registrados según el artículo 12 del Exchange Act (generalmente cotizables o negociados en forma pública) debe informar periódicamente respecto de tal propiedad a la sociedad emisora, la SEC y a los otros mercados de valores mobiliarios. Otras normas relativas al deber de informar se aplican a los ofrecimientos públicos de compra.

PROBLEMS OF MULTINATIONAL ENTERPRISES IN SELLING SECURITIES IN EUROPE

William Haney and Sylvie Durant des Aulnois

Mr. Haney is a partner in the law firm of Rogers & Wells. He is currently resident in Rogers & Wells head office in New York, and from 1975 to 1983 was resident in that firm's Paris office. Mr. Haney holds a J.D. degree from the Harvard Law School.

Ms. Durant des Aulnois is an Associate with the law firm of Rogers & Wells, in New York, where she practices principally in the area of business and securities law for domestic as well as foreign clients of the firm. Ms. Durant des Aulnois holds a Master in Comparative Jurisprudence from New York University and a Maitrise in Business Law from the University of Paris (II).

I. INTERNATIONAL CAPITAL MARKETS IN EUROPE -- A REGULATORY OVERVIEW

The international market in securities, both in Europe and elsewhere in the world, has been and continues to be principally a market in debt obligations -- in particular the so-called Eurobond market. The Eurobond market as it has developed over the past twenty years is a truly transnational market with a well developed distribution system capable of placing and trading securities in financial centers throughout Europe and the world, with Cedel and Euroclear providing centralized clearing services. This market is also to a surprising extent an unregulated, or self-regulated, one. This results from the tradition -- one might say the fiction -- that Eurobond issues are private placements and from the related fact that Eurobonds are usually not widely listed or traded on stock exchanges, even though, for marketing reasons, virtually all issues are nominally listed on at least one exchange, most often Luxembourg, in order to qualify as permitted investments for various institutional investors. As will be seen, securities regulation in Europe is to a large degree in the hands of the various stock exchanges; to that extent the Eurobond market escapes regulation.

Alongside the Eurobond market, properly so-called, there exists a very important volume of bonds denominated in the local currency and offered in domestic markets by foreign issuers. Such issues are, of course, subject to regulation to the same extent as offerings by domestic issuers and are often subject to additional restrictions or authorizations.

The information contained in this article was current when presented at the Conference on Reorganization of Multinational Entreprise in October 1984. The authors have not attempted to incorporate developments occurring between that date and the date of publication.

The international market in equity securities is growing rapidly, but is still in its infancy compared to the market for debt securities. Also, while an increasing amount of direct trading among institutions in different countries takes place, the international equity market is still handicapped by the absence of central clearing and (except for a recently instituted, limited-scale prototype system among several European stock exchanges) quotation systems. The market may be characterized as multinational rather than transnational; an issuer's ability to sell its equity securities in foreign markets depends to a large degree upon the securities being listed on the stock exchanges or organized over-the-counter markets in those countries, with the resulting need to comply with the national regulations of those countries.

II. COMPARATIVE SECURITIES LAW AND PRACTICE IN SELECTED EUROPEAN COUNTRIES (UNITED KINGDOM, FRANCE, GERMANY, NETHERLANDS & SWITZERLAND).

A. Restrictions on Access to Capital Markets

Although the Treaty of Rome establishes the principle of free movement of persons, goods, services and capital, most countries still impose restrictions on access to their respective national capital markets. Two categories of restrictions are common: (1) currency regulations which generally apply to resident purchasers of foreign issuers' securities, and (2) administrative authorizations geared towards control of capital exports which apply more specifically to foreign issuers.

(1) Turning to currency restrictions, among the surveyed countries, only France has strict rules. Accordingly, except in France, residents are free to purchase any securities they wish on foreign securities markets. The French Circulaire of May 21, 1981 requires French investors to deposit all foreign securities with approved intermediaries ("intermédiaires agréés", including most banks and the Stockbrokers' Association). It further provides that all foreign securities transactions must be made through an approved intermediary and must be paid for in foreign currency held by French residents as proceeds of the sale of foreign securities. These special holdings of foreign currency, referred to as "devise-titre", are separately traded on the French exchange market, at a

heavy premium over the commercial rate. All proceeds from the sale of foreign securities and all income from such securities must be either reinvested or repatriated to France and exchanged within one month of the receipt of such funds. The result of these measures has been to freeze the aggregate holdings of foreign securities held by French residents, and generally to render purchases of foreign securities unattractive to French residents.

Other countries have eliminated limitations applicable to either issuers or purchasers. The United Kingdom abolished all exchange controls in 1979 although the enabling legislation remains in effect. Switzerland is well known for its absence of any such regulation; Germany lifted exchange control restrictions in 1974 and the Netherlands' Foreign Financial Relations Act of May 1, 1981 does not impose any significant restrictions on either issuers or purchasers of foreign securities.

(2) If progress has been made in freeing the markets from exchange controls with regard to the convertibility and holding of foreign currencies by nationals, restrictions on public and private offerings by foreign issuers remain through a variety of administrative authorizations applicable in some cases to foreign issuers alone, and in other cases to both foreign and domestic issuers. The "issue, listing or sale of securities" by a foreign issuer in France is subject to the prior authorization of the Treasury (Decree No. 67-78 of January 27, 1967, art. 5). This requirement is relaxed and consists of a mere notification procedure with respect to issuers which are nationals or residents of EEC countries; however, the delay (usually two months) which it entails severely restricts access to the market. In the United Kingdom, the Treasury's permission must be secured for all borrowing transactions effected by or on behalf of nonresidents which concern the issue of sterling securities. The Bank of England also exercises control over the timing of all issues, by foreign and domestic issuers, exceeding £3 million "in order to maintain an orderly new issue market". A similar queueing system is effectively applied in Germany by the German banks' Central Capital Market Subcommittee with respect to all foreign bond issues, coupled with a general understanding that all Deutch Mark foreign issues must be led managed by a German bank. In the Netherlands, prior approval of the Dutch Central Bank must be secured for all straight Guilder bond issues (but not

"equity linked" issues) over Dfls. 10 million (authorization is routinely granted but there is a "calendar" for issues in excess of Dfls. 50 million), and all borrowing transactions involving nonresidents must be reported, irrespective of the amount. Additionally, where the amount of redemption or interest of a foreign security is to any extent linked to the Guilder's exchange rate against the foreign currency involved, prior authorization from the Dutch Central Bank must be obtained, regardless of whether the securities are offered in a private or public placement. The Dutch Central Bank also imposes limits on all borrowings by foreign issuers, which are subject to a two-tier cap of Dfls. 100 million per transaction and Dfls. 400 million per calendar half-year. Even Switzerland reserves the right of the National Bank to take necessary measures to protect the Swiss Franc and to impeach or deter nonresidents' placement. For example, capital exports by banks and financial institutions of more than Swfr. 10 million for a period of more than one year are subject to the (rarely exercised) veto of the National Bank and the maximum permissible amount for each public bond offering is Swfr. 200 million. The queueing system formerly in effect for foreign issuers was abolished at the beginning of 1984.

B. Registration, Prospectus and Listing Requirements

The EEC Directives governing the conditions of admission of securities to listing (Second Directive or "Listing Directive" 79/279 of March 5, 1979) and prospectus disclosure (Sixth Directive or "Prospectus Directive" 80/390 of March 17, 1980 and Proposed Directive of January 13, 1981, amended July 12, 1982) constitute a comprehensive registration and disclosure system. It should be noted, however, that as of today, the system is applicable only to listed securities. The Proposed Directive would make similar standards applicable to private placements as well, but has not yet been adopted by the EEC Council. The following is an attempt to summarize briefly the respective (1) registration, (2) listing and (3) prospectus requirements applicable in the United Kingdom, France, the Netherlands, Germany and, outside the Community, Switzerland. Departure from the standards established by the EEC Directives will be underscored where appropriate.

(1) The Second Directive provides that each member state shall designate a competent authority to review and approve prospectuses prepared in connection with the listing of new issues on a stock exchange. The Sixth Directive makes it unlawful for securities (debt or equity) to be quoted on a stock exchange unless a prospectus has been registered with, and approved by, the competent supervisory authority, and has been published. The scope of these Directives is, however, limited to listed securities, and also excludes securities issued or guaranteed by a member state, securities issued by companies which benefit from state monopolies or operate under special law, and securities resulting from the conversion of convertible debt securities, the exercise of warrants or the distribution or exchange free of charge to holders of securities already listed. The Sixth Directive also purports to set forth the information which is included in the prospectus. Despite the limited scope of the Sixth Directive, implementing national legislation had been passed only in the Netherlands (Law of June 15, 1983 and Ministerial Decree of November 1, 1983), along with Denmark. France maintains that its existing regulations conform with this Directive. Although all the other member states are currently working to bring their legislation in line with the Directive, the Commission has threatened to institute infringement procedures against them because of their delay in implementation. Except for the French Commission des Opérations de Bourses (the "COB"), the surveyed countries have no governmental agency specifically devoted to regulation, although the Department of Trade does exercise some regulatory authority in this field in the United Kingdom, and, except in France and to some extent the United Kingdom, the closest analogy to registration in the U.S. sense is the process of applying for listing on the stock exchange. The task of processing applications is handled by the respective stock exchange admission boards.

France requires that all issues offered to the public be registered with the COB (Ord. No. 67-883 of Sept. 28, 1967) and that an announcement be published in the Official Gazette (BALO) before securities may be offered to the public. (L. No. 66-537 of July 24, 1966, art. 483; L. of Jan. 30, 1907, art. 3, as amended). Additionally, all foreign issuers issuing securities in France must file copies of their corporate constituting documents (translated if necessary) with the clerk of the Commercial Court. (Id.) Although English law does not mandate registration of new issues as such, it requires the filing with the Registrar of Companies of any printed material which qualifies under the statutory definition as a "prospectus" used in connection with the "offer of securities to the public" (Companies Act of 1948, §§ 41 and 417). In both France and the United Kingdom, the applicability of these provisions depends upon whether an offer is made "to the public". In France, the 1966 Company Law raises a presumption of a public offering in the case of listed securities, securities placed through a broker or other financial intermediary and securities "advertised" by the issuer. In both jurisdictions, the characterization of an issue as being made to the public also depends on an analysis of the facts and the degree or likelihood of dissemination of the securities outside of a limited number of offerees selected by the issuer or the underwriter. In addition to the private placement exception discussed above, exemptions are available in both France and the United Kingdom for securities similar to securities already listed on a stock exchange; in France for securities issued for consideration other than cash and securities issued or guaranteed by the state or by a government entity owned or controlled by the state; and in the United Kingdom where, having regard to the size and other circumstances of the issue and to the persons to whom it is made, registration is found to be unduly burdensome.

Although no registration requirement exists in Germany or the Netherlands, essentially the same result is achieved for debt issues in the national currency by the requirement that such issues be listed. This requirement exists as a result of a gentlemen's agreement among the banks in Germany, and as a matter of law in the Netherlands for issuers other than banks unless the denomination of the securities exceeds Dfls. 100,000.

While Swiss Law mandates the publication of a prospectus with specified (and rather minimal) contents in connection with a public offering of securities (Swiss Code of Obligations §§ 631, 651, and 1156), the prospectus is not required to be filed with any central authority. In Germany, the publication and distribution of a prospectus is a contractual obligation arising from listing agreements and is, therefore, restricted to issuers seeking admission to the stock exchange. The German Investment Company Act of 1957 and Foreign Investment Company Act of 1969, which apply to domestic mutual funds and foreign investment companies, respectively, constitute the only exceptions to the legal vacuum otherwise existing in this field.

Under these statutes, accredited investment companies, in order to qualify for preferred tax treatment, must comply with strict disclosure provisions, including the semiannual filing of financial statements and the distribution of a prospectus to each investor. However, it seems unlikely that Germany will take any further action in this direction in the near future. A legislative bill governing the distribution of securities and mandating registration of all securities offered to the public and the filing of a prospectus and of periodic reports was introduced in 1978, but failed to receive the necessary support. An amended proposal was reintroduced last year in an effort to implement the EEC Directives but was once again rejected.

(2) The existing legislation of most European countries does not deal with prospectus disclosure, but rather leaves the stock exchanges free to elaborate their own standards. The content of the prospectus will be examined as one of the conditions of admission to listing. Before discussing information required in a prospectus, some of the additional requirements applicable to admission of a security to listing on a stock exchange should be mentioned. Additional details also appear in Exhibit I attached.

First, all stock exchanges require that an application for listing be sponsored by a member of the stock exchange. Because stock exchanges are in general selective clubs closed to foreigners, domestic stockbrokers and banks enjoy an almost uncontested monopoly on all new issues. By the end of next year, however, London, in its effort to deregulate its market, will allow foreign members on the stock exchange.

Second, minimum market capitalization and distribution standards apply to ensure minimum liquidity of the securities.

Third, issuers are required to enter into a listing agreement or undertaking in which they obligate themselves to comply with all the rules of the stock exchange, including reporting and prospectus requirements. The main purpose of listing agreements is to ensure that information which will enable investors to make an informed investment decision will be communicated to the stock exchange and the public at the time of the issue and on a regular basis in the future. To that effect a prospectus is always required. With respect to foreign issuers of debentures, listing agreements also often mandate the designation of a paying agent. Violation by an issuer of any of its obligations constitutes a default under the listing agreement sanctioned by the delisting of the securities at the option of the stock exchange authority, in addition to any applicable statutory penalty.

(3) Finally, issuers must submit and publish a prospectus. Schedules A (equity) and B (debt) to the Sixth Directive specify in detail the information which should be made available to investors in this document. What is striking in the Sixth Directive is the departure from earlier practice; issuers operating in what used to be a relatively unregulated market will now have to comply with disclosure rules almost as strict as those established by the Securities Act of 1933 in the United States. Although it is not our purpose here to compare U.S. and European disclosure requirements, it should be noted that the standards of the U.S. securities laws are, as a general rule, higher than the standards of most other countries. American public companies wishing to enter the European capital markets will thus not be surprised. However, they may find raising capital in Europe more expensive than in the past, particularly if the EEC adopts the Proposed Directive which would extend the prospectus and registration requirements to all offering of securities to the public (as defined in the Directive), whether or not the securities are listed on a stock exchange. Member states were given until June 30, 1983 to conform their respective national legislation to the Sixth Directive. As mentioned above, only the Netherlands has done so, while prior regulations in France and, to a lesser extent in the United Kingdom, approach the EEC standards. Discrepancies remain nonetheless.

The attached Exhibit II contains a detailed, although not exhaustive, analysis of the information required by each country. To touch briefly upon some of the major items which must necessarily be included in listing particulars under current practice:

a. the required description of the issue and terms of the offering usually complies with the standards of the Sixth Directive;

b. except in the United Kingdom and the Netherlands, information relating to capital, and in particular, risks of dilution of shareholders' rights, falls short of the EEC standards;

c. although the Sixth Directive requires financial disclosure for the three preceding years, under existing standards German and Swiss investors are only provided with information relating to the previous year, whereas the British investor is provided with the issuer's financial picture over the last five years; and

d. only France, the United Kingdom and the Netherlands meet EEC standards for disclosure of conflicts of interest between directors and shareholders.

C. Continuing Disclosure Requirements

While the Second and Sixth Directives prescribe the minimum information to be given to investors at the time the securities are admitted to official quotation, and annually thereafter, the Reporting Directive (unnumbered Directive 82/121 of February 15, 1982) completes these measures by providing investors with information about the issuers' first six months of the financial year during the entire period that the securities are listed. Pursuant to these provisions, issuers are required to make available to the public their annual accounts, semi-annual reports of their financial situation and any information of exceptional nature which is price-sensitive. It should be noted, however, that issuers of straight debentures are not subject to the half-yearly report requirement. Exhibit III attached lists the principal requirements of the EEC Directives, as well as the major features of the national legislation of the countries surveyed here.

A rapid glance at the legislation shows that companies in all the countries with which we are concerned must publish their annual accounts. However the degree of mandatory disclosure varies widely from one country to the other. The United Kingdom has by far the most stringent requirements in that it forces companies to disclose not only their financial position but also data regarding shareholders and directors, payments to directors and highest paid executives, borrowing of the company and contingent liabilities, as well as the auditors' report. In France, the 1966 Company Law provides for extensive disclosure to existing shareholders, but limits the information made available to the public at large to a mere balance sheet and income statement unless the company is listed on the stock exchange, in which case it must also publish a statement of contingent liabilities, its operating income statement and profit and loss accounts. Auditors' reports are made public only in Germany, the United Kingdom and the Netherlands. As a general remark, it should be emphasized that in most cases existing national legislation mandates the filing in the public records of companies' annual accounts but that publication of such information is required as a matter of law only in Germany, the Netherlands and France (for listed companies). Implementation only partially achieves the wide diffusion in the information enabling the public to make an intelligent investment decision which the publication provisions of the Directives purport to accomplish.

Interim reports are required by statute in France and the Netherlands. In other countries semi-annual or quarterly financial disclosure is either voluntary, as in Germany, or required by listing agreements, as in Switzerland and the United Kingdom. The same is applicable to information likely to influence the value or trading of the securities listed.

D. Accounting Standards

A major, if not the principal problem encountered by an issuer selling securities in a foreign market is the differences in accounting standards among various countries. Multinational companies are required to conform, at least within certain tolerances, with the rules of each country in which they operate or in which their securities are quoted on a stock exchange. Adjusting to different accounting standards, which can involve the complete restatement of accounts and the adoption of different auditing practices, can drastically increase the cost of issuing securities abroad.

The financial and accounting community has been working towards harmonization over the last decade. One of the most tangible results of this international cooperation is the adoption of the EEC Fourth Directive (the "Accounting Directive," 78/660 of July 25, 1978) with respect to annual accounts, and more recently the Seventh Directive (the "Consolidated Accounts Directive," 83/349 of June 13, 1983) with respect to consolidated accounts. The Fourth Directive was originally supposed to be implemented into national law by January 1, 1982. In view, however, of the complexity of the Seventh Directive and of the absence in Europe (except for the United Kingdom and Germany at the domestic level) of a tradition of consolidation of accounts and the resulting need for accountants to be trained in new techniques, member states have been given until January 1, 1988 to bring their legislation into line, while groups of companies have until January 1, 1990 to prepare their consolidated accounts.

So far, only the United Kingdom and the Netherlands have enacted legislation fully applying the Fourth Directive. France has made progress towards implementation by means of two laws of April 1982 and April 1983, the Decree of November 29, 1983 and the publication of a revised "chart of accounts." As for Germany, legislative proposals were rejected twice by the Council of States, in 1982 and 1983, largely because of the requirement of the Fourth Directive that the new standards apply to limited liability companies ("GmbH") and certain limited partnerships ("KG"), as well as to stock companies ("AG"). The EEC standards are not controversial with respect to AGs, which already largely follow these rules. Outside of the Community, standards applicable in Switzerland are said to be relatively general and broadly interpreted.

E. Insider Trading

A rapid survey of the legislation of the countries which we have selected and of the action taken at the EEC level reveals that efforts have been concentrated on complete and timely disclosure rather than insider trading.

The statutes are generally silent on this subject. The EEC issued a recommendation in 1977, but this text has no binding effect on the member states. The EEC is also currently working on a proposed directive but there is no indication as to whether or when it will be published. Switzerland and the Netherlands have no legislation dealing with this matter, although both are working on proposed regulations. France, Germany and the United Kingdom impose restrictions on insider trading; each of them, however, has opted for a different approach. France stands for a full-fledged statutory system characterized by heavy criminal penalties, while Germany has a rather peculiar contractual self-regulatory system among the stock exchange, banks and industry; and the United Kingdom offers a combination of both. Details of these three solutions are presented in synoptic table in the attached Exhibit IV.

It appears from the German experience that voluntarism leaves out a large number of potential insiders, in that only signatories are bound by a contractual gentlemen's agreement. Although all banks are bound, only half of the companies admitted to the stock exchange are covered. Moreover, sanctions are mild and publicity unlikely.

Also, as a practical matter, European enforcement of insider dealing regulations is often sporadic due to lack of means and understaffing. It appears to be the COB's practice to conduct an investigation only when substantial evidence of an irregular transaction is affirmatively presented to it or in flagrant cases.

Finally, internationalization of insider trading has stymied enforcement in many cases. The COB and the London Stock Exchange have repeatedly reported that their investigations have come to a dead end when faced with the wall of the Swiss bank secrecy. Under pressure from the U.S. Securities and Exchange Commission, Switzerland and the United States signed in 1982 a Memorandum of Understanding pursuant to which Switzerland and member banks of the Swiss Bankers' Association agree to assist the United States in tracing insider trading originating from Switzerland which affects the U.S. Market. France and the United Kingdom are currently negotiating similar cooperation agreements with Switzerland. The latter is also presently working on legislation on the matter to curb, or at least deter, irregular transactions. The principal effect of such measures, however, may be to shift insider trading transactions to other, less fastidious, financial centers, a development which is reportedly already underway.

F. Proxy Solicitation

There is no legislation or proxy solicitation as such in any of the countries which we have surveyed and proxy contests are very rare. In particular, proxy statements in the U.S. sense of the term are not significantly employed as a regulatory tool to require corporate disclosure. As a practical matter, communication with shareholders is made difficult by the fact that, in the surveyed countries other than the United Kingdom and, as a result of recent legislation, France, most shares are held in bearer form. Company laws do as a general rule recognize a shareholder's right to be represented by proxy at a meeting and, in some cases, impose certain requirements as to form and content of proxies and accompanying materials. A company whose shares are traded in a foreign country is not, however, generally subject to the company law requirements of the latter country and the diverse national laws relating to proxies do not constitute a significant impediment to cross-border sales of securities.

* * * * * * * * * *

The foregoing discussion is far from an exhaustive survey of securities regulation in Europe, or even in the countries surveyed. It is hoped, however, that the discussion does provide an overview and a frame of reference for consideration of the diverse and sometimes conflicting regulatory schemes with which a multinational enterprise must cope when it wishes to sell its securities on the international capital markets of Europe.

IBIT I

REGISTRATION AND LISTING REQUIREMENTS

UNITED KINGDOM	FRANCE	NETHERLANDS	SWITZERLAND	GERMANY	EEC
When is registration required? Exemptions.					
-In connection with listing on a stock exchange -Filing of "prospectus" used in connection with "offers to the public" -Exemptions available for securities similar to securities already listed; and where "having regard to the size and other circumstances of the issue and to the persons to whom it is made, registration is found to be unduly burdensom" (certificate exemption)	-In connection with "offer to the public" i.e.,listed securities, securities placed through a broker or other financial intermediary, "advertised" securities and "offers made to persons not related to the issuer or to each others" -Exemptions available for securities issued or guaranteed by the State, governmental agencies, or state-owned corporations and for securities similar to securities already listed	-In connection with listing on a stock exchange	-In connection with listing on a stock exchange	-In connection with listing on a stock exchange -Mutual funds which are granted tax preferred status	-In connection with listing on a stock exchange -Exemptions available for securities issued by States, governmental agencies, international organizations and for securities similar to securities already listed
Where is registration made?					
-Stock exchange -Filing with the Registrar of Companies	-Commission des Operations de Bourse ("COB")	-Stock Exchange	-Stock Exchange	-Stock Exchange -Trade Register	-Competent supervisory authority designated by member state

UNITED KINGDOM	FRANCE	NETHERLANDS	SWITZERLAND	GERMANY	EEC
Additional requirement					
-Foreign Companies doing business in the U.K. must file their corporate constituting documents with the Registrar of Companies	-Foreign issuers must file their corporate constituting documents with the Clerk of the Commercial Court -Publication of announcement in Official Gazette ("BALO")			-Publication of notice of filing of an application for listing	
Listing Requirements					
-Sponsored by broker -Aggregate market value of all securities of same issuer at least £500,000, and at least £200,000 per security with 25% in public hands (10% if listed on the USM); 5 years trading record (3 Years on USM) -Listing agreement -Prospectus	-Sponsored by broker and favorable opinion Stockbrokers' Assn' -Minimum FF 1.5 million share capital with at least 25% in public hands (10% if listed on the Secondary Market) -Undertaking to provide the COB with, and to publish, required information -Prospectus	-Sponsored by member of stock exchange (broker or bank) -Dfls 2.5 million share capital market value -Minimum maturity of 7 years (convertible debt); 10 years (bonds); 5 years (euroguilder Notes) -Listing Agreement -Prospectus	-Sponsored by bank -Minimum amount of issue Swfr.20 million (debt) or 5 million (equity); at least Swfr 50 million previously traded between banks in at least 250 portfolios -First-class issuer; dividend or interest free of charge -Undertaking by the	-Sponsored by German bank -DM 500,000 aggregate par value of securities to be listed (or 1,000 shares if no par value shares) with at least 25% in the public; trading record and dividend history -Undertaking to maintain paying agent -Prospectus; notice of referral if prospectus	-Minimum market capitalization and distribution 200,000 ECU (debt) or 1 million ECU and at least 25% of the subscribed capital in public hand (equity) -Publication of information relating to shareholders' right; equal treatment of all shareholders -Prospectus

BIT I (Con't)

UNITED KINGDOM	FRANCE	NETHERLANDS	SWITZERLAND	GERMANY	EEC
ing Requirements (Con't)					
-Bank of England's approval for issues over 13 million	-COB's approval ("VISA")	-Dutch Central Bank's approval for debt issues over Dfls 10 million; queueing system for issues over Dfls 50 million	sponsor to provide the stock exchange with annual reports and report of corporate changes -Prospectus -Swiss Central Bank's approval for all capital exports of more than Swfr 10 million	was published within 1 year prior to issue -Approval of the Central Capital Market Subcommittee (queueing system) for all debt issues	

BIT II

CONTENT OF PROSPECTUS

(Unless otherwise indicated by (a) for equity or (b) for debt, applicable to both)

UNITED KINGDOM	FRANCE	NETHERLANDS	SWITZERLAND	GERMANY	EEC
STATUTORY AUTHORITY					
-4th schedule to Companies Act of 1948 -Schedule II to Rules and Regulations of the Stock Exchange -Rules of the Stock Exchange for the USM	-COB Ins. of Feb. 2, 1982	-Law of June 15, 1983 and Ministerial Degree of Nov. 1, 1983 adopting the ECC Second, Sixth and Reporting Directives (see EEC section for description)	-Rules of the Stock Exchange	-Stock Exchange Rules relating to Admission of Securities, § 4	-Sixth Directive 80/390 of 3/17/80 -Proposed Directive of 1/13/81, amended 7/19/82
CONTENT					
General Information					
-Name; address; law of incorporation -"True and accurate" statement	-Name; registry number; address; law of incorporation; company's purpose; fiscal year -Listings or applications for listing -Paying agent -Reference to notice published in the official Gazette (BALO) -COB's approval (visa)		-History of the Company -Corporate structure, name and place of registration	-History of the company giving at least the year of its foundation -Object of the company	-Name; registry number; law of incorporation; address; company's purpose -Listings or application for listing on stock exchange of a member state; traded but not listed -Listings or application

[BIT II (cont'd)

UNITED KINGDOM	FRANCE	NETHERLANDS	SWITZERLAND	GERMANY	EEC
Information Relating to Issue					
-Nature, amount and terms of the offering	-Nature, amount and terms of the offering		-Description of the terms of the issue	-Designation of the securities'; procedure of issue; authorization of issue; terms of subscription	-Nature, amount and authorization of the issue:
-Rights of securities' holders; power of management to modify rights of securities' holders	-Rights of securities' holders		-Authorization of the issue		-(a) Description of shares; description of shareholders' rights; restriction on transaction
	-Purpose of the offering				
-Tax applicable	-Underwriters' name and amount of commission		-(b) Interest; repayment; guaranties; representation of the creditors' syndicate	-(b) Redemption; detailed terms of the loan	
-Underwriters; commissions paid to underwriters or brokers in the last 2 years	-Authorization of the issue		-Termination of the offering	-Paying offices and depositories	-(a) Nominal value of share; right of preemption; discount
	-Preemptive rights		-Contribution in kind and concession of particular advantages	-Use of proceeds	
	-Termination of the offering				-Underwriters; underwriters' commission
					-Withholding tax
	-(b) Denomination; redemption; term; interest rate; yield				-(b) Conditions to the loan; nominal value redemption price; interest rate; term yield
	-(b) Tax status				
	-(b) Amortization; guarantees; debtholders' representation				-(b) Amortization; trustee guarantees; subordination
					-Net proceeds; use of proceeds
					-Offering period

UNITED KINGDOM	FRANCE	NETHERLANDS	SWITZERLAND	GERMANY	EEC
Information Relating to Capital					
-Information required with respect to both the company and its subsidiaries	-Amount of share capital; classes of shares and rights attached thereto		-Outstanding capital stock; classes of shares; face value and rights attached thereto	-Development, nominal value and classification of capital stock	-(a) Issued capital; classes of shares; paid-up capital
-Authorized, issued and paid-up capital; description and nominal value of shares	-Outstanding convertible debentures		-Outstanding nonvoting stock	-Outside participations of over 25% or 50% and references to intercompany agreements (re controlling interests and paying over of profits)	-(a) Unissued capital; pre-emption rights; conditions to change in capital structure
	-Changes in capital structure over last 5 years				
-Outstanding borrowing	-Authorized and issued capital; conditions to new issues; number of shares listed or traded in France or held by French residents (for foreign companies only)		-Outstanding debt borrowing		-(a) Outstanding debentures, including convertible debt
-Statement that no issue which would alter control of the company will be made without shareholders' consent				-Substantial participations	-(a) Controlling shareholders
-Description of issues made in the last 2 yrs.	-Treasury shares; shareholders directly or indirectly holding 5% or more of share capital; shares held by directors, management and/or employees.				-(a) Majority holdings, directly or indirectly in other companies
-Alterations to capital structure					
	-Participations (over 10%) in other companies				

UNITED KINGDOM	FRANCE	NETHERLANDS	SWITZERLAND	GERMANY	EEC
Description of Issuer's Business					
-Nature of the business; relative importance of each activity	-Nature of business; business analysis, geographically and per activity			-Gross proceeds from sales over the last 3 years	-Activity; location of principal establishments
-Turn-over for the last 5 years (3 years for companies listed on the U.S.M.)	-Turn-over for last 3 years; market analysis			-Production and sales data, as far as possible	-Turn-over during the last 3 years
					-Labor
-Material contracts	-Main investments; research and development policies				-Research and development policies
					-Investment policy; material investments, their location and method of financing; proposed investments
	-Employees				
	-Material contracts; suppliers				
	-Litigations				

BIT II (cont'd)

UNITED KINGDOM	FRANCE	NETHERLANDS	SWITZERLAND	GERMANY	EEC
Financials					
-Consolidated accounts if available	-Consolidated accounts if available		-Last statement of income and last balance sheet; "brief" statement of outstanding liabilities; outstanding debentures; "brief" statement of changes in the financial position of the issuer since the last financial statements	-Last financial statement (not more than 13 months old) with interim report	-Consolidated accounts if available
-Balance sheets and profit and loss accounts for the last 5 years (3 years if the company listed on U.S.M.)	-Balance sheets and profits and losses account for the last 3 years; 6 month update if available		-Auditors' report	-Explanation of all major items on the balance sheet; list of all liabilities not shown on balance sheet	-Balance sheets and profit loss accunt for the last 3 years
-Auditors' report	-Auditors' report		-Dividends track record for the last 5 years	-Appropriation of pro- in accordance with the Art. of Association and data on dividends paid within the last 5 years	-Profit and loss per share
-Dividend per share and total amount of dividends distributed for the last 5 years (3 years if company listed on U.S.M.)	(a) Dividend tract record for the last 5 years; highest and lowest quotations; volume of shares traded in last 2 years				-Dividend per share for the last 3 years
-Table of source and application of funds	(b) Yield for the last 2 years				-Interim report
-Statement by the directors that the company has sufficient working capital	-Table of source and application of funds				-Table showing sources and application of funds over the past 5 years
-Forecasts or projections are permissible if accompanied by by auditors	-Report of directors on financial situation and prospects of the company				-Financials information relating to subsidiaries likely to have effect on the valuation of the company's assets
	-Projections together with assumptions				-Recent development and prospects of the issuer

UNITED KINGDOM	FRANCE	NETHERLANDS	SWITZERLAND	GERMANY	EEC
-(b) If fixed income securities, statement by directors that profits will be sufficient to pay dividend/interest and particulars of net tangible assets					
-No tax liability or adequate reserve therefor					
Management					
-Name, address and qualification of directors and secretary	-Name, address and functions of directors and officers		-Composition of the board of directors, principal officers and auditors	-Composition of the managing board and the board of directors	-Names, addresses and functions of members of the administrative, management or supervisory bodies
-Directors' shareholdings in the company	-All amounts paid to administrators and directors during the previous year				-Directors' shareholding in the company (aggregate)
-Full disclosure of interested transactions	-Interested transactions				-Remuneration and benefits in kind received by directors
-Aggregate emoluments of the directors for the last year, and estimate for the current year	-Stock option plans				-Interested transactions, including loans and guarantees

UNITED KINGDOM	FRANCE	NETHERLANDS	SWITZERLAND	GERMANY	EEC
EXCEPTIONS					
-With respect to Euro-currency securities, the prospectus must comply with "the format and content generally recognized and accepted in the international Euro-currency securities market"	-The summary information card distributed to the public may be used for registration purposes where the company otherwise discloses the required information			-Where a prospectus has been published in the last 12 months the issuer may use a "Notice of Referral"	-Any information may be omitted if its disclosure is considered to be contrary to the public interest or detriment the issuer, provided that the omission is not likely to mislead the public -Information of minor importance may be omitted if not bearing on the evaluation of the issuer's assets and liabilities, financial position, profits and losses and future outlook
PUBLICATION					
-Publication of abridged particulars in two London newspapers and circulation by Extel Statistical Services Limited (one newspaper and circulation of an advertisement in case of a placing)	-Publication of announcement of the offering in the Official Gazette (BALO) prior to the beginning of the offering (criminal sanctions L.No. 66-537 of July 24, 1966, Art. 483)			-Announcement of the filing of an application -Publication in full in the Federal Gazette and in a journal carrying stock exchange announcements	-By insertion in a national newspaper; free brochure available at stock exchange, the issuer's offices and the underwriter's offices

BIT II (cont'd)

UNITED KINGDOM	FRANCE	NETHERLANDS	SWITZERLAND	GERMANY	EEC
				-Publication must be made at least 3 working days prior to listing	-In lieu of the full listing particulars publication of a notice stating where the complete particulars may be obtained -Publication must be made within a reasonable time prior to issue

BIT III

CONTINUING DISCLOSURE REQUIREMENTS
(Unless otherwise indicated by (a) for equity or (b) for debt, applicable to both)

UNITED KINGDOM	FRANCE	NETHERLANDS	SWITZERLAND	GERMANY	EEC
	(Apply to S.A.'s, whether or not listed)			(Apply to AG's, whether or not listed)	
-Companies must file their Annual Return with the Registrar of Companies, including: .information regarding .capital stock .list of shareholders and their shareholdings .directors & secretaries .indebtedness and contingent liabilities of the company .certified copy of annual accounts .accounting policies .transactions with affiliates .remuneration of Directors and officers (in the aggregate except for the Chairman; exemption for officers who discharge their duties abroad). .group accounts .auditors' report -Listed companies must provide stock exchange	-Annual accounts submitted to shareholders include: .balance sheet .income statement .profit & loss account .report of the Board .report of auditors .remuneration of the highest paid individuals .financial information for the 5 preceding years .dividend for the 3 preceding years .acquisition of 10% shareholding in another company -Information available to the public (filed with the Clerk of the Commercial Court): .balance sheet .income statement -Additional disclosure for listed companies (to be published in the Official Legal Gazette): .statement of contingent liabilities	-Ministerial Decree of November 1, 1983 implements the EEC reporting requirements -Annual accounts to be filed with the Trade Register include: .balance sheet .income statement .explanatory notes .statement of changes in financial position .auditors' report -All of the above, together with "all information which may be of importance to securities holders" must be submitted to the Amsterdam Stock Exchange, if possible prior to the publication of such information.	-(a) Annual report including balance sheet and statement of income -(a) Listed companies must comply with stock exchange's requirements which are more stringent, i.e., quarterly and semi-annual statement of income. -(b) No mandatory disclosure requirements. However, public offering entails sponsors' (banks) responsibility for disclosure and specific requirements will be included included in the prospectus (i.e. annual report)	-Announcements in the Federal Gazette and a widely distributed financial journal: .shareholders' meetings .dividends .subscription rights and stock splits .audited balance sheet and income statement (must also be filed with trade egister, together with the auditors' and Board's reports) .group accounts -Foreign investment companies must additionally publish a semi-annual report. -Listed companies voluntarily submit to the stock exchanges regular (quarterly or semi-annually) reports about the situation of the Company.	-Annual accounts and annual report -Semi-annual report of activity and profit and losses -New developments in the industry which may affect substantially the value of the shares. -Include: (1) balance sheet (2) profit & loss account (3) net turn-over (4) interim dividend (if any) (5) explanatory statement -Annual accounts should be audited -Publication or availability in places indicated in an announcement; send to competent authority.

[BIT III (cont'd)

UNITED KINGDOM	FRANCE	NETHERLANDS	SWITZERLAND	GERMANY	EEC
with semi-annual reports and preliminary announcements of any "price sensitive information" such as acquisition, dividend, profit and loss, capital structure.	.operatng income statement .profit and loss statement .turn-over (quarterly) .semi-annual report -All of the above should be reported to the COB, as well as "any information likely to influence trading of the securities."			-Foreign companies listed on a German stock exchange must undertake to publish an annual financial report, including profit & loss statement in a German newspaper. -(b) Publication limited to yearly financial statements and notices of calling or drawing of bonds list of bonds drawn but not yet presented.	-(b) Counsel Directive 82/121 specifically excludes debentures from semi-annual report requirement; convertible debentures covered to the extent that warrants may be admitted only if the related shares are already listed.

IBIT IV

INSIDER TRADING

UNITED KINGDOM	FRANCE	NETHERLANDS	SWITZERLAND	GERMANY	EEC
Source					
-Companies Acts 1980 & 1981 -Model Code of Securities Transacting by Directors of Listed Companies	-Ordinance of 1967 as amended by Laws of 1970 and 1983	-No specific legislation -Proposed amendments to the Penal Code (the following pertains to proposed legislation)	-No specific legislation -Proposed amendments to Penal Code, Art 161 and Code of Obligations Art. 726a and b, 902a and 903 (the following pertains to proposed legislation)	-Insider Trading Guidelines as of 1976 -(Contract between the stock exchange, banks and industry)	-European Code of Conduct of 1977 -Proposed Directive (not binding)
Characteristic					
-Legal regulation -Self-regulation	-Legal regulation	-Legal regulation	-Legal regulation	-Self-regulation	-Voluntary Code
Insiders					
-Directors -Person "knowingly connected with a company" or who was so within the past six months, i.e., officers, employees -Any person who acquires inside information through his professional or business relationship with a company	-Directors -Spouse of director -Persons who, by their profession, acquire privileged information, i.e., employees, accountants, lawyers, bankers, journalists, brokers, civil servants -Tippor, but not tippee, liable	-Persons who, by reason of their functions or profession, acquire privileged information -Tippor, but not tippee, liable	-Directors, executive officers, auditors, fiduciaries (whether of the company itself or controlling company) and employees -Federal and state officials; employees of governmental agency -Any person owing a duty of "commercial secrecy" (civil penalty only)	-Directors -Affiliated companies -Shareholders with more than 25% holding -Employees who, as such, typically acquire inside information -banks and their employees	-Includes affiliated companies -Shareholders able to exercise a determining influence on the management -Employees with regular access to inside information -Financial intermediaries and their employees

IBIT IV (Con't)

UNITED KINGDOM	FRANCE	NETHERLANDS	SWITZERLAND	GERMANY	EEC
iders (Con't)					
-Tippor -Tippee -Any person who trades on the basis of price-sensitive information or communicates such information, is subject to CSI investigation	-Affiliated companies				-Persons who have a professional fiduciary or business relationship with the company -Public officials -Journalists -Spouses of the above
Inside Information					
-Privileged information which could materially affect the price of the securities	-Privileged information relating to the prospects or the situation of the issuer, whether it is on the technical, commercial or financial functioning of the company or facts likely to bear on the operation or situations of the securities market, or on the performance of a security	-Privileged information, the publication of which is likely to influence the value of shares	-Privileged information; the publication of which is likely to influence the value of shares	-Information on not-yet-published or not-yet-known circumstances likely to influence the value of the securities	-Unpublished price-sensitive information relating to a company the market in its securities or any event which is price-sensitive
Securities					
-Securities listed on a stock exchange	-Securities of any kind traded on a stock exchange	-Listed securities	-All securities listed or traded	-Stock, stock options, bonds issued by the...	-Transferable securities subject of dealings...

UNITED KINGDOM	FRANCE	NETHERLANDS	SWITZERLAND	GERMANY	EEC
Securities (Con't)					
-Private placement -Does not apply to Eurobonds dealings in good faith				...company or an affiliated company and which are admitted to official or quasi-official stock exchange listing	...in an organized market
Prohibition					
-Transaction in any securities on the basis of privileged information on a stock exchange -Communicate a privileged information to a third party knowing, or with reasonable cause to believe, that such third party would use that information in dealing in any securities on a stock exchange -Counsel any other person to deal in any such securities on a stock exchange	-Transaction on the securities market on the basis of inside information and giving the information to another person so that he may profit from it before the information becomes public	-Sale or purchase of shares on the basis of inside information	-Transaction for insider's own financial interest	-Transaction of insiders in securities in which inside information is used for their own profit or the profit of third parties	-Transactions, on the basis of inside inmation -Giving the information to another person so that he may profit from it

BIT IV (Con't)

UNITED KINGDOM	FRANCE	NETHERLANDS	SWITZERLAND	GERMANY	EEC
Sanctions					
-Imprisonment up to 2 years and/or fine	-Imprisonment from 2 months to 2 years and/or fine from FF6,000 to 5 million or more, up to 4 times any profit obtained, but in no event less than such profit	-2 years imprisonment and/or fine up to Dfls 100,000 or 4 times any profit obtained	-Imprisonment and/or fine -Profit to be claimed by the company -Damages to any injured party	-Profit to be claimed by the company -Costs of inquiries proceedings -Notification to the Board of the company -Publication in case of gross violation	-To be left to member states
Enforcement					
-Investigation by the Council for Securities Industry -Investigation and prosecution by the Department of Trade or the Director of Public Prosecutions	-Investigation by the Commission des Operations de Bourse -Prosecution in penal court by the Public Prosecutor	-Penal courts	-Penal courts		-To be left to member states

RÉSUMÉ EN FRANÇAIS

PROBLÈMES DES MULTINATIONALES DANS
LA VENTE DES VALEURS EN EUROPE

Le rapport qui précède donne un aperçu des législations nationales et des directives européennes qui affectent l'émission de capital ou d'obligations par les sociétés étrangères sur les marchés nationaux français, britannique, allemand, hollandais et suisse. Plus particulièrement, les juristes et financiers intéressés par la situation de ces marchés trouveront lá une liste comparative des principales restrictions et conditions applicables aux valeurs mobilières etrangères émises ou cotées sur l'un des marchés nationaux étudiés.

L'analyse est divisée en six sujets á l'intérieur desquels les législations nationales sont brièvement décrites et comparées aux standards européens: (A) Mesures protectionnistes limitant l'accès aux marchés des capitaux´(B) Enregistrement préalable, circulaire et inscription à la cote (C) Publication obligatoire de l'information à intervalles réguliers, (D) Principes comptables´(E) Spéculations des initiés et (F) Sollicitation de pouvoirs auprès des actionnaires. Les détails techniques indispensables à la compréhension de l'exposé, mais qui auraient par trop alourdi le texte, sont présentés en annexe sous forme de tableaux synoptiques.

En guise d'avertissement, il est important de souligner que cet article a seulement pour but d'informer le lecteur des problèmes auxquels les sociétés étrangères qui désirent pénétrer certains marchés de capitaux européens sont le plus souvent confrontées. Cet article ne prétend donc pas du tout faire une analyse exhaustive des législations et des jurisprudences dans une matière en rapide évolution.

RESUMEN EN ESPAÑOL

PROBLEMAS DE LAS MULTINACIONALES CON LA VENTA DE VALORES EN EUROPA

El informe precedente presenta un cuadro de las legislaciones nacionales y de las directivas europeas, que conciernen la emisión de capital o de obligaciones por empresas extranjeras sobre los mercados nacionales franceses, británicos, alemanes, holandeses y suizos. En particular, los juristas y financistas interesados en la situación de esos mercados encontrarán una tabla comparativa de las principales restricciones y condiciones aplicables a los valores mobiliarios extranjeros emitidos o cotizados en los mercados nacionales objeto de este estudio.

El análisis se divide en seis temas, en cada uno de los cuales la respectiva ley local es brevemente comentada y comparada con el modelo europeo: (A) Medidas proteccionistas limitando el acceso a mercados de capitales; (B) Registro previo, prospecto e inscripción para la cotización; (C) Publicación obligatoria de la información en intervalos regulares; (D) Principios contables; (E) Especulación desleal; y (F) Solicitud de poderes ante los accionistas. Los detalles técnicos indispensables para la comprensión del informe, pero que hubieran tornado dificultosa la lectura del texto, se ofrecen en un apéndice en forma de cuadro sinóptico.

A modo de advertencia, es importante destacar que este artículo sólo se propone informar al lector sobre los problemas que mas frecuentemente puede encontrar una empresa extranjera deseosa de penetrar ciertos mercados de capitales europeos. Este artículo no pretende, por lo tanto, hacer un análisis exhaustivo legal y jurisprudencial de una materia en rápida evolución.